LEGAL RESEARCH & WRITING

THIRD EDITION

ESSENTIALS OF CANADIAN LAW

LEGAL RESEARCH AND WRITING

THIRD EDITION

TED TJADEN

National Director of Knowledge Management
McMillan LLP

IRWIN
LAW

Legal Research and Writing, third edition
© Irwin Law Inc., 2010

Published in 2010 by

Irwin Law Inc.
14 Duncan Street
Suite 206
Toronto, ON
M5H 3G8

www.irwinlaw.com

ISBN: 978-1-55221-176-2

Library and Archives Canada Cataloguing in Publication

Tjaden, Ted
    Legal research and writing / Ted Tjaden. — 3rd ed.

(Essentials of Canadian law)
Includes bibliographical references and index.
Issued also in electronic format.
ISBN 978-1-55221-176-2

    1. Legal research—Canada. 2. Legal composition. 3. Legal research—Canada—Computer network resources. 4. Information storage and retrieval systems—Law—Canada. I. Title. II. Series: Essentials of Canadian law

KE250.T53 2010   340.072'071   C2010-903178-4
KF240.T53 2010

The publisher acknowledges the financial support of the Government of Canada through the Book Publishing Industry Development Program (BPIDP) for its publishing activities.

We acknowledge the assistance of the OMDC Book Fund, an initiative of Ontario Media Development Corporation.

Printed and bound in Canada.

1 2 3 4 5   14 13 12 11 10

SUMMARY
TABLE OF CONTENTS

DETAILED
TABLE OF CONTENTS

CHAPTER 3:

RESEARCHING LEGISLATION 66

CHAPTER 6:
LEGAL RESEARCH DATABASES AND CD-ROMS   *136*

LIST OF FIGURES

LIST OF TABLES

PREFACE
To the Third Edition

Change continues to dominate the legal research field. There have been many developments in the legal publishing and legal research community in Canada since the second edition was published in late 2004. Most of these changes have occurred in three areas: (i) new print materials; (ii) new and improved "fee" and "free" online research materials, particularly the improvement to legislation and case law for free on the website of the Canadian Legal Information Institute; and (iii) the advent of Web 2.0 technologies that are essential to legal research, including the use of blogs, wikis, and RSS feeds.

More particularly, some of the new content in the third edition includes:

- Updated content in every chapter
- A new chapter on knowledge management in law firms
- Updates to new developments for some of the major legal publishers and their products, including Westlaw Canada, LexisNexis Quicklaw, Canada Law Book, CCH Online, and Irwin Law
- The increasing digitization of all legal materials, including e-books
- Expanded coverage of free legal resources, including CanLII
- Updates to legal encyclopedias, now including *Halsbury's Laws of Canada* and *JurisClasseur Québec*, in addition to the *Canadian Encyclopedic Digest*
- Improved coverage for Québec, the UK, Australia, and New Zealand
- Coverage of Web 2.0 tools (such as blogs and wikis) for legal research

- Extensive updates to resources in Chapter 8 on Legal Research by Topic
- Updates to reflect a new edition of the McGill Guide (6th ed.)
- New cases added on the recoverability of online search charges (Chapter 1), legal research and writing malpractice (Chapter 11), and restrictive covenants in the sale of a business (Appendix A, sample problem)
- New and updated illustrations and tables
- A new sample research problem and research memo (on the topic of restrictive covenants in sale of a business)

Without the support and patience of my wife Reiko and daughter Hannah, none of this would have been possible.

Thanks also to my law firm McMillan LLP where legal research and writing is taken seriously and valued at all levels of the firm. Particular thanks go to my staff, including Danielle Beaudoin, Stephanie Dutra, John Loosemore, Mary Kelly, Janette Nicholson, Katharine Thompson, Alison Walker, and Brenda Wong. In addition, I am grateful to the students at the firm and to Marlene Kane and Lisa Kerbel Caplan for their insights on legal research and writing. Katharine Thompson, in particular, provided feedback on and ideas for this new edition.

John Papadopoulos and Sooin Kim at the Bora Laskin Law Library also provided helpful comments and insights on legal research and writing.

I am indebted to the group of Toronto-based legal research lawyers who tolerate my presence at their informal meetings.

I am also indebted to all of these people for their ideas, their teachings, and their commitment to legal research and writing. I have borrowed liberally from all of them, not all of which can be properly documented; hence this form of general acknowledgement.

A special word of thanks to Anita Levin whose expertise in editing and knowledge of legal research and writing made this third edition much better than when I started it. Finally, thanks also to Jeff Miller and Alisa Posesorski of Irwin Law. I cannot imagine a better publisher —I am extremely impressed by the dedication of the Irwin Law staff and the quality of their publications.

Ted Tjaden
February 2010
Toronto, Ontario

INTRODUCTION TO LEGAL RESEARCH AND WRITING

Legal research is a practical skill needed by lawyers, law students, paralegals, judges, law librarians, and members of the public who must find and use law-related information such as court cases, legislation, commentary, and sample court documents and agreements. With the advent of the Internet and online legal databases, legal research now encompasses the need to use and master both print and online resources. Computer technology has changed much in legal research in Canada with the increase in the amount of law-related information available online and improvements in search and retrieval software. With these changes comes the need for many to learn new techniques and discover new sources for finding law-related information.

Related to legal research is legal writing, also a practical skill that requires clarity, precision, and an understanding of some basic legal writing requirements. Legal writing involves the drafting of a number of law-related documents, including legal research memos, opinion letters, business agreements, and court pleadings and factums. Fortunately, much has been written about legal writing in the past few years, and even though legal writing is not always taught well in law school, this book provides readers with a brief overview of effective legal writing.

For many lawyers and law students, legal research and writing is a bad memory of first-year law school since, despite the efforts of dedicated law librarians, most law school deans in Canada do not devote enough attention to legal research and writing. For first-time legal researchers, finding relevant cases and legislation can be difficult; ensuring that a particular case or statute has not been reversed or amended can be seemingly impossible for the uninitiated (it is not). Finding and drafting relevant and effective court documents and other law-related documents poses its own challenges. While the introduction of computer technology has in many cases improved access to legal information, computer technology also introduces the spectre of "information overload" and the danger of being bogged down with too much information. The need now is to be able to effectively sift through this mass of information to distil the particular information relevant to the question being researched.

This book—aimed at lawyers, law students, paralegals, judges, law librarians, and members of the public—seeks to explain the practical skills needed for print and online legal research and for legal writing. It provides a current and comprehensive look at the topic, consolidating information on legal research and writing into one handy, easy-to-use resource. This chapter introduces legal research and writing by discussing the following topics: (i) the importance of legal research and writing literacy to the legal profession, (ii) basic legal research techniques and resources, (iii) recovery of online research costs, (iv) legal citation, and (v) copyright issues affecting legal research and writing.

A. THE IMPORTANCE OF LEGAL RESEARCH AND WRITING LITERACY

There should be no need to argue the importance of legal research and writing, but considering the short shrift it is often given in law school, it is understandable that some lawyers may not regard legal research as important as other skills, such as advocacy and negotiation. In fact, much has been written on the reasons why law schools graduate students with such poor legal research and writing skills.[1] Many law stu-

---

1   See Robert C. Berring, Jr., "Twenty Years On: The Debate over Legal Research Instruction" (2008) 17 Perspectives: Teaching Legal Research and Writing 1; Daniel Perlin, "Law Students and Legal Research: What's the Problem?" (2007) 32 Can. Law Library Review 18; Roy M. Mersky, "Legal Research versus Legal Writing within the Law School Curriculum" (2007) 99 Law Library Journal 295; Connie Crosby, "Students Still Unprepared for Legal Research" *The Lawyers Weekly* (21 July 2006) 14; Emily Grant, "Toward a Deeper Understanding of Legal Research and Writing as a Developing Profession" (2003) 27 Vt. L. Rev. 371; Maureen F. Fitzgerald, "What's Wrong with Legal Research and Writing? Problems and Solutions" (1996) 88 Law Library Journal 247; Donald J. Dunn, "Why Legal Research Skills Declined, or When Two Rights Make a Wrong"

dents are able to graduate from law school without having done very much original research. First-year students, for example, are often provided pre-made casebooks containing much of the law they need to read, lessening or eliminating the need to find their own relevant cases. In addition, since legal research and writing is often taught on a "pass-fail" basis, many students will regard such courses as being less important than the substantive, graded courses they are required to take. And since most law school courses are taught as discrete subjects, there is a false sense given to students that legal problems fall nicely into well-defined categories when in fact the reality is that legal problems are not always so easily categorized, problems that in real life must be correctly analyzed if the research being performed is to be meaningful and effective.

1) Competent Lawyers Know How to Research

What is it then that lawyers do, and why would legal research and writing be so important to their work? Simply put, lawyers are licensed professionals who are given a monopoly to provide legal advice to clients. Given that modern society is unfortunately complex with numerous (and sometimes conflicting) rules that govern relationships between individuals, there is a role to be played by lawyers in helping people understand their legal rights and structure their affairs to comply with these complex rules. The role that lawyers play therefore involves two basic tasks: (i) *understanding* the law, which requires legal research skills, and (ii) *communicating* the law to the clients or to judges, which requires, among other things, legal writing skills.

(1993) 85 Law Library Journal 49; Ron M. Mersky, "Rx for Legal Research and Writing: A New Langdell" (1991) 11 Legal Reference Services Quarterly 201; Joan S. Howland & Nancy J. Lewis, "The Effectiveness of Law School Legal Research Training Programs" (1990) 40 J. Legal Educ. 381; Christopher G. Wren & Jill Robinson Wren, "The Teaching of Legal Research" (1988) 80 Law Library Journal 7; Helene S. Shapo, "The Frontiers of Legal Writing: Challenges for Teaching Research" (1986) 78 Law Library Journal 719; Leonard J. Baird, "A Survey of the Relevance of Legal Training to Law School Graduates" (1978) 29 J. Legal Educ. 264 at 273, table 3; Robin K. Mills, "Legal Research Instruction in Law Schools, the State of the Art Or, Why Law School Graduates Do Not Know How to Find the Law" (1977) 70 Law Library Journal 343; Sandra Sadow & Benjamin R. Beede, "Library Instruction in American Law Schools" (1975) 68 Law Library Journal 27; Robert A.D. Schwartz, "The Relative Importance of Skills Used by Attorneys" (1973) 3 Golden Gate U.L. Rev. 321.

The Law Society of Upper Canada has recognized the importance of legal research and writing in its definition of a competent lawyer in Rule 2.01(1) of its *Rules of Professional Conduct*:[2]

> "competent lawyer" means a lawyer who has and applies relevant skills, attributes, and values in a manner appropriate to each matter undertaken on behalf of a client including:
>
> (a) knowing general legal principles and procedures and the substantive law and procedure for the areas of law in which the lawyer practises,
>
> (b) investigating facts, identifying issues, ascertaining client objectives, considering possible options, and developing and advising the client on appropriate courses of action,
>
> (c) implementing, as each matter requires, the chosen course of action through the application of appropriate skills, including,
>
> (i)   legal research,
>
> (ii) analysis,
>
> (iii) application of the law to the relevant facts,
>
> (iv) writing and drafting,
>
> . . .
>
> (viii) problem-solving ability

With this definition, the Law Society of Upper Canada is recognizing that, to be competent, lawyers need legal research and writing skills. Implicit in this definition is a slightly broader skill, that of legal information literacy.

2) Legal Information Literacy

To equate lawyer competency with the ability to conduct legal research is not too surprising. Likewise, understanding some of the standard techniques of legal research, such as starting with secondary resources before consulting primary resources, is fairly basic advice. However, there can be a tendency when discussing legal research to think only of legal literature and its specialized materials and resources. Yet, conducting effective legal research also requires more general information literacy, including an ability to "recognize when information is needed and have the ability to locate, evaluate, and use effectively the needed information."[3]

---

2   Law Society of Upper Canada, Rules of Professional Conduct, Rule 2.01(1), online: Law Society of Upper Canada, www.lsuc.on.ca/regulation/a/profconduct/rule2/

3   The American Library Association, *Presidential Committee on Information Literacy, Final Report* (10 January 1989), online: American Library Association, www.ala.org.

Information literacy also includes the ability to assess the social, cultural, and philosophical impact of information.[4]

When applied to legal research, information literacy includes a number of skills:

- *Recognizing when information is needed.* In some situations, the effective legal researcher will know when a particular problem requires information that needs to be looked up in print materials or online sources versus simply talking to someone knowledgeable about the problem. Stated differently, not all problems lend themselves to traditional print or online research. Knowing when to research and knowing when to talk to someone first can save a lot of time. Remember the Chinese proverb: A single conversation across the table with a wise person is worth a month's study of books.
- *The ability to locate information.* One thing that often separates law librarians from lawyers is that law librarians have a richer understanding of the sources of legal information. As such, to improve your information literacy, develop a sense of where the best information is likely to be found. For example, in many situations, if you are looking for academic commentary on a fairly recent topic, journal literature or law-related blogs (discussed in more detail in Chapter 5) may be better sources than textbooks or encyclopedias. On the other hand, if you were looking for more practitioner-oriented information, you might do better searching for seminar papers in the *Canadian Legal Symposium Index* database on LexisNexis Quicklaw.
- *The ability to evaluate information.* Information-literate researchers also know how to critically evaluate their research results. At a basic level, it might simply be knowing who the good authors or publishers are. In other situations, you would look to see how well-researched the material is that you are relying upon — has that author provided her own footnotes to source material? How current is the information? With legal information in particular, the quality of your information can often be impacted by how current or recent it is. A good researcher will therefore ensure to "note up" his research to check that none of the cases being relied upon have been overturned on appeal or criticized by subsequent judges, and that any legislation being relied upon has not been repealed or amended or interpreted in an unfavorable manner.

---

4   Jeremy Shapiro & Shelley Hughes, "Information Literacy as a Liberal Art" (1996) 31 Educom Review, online: http://net.educause.edu/apps/er/review/reviewArticles/31231.html.

- *Knowing sources of non-legal information.* For legal research, it is generally no longer sufficient to limit yourself to only the "pure" legal literature. Increasingly, in order to effectively advise clients, legal information literacy means that you will need to be aware of business and economic information or other non-legal research sources. Many disputes, for example, may involve medical issues that will require the ability to research medical information. Or they may involve economic/actuarial issues that will involve an understanding of financial issues. In many situations, there will be outside experts providing advice on non-legal issues; regardless, even where that occurs, most lawyers will need to educate themselves on these non-legal issues and it will always be in their interest to develop as much literacy with non-legal information as is reasonable.
- *Understanding the social, cultural, and philosophical impact of information.* Although it may be more likely for lawyers working in academia or non-profit institutions to be more overtly concerned with the social, cultural, and philosophical impact of information, lawyers in the private sector also encounter these issues regularly. Almost any legal issue has some social, cultural, or philosophical informational impact, including such practice areas as privacy law, copyright law, family law, and elder law. The *pro bono* work that many lawyers voluntarily undertake addresses the impact that information can have on citizens: one reason our legal system is sometimes too complex for non-lawyers is the difficulty in finding and understanding relevant legal principles or rules; to the extent that lawyers help bridge the gap between the client and the complicated world of legal information, they are engaged in these social, cultural, and philosophical issues involving information.

If legal research is an important skill for all lawyers, and if lawyers need a broader legal information literacy, what are some of the basic techniques of legal research?

B. SOME BASIC LEGAL RESEARCH TECHNIQUES

This section of the book sets out some basic legal research techniques, all of which are touched upon or actually discussed in more detail throughout the book.

Primary resources versus secondary resources. As a starting point, it helps to understand that law-related information can be divided into two basic categories: primary legal resources versus secondary legal resources. Primary legal resources consist of legislation (statutes and regulations) and case law (the decisions of courts and administrative tribunals). Secondary legal resources, on the other hand, are background materials that comment on or help explain how to use or find primary legal resources. Secondary legal resources include such things as textbooks, legal journals, encyclopedias, case law digests, dictionaries and word and phrases services, Web guides, and various current awareness tools. While secondary legal resources may carry some *persuasive* value with courts, it is ordinarily only primary legal material that will bind a court and directly affect a person's legal rights. Thus, just as a doctor will not diagnose a patient without first conducting a physical examination of the patient, a lawyer should not render a legal opinion to a client without at least having consulted primary legal resources. Having said this, however, smart legal researchers will *start* their legal research with secondary legal resources (because of their broad overview and identification of relevant cases or legislation) and then *finish* their research by consulting and verifying primary sources of law.

Use of dictionaries and words and phrases services. Legal dictionaries and words and phrases services are discussed in more detail in Chapter 2 and are useful for not only defining Latin and legal phrases, but in some cases, for finding cases or legislation in which particular terms have been defined. For those who cannot afford the cost of the hardbound version of these dictionaries, the publishers of these dictionaries usually offer softcover, abridged versions of their dictionaries at a cheaper price (see Chapter 2 for a list of some of these pocket dictionaries). Both LexisNexis Quicklaw and Westlaw Canada now have online words and phrases services.

Identifying the issue; starting broadly. A critical first step in legal research is correctly identifying the relevant factual and legal issues that one must research. Sometimes, the issue will be obvious or specific, such as "On what grounds can the police search a car trunk without a warrant?" In other cases, the issue may be less obvious and require some analysis to ensure that one has identified the relevant areas of law. It is also important to keep your initial analysis and research broad. There can be a danger in too quickly narrowing one's legal research, thereby overlooking other possible relevant considerations.

Figure 1.1
Screenshot from Westlaw Canada's Words and Phrases Database

Reprinted by permission of Carswell, a division of Thomson Reuters

Legal research as a three-step process. Another useful technique is to realize that most legal research involves a three-step process, regardless of the particular resources being used:

1. *Finding.* The first step involves finding the relevant information by using an index, table of contents, catalogue, or other finding tool for print resources and by typing in your keywords or search criteria for online resources.

2. *Reading.* The second step is to then read the relevant material found using step one above. The information read in this step could include a case, a statute, or a passage from a book or encyclopedia, for example.

3. *Noting-up.* The third and final step in most legal research is to "note-up" the information consulted in step two above. Noting-up involves verifying your information by ensuring that the information, be it a case, a statute, or a passage from an encyclopedia, has not been reversed or amended. The technique of noting-up is discussed in more detail later in the book. For now, it is sufficient to realize that noting-up might entail different procedures or techniques, depending on the particular resources being used and whether it is in print or online format. For some print looseleaf resources, such as the *Canadian Encyclopedic Digest*, noting-up involves checking supplemental yellow pages at the front of the tab or book. Other material involves consulting a cumulative supplemental volume. Many

American print resources have a "pocket" on the inside of the back cover which contains a cumulative paper update. Online resources, on the other hand, are often already up-to-date or simply offer a "button" or "link" on which one can click to note-up the information being researched.

Online computer skills. Like it or not, the world has moved in the direction of computer technology and lawyers increasingly will need to become computer literate to access online information. Fortunately, with the improvement in computer software, computers are becoming more intuitive to use. Basic keyboarding skills, the ability to use and control a mouse, and a flexible attitude are the basic online computer skills that lawyers and others conducting legal research will need to have.

Practise, practise, practise. For most people, legal research and writing is an applied skill that only improves through regular use and practise. Reading a book about how to play the piano or attending a lecture on playing the piano will not make you a good piano player unless you actually put to use what you have read or learned through hands-on practise. It is the same with legal research and writing.

The legal research process. There is a tendency to treat legal research as a discrete activity involving various techniques on how to use law books or online databases. In reality, however, legal research is not just the application of techniques in using a particular resource but the process that one takes in first correctly analyzing the facts and issues related to the problem being researched and correctly applying the research to those facts and issues. Unlike in law school when legal research problems are often given in discrete subject areas (a "criminal law" problem, for example), real-life problems do not come bundled in a box with all of the relevant facts and issues set out in advance.

The legal research process is often described in the legal literature as a multi-step process that requires the researcher to think systematically about what is being researched. A common approach is to break the research process into the following steps, described by Fitzgerald as the "FILAC" approach (based on the first letter for each of the five steps):[5]

1. *Facts*: The first step in this legal research process is to correctly identify the *relevant* facts. In some research situations, the relevant

---

5   Maureen F. Fitzgerald, *Legal Problem Solving: Reasoning, Research and Writing*, 4th ed. (Toronto: Butterworths, 2007) at 2–4 and cc. 2, 3, and 10. See also Christoper G. Wren & Jill Robinson Wren, *The Legal Research Manual: A Game Plan for Legal Research and Analysis*, 2d ed. (Madison, WI: Legal Education Publishing, 1986).

facts will be obvious or will be provided and can be taken as a given. In other situations, the relevant facts may not be so obvious and may only be identified after one has gotten further along in the research process, thereby requiring the researcher to maintain a flexible attitude and a willingness to continually "run through" this research process in search for new, different information. Relevance of facts will also vary from problem to problem. In a breach of contract problem, the age of one of the parties is likely irrelevant (unless the party is an infant) but in a wrongful dismissal problem, the age of the employee may be relevant if the employee is older, a long-time employee and unlikely to be easily re-hired. Section E of Chapter 12 discusses writing legal research memos and suggests that an important aspect of a research memo is briefly setting out the relevant facts so that the person reading the memo can have some context for the opinion that is being provided.

2. *Issues*: After the relevant facts have been identified in step 1, the next step is for the researcher to identify the relevant issues to be researched. These issues will quite obviously arise from the facts identified and should ordinarily be stated in the form of legal questions that the client needs answered. In some research situations, the issue may be fairly broad—is there a common law tort for the invasion of privacy in Ontario? More often, the issue to be identified will be narrower and specific to the client's situation: what are the procedures, if any, to appeal a decision by a university to expel a student for an alleged violation of the university's e-mail policies? Like the situation in identifying relevant facts, identifying relevant issues can be a fluid process where the issues may change slightly as the research is undertaken and new approaches or issues are identified.

3. *Law*: Once the facts and issues are identified, the researcher must find the relevant law, a process described in detail throughout this book. Ordinarily, it is prudent to begin the finding process using secondary resources (such as books, journal articles, and encyclopedias) to gain a broad overview of the applicable law. This is then followed by narrowing in on relevant primary sources of law (legislation and case law). The competent researcher keeps a checklist or notes of the resources consulted to make it easier to later update the research or to allow a different researcher to carry on the work.

4. *Analysis/Application of Law to Facts*: The next step in the legal research process is to then apply the relevant law to the facts to analyze the way in which a judge would decide the matter given the same set of facts. At this stage, if the researcher is preparing a memo,

it is usually wise to analyze the facts and the law from multiple viewpoints, not just from the viewpoint of the client. This allows one to anticipate the arguments to be made by the opposing party and to assess the strengths and weaknesses of those arguments.

5. *Conclusions*: If the foregoing steps have been followed, it should ordinarily be quite easy to answer the questions raised in the legal research problem. In some cases, the researcher can be relatively confident of the conclusions reached by speaking in terms of a "strong likelihood" of success. In other situations, the law may be unsettled and the conclusions reached must be couched in appropriate terms that identify the unsettled nature of the law and the relevant factors that might influence the outcome one way or the other.

Understanding the legal research process is a very important part of being an effective legal researcher. There is a short legal research checklist in Chapter 11, Section E, to help researchers be systematic in the approach they take to legal research.

C. THE RECOVERY OF ONLINE LEGAL RESEARCH COSTS

Although legal research still involves the use of printed materials, the trend is clearly towards using online resources. One of the ways in which the importance of legal research has been recognized is when a court or taxing officer has allowed recovery of the costs of online research.[6] The issue arises in two circumstances: (i) where a client is challenging the bill of its own lawyer and (ii) where the losing party is obliged to pay the winning party's costs but objects to having to pay the online charges or argues that the amounts are excessive.

In the first scenario, courts (or taxing officers) will tend to favour the client and not require the client to reimburse the client's law firm for the online research disbursements unless (i) the law firm has clearly indicated in its retainer agreement with the client that the law firm may incur such charges on behalf of the client and pass those costs on to the

---

6   See Lisa A. Peters, "Recovery of Legal Research Expenses in Taxations and Assessments of Costs" (1997) 55 Advocate 79 at 80–81, citing, among other cases, *Xidos v. Tim Hill and Associates* (1990), 97 N.S.R. (2d) 212 at paras. 15–17 (T.D.) [*Xidos*] where the court encouraged lawyers to conduct research since it helps the court in its decision making. Also see Stephen A. Thiele, "The Costs of Legal Research: Changing Attitudes in the Profession" (2004) 29 Advocates' Q. 324.

client, and (ii) the costs were necessary and reasonable. For example, in *Oliver & Co. v. Choi*,[7] the court held that the client was responsible to reimburse her lawyers for Quicklaw search charges, but the amount was reduced since it was excessive and was not mentioned in the retainer agreement.[8] In *Shagoras Enterprises Ltd v. Lindsay Kenney LLP*,[9] the court did not require the client to pay the online research charges since the firm was not able to justify them.[10] Likewise, in *Ramsay Lampman Rhodes v. Calvin*,[11] the court disallowed recovery of online research charges by the law firm since the firm did not provide evidence that the charges to the client were necessary or reasonable.[12] In several cases, the court either denied recovery by the law firm[13] or reduced the amount to be reimbursed by the client[14] on the basis that the law firm had a flat rate arrangement with the online providers. In *Berge Horn v. Ziebler*,[15] for example, the retainer agreement obliged the client to "to pay, as and when they are incurred, any expense, disbursements and applicable taxes." The law firm in question had a monthly flat rate agreement with each of Quicklaw and Westlaw but billed the client the notional search charges generated by both databases. Since the law firm did not "incur" these notional search charges (but instead paid its usually monthly flat rate), the charges were held to not be payable under the retainer agreement.

However, in most situations where law firms are conducting research on one or more of the commercial online databases, the research is specific to that client and hence not overhead in the same way that a law firm's general print library materials would be. In addition, the client will ordinarily be benefitting from the specific online research that would be much more expensive to the client if done in print (or in many cases, trying to conduct the research using print resources may not even be feasible). As such, clients should be required to pay such charges where the cost is reasonable. However, the onus is on the law

---

7   2002 BCSC 152.
8   For a similar result, see *Fasken Martineau DuMoulin LLP v. Bastion Development Corp.*, 2001 BCSC 1694 [*Fasken Martineau*].
9   2008 BCSC 950.
10 *Ibid.* at para. 173.
11 2008 BCSC 1118.
12 *Ibid.* at para. 87.
13 For example, see *LeClair v. Blenk*, 2009 BCSC 926 at para. 22 and *Berge Horn v. Ziebler*, 2008 BCSC 72 at paras. 55–59 [*Berge Horn*].
14 *Denmar Equipment Rentals Ltd. v. 342699 B.C. Ltd.*, 2004 BCSC 1169 paras. 53–56.
15 *Berge Horn*, above note 13 at paras. 55–59.

firm to explain in clear terms to the client in the retainer agreement the purpose of such research and how it will be priced. For example, if the firm has a flat rate contract with online providers and the firm will be passing on the cost of research based on the provider's notional search costs, this should be disclosed to the client.

In the second scenario—where the losing party objects to having to pay the online research charges of the winning party (or argues that the amount is excessive)—the trend (except in Alberta) is towards allowing the winning party to recover the costs of legal research, including the cost of LexisNexis Quicklaw or Westlaw Canada online search charges. There are a number of cases from each of British Columbia,[16] Manitoba,[17]

---

16 *Canada Deposit Insurance Corp. v. Commonwealth Trust Co.*, 2009 BCSC 1493 [allowed, law firm not making "secret profits" on disbursements, including Quicklaw charges]; *Encorp Pacific (Canada) v. B.C. Bottle Depot Assn.*, 2009 BCSC 1657 [Quicklaw charges allowed since online searching was efficient but reduced by half since cost included part of firm's overhead]; *McKnight v. Hutchison*, 2008 BCSC 101 [Quicklaw charges substantially reduced since amount billed represented more than two times lawyer's monthly flat-rate fee, not reasonable to ask losing party to pay overhead costs of the winning party's lawyer]; *Parsons v. Finch*, 2007 BCSC 59 [Quicklaw charges reduced to $450 since party did not establish the actual cost of the Quicklaw research done but only the amount billed]; *Summers v. McGinnis*, 2005 BCSC 523 [charges were necessary and proper, and cost was reasonable, not overhead]; *Rohani v. Rohani*, 2004 BCSC 353 [charges reduced, lack of evidence on how it was used]; *Bridgewater Financial Services Ltd. v. 347451 B.C. Ltd.*, 2004 BCSC 21 [reduced from $683.68 to $200 since no evidence by law firm of the necessity of the research]; *McNulty v. Noordam*, [2003] B.C.J. No. 2166 (Prov. Ct.) [online search charges allowed]; *Fasken Martineau*, above note 8 [online searches provide a benefit to client, costs allowed but reduced because excessive]; *Girocredit Bank Aktiengesellschaft Der Sparkassen v. Bader* (1999), 118 B.C.A.C. 204 (C.A.) [especially at the appellate level]; *Lang Michener Lawrence & Shaw v. Hui*, [1999] B.C.J. No. 2505 (S.C.) [unusual legal issues]; *Parsons v. Canada Safeway Ltd.*, [1995] B.C.J. No. 1947 (S.C.) [Quicklaw disbursements of $214.30 allowed for occupier's liability research, many unreported decisions are available only on Quicklaw].

17 *Westco Storage Ltd v. Inter City Gas Utilities Ltd.*, [1988] 4 W.W.R. 396 (Q.B.) [computer research costs of $1,593.52 held to be reasonable].

Ontario,[18] Nova Scotia,[19] and the Federal Court[20] where the winning

---

18   *Wells v. White*, 2009 CarswellOnt 4992 (S.C.J.) [Westlaw charges reduced since no
supporting evidence of searches conducted]; *Esterreicher v. Non-Marine Under-
writers, Members of Lloyd's*, 2009 CarswellOnt 4435, [2009] O.F.S.C.D. No. 89 at
para. 21 (F.S.C.O.) [charges allowed since reasonable and "although Commission
decisions are available free of charge, a prudent researcher would also want to be
aware of Court decisions and relevant decisions of other jurisdictions"]; *Santos
v. Szlachta*, 2008 CarswellOnt 430 (S.C.J.) [allowed, charges reasonable given
complexity of the trial]; *Davies v. Clarington (Municipality)*, 2007 CarswellOnt
7413 (S.C.J.) [Quicklaw charges of $3,734.91 allowed since amount reasonable for
a complex trial]; *Caneast Foods Ltd. v. Lombard General Insurance Co. of Canada*
(2007), 55 C.C.L.I. (4th) 66 (Ont. S.C.J.) [Quicklaw charges of $274.19 payable
by losing party since winning party passed on the cost to its client]; *Thangarasa
v. Gore Mutual Insurance Co.*, 2005 CarswellOnt 8352 (F.S.C.O.) [important for
counsel to do online research to be properly prepared, especially for complex mat-
ters]; *Moon v. Sher* (2004), 246 D.L.R. (4th) 440 (Ont. C.A.) [Quicklaw and similar
search vehicles have become convenient aids to research and their costs should
be recoverable as disbursements provided they are not excessive and have been
charged to the client]; *Mandic v. See-Me Auto Leasing Ltd.*, 2004 CarswellOnt 5260
at para. 15 (S.C.J.) ["I do not understand the nature of the objection or have any
concern as to why a legal research service should not be a recoverable disbursement. In this day and age, it likely represents the most cost effective way to locate
and copy cases."]; *Bakhtiari v. Axes Investments Inc.* (2003), 66 O.R. (3d) 284 at
para. 52 (S.C.J.), var'd on other grounds (2004), 69 O.R. (3d) 671 (C.A.), leave to
appeal to S.C.C. refused, 2004 CarswellOnt 3779 [online research charges allowed:
"All of these items are everyday costs in running any litigation and are case-specif-
ic, rather than mere overhead, as for example, the cost of local telephone service is.
If they are not included expressly, they are certainly disbursements 'reasonably necessary for the conduct of the proceeding' within Tariff item 35, and I so order."];
Sellors v. Total Credit Recovery Ltd., [2001] O.J. No. 2337 (S.C.J.); *Lawyers' Professional Indemnity Co. v. Geto Investments Ltd.* (2002), 17 C.P.C. (5th) 334 (Ont. S.C.J.)
[Quicklaw expenses are time and cost effective, and efficient, allowed]; *Nordlander
v. Nordlander Estate (Executor and Trustee of)*, [1999] O.J. No. 117 (Gen. Div.) [but
reduced by the court]; *Marchese (c.o.b. Dooney's Café) v. Hix*, [1997] O.J. No. 3186
(Gen. Div.); *LDR Contracting Inc. v. Filion*, [1996] O.J. No. 2768 (Gen. Div.); *Gaudet
v. Mair*, [1996] B.C.J. No. 2547 (Prov. Ct.); *Denzler v. Aull* (1994), 19 O.R. (3d) 507
(Gen. Div.) [Quicklaw disbursements of $118.55 allowed on solicitor-client cost
award]; *Lau v. Tung*, [1994] O.J. No. 1873 (Gen. Div.) [Quicklaw search charges
allowed, "reasonably necessary for the conduct" of litigation]; *Kawartha Feed Mills
(1980) Inc. v. Goldie*, [1992] O.J. No. 3739 (Gen. Div.); *Re Solicitor*, [1973] 1 O.R. 870
(S.C.) [fifty hours of research reasonable for complicated criminal defence].

19   *Coleman Fraser Whittome & Parcells v. Canada (Department of Justice)*, [2003]
N.S.J. No. 272 (S.C.) [online search charges allowed, but reduced; research
involved case law and case reports that would not normally be expected to be in
the office library of the law firm]; *Keddy v. Western Regional Health Board*, [1999]
N.S.J. No. 464 (T.D.) [reasonable amount for Quicklaw searches allowed, online
research is generally cost-effective]; *Xidos*, above note 6 at paras. 15–17.

20   *AstraZeneca AB v. Apotex Inc.*, 2009 FC 822 [Quicklaw charges allowed but

party was successful in passing on all or part of its costs of conducting online research.[21]

In *Sellors v. Total Credit Recovery Ltd.*,[22] for example, the court allowed Quicklaw charges on the basis that they were cost and time effective:

> The Quick Law [sic] research expense is a legitimate solicitor and client disbursement. I could be tempted in calling the charges items of overhead consumed in the time-keeper's hourly rate and simply the cost of doing business. It is an interesting argument.
>
> I believe that these particular disbursement expenses are created for a specific client in a specific proceeding touching on issues and law specifically relating to that client's case. Quick Law [sic] is generally time and cost effective and efficient. The incurrence of the expense is neither unreasonable nor unnecessary.
>
> Involvement with this cost is specifically for the benefit of the client. All reasonable and necessary disbursement expenses within the four corners of this litigation should be assessable. Quick Law

---

reduced]; *Simpson Strong-Tie Co. v. Peak Innovations Inc.*, 2009 FCA 202 [charges allowed since searches attributed to a specific file]; *Bayer AG v. Novopharm Ltd.*, 2009 FC 1230 [allowed since done for specific matter but reduced since duplicate searches were done on multiple databases]; *Métis National Council of Women v. Canada (Attorney General)*, 2007 FC 961 [allowed but reduced since the dates of some searches related to other matters]; *Brilliant Trading Inc. v. Wong*, 2006 FC 254 [charges allowed but reduced due to insufficient evidence of relevancy or importance]; *Englander v. Telus Communications Inc.*, 2004 FC 276 [reduced to $2,100, the absence of search parameters which might permit confirmation that the work done was not predicated on irrelevant considerations]; *Early Recovered Resources Inc. v. Gulf Log Salvage Co-Operative Assn.*, 2001 FCT 1212 [computer assisted research of $110.29 allowed]; *Boots v. Mohawk Council of Akwasasne*, [2000] F.C.J. No. 312 (T.D.); *Pharmacia Inc. v. Canada (Minister of National Health and Welfare)*, [1999] F.C.J. No. 1770 (T.D.) [online research necessary because of a "change of research needs and techniques"]; *Ager v. International Brotherhood of Locomotive Engineers*, [1999] F.C.J. No. 909 (C.A.) [allowed, but reduced due to lack of evidence on necessity of online research]; *Maison des pâtes Pasta Bella Inc. v. Olivieri Foods Ltd.*, [1998] F.C.J. 1171 (T.D.) [online searches allowed as reasonable, represent a change in research needs and techniques]; *Canada v. W. Ralston & Co. (Canada) Inc.*, [1997] F.C.J. No. 291 (T.D.); *C & B Vacation Properties v. Canada*, [1997] F.C.J. No. 1660 (T.D.); *Canastrand Industries Ltd. v. Lara S (The)*, [1995] F.C.J. No. 1157 (T.D.) [computer-aided research was essential]; *CNR v. Norsk Pacific Steamship Co.*, [1994] F.C.J. 1293 (T.D.) [costs allowed for online searches where the decision to incur the cost was a prudent representation of the client, even if nothing of use was found in the search]; *Prouvost S.A. v. Munsingwear Inc.*, [1994] F.C.J. No. 1289 (T.D.).

21 See also Mark M. Orkin. *The Law of Costs*, 2d ed., looseleaf (Aurora, ON: Canada Law Book, 1987) at para. 219.6(9).

22 Above note 18.

[sic] research disbursement expense is not overhead expense within the meaning and intent of a solicitor and client award of costs.[23]

Likewise, in *Boots v. Mohawk Council of Akwasasne*,[24] the court allowed Quicklaw disbursements on the basis that the research was necessary and the costs were reasonable:

> As to the matter of disbursements, and as I explained at the assessment, an issue has arisen from time to time about computer research costs, in this case Quicklaw searches, and whether they are distinguishable from the overhead costs of a law firm, the premise being that overhead costs are already reflected in counsel fees. I am satisfied from counsel's explanation, however, that the research conducted in respect of this particular counterclaim was necessary and the costs claimed by the Defendant were reasonably incurred. The other disbursements are supported by the evidence contained in the affidavit of K. Melanson sworn on July 5, 1999. They appear to be reasonable and necessary in the circumstances of these proceedings and are allowed with the following exceptions.[25]

In *Atkinson v. McGregor*,[26] the court thought that online research, where necessary, should be promoted within the industry by allowing the recovery of online search fees:

> I agree with the decision in *Parsons*: charges for Quicklaw are a cost of doing business for lawyers. Since a law firm might charge a disbursement for legal research done by an outside agency; it does seem odd that a law firm that has the capacity to do in-house research cannot claim the computer charges. Indeed, as I said in *Kelly v Lundgard*, a memorandum on costs issued on [sic] 1997 which did not find its way into Quicklaw, it is a cost which should be encouraged because it improves the quality of research at a very minimal cost to the client. I issued that decision as a Memorandum, and not Reasons, because I was of the view that the issue of charges for computer research was not a new topic in Alberta, having already been discussed in *Wenden*. In *Kelly*, I said:
>
> > ... *there is a strong public policy argument for supporting computer research and by making that support practical by awarding costs for access to computerized legal research. Done responsibly, computer access to data bases will give lawyers,*

---

23   *Ibid.* at paras. 56–58.
24   Above note 20.
25   *Ibid.* at para. 8.
26   *Atkinson v. McGregor* (1998), 66 Alta. L.R. (3d) 289 (Q.B.).

*and therefore litigants, much quicker access to applicable case
law than can be achieved by the traditional, labour intensive,
methods of legal research. The dramatic savings in time spent
result in major savings to the clients. In addition, computerized
legal research gives access to current case law, months before
any of those cases would be published by traditional means. It
may be too soon to declare that the normative standard for legal
research is computer research, but the day on which courts will
make that pronouncement cannot be far off.*

That is not to say, however, that costs for computer research, like
all other costs, will never be excessive. We are entitled to assume
that lawyers have not only some general background in law, but that
they have some general background in obtaining information from
electronic data bases and are using appropriate means to acquire that
information.

Moreover, as pointed out in *Parsons*, Quicklaw contains many
decisions which are not otherwise reported . . .[27]

To the contrary, however, are several cases in which the courts have
not allowed legal research costs or have reduced the costs to be awarded
for legal research where the research was held to be unnecessary or not
conducted in a reasonable manner[28] or held to be overhead and hence

---

27   *Ibid.* at 293–94 [emphasis added].
28   *Neighbourhoods of Windfields Ltd. Partnership v. Death* (2009), 54 M.P.L.R.
     (4th) 247 (Ont. S.C.J.), aff'd 2009 ONCA 277 [Westlaw charges of $4,473.72
     disallowed, no evidence to support their need for conduct of the proceedings];
     McKnight v. Hutchison, 2008 BCSC 101 [online research charges reduced since
     plaintiff did not lead sufficient evidence and the charges appeared to be basic
     office overhead]; *Cherubini Metal Works Ltd. v. Nova Scotia (Attorney General)*,
     2008 NSSC 323 [online research charges disallowed, no evidence led that dis-
     bursement was just and reasonable]; *Prehara v. Royer*, 2007 BCSC 912 at para. 41
     [charges can be recovered but here disallowed since evidence scant: "As I have
     ·decided in other cases, Quicklaw can be a necessary and proper disbursement
     but that is not a given. There must be some evidence justifying its use. The de-
     fendants submit that any authority is available through the free services of the
     courthouse library website, CanLII, or a hard cover report series. Furthermore,
     this case did not involve any unusual legal issues requiring Quicklaw's use."];
     Swityk v. Priest, 2006 BCPC 519 [disallowed since unclear how amount was
     calculated]; *Bank of Montreal v. Binder* (2005), 20 C.P.C. (6th) 383 (N.S. Small
     Cl. Ct.) [lack of evidence of actual cost]; *Mitchell v. Canada (Minister of National
     Revenue)*, 2003 FCA 386 [Quicklaw searches allowed but not the cost of outside
     counsel retained to conduct the searches]; *Boyne Clarke v. Steel*, [2002] N.S.J.
     No. 186 (T.D.) [online search charges not allowed, research involved Supreme
     Court of Canada cases and other materials easily available in print]; *Bank of
     Montreal v. Scotia Capital Inc.*, 2002 NSSC 274 [not appropriate for party and

not recoverable as a disbursement.[29]

In particular, Alberta courts tend to be the most restrictive on the basis that online charges are already covered in that part of the costs tariffs dealing with trial preparation. Although there were some older Alberta decisions allowing recovery of online charges,[30] the more recent cases in Alberta are quite clear in denying recovery.[31] In *Marshall*

---

party costs]; *Rankin v. Menzies*, [2002] O.J. No. 1280 (S.C.J.) [Quicklaw charges not allowed where student credited with 15.8 hours of legal research under tariff]; *Jeff (Guardian ad litem of) v. Kozak*, 2002 BCSC 103 [Quicklaw searches not properly attributable to losing party where purpose of the search was to check out judge assigned to the hearing]; *Kuchma v. 1028719 Ontario Ltd. (c.o.b. Ryland Homes)*, [1999] O.J. No. 3068 (S.C.J.) [amounts not shown to be reasonable]; *Hennings v. Hennings* (1999), 49 R.F.L. (4th) 295 (Ont. S.C.J.) [not allowed due to lack of evidence regarding whether necessary]; *Zwicker v. Schubert*, [1999] 12 W.W.R. 273, 184 Sask. R. 35 (Q.B.) [no reasons given]; *Royal Bank of Canada v. Hayter*, [1999] O.J. No. 1621 (Gen. Div.) [no reasons given]; *Moin v. Collingwood (Township)*, [1998] O.J. No. 1522 (Gen. Div.) [no reasons given]; *Powar v. British Columbia (Ministry of Transportation and Highways)*, [1995] B.C.J. No. 706 (S.C.); *Re Briand Estate* (1995), 10 E.T.R. (2d) 99 (Ont. Ct. Gen. Div.), aff'd (1999) 122 O.A.C. 295 (Div. Ct.) [legal research costs for estate work reduced as not being justified]; *Knight v. Millman Estate* (1990), 66 Man. R. (2d) 275 (Q.B.); *Lee v. Leeming* (1985), 61 A.R. 18 (Q.B.) [no reasons given].

29   *Towcon Holdings Inc. v. Pinnacle Millwork Inc.*, 2007 CarswellOnt 5116 (S.C.J.) [Quicklaw charges of $1,239.50 disallowed as being overhead]; *Alcock v. Mc-Dougald* (2005), 14 M.P.L.R. (4th) 211 at para. 34 (Ont. S.C.J.) [disallowed, "I do not think we have reached the stage where counsel are entitled to eliminate their libraries and pass on to an opposing party the total cost of retrieving case law"]; *Shahshahani v. Shamsuzzoha*, 2005 CarswellOnt 15 (S.C.J.) [disallowed since firm paid a flat rate making it part of the firm's overhead]; *Elliott v. Nicholson* (1999), 179 N.S.R. (2d) 264 (S.C.) [part of office overhead]; *Nebete Inc. v. Sanelli Foods Ltd.*, [1999] O.J. No. 859 (Gen. Div.) [Quicklaw disbursements not allowed since should be included in the lawyer's hourly rate].

30   *Atkinson v. McGregor*, above note 26 [allowed for the physical cost of putting information into a computer and transmitting it to counsel]; *Holmes (Re)* (1991), 80 Alta. L.R. (2d) 373 (Q.B.) [disbursements for computer research allowed].

31   *Marshall RVR (2000) Ltd. (c.o.b. Budget Rent a Car) v. Gorman*, 2007 ABPC 313 [*Marshall*]; *Davidson v. Patten*, 2005 ABQB 521 [not allowed as a disbursement under the tariff]; *Milsom v. Corporate Computers Inc.*, 2003 ABQB 609 [disbursement to a legal research firm not allowed, cost already built into tariff in the form of trial preparation]; *Edmonton (City) v. Lovat Tunnel Equipment Inc.*, [2002] A.J. No. 1440 (Q.B) [computer search charges not allowed since included in the costs awarded for trial preparation]; *Standquist v. Coneco Equipment*, 2000 ABCA 138 [online search charges not allowed, a substitute for lawyer's work covered elsewhere in tariff]; *Hughes v. Gillingham*, 1999 ABQB 747 [not allowed since a technological substitute for the time spent in trial preparation]; *Dornan Petroleum Inc. v. Petro-Canada* (1997), 199 A.R. 334 (Q.B.); *Lalli v. Chawla* (1997), 53 Alta. L.R. (3d) 121 (Q.B.) [not allowed in this particular case]; *Sidorsky v. CFCN*

RVR (2000) Ltd. (c.o.b. Budget Rent a Car) v. Gorman, for example, the court regarded Westlaw charges as unreasonable and not recoverable under the tariff in Alberta:

> I am not prepared to approve the claim of $1,279.04 for Westlaw Research. With respect, I am of the view that this is not reasonable. Perhaps showing generational differences, lawyers normally would pay for and maintain a library within their office. Those that choose not to do so could have recourse to the library maintained by the Law Society at the Court House in Grande Prairie. All of the authorities cited to me were readily available in the normal law reports found within the Court House library. Where lawyers choose to utilize electronic means of research, they do so in my view at their own expense. I have concluded that the claim for Westlaw Research is not reasonable and is not recoverable.[32]

More recently, in *Aram Systems Ltd. v. NovAtel Inc.*,[33] Justice Macleod of the Alberta Court of Queen's Bench questioned the reluctance by Alberta courts to allow recovery of online legal research costs (where warranted). His concern was that the Alberta position—of generally not allowing recovery—was out of touch with modern legal practice given that legal research was increasingly being done online. He has called upon the Alberta Court of Appeal to revisit the issue:

> With great respect to those decisions made at an earlier time, I think that the view of computerized legal research as a mere alternative is no longer consonant with the reality of current legal practice. Such research is now expected of counsel, both by their clients, who look to counsel to put forth the best possible case, and by the courts, who rely upon counsel to present the most relevant authorities. Indeed, it might be argued that a lawyer who chooses to forgo computerized legal research is negligent in doing so. This is particularly so given that many law firms and indeed governments are now cancelling hard copy subscriptions to legal resources in favour of the electronic versions. The practice of law has evolved to the point where computerized legal research is no longer a matter of choice.

Communications Ltd. (1995), 167 A.R. 181, rev'd in part on other grounds (1997), 206 A.R. 382 (C.A.) [online research charges considered a part of the fees taxed and recovered and therefore not a matter for taxation as a disbursement]; *Argentia Beach (Summer Village) v. Warshawski and Conroy* (1990), 106 A.R. 222 (C.A.) · [not allowed here, but might be allowed due to extent or difficulty of research].

32   *Marshall, ibid.* at para. 23.

33   2010 ABQB 152.

. . . I would point out that the disbursement claimed in these cases is for access to the legal databases and is based upon the time spent doing research for the particular client on the particular matter. There is no suggestion that the disbursement is meant to reimburse the law firm for the cost of computers as capital assets. In my view, disbursements for electronic legal research are similar to disbursements for photocopying; it is the copies, not the copiers, that are being paid for.

Nevertheless, I am bound by the weight of authority and must therefore refuse to allow the disbursement. Perhaps the time has come for our Court of Appeal to revisit this issue, but in light of the existing authority, I am not in a position to do so.[34]

Some of these decisions where online search charges have not been allowed must be taken with some caution. There is a difference between not allowing online search charges where the cost is unreasonable or unnecessary (something which makes sense) versus not allowing online search charges simply because they represent some "new fangled technology" (a view that is backwards-looking and out of touch with the way law is and will be practised). In some of the decisions where the court refused to order the losing party or client to pay the cost of the online research charges a comparison is made to the general overhead costs that lawyers or law firms carry to maintain a print law library, costs that are not generally charged to a client on specific files. But there is a major difference between the general costs of maintaining a print law library which will be used repeatedly for a variety of research tasks over time versus a specific charge for a specific client at a particular point in time, a charge that is related to the file at hand and involves research that is not likely of benefit to other lawyers or clients at the firm. As such, online search charges are not like the costs to maintain a print law library and should be recoverable.[35] Moreover, it has been argued that not allowing recovery of these online charges may result in unequal access to the law since poorer clients may be reluctant to incur these online charges if they will not be reimbursed by the losing party if successful at trial.[36] Finally, the commercial online databases are sometimes the only source of case law or other information, or can be the only effective way of locating particular items (through advanced online searches that would be impossible to replicate or would

---

34   *Ibid.* at paras. 23–25.
35   Peters, above note 6 at 85.
36   *Ibid.*

take much longer using print resources); in these situations, the costs of online searches should clearly be recoverable.

Thus, where a party is seeking to recover the solicitor-client costs of research or the disbursement cost of online searches, it will be necessary to show that the research conducted was reasonable and necessary. Even though there are contradictory decisions regarding whether online computer search charges should be allowed as taxable disbursements to be paid by the losing party, it is clear that courts will allow such charges—and the costs of conducting any type of print or online legal research—where it can be established that the research was necessary, and that the costs or time incurred was reasonable under the circumstances, given the applicable issues facing the lawyer. In seeking to recover legal research costs and online search disbursements, the lawyer should be prepared to lead evidence regarding the necessity and complexity of the research, the advantages of using online research databases for the research, and the agreement of the client to incur such costs.

D. LEGAL CITATION

Legal citation involves standardized rules for the way in which one refers to court cases, legislation, and other legal materials. For example, in Canada, it is standard to cite a court case in the following typical pattern: case name (in italics), year (in square brackets or round parentheses, depending on the reporter), volume number of reporter, reporter name, reporter series (if any), page number of the first page of the decision, and then the level of court:

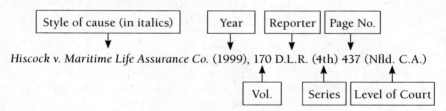

Standardized legal citation is important for several reasons: (i) information from the citation can be used to quickly identify whether the material is worth pursuing, for example, by looking at the year of the case and the level of court; (ii) the citation can be used to easily retrieve the full text from the shelf or from an online database such as the Canadian Legal Information Institute (CanLII, www.canlii.org) or an online commercial database; and (iii) using proper citation lends credibility to your written work and makes it easier for readers to find the information being cited.

In Canada, the leading style guide is the *Canadian Guide to Uniform Legal Citation*,[37] which is generally referred to by its more common name—the "McGill Guide"—since it is a publication by the editors of the *McGill Law Journal*. The McGill Guide covers a wide range of citation questions, including rules on footnoting (Rule 1.3) and rules on citing legislation (Chapter 2), case law (Chapter 3), government documents (Chapter 4), international materials (Chapter 5), and secondary materials (Chapter 6). The McGill Guide is published as one book in both English and French and contains a number of useful appendices, including information on courts, court levels, case law reporters, and their abbreviations.

In the United States, legal researchers use *The Bluebook: A Uniform System of Citation* (the "Bluebook"), which has in many situations a different style format than the McGill Guide.[38] As a result, Canadian legal researchers should ordinarily use the McGill Guide when citing legal materials from any jurisdiction (including the United States). There are, however, two situations when Canadians may need to refer to *The Bluebook*: (i) when required to do so by an American publisher if submitting something for publication in an American legal publication or (ii) when referred to *The Bluebook* by the McGill Guide, which happens a few times (as, for example, in Rule 2.3.2.2 of the McGill Guide).

For matters of citation not included in the McGill Guide, refer to more general style guides such as *The Redbook: A Manual on Legal Style*,[39] *The Chicago Manual of Style*,[40] or *A Manual for Writers of Term Papers, Theses, and Dissertations*.[41]

In recent years, especially with the proliferation of case law online where the court is—in essence—publishing its own decision, there

---

37   6th ed. (Toronto: Carswell, 2006). In anticipation of a new 7th edition, the editors of the McGill Guide circulated a survey to the Canadian law library community in March 2009. One of the questions in the survey asked for user preferences for a possible online version for a new edition.

38   18th ed. (Cambridge, MA: Harvard Law Review Association, 2005). *The Bluebook* now offers an online subscription at www.legalbluebook.com. An alternative American citation guide that is gaining popularity due to its simpler approach is Darby Dickerson, *ALWD Citation Manual: A Professional System of Citation*, 3d ed. (New York: Aspen, 2006). There is also a free online American citation guide called *Introduction to Basic Legal Citation*: see www.law.cornell.edu/citation/.

39   (St. Paul, MN: West Group, 2002).

40   15th ed. (Chicago: University of Chicago Press, 2003).

41   Kate L. Turabian, 7th ed., revised by Wayne C. Booth *et al.* (Chicago: University of Chicago Press, 2007).

has been a move towards "neutral citation" that provides for a standard citation for court decisions by case name, year, court, decision number, and paragraph numbers:

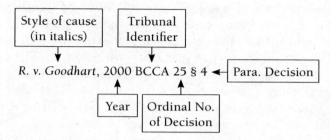

The citation is "neutral" to the extent it follows universal patterns and is not "dependent" on citations used by the commercial legal publishers for cases they publish in print or on their commercial databases. The Canadian Citation Committee has developed these neutral citation formats, currently embodied in their online guide called *The Preparation, Citation and Distribution of Canadian Decisions*.[42] In addition, the Supreme Court of Canada has special rules governing the citation of electronic versions of decisions of the Supreme Court of Canada and other courts.[43]

What follows next in this section is a list of answers to the most frequently asked questions about legal citation:

Do I need to italicize the "v." in the style of cause?
The "v." (or "c." in French) in the style of cause is an abbreviation for "versus" (*Smith v. Jones*) and is pronounced "v" or "and." Although prior editions of the McGill Guide did not italicize the "v." (or "c." in French), Rule 3.2.2 of the McGill Guide now authorizes the reader to italicize the "v.," something which many authors and publishers already did since the names of the parties in the style of cause must also be italicized and it is easier—when typing—to also italicize the "v." (or "c." in French) as well.

---

42   Frédéric Pelletier, Ruth Rintoul, & Daniel Poulin, eds., *The Preparation, Citation and Distribution of Canadian Decisions* (2 April 2009), online: www.lexum. umontreal.ca/ccc-ccr/preparation/en/.

43   Supreme Court of Canada, *Bulletin* (6 October 2000), online: http://scc.lexum. umontreal.ca/en/bulletin/2000/00-10-06.bul/00-10-06.bul.html. See also Rule 44 of the *Rules of the Supreme Court of Canada*, S.O.R./2002-156, which, through mention of electronic versions of legislation and case law, authorizes the use of electronic versions.

When citing a case, when do I use square brackets vs. round parentheses for the year?
This is somewhat surprisingly the most confusing citation issue for law students and those new to legal research. **Round parentheses** are used for the year when citing cases that are reported in case law reporters that are published by the volume number—in other words, use round parentheses to indicate the year of the decision: McGill Guide, Rule 3.2.4.1. The comma follows the round parentheses. Example (emphasis added): *Bingo Enterprises Ltd. v. Plaxton* **(1986)**, 41 Man. R. (2d) 19 (C.A.). **Square brackets** are used for the year when citing cases that are reported in case law reporters that are published annually or by the year—in other words, use square brackets to indicate the year of the reporter: McGill Guide, Rule 3.2.4.2. The comma precedes the square brackets. Example (emphasis added): *R. v. Noble*, **[1997]** 1 S.C.R. 874.

Table 1.1 sets out a list of some popular Canadian case law reporters that use either square brackets or round parentheses.

What are parallel citations and do I need to use them?
Many important cases are published in print in multiple case law reporters (and online). A decision on tort law from the Supreme Court of Canada that arose in British Columbia may likely be reported in the *Supreme Court Reports*, the *Dominion Law Reports*, the *British Columbia Law Reports*, and the *Canadian Cases on the Law of Torts*. Rule 3.2.9 of the McGill Guide requires the researcher to include citations to multiple case law reports where possible. This is done as a courtesy to the reader who may have access to only one of the several case law reporters listed in the citation. Thus, in a parallel citation, what is being cited is one single decision, a decision that has been reported in a string or list of multiple case law reporters—it is not necessary to consult each individual reporter listed in a parallel citation since they are each reporting the same decision. An example of a parallel citation is as follows: *Wenden v. Trikha* (1992), 1 Alta.L.R. (3d) 283, 124 A.R. 1, 6 C.P.C. (3d) 15 (Q.B.)—in this example, the same trial decision in *Wenden v. Trikha* is reported in three different case law reporters (i.e., the *Alberta Law Reports*, the *Alberta Reports*, and *Carswell's Practice Cases*).

How do I cite unreported decisions?
Increasingly, lawyers and judges regularly use and cite decisions from online databases. If the case is unreported (i.e., not available in a print case law reporter), the McGill Guide sets out rules on how to cite unreported decisions, whether by citing to the court file (Rule 3.2.13) or to an online database (Rule 3.10). The format follows the general pattern

Table 1.1
Sample Citations: Square Brackets vs. Round Parentheses

Popular Canadian Case Law Reporters Published by Year
[Use Square Brackets]

Reporter	Example
Supreme Court Reports [1923–current]	Douglas v. Tucker, [1952] 1 S.C.R. 275 (S.C.C.)
Federal Court Reports [1923–current]	"Donnacona II" (The) v. Montship Lines Ltd., [1961] Ex. C.R. 249 or Feherguard Products Ltd. v. Rocky's of B.C. Leisure Ltd., [1993] 3 F.C. 619 (C.A.)
Dominion Law Reports [1923–1955]	Canadian Performing Rights Society Ltd. v. Ming Yee, [1943] 4 D.L.R. 732 (Alta. Dist. Ct.)
Western Weekly Reports [1923–1955] [1971–current]	Bradshaw v. Epp, [1937] 3 W.W.R. 577 (Man. C.A.) Waldron v. Royal Bank, [1991] 4 W.W.R. 289 (B.C.C.A.)
Ontario Reports [1931–1973]	Mitchell v. Jolly, [1960] O.R. 470 (C.A.)

Popular Canadian Case Law Reporters Published by Volume
(Use Round Parentheses)

Reporter	Example
Supreme Court Reports (1867–1922)	Francis v. Allan (1918), 57 S.C.R. 373 (S.C.C.)
Exchequer Court Reports (1875–1922)	Canadian Vickers Ltd. v. "Susquehanna" (The) (1919), 19 Ex. C.R. 116 (C.A.)
Dominion Law Reports (Vol. 1, 1912–Vol. 64, 1922) (Vol. 1, 1956–Vol. 70, 1968) (2d) (Vol. 1, 1969–Vol. 150, 1984) (3d) (Vol. 1, 1985–current) (4th)	Pratt v. Lovelace (1913), 11 D.L.R. 385 (Sask. C.A.) Morrison v. Mills (1963), 38 D.L.R. (2d) 489 (Alta. T.D.) R. v. Zaduk (1978), 98 D.L.R. (3d) 133 (Ont. C.A.) Wadsworth v. Hayes (1996), 132 D.L.R. (4th) 410 (Alta. C.A.)
Western Weekly Reports (Vol. 1, 1912–Vol. 10, 1916) (Vol. 1, 1951–Vol. 75, 1970) (N.S.)	Drinkle v. Regal Shoe Co. (1914), 7 W.W.R. 194 (B.C.S.C.) Gordon v. Hipwell (No. 2) (1952), 5 W.W.R. (N.S.) 635 (B.C.C.A.)
Ontario Reports (1974–current)	Boehmers v. 794561 Ontario Inc. (1995), 21 O.R. (3d) 771 (C.A.)

Note 1:   This chart is not an exhaustive list of reporters.

Note 2:   Some reporters, such as the Dominion Law Reports, Ontario Reports, and Western Weekly Reports, have changed over time from publishing by year [square brackets] to publishing by volume (round parentheses).

Note 3:   All LexisNexis Quicklaw unreported decisions use square brackets around the year of the decision — example: Parsons v. Canada Safeway Ltd., [1995] B.C.J. No. 1947 (S.C.) (QL).

for reported cases (style of cause, year, "source," and level of court). Unfortunately, the McGill Guide does not provide examples for every possible source of online law-related materials.

A typical decision on LexisNexis Quicklaw that is not reported in a print case law reporter would be cited thus (where "O.J." represents the Ontario Judgments database on which the case was found and the "No. 1723" being the unique number LexisNexis Quicklaw has assigned to that case for that database for that year):

> *R. v. Zborovsky*, [1992] O.J. No. 1723 (Ont. Prov. Ct.) (QL)

A typical decision on Westlaw Canada that is not reported in a print case law reporter would be cited thus:

> *Clarke v. Action Driving School Ltd.*, 1996 CarswellBC 1004 (S.C.) (Westlaw)[44]

I used an online database to find a case — can I cite to only the online version even if the case is also published in print?
Where a case is available in print *and* online, Rule 3.1 of the McGill Guide requires the researcher to cite to the print version (and to also cite to the electronic database). The rationale for this is obvious: not all readers will have access to the online version and not all online versions of material allow for easy "pinpoint" citations if there are no paragraph numbers provided in the online version; as a courtesy to the reader, therefore, one should prefer a citation to print material. The suggestion in the McGill Guide to cite to both the print *and* the online version is good but is not always done in practice since most sophisticated researchers will know (or readily assume) whether a particular case in print is available online (and recent cases will most likely be online for free on CanLII), so it is usually sufficient to cite to only the print version.

How do I cite to the *Canadian Encyclopedic Digest*?
Unfortunately, Rule 6.5 of the 6th edition of the McGill Guide provides examples for only *Halsbury's Laws of England* and *American Jurisprudence* but not for the *Canadian Encyclopedic Digest* (CED) (encyclopedias are discussed in Chapter 2). Based on the examples provided, you can create a citation to the CED as follows:

---

44   Rule 3.10.2.1 of the 6th edition of the McGill Guide currently suggests using (WLeC) to identify what was called WestlaweCARSWELL (now called Westlaw Canada). In the example above, I have used simply Westlaw pending a decision by the editors of the next edition of the McGill Guide on how to abbreviate Westlaw Canada.

Title of encyclopedia, volume, edition (place of publication: publisher, year of publication), "title of chapter," (optional) pinpoint.

Canadian Encyclopedic Digest, Vol. 31, 3d ed. (Toronto: Carswell, 1988) "Torts," §126.

If citing to only the online version of the CED, this is more complicated since the online version does not use volume numbers. For online, drop the volume number but keep the edition (and realize the publisher is in the process of publishing a new print 4th edition).

How do I cite to a seminar paper from a CLE conference?
The examples given by the McGill Guide in Rule 6.3 for "Collection of Essays" and Rule 6.11 for "Addresses and Papers Delivered at Conferences" do not address the typical seminar paper from a continuing legal education (CLE) conference put on by, say, the Canadian Bar Association. For those types of seminar papers, consider using the following form (where the symposium or conference was called "Advanced Real Estate"):

Morton G. Gross, "Ground Leases and their Financing" in *Advanced Real Estate* (Toronto: Canadian Bar Association, Ontario, 1988).

A few final tips on legal citation:

- Don't guess and don't be lazy—look it up in the McGill Guide if you are not certain.
- You can often safely rely upon the way in which a reputable publisher has cited a case or a statute in its publication by simply copying how the publisher has cited the material. If your document is important, however, check the McGill Guide.
- Appendix G (case law reporters) and Appendix H (periodicals and yearbooks) to the McGill Guide provide examples of how to abbreviate titles.

E. COPYRIGHT ISSUES AFFECTING LEGAL RESEARCH AND WRITING

Related to issues of citation are issues of copyright law. In Canada, copyright law is governed by the *Copyright Act*.[45] Under that Act, the owner of the copyright in a literary work (i.e., a legal textbook, for example) has

---

45   R.S.C. 1985, c. C-42.

the sole right to produce or reproduce the work or any substantial part thereof in any material form.[46] Users are given relatively limited rights to copy protected works. One exemption to copyright is the defence of "fair dealing" for the purpose of research or private study (with various conditions attached).[47] Therefore, for legal researchers, the issue that arises is determining when permission from the copyright owner is needed for the use of law-related resources.

For government works, the issue is affected Crown copyright, which states that the government retains copyright in any work that has been prepared or published by or under the direction or control of Her Majesty or any government department.[48] The notion that the government would insist upon Crown copyright over legislation and cases has been criticized by academic commentators.[49] A more preferable viewpoint would be that all works produced under authority of the government are in the public domain for the benefit of all to use, subject possibly to the right of the government to claim any "moral rights" in its works when necessary to protect the accuracy or representation of the work.[50] Alternatively, if the government insists on maintaining a Crown copyright in its works, an argument could likely be made on philosophical grounds that all citizens, as taxpayers, have an implicit, royalty-free licence to use government works.

Fortunately, the Canadian federal government has largely resolved some of these issues as they affect legal research materials through its issuance of the *Reproduction of Federal Law Order*[51] which allows cases and legislation issued under authority of the government to be freely

---

46   *Ibid.*, s. 3(1).

47   *Ibid.*, s. 29.

48   *Ibid.*, s. 12.

49   See, for example, David Vaver, *Intellectual Property Law* (Toronto: Irwin Law, 1997) at 59–60. See also Ted Tjaden, "Chapter 4: The Impact of Crown Copyright on Access to Law-Related Information" in *Access to Law-Related Information in Canada in the Digital Age* (LL.M. Thesis, 2005, University of Toronto, Faculty of Law, 2005), online: www.slaw.ca/resources/tjaden-thesis/, in which the author rants against Crown copyright as being a dated, paternalistic, and unnecessary concept (given the fact, for example, that the United States has not suffered any catastrophes as a result of not having Crown copyright).

50   This in fact is consistent with Recommendations 10, 11, and 12 of the House of Commons Standing Committee on Communications and Culture, *Report of the Sub-Committee on the Revision of Copyright: A Charter of Rights for Creators* (Ottawa: Supply & Services, 1985) at 10–12.

51   S.I./97-5.

used so long as any reproductions are accurate and not represented as official versions:[52]

> Anyone may, without charge or request for permission, reproduce enactments and consolidations of enactments of the Government of Canada, and decisions and reasons for decisions of federally-constituted courts and administrative tribunals, provided due diligence is exercised in ensuring the accuracy of the materials reproduced and the reproduction is not represented as an official version.

For private legal publishers, the issues are slightly different. Most, if not all, of these publishers will own copyright in their textbooks, case law reporters, and other law-related publications. Technically, unless one were able to rely upon the "fair dealing" provisions of the Act—which are relatively narrow—it would be necessary, for example, to obtain the permission of the applicable publisher to photocopy material for court or to cite passages in one's court factum from a publisher's textbook. As a practical matter, legal publishers have not pursued copyright infringement claims against individual lawyers or law firms, although Access Copyright,[53] the national copyright collective in Canada that represents authors, has in the past announced a collective photocopying licence for law firms that it intends to negotiate with lawyers that would, for a negotiated flat fee, give permission for lawyers and employees at the firm to photocopy from published works. The Federation of Law Societies of Canada, however, has taken a cautious approach to such licences.[54]

Of particular interest to the legal community is the recent Supreme Court of Canada decision in *CCH Canadian Ltd. v. Law Society of Upper Canada*,[55] arising from a ten-year dispute between several Canadian legal publishers and the Law Society of Upper Canada. The publishers alleged, among other things, that the photocopying service provided

---

52   The Ontario government also has a policy on copyright of legal materials that allows any person "to reproduce the text and images contained in the statutes, regulations and judicial decisions without seeking permission and without charge" but the materials "must be reproduced accurately and the reproduction must not be represented as an official version." A copyright notice in favour of the Queens Printer for Ontario must also be provided. See Ontario, "Policy on Copyright on Legal Materials," online: Government of Ontario, www.ontario. ca/en/general/004222.

53   See online: www.accesscopyright.ca.

54   Federation of Law Societies of Canada, National Copyright Committee, "Copyright Notice" (January 2001).

55   *CCH Canadian Ltd. v. Law Society of Upper Canada*, 2004 SCC 13, rev'g 2002 FCA 187, rev'g [2000] 2 F.C. 451 (T.D.).

by the Law Society's law library infringed the copyright of these legal publishers.

Chief Justice McLachlin, speaking for the Court, ruled largely in favour of the Law Society. It was held that, although copyright existed in the publishers' works under consideration, the copying done by the Great Library was fair dealing with the publishers' works. In addition, the Court also ruled that the Great Library did not authorize copyright infringement by the mere fact of supplying self-service photocopiers in its library. The Court also ruled that fax transmissions of photocopy requests to individual patrons were not "communications to the public."

On the issue of the extent of copyright in the court decisions and headnotes, McLachlin, C.J., adopted a test of "skill and judgment" in defining the degree of "originality" a work must have to be subject to copyright:

> For a work to be "original" within the meaning of the *Copyright Act*, it must be more than a mere copy of another work. At the same time, it need not be creative, in the sense of being novel or unique. What is required to attract copyright protection in the expression of an idea is an exercise of skill and judgment. By skill, I mean the use of one's knowledge, developed aptitude or practised ability in producing the work. By judgment, I mean the use of one's capacity for discernment or ability to form an opinion or evaluation by comparing different possible options in producing the work. This exercise of skill and judgment will necessarily involve intellectual effort. The exercise of skill and judgment required to produce the work must not be so trivial that it could be characterized as a purely mechanical exercise. For example, any skill and judgment that might be involved in simply changing the font of a work to produce "another" work would be too trivial to merit copyright protection as an "original" work.[56]

In looking at the exercise of "skill and judgment" needed to compile reported judicial decisions, the Court concluded that the compilation of the headnotes, case summaries, topical index, and reported judicial decisions in issue met this test and that the legal materials in this case were "original" works covered by copyright.[57]

On the issue of whether the Law Society authorized infringement of copyright by providing self-service photocopiers in the Great Library, however, the Court ruled in favour of the Great Library:

---

56   *Ibid.* at para. 116 (S.C.C.).
57   *Ibid.* at paras. 29–36.

[A] person does not authorize copyright infringement by authorizing the mere use of equipment (such as photocopiers) that could be used to infringe copyright. In fact, courts should presume that a person who authorizes an activity does so only so far as it is in accordance with the law. Although the Court of Appeal assumed that the photocopiers were being used to infringe copyright, I think it is equally plausible that the patrons using the machines were doing so in a lawful manner.

. . . The Law Society's posting of the notice over the photocopiers does not rebut the presumption that a person authorizes an activity only so far as it is in accordance with the law. Given that the Law Society is responsible for regulating the legal profession in Ontario, it is more logical to conclude that the notice was posted for the purpose of reminding the Great Library's patrons that copyright law governs the making of photocopies in the library.

Finally, even if there were evidence of the photocopiers having been used to infringe copyright, the Law Society lacks sufficient control over the Great Library's patrons to permit the conclusion that it sanctioned, approved or countenanced the infringement. The Law Society and Great Library patrons are not in a master-servant or employer-employee relationship such that the Law Society can be said to exercise control over the patrons who might commit infringement . . . . Nor does the Law Society exercise control over which works the patrons choose to copy, the patron's purposes for copying or the photocopiers themselves.[58]

Even though copyright existed in the works in question, the Court took a broad view of "fair dealing" and held that the photocopying done by the Great Library constituted fair dealing in these circumstances. In so deciding, the Court made a number of significant rulings:

- The scope of fair dealing must not be interpreted restrictively.[59]
- The section 29 fair dealing exception is always available to a defendant: "Simply put, a library can always attempt to prove that its dealings with a copyrighted work are fair under section 29 of the *Copyright Act*. It is only if a library were unable to make out the fair dealing exception under section 29 that it would need to turn to section 30.2 of the *Copyright Act* to prove that it qualified for the library exemption."[60]

---

58   *Ibid.* at paras. 43–45.
59   *Ibid.* at para. 48.
60   *Ibid.* at para. 49.

- If the copying is being done for the purpose of "research," the meaning of "research" must be given a large and liberal interpretation in order to ensure that users' rights are not unduly constrained, even where the research is "for profit" (as in the practice of law).[61]
- To determine whether the copying (or "dealing") of the work is "fair," the Court has proposed a number of factors: "(1) the purpose of the dealing; (2) the character of the dealing; (3) the amount of the dealing; (4) alternatives to the dealing; (5) the nature of the work; and (6) the effect of the dealing on the work."[62]

In concluding that the Great Library dealt fairly with the publishers' works, the Court placed emphasis on the fact that the Great Library's "Access to the Law Policy" placed self-imposed restrictions on the library to help ensure compliance with copyright law:

> The factors discussed, considered together, suggest that the Law Society's dealings with the publishers' works through its custom photocopy service were research-based and fair. The Access Policy places appropriate limits on the type of copying that the Law Society will do. It states that not all requests will be honoured. If a request does not appear to be for the purpose of research, criticism, review or private study, the copy will not be made. If a question arises as to whether the stated purpose is legitimate, the Reference Librarian will review the matter. The Access Policy limits the amount of work that will be copied, and the Reference Librarian reviews requests that exceed what might typically be considered reasonable and has the right to refuse to fulfill a request. On these facts, I conclude that the Law Society's dealings with the publishers' works satisfy the fair dealing defence and that the Law Society does not infringe copyright.[63]

Although there were a number of other procedural rulings by the Court on issues between the parties, one additional ruling, albeit likely in *obiter*, was that the Great Library was entitled to rely upon the "library exemption" under section 30.2(1) of the *Copyright Act*, which allows a library to copy a work on behalf of a patron where that patron was able to rely upon the fair dealing exceptions:

> In 1999, amendments to the *Copyright Act* came into force allowing libraries, archives and museums to qualify for exemptions against copyright infringement. Under s. 30.2(1), a library or persons acting

---

61   *Ibid.* at para. 51.
62   *Ibid.* at para. 53.
63   *Ibid.* at para. 73.

under its authority may do anything on behalf of any person that the person may do personally under the fair dealing exceptions to copyright infringement. Section 2 of the *Copyright Act* defines library, archive or museum. In order to qualify as a library, the Great Library: (1) must not be established or conducted for profit; (2) must not be administered or controlled by a body that is established or conducted for profit; and (3) must hold and maintain a collection of documents and other materials that is open to the public or to researchers. The Court of Appeal found that the Great Library qualified for the library exemption. The publishers appeal this finding on the ground that the Law Society, which controls the library, is indirectly controlled by the body of lawyers authorized to practise law in Ontario who conduct the business of law for profit.

I concluded in the main appeal that the Law Society's dealings with the publishers' works were fair. Thus, the Law Society need not rely on the library exemption. However, were it necessary, it would be entitled to do so.[64]

With the increase in online legal resources, many publishers are protecting their intellectual copyright through licences that their customers must sign in order to use their products. In most of these agreements, the vendors contractually restrict the use of their data by their customers and control the downloading, storage, and use of the data. Persons or organizations who enter into these licence agreements for online legal resources should take some care in ensuring that the terms of the licence conditions are understood by all persons within the organization who will be accessing the information. Section E of Chapter 9 provides more information on negotiating licences for law-related resources in electronic format.

F. CONCLUSIONS

Legal research and writing is an important skill. Finding, applying, and communicating the relevant law for a particular issue is a basic function of lawyering. Fortunately, the basic techniques of legal research are relatively straightforward. What follows in the next chapter is a discussion of secondary or background legal resources — such as textbooks, legal journals, encyclopedias, case law digests, and other reference tools — usually a good starting point for all legal research.

---

64   *Ibid.* at paras. 83–84.

G. LEGAL RESEARCH AND LEGAL CITATION GUIDES

Canada

Appleby, Eric. *Legal Research Guide to Statutes 2007.* Fredericton, NB: Maritime Law Book Ltd., 2007, online: www.mlb.nb.ca/site/ffiles/statute.pdf.

Banks, Margaret. *Using a Law Library: Canadian Guide to Legal Research.* 6th ed. Toronto: Carswell, 1994.

Beaulac, Stéphane, ed. *Legal Style Guide / Guide de style juridique.* Markham, ON: LexisNexis, 2006.

Fish, Bonnie. *Fish on Legal Research.* Aurora, ON: Canada Law Book, 2010 (DVD).

Fitzgerald, Maureen F. (with Melinda Renner). *Legal Problem Solving: Reasoning, Research and Writing.* 4th ed. Toronto: Butterworths, 2007.

Gordon, Suzanne & Sherifa Elkhadem. *The Law Workbook: Developing Skills for Legal Research and Writing.* Toronto: Emond Montgomery, 2001.

Kerr, Margaret *et al. Legal Research: Step by Step.* 3d ed. Toronto: Emond Montgomery, 2009.

Lafond, Pierre-Claude & Philippe Samson. *Techniques de repérage des sources documentaires du droit: guide pratique.* 3e éd. Cowansville, QC: Éditions Y. Blais, 2004.

LeMay, Denis. *The Civil Code of Québec in Chart Form.* Montréal: Wilson & Lafleur, 2006.

LeMay, Denis & John Eaton. *Essential Sources of Canadian Law / Les références essentielles en droit canadien.* Toronto: Irwin Law, 2009.

LeMay, Denis *et al. La recherche documentaire en droit.* 6e éd. Montréal: Wilson & Lafleur, 2008.

MacEllven, Douglass *et al. Legal Research Handbook.* With special assistance by Denis LeMay. 5th ed. Toronto: Butterworths, 2003.

McCallum, Margaret E. *et al. Synthesis: Legal Reading, Reasoning and Writing in Canada.* 2d ed. Toronto: CCH Canadian, 2008.

McGill Law Journal, eds. *Canadian Guide to Uniform Legal Citation*. 6th ed. Toronto: Carswell, 2006.

McCormack, Nancy *et al*. *The Practical Guide to Canadian Legal Research*. 3d ed., Toronto: Carswell, 2010.

Yogis, John A. & Innis M. Christie. By Michael J. Iosipescu & Michael E. Deturbide. *Legal Writing and Research Manual*. 6th ed. Toronto: Butterworths, 2004.

Zivanovic, Aleksandra. *Guide to Electronic Legal Research*. 2d ed. Toronto: Butterworths, 2002.

United States

Barkan, Steven M. *et al*. *Barkan, Mersky and Dunn's Fundamentals of Legal Research*. 9th ed. Westbury, NY: Foundation Press, 2009.

Berring, Robert C. & Elizabeth Edinger. *Finding the Law*. 12th ed. St. Paul, MN: West Group, 2005.

Cohen, Morris L. & Kent Olsen. *Legal Research in a Nutshell*. 9th ed. St. Paul, MN: West Group, 2007.

Dickerson, Darby. *ALWD Citation Manual: A Professional System of Citation*, 3d ed. New York: Aspen, 2006.

Elias, Stephen & Susan Levinkind. *Legal Research: How to Find and Understand the Law*. 15th ed. Berkeley, CA: Nolo Press, 2009.

Kunz, Christina *et al*. *The Process of Legal Research*. 7th ed. New York: Aspen Law & Business, 2008.

Schmedemann, Deborah A. & Christina L. Kunz. *Synthesis: Legal Reading, Reasoning and Writing*. 3d ed. Aspen Law & Business, 2007.

United Kingdom

Knowles, John. *Effective Legal Research*. 2d ed. London: Sweet & Maxwell, 2009.

Australia

Bott, Bruce & Ruth Talbot-Stokes. *Nemes and Coss' Effective Legal Research*. 4th ed. Chatswood, NSW: LexisNexis Butterworths, 2009.

Watt, Robert & Francis Johns. *Concise Legal Research*. 6th ed. Sydney: Federation Press, 2009.

CHAPTER 2

SECONDARY LEGAL RESOURCES

The goal of legal research is to find relevant legislation or judicial decisions (i.e., primary legal resources) that apply to the particular legal problem being researched because only legislation or judicial decisions have the power to affect legal rights. However, finding relevant statutes and cases can be a challenge for first-time legal researchers.

Therefore, an effective legal research technique when starting to research a particular problem is to first consult secondary legal resources to gain a broad overview of the topic. Secondary legal resources include such things as textbooks, law journals, seminar papers, encyclopedias, case law digests, Web guides, and other reference tools. Starting with secondary legal research resources has several advantages:

- Secondary legal resources generally provide a good synopsis of the law and provide footnotes or links to relevant legislation or case law.
- They are usually written by experts in their field, allowing the researcher to take advantage of someone else's work.
- Most materials are relatively current, especially if they are in loose-leaf format or online.
- Some secondary legal resources, such as leading textbooks or well-researched law journal articles, are highly persuasive in court.

This chapter provides a brief overview of textbooks, law journals, CLE/seminar papers, legal encyclopedias, case law digests, and general legal reference resources (law dictionaries, legal citation guides, legal directories, forms and precedents, court rules, current awareness tools, and Web guides). The emphasis will be on Canadian materials, with discussion of British, American, and Australian materials where relevant, since these are usually the other jurisdictions of most interest to Canadian legal researchers.

A. TEXTBOOKS

Lawyers, judges, academics, and other researchers have written books on most, if not all, legal topics imaginable. If you find a relevant book covering your area of legal research, you will have saved yourself a lot of time by leveraging the research of experts on the topic (the notion of "standing on the shoulders of giants").

You can find law-related textbooks at most courthouse, law society, and law school law libraries. Many law firms also own their own law-related textbooks relevant to their own areas of practice (for information on selecting or acquiring law-related resources, see Chapter 9). Searching for law-related textbooks has been made easy with the advent of the Internet. Catalogues for major law libraries in Canada (and throughout the world) can now be found online (see Table 2.1). Searching these online library catalogues by author, title, subject, or keyword can help you identify relevant materials for your topic to help you decide if you want to try to borrow the material or buy it for yourself.

Table 2.1
Chart of Online Canadian Library Catalogues Containing
Law-Related Material

Law Library	WWW Address for Catalogue
Diana M. Priestly Law Library (UVic)	http://library.law.uvic.ca
UBC Law Library	www.library.ubc.ca
B.C. Courthouse Library Society	www.courthouselibrary.ca
U of Calgary Law Library	http://osiris.lib.ucalgary.ca
John A Weir Memorial Law Library (U of Alberta)	www.library.ualberta.ca
U of Saskatchewan Law Library	http://sundog.usask.ca
E.K. Williams Law Library (U of Manitoba)	www.umanitoba.ca/libraries
U of Western Ontario Law Library	www.lib.uwo.ca
U of Windsor Law Library	http://cronus.uwindsor.ca/library

Law Library	WWW Address for Catalogue
Osgoode Hall Law School (York U)	www.library.yorku.ca
Law Society of Upper Canada	http://library.lsuc.on.ca
Bora Laskin Law Library (U of Toronto)	www.library.utoronto.ca
Supreme Court of Canada Law Library	http://catalogue.scc-csc.gc.ca
William R. Lederman Law Library (Queens U)	http://library.queensu.ca
U of Ottawa Law Library	http://orbis.uottawa.ca
Nahum Gelber Law Library (McGill U)	www.mcgill.ca/library
U of Montreal Law Library	www.bib.umontreal.ca/Atrium
U of Sherbrooke Law Library	www.usherbrooke.ca/biblio
U of Laval Law Library	http://ariane.ulaval.ca
Gerald V. La Forest Law Library (UNB)	https://quest.unb.ca
U of Moncton Law Library	www.umoncton.ca umcm-bibliotheque-droit
Sir James Dunn Law Library (Dalhousie U)	www.library.dal.ca
National Library of Canada	www.collectionscanada.gc.ca/amicus

Searching online library catalogues is relatively straightforward, depending on the catalogue software being used by the library. Many inexperienced researchers fail to appreciate the value of searching on the "controlled vocabulary" used by library cataloguers in the catalogue to describe materials held by the library. Library of Congress Subject Headings are one of the more common controlled vocabularies. If, like most people (including some librarians), you are not exactly sure of the Library of Congress Subject Heading for your topic, try conducting a "title keyword" search to find any relevant record in the catalogue. Once you find an item of interest, browse through the detailed catalogue record for that item to see what the Library of Congress Subject Headings are for that item and then conduct a "related search" by clicking on the Library of Congress Subject Heading link (if you are in a Web browser version of the catalogue) or by retyping the *actual* Library of Congress Subject Heading and rerunning your search. This will then result in a list of *all* materials held by that library on that topic. For example, searching on "defamation" and "law" in a title keyword search brings up lots of catalogue records, one of which will be *The Law of Defamation in Canada*, 2d ed. (Carswell), a four-volume looseleaf. Clicking on the "full record" for that entry reveals that the official Library of Congress Subject Heading for that topic is in fact "Libel and slander—Canada" (as opposed to using the term "defamation" as part of the official subject heading). Clicking on that Subject Heading will then generate a list of all books held by the library on Canadian defamation (or libel and slander) law.

Another useful technique when searching online library catalogues is to sort your search results by *reverse chronological order* or *most recent first* (if this option is available on the catalogue) on the assumption—generally true for legal materials—that more recent material is better than older, dated material.

There are a number of criteria that can be applied in assessing the quality of law-related textbooks. Some of these criteria include the following points:

- The *content* of the material—is the law applicable to your jurisdiction or area of practice?
- The *expertise of the author*—what credentials, experience, or reputation does the author have?
- The *currency* of the material—how recent is the book? If it is a loose-leaf or in electronic format, how often is it updated?
- The *format* of the material—does the material have an index or table of contents? If so, is the index or table of contents reliable? If the resource is in electronic format, how easy is it to search or save search results?
- The *publisher* of the material—does the publisher have a reputation for quality?

Some of the leading publishers in Canada of print law-related textbooks include Butterworths, Canada Law Book, Carswell, CCH Canadian, E. Montgomery, Éditions Yvon Blais, Irwin Law, Maritime Law Book, and Wilson and LaFleur, although there are also a number of other important specialty publishers of law-related material, including the various provincial and federal bar associations and the federal and provincial governments. Law reform commission reports are an excellent source of legal information since lawyers or researchers acting on behalf of the law reform commission have already done fairly exhaustive research on your behalf. These reports are usually prepared on legal topics of general interest and can be found in library catalogues of academic law libraries or by searching the web-site of the BC Law Reform Group, which has an excellent online database of law reform commission reports from jurisdictions around the world.[1]

---

1   See BC Law Reform Group, Law Reform Database, online: www.bcli.org/bclrg/law-reform. See also Manas Media Inc., *World Law Reform Collection: Jurisdiction*

Important publishers of British secondary legal materials include Ashgate, Butterworths U.K., CCH, Hart, Informa Professional, Jordan, Oxford University Press, Routledge-Cavendish, and Sweet & Maxwell. In Australia, there is Butterworths Australia, Cavendish, CCH, Federation Press, and Thomson Reuters. In the United States, there is West Publishing, Matthew Bender, Aspen Law, Bureau of National Affairs, Oceana Publications, and CCH, to name a few.

The American Association of Law Libraries has a useful page setting out information and links on the three major legal publishers (Thomson, Reed Elsevier, and Wolters Kluwer), including an explanation of the relationship among various publishers within the three major groups and including a list of other independent publishers.[2]

Increasingly, publishers are willing to publish their textbooks in electronic format, either on CD-ROM or through their commercial online databases. There are over 150 Canadian law-related books available in electronic format, covering over thirty legal subject areas, ranging from administrative law to tort law.[3] Some recent examples of Canadian books in electronic format include:

- *Irwin Law*: Irwin Law has partnered with ebrary to make all of the Irwin Law titles available online (by subscription). The online versions maintain the look and feel of the print versions while at the same time being full-text searchable. Page numbers in the index are clickable (to take users to the applicable page), and website URLs in the text are also clickable. See Figure 2.1 for a screenshot of the Irwin Law e-Library. Subscribers can also digitally highlight, bookmark, and annotate pages. Within the InfoTools feature, users can also highlight a caselaw citation, then link to a caselaw database to search for a full-text version of the case.
- *Carswell*: Carswell makes a number of its books available via subscription on Westlaw Canada, CD-ROM, and its eReference Library (www.carswellreference.com). The e-books on Westlaw Canada are currently "packaged" by their "Source" products, by topic (for example, the Carswell looseleaf *Bankruptcy and Insolvency Law of*

---

and *Subject Index* (Kanata, ON: Manas Media Inc., 2002) (updated periodically; online subscription available at www.manasmedia.com).

2   See "A Legal Publishers List: Corporate Affiliations of Legal Publishers," 2d ed., online: www.aallnet.org/committee/criv/resources/tools/list (last updated 1 May 2006).

3   Ted Tjaden, "Update re Law-Related Books," The SLAW Blog, comment posted 7 January 2009, www.slaw.ca/2009/01/07/update-re-law-related-e-books.

Canada is also available online on Westlaw Canada as part of their InsolvencySource database). E-books are also available for such topics as criminal law, estates and trusts, family law, bankruptcy and insolvency, and securities law.

- *LexisNexis Canada*: Treatises published by LexisNexis Canada are increasingly available on LexisNexis Quicklaw as e-books, including such titles as Wlaker's *Canadian Conflict of Laws*, 6th ed., and Swan's *Canadian Contract Law*, 2d ed.
- *Canada Law Book*: The popular Brown and Beatty textbook, *Canadian Labour Arbitration*, is available by Web subscription or CD-ROM, as are several other titles, including Salhany's *Canadian Criminal Procedure*, 6th ed.

Figure 2.1
Screenshot of the Irwin Law e-Library

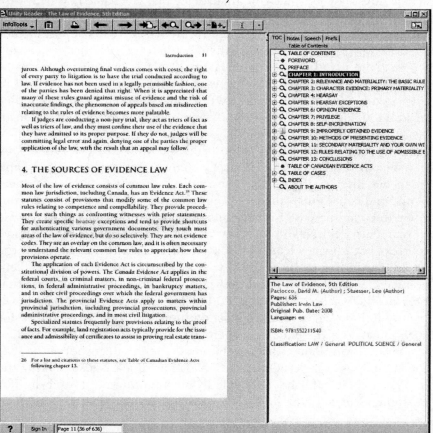

The importance of starting your legal research by consulting a good book cannot be overlooked, whether using a print or online version. Chapter 8 provides a list of Library of Congress Subject Headings for the major law-related topics, along with a list of the leading textbooks in Canada, arranged by topic, and can be a useful starting point for any legal research project.

B. LAW JOURNALS

Law journals are another excellent source of background material on law-related topics. Articles can range from very practitioner-oriented, often written by lawyers or judges, to more theoretical or policy-based, often written by academics or other scholars. Regardless of the type of article, most law journals contain articles that cite some law, be it case law or legislation, and can be a great way to legitimately leverage someone else's research. Increasingly, courts are receptive to counsel including relevant journal articles in their books of authorities, especially where there may be ongoing debate or analysis on substantive areas of law. Due to the publishing cycle of books, journal articles tend to discuss more current or timely issues than is possible in monographs; in addition, journal articles will often go into more specific detail on an issue than is possible in a book.

Law journals are published in print and online by law schools, by law societies and bar associations, by commercial legal publishers, and by special interest groups. Print law journals can be found in most academic and courthouse libraries. There has recently been and will continue to be an increase in the availability of law journals in electronic format. Both LexisNexis Quicklaw and Westlaw Canada have extensive full-text law journals from Canada, the United States, and around the world (depending on the scope of your subscription). Another excellent commercial database of online journals is HeinOnline,[4] a database that provides PDF access to over 1,200 law journal titles (comprising over twenty million pages of text), most dating back to the first volume for each journal on the database. There are currently over fifty Canadian law journals on HeinOnline (see Figure 2.2 for a screenshot of the Law Journal Library on HeinOnline). Canada Law Book is also making the law journals it publishes available by subscription on its website (for example, *Criminal Law Quarterly*). Individual journal publishers, such

---

4   HeinOnline, online: www.heinonline.org.

as Oxford University Press,[5] also make recent volumes of its law journals available online by subscription.

The "best practice" in finding law journal articles is to search journal indexes, many of which are increasingly in electronic format, which allow for keyword searching by author, title, and subject. Regardless of whether the journal index is in print or electronic format, they allow the researcher to find citations to relevant law-related journals articles, are extremely easy to use, and usually contain their own guide on how to use them. Since most online journal indexes only catalogue journal articles from the mid 1980s to the most recent articles, researchers must not overlook the need to use older print format journal indexes to help locate pre-1980s journal articles.

Figure 2.2
Screenshot of HeinOnline's Law Journal Library

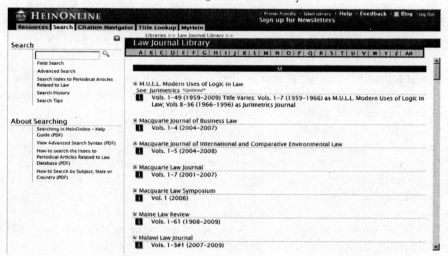

In Canada, there are two main journal indexes:

- *Index to Canadian Legal Literature.* Toronto: Carswell, 1981 [updated quarterly]. Available in print (as part of Carswell's *Canadian Abridgment*) and online through Westlaw Canada or LexisNexis Quicklaw.
- *Index to Canadian Legal Periodical Literature.* Montreal: Canadian Association of Law Libraries, 1963 [updated irregularly]. Available in print only.

---

5   See, for example, Oxford University Press's list of online journals at www. oxfordjournals.org/subject/law.

Canadian journal literature is also indexed in Wilson's *Index to Legal Periodicals & Books*, available in print and held by most large academic law libraries. This index, which provides coverage from 1981 to the present, also provides extensive citations to American legal journal literature, as well as coverage of journals from Puerto Rico, Great Britain, Ireland, Canada, Australia, and New Zealand.[6] Similar journal coverage, including Canadian, is also provided by *LegalTrac*, an online law journal index published by the Gale Group and available in print as the *Current Law Index* (coverage from 1980). For users with access to HeinOnline, there is the *Index to Periodicals Related to Law* (IPRL) that indexes articles relating to legal topics that are published in non-law periodicals (i.e., publications not indexed in the standard legal indexes such as the *Index to Legal Periodicals* and *LegalTrac*). An example of a citation indexed in the IPRL is the following title from a periodical called *Accounting Review*, found under the topic "Securities":

> The effects of Sarbanes-Oxley on auditing and internal control strength. Patterson, Evelyn R. and Smith, J. Reed. Accounting Review. 82(2):427–455. March 2007.

Legal Journals Index, available in print and via online subscription from Sweet & Maxwell and available on Westlaw Canada, indexes more than 430 law journals from or about the United Kingdom and the EU.

One of the major Australian and New Zealand law journal indexes is *AGIS: Attorney-General's Information Service*, available in print and via online subscription (held by many major academic law libraries).

The *Index to Foreign Legal Periodicals*, produced by the American Association of Law Libraries, provides access to legal literature outside of the United States, England, Canada, and Australia, covering the period from 1960 to the present (in print). An online version, from Ovid Technologies, provides coverage from 1985 to the present.

In addition to finding relevant journal articles by searching in a print or online journal index, it is also possible to search the full text of journals on LexisNexis Quicklaw, Westlaw Canada, or HeinOnline. When searching full-text law journal databases, however, it is important to realize that you are usually never searching the entire "universe" of law journal articles since even the most extensive online law journal database does not have every law journal, and even for the ones online, they often do not go back very far (except for HeinOnline, which

---

6   Some academic law libraries may also have a subscription to Wilson's online *Index to Legal Periodicals Full Text* (www.hwwilson.com/databases/legal.htm), which has the added feature of having the full text of over 325 select periodicals dating back as far as 1994.

has excellent historical coverage).[7] Hence the advantage of using both journal indexes and full-text searches to ensure the widest possible coverage of material.

Another potential disadvantage of searching full-text journals is the risk of getting "false hits" unless your search criteria are precise and accurately set out. A useful technique when searching full-text law journals is to search by "field" or "segment" to limit your search terms to a particular part of the article, such as title or author. For example, searching full-text law journals on the word "internet" may retrieve articles where the main focus is not the Internet (simply because the word "internet" is mentioned somewhere in the text), whereas searching the word "internet" in the title field or segment will more likely retrieve articles focusing on the issue of the Internet on the assumption that an article where the search term appears in the title will likely be on that topic.

To be exhaustive, the effective legal researcher will therefore search both journal indexes and full-text journal databases.

C. CLE/SEMINAR PAPERS

Whereas university law reviews or journals tend to be more academic or scholarly, there is a body of literature in the form of continuing legal education (CLE) seminar papers that tend to be more practitioner-focused. Attendees of CLE seminars will ordinarily be given a binder containing copies of the papers presented at the seminar; these binders are then typically added to the law firm's internal library or kept by the lawyer in her office. Seminar topics are usually on either current issues facing the profession (e.g., *Civil Litigation: Your Passport to the New Rules: Hit the Ground Running*) or on practical, substantive areas of law important to practising lawyers (e.g., *Real Property Law: Closing the Deal*). Increasingly, CLE seminars are making their materials available online.[8]

The *Canadian Legal Symposia Index* on LexisNexis Quicklaw is the best way to search for CLE papers (this database indexes CLE papers from 1986 to current). You can search by keyword and then check the

---

7   If you are searching on fairly specific keywords—such as a case name or author—a full-text law journal database search can sometimes find discrete references, where your keywords appear in a footnote, for example, resulting in hits that you might not likely find using law journal indexes.

8   In Ontario, for example, AccessCLE provides online access (for a fee) to a large number of CLE papers from Law Society of Upper Canada seminars. See: http://ecom.lsuc.on.ca/home/accesscle.jsp. There are currently about 2,500 seminar papers available ranging across a dozen different practice areas or topics.

"Subjects" of records in your search results and revise your search, as needed, to search on the official "Subject" descriptors. Alternatively, LexisNexis Quicklaw currently allows you to search by the "Title" or "Author" segments of the results record, which can focus your search if you limit your keywords to the "title" of the paper or if you are searching for a known author.

Figure 2.3 shows the contents of a typical search result on the Canadian Legal Symposia Index, with five headings: Title, Author, Publisher, Subjects, and Symposium.

Figure 2.3
Contents of Sample Entry from the *Canadian Legal Symposia Index* on LexisNexis Quicklaw

Title\Titre:	Negotiating and drafting a bulletproof shareholder agreement.
By\Par:	Whitcombe, Michael P.
Publ\Editeur:	Toronto, Ont. : Insight Information, 2009.
Subjects\Sujets:	Contracts -- Canada.
	Corporation law -- Canada.
	Commercial law -- Canada.
	Contrats -- Canada.
	Sociétés -- Droit -- Canada.
	Droit commercial -- Canada.
Symposium:	Negotiating and drafting major business agreements : bulletproof your documents.

Actually getting a copy of a particular CLE paper is a two-step process, starting with searching by keyword in the *Canadian Legal Symposia Index* on LexisNexis Quicklaw and then checking to see if your law library has a copy of the particular CLE binder in which the paper is found. To do this second step, you usually need to search on the name of the Symposia (e.g., "Negotiating and drafting a bulletproof shareholder agreement" in the example in Figure 2.3) since most libraries catalogue CLE seminar conferences only to the level of the name of the Symposia (as title) and Chairpersons of the conference (as authors) and not necessarily at the level of individual paper titles and authors of individual paper titles.

Using the example in Figure 2.3, I would recommend citing CLE papers as follows:[9]

---

9   As mentioned in Chapter 1, Section D, the 6th edition of the McGill Guide does not provide a good example of typical CLE papers, so I have adapted Rules 6.3 and 6.11 to come up with the style example above.

Michael P. Whitcombe, "Negotiating and Drafting a Bulletproof Share-holder Agreement" in *Negotiating and Drafting Major Business Agreements: Bulletproof Your Documents* (Toronto: Insight Information, 2009).

You can also try to find CLE papers by topic using either or both of the "free" techniques below, but these techniques will usually be less exhaustive than searching the *Canadian Legal Symposia Index* on LexisNexis Quicklaw:

- The Great Library of the Law Society of Upper Canada now catalogues CLE seminar binders not only by the "symposia" or seminar title but also at the individual paper/author level. To locate CLE papers in their catalogue,[10] select the "Guided Keyword Search" and select "search in" Table of Contents from the drop-down menu and input your keywords you want to be found in the title or author name of your desired research topic.
- You can also search or browse the websites of the major CLE conference providers, listed below, or try searching law firm websites for their bulletins and publications using the specialized search engines discussed in Section F(6), below in this chapter.

The major CLE providers in Canada organized through or on behalf of the profession are listed below by jurisdiction, nationally and then west to east:

- **National:** Canadian Bar Association — Professional Development www.cba.org/pd/index.aspx
- **BC:** Continuing Legal Education Society of British Columbia www.cle.bc.ca
- **Alberta:** Legal Education Society of Alberta www.lesa.org
- **Saskatchewan:** Saskatchewan Legal Education Society www.sasklegal.ca
- **Manitoba:** Continuing Professional Development www.lawsociety.mb.ca/education
- **Ontario:** Law Society of Upper Canada: CLE Home http://rc.lsuc.on.ca/jsp/home/cleHome.jsp
- **Ontario:** Ontario Bar Association: Programs www.softconference.com/oba/allprogram.aspx
- **Ontario:** Osgoode Professional Development www.law.yorku.ca/clehome.html

---

10   Law Society of Upper Canada, Great Library catalogue, online: http://library.lsuc.on.ca.

- **Quebéc**: Continuing Legal Education
  www.barreau.qc.ca/formation
- **Newfoundland**: Continuing Legal Education
  www.lawsociety.nf.ca/offerings.asp
- **Nova Scotia**: Barrister's Society CLE
  www.nsbs.org/development.php

In addition, a number of other organizations provide CLE, listed below in alphabetical order:

- **Canadian Institute**
  www.canadianinstitute.com
- **Canadian Tax Foundation**
  www.ctf.ca
- **Federated Press**
  www.federatedpress.com
- **Insight Information**
  www.insightinfo.com
- **Insolvency Institute of Canada**
  www.insolvency.ca

In the United States, the Practising Law Institute[11] and West Legal EdCenter[12] are two major providers of online CLE for lawyers.

D. LEGAL ENCYCLOPEDIAS

Legal encyclopedias are another excellent starting point for legal research because of their relatively exhaustive scope and broad overview of law-related topics.

In Canada, there are now three major legal encyclopedias:

- *Canadian Encyclopedic Digest* (3d ed.) (Carswell)
- *Halsbury's Laws of Canada* (LexisNexis Canada)
- *JurisClasseur Québec* (LexisNexis Canada)

Although all three of these titles are available in hard copy versions, they are increasingly being used online (by subscription). The online versions have a number of advantages: (i) they are updated automatically, eliminating the need for manual updating of pages in the looseleaf versions, (ii) they are full-text searchable, and (iii) they have

---

11   Practising Law Institute: www.pli.edu.
12   Online: http://westlegaledcenter.com.

interactive hypertext links to the full-text of cases and legislation cited in their footnotes.

1) *Canadian Encyclopedic Digest*

The *Canadian Encyclopedic Digest*, known as the CED, is published by Thomson Reuters as a looseleaf in two separate editions, a brown Western edition and a green Ontario edition (although some titles from both editions, such as administrative law, are identical). As of the date of publication of this book, Thomson Reuters is in the process of publishing a new, updated fourth edition of the CED. The discussion that follows refers to the existing third edition.

The CED contains Vol. 1 (Absentees to Agency) to Vol. 34 (Weights and Measures to Young Offenders), plus a Research Guide and Key. Each topic can be found under a "tab" (called a "title"). Each topic or "title" is written by a lawyer who has some expertise in that area; hence, (i) titles are updated on an *ad hoc* basis, title by title, and (ii) the quality can vary from title to title, although the overall quality of the CED is quite good. The text is supplemented by yellow update sheets, found at the *front* of each title; thus, to note up your CED research, you must check the relevant paragraph number in the yellow supplemental sheets.

First-time users should consult the Research Guide and Key to obtain an overview of the publication, which is very simple to use. Access is most often by subject, via the index; if you have a case name on point, you can check the Table of Cases from the relevant title for that case and then refer to the paragraph cross-references where the known case is mentioned in the text and find other (similar) cases that may be relevant to your research.

The CED is also available on CD-ROM, a product which has a number of advantages over the print product:

- the CD-ROM contains both the West and Ontario editions
- there is no need to update "looseleaf" pages with the CD-ROM
- the CD-ROM is easy to search and does not take up shelf space

However, most users are now using the online version of the CED on LawSource on Westlaw Canada. This Internet version has added functionality over the print or CD-ROM version in that cases or legislation mentioned in the footnotes on Westlaw Canada are "clickable" and will launch the full text of the decision (see Figure 2.4 for a sample entry from the CED on Westlaw Canada).

One advantage that the CED has is that, as part of the development of the new fourth edition, Carswell will be providing links from particular

CED paragraphs to the corresponding case law digest from the Canadian Case Digests on Westlaw Canada (discussed in Section E, below in this chapter). For example, §339 of the "Animals" title on the CED (dealing with liability for injuries afflicted by dogs) has a cross-reference above the paragraph as follows (with a hypertext link provided): "See *Canadian Abridgment*: TOR.XVI.10.a.iii Torts—Negligence—Liability of owner or possessor of animals—Injury by domestic animals—Injury by dog." These cross-reference links from the CED to the relevant *Canadian Abridgment* section are a nice improvement recently added by the publisher.

Figure 2.4
Sample Entry from Carswell's *Canadian Encyclopedic Digest* on Westlaw Canada

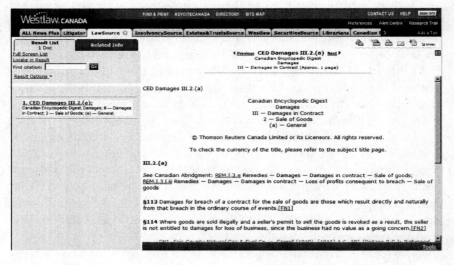

Reprinted by permission of Carswell, a division of Thomson Reuters.

2) *Halsbury's Laws of Canada*

In late 2006, LexisNexis Canada announced the launch of *Halsbury's Laws of Canada*, a new multi-volume encyclopedia mirroring their other *Halsbury's Laws* encyclopedia series (with the main one being from England, discussed in Section D(4), below in this chapter).[13] At the time of publication of this book, there are currently thirty-five print volumes, ranging from "Access to Information and Privacy" to "Wills

---

13   For a discussion of this new encyclopedia—and for a brief comparison to the CED—see Amy Kaufman, "*Halsbury's Laws of Canada* in Context" (2008) 33 Canadian Law Library Review 416.

and Estates" (some volumes contain more than one topic). Their plan is to complete fifty-seven hardbound volumes that will cover about 100 subject areas. The editors of each subject area are usually lawyers or academics who are experts in their field (for example, the "Conflicts of Law" title is edited by Professor Janet Walker, one of the leading commentators in Canada on that topic).

Although initially published only in print, *Halsbury's Laws of Canada* is now available by subscription on LexisNexis Quicklaw. The online version is both searchable and browsable, with hypertext links to the full text of sources cited in footnotes to each paragraph of commentary.

3) *JurisClasseur Québec*

Just as LexisNexis Canada mirrored their *Halsbury's Laws of Canada* encyclopedia on their much older British equivalent title (*Halsbury's Laws of England*), so has LexisNexis Canada mirrored JurisClasseur Québec on their much older French equivalent title (*JurisClasseur France*).

As of the date of publication of this book, there are currently the following topics for *JurisClasseur Québec*: civil law, contracts, and evidence. Eventually this suite of looseleaf services will be expanded to include employment law, sentencing, business law, and public law.

4) Encyclopedias for Other Jurisdictions

For researching British law, *Halsbury's Laws of England* is an authoritative encyclopedia published by Butterworths that dates back to 1907. Currently available in a brown fourth edition in print, it is now available by subscription on LexisNexis Quicklaw. *Halsbury's Laws of England* in print is a multi-volume encyclopedia, arranged by topic alphabetically. Each topic is organized into numbered paragraphs with extensive footnotes that provide links to supporting case law and legislation from England and the European Union. This pattern is repeated in the online version. Some Canadian academic law libraries may still subscribe to the green third edition of *Halsbury's Laws of England*, which has two advantages for Canadian legal researchers. First, the third edition tends to emphasize more British common law, whereas the newer fourth edition tends to highlight more of the legislative developments in England in recent years, something of less interest to most Canadian legal researchers. Second, the third edition has "Canadian converter" volumes that provide citations to Canadian case law, which can be useful for some legal research topics that are based on common law principles (however, it is reasonable to assume that with the advent of a *Hals-*

bury's Laws of Canada, there will be less need for Canadian converter volumes).

For researching American law, there are two major enyclopedias:

- *Corpus Juris Secundum* (West Publishing) (print and online): The "CJS," as it is known, is available in print in a multi-volume set, organized alphabetically by over 400 topics. Information is kept current by annual, cumulative "pocket parts" in the back of each volume. Information is organized by numbered topics, supported by extensive footnotes to case law and legislation, with "key-number" references to the West *Digest* system to find more case law by topic.
- *American Jurisprudence*, 2d ed. (West Publishing) (print and online): "AmJur," as it is known, is another American legal encyclopedia that was originally published by the Lawyers Cooperative. It is available in print and online and is also divided into over 400 topics. Unlike CJS, which attempts to cite as many federal and states cases as possible, AmJur generally provides links to only leading cases.

Another "encyclopedic" American work is the series *American Law Reports* (West Publishing). This series provides a collection of articles or annotations of important or leading cases. There is both a federal and state version; it is available in print and online. The print Index is relatively easy to use and goes into a fair degree of detail (e.g., "Automobiles and Highway Traffic—Air bag systems defective, product liability"). If one is able to identify one's topic in the Index, one is led to a fairly exhaustive article covering all relevant U.S. case law, legislation, and other authorities on point. Articles are kept current by way of updates or supplements in the "pocket part" at the back of each individual volume.

For researching Australian law, there are two major Australian law-related encyclopedias: (i) *Halsbury's Laws of Australia* (LexisNexis Australia, print and online subscription), mirrored after *Halsbury's Laws of England*, and (ii) *Laws of Australia* (Thomson, print and online subscription).

There are also other *Halsbury's* encyclopedia titles, including

- *Halsbury's Laws of Hong Kong*
- *Halsbury's Laws of India*
- *Halsbury's Laws of Malaysia*
- *Halsbury's Laws of Singapore*

Law-related encyclopedias are critical research tools and should be consulted for all questions since they can provide a quick overview of most legal topics and link to relevant case law, legislation, or other commentary on the topic.

E. CASE LAW DIGESTS

Case law digests contain summaries of court cases, usually organized by topic, that allow the researcher to locate relevant case law within the jurisdiction. Unlike legal encyclopedias, which may only refer the reader to significant or leading cases, case law digests usually attempt to provide an exhaustive list of cases for the particular jurisdiction. In print, these case law digests can be quite formidable, due to the volume of case law, which is always increasing with time. Fortunately, there are also a number of case law digests in electronic format that can be searched by keyword or sometimes browsed by topic.

In Canada, the most comprehensive print case law digest is the *Canadian Abridgment* (3d ed.), a multi-volume green and blue set published by Thomson Reuters, which is also available on CD-ROM and as "Canadian Case Digests" on LawSource through Westlaw Canada. The *Canadian Abridgment* in print is in fact more than just a service providing digests of case law; there are various components:

- *Canadian Case Citations*: in print, this red, multi-volume component acts as a "note-upper" for Canadian cases, providing case history, judicial treatment and citation information.
- *Canadian Statute Citations*: in print, this grey, multi-volume component provides citations to Canadian cases that have considered or applied particular sections of Canadian federal and provincial statutes and rules of practice (and selected international treaties).
- *Index to Canadian Legal Literature*: in print, this green, multi-volume component—discussed above in more detail—provides an index to major Canadian law journal articles and other Canadian legal literature.
- *Words & Phrases*: in print, this blue, multi-volume component—discussed in more detail in Section F(1), below in this chapter—provides extensive definitions of words and phrases as defined by Canadian courts.

It is possible to buy individual components or even individual volumes of the *Canadian Abridgment* only on specific legal topics. The case law coverage in the *Canadian Abridgment* dates back to the 1800s. Access is primarily by topic using the *Key and Research Guide* or by keyword using the *General Index*. Once the topic is found using either resource, the user is led to the main volume for that topic and paragraph number range; to update the research, the user then consults the paper supplements, which typically include a cumulative supplement and individual monthly supplements. Indexes are found in the back of every volume, including supplements. One major change with the third edition is an updating and consolidation of the subjects or topics into which case summaries are organized.

The *Canadian Abridgment* contains its own classification system that organizes cases into ever discrete topics. These topics are assigned classification numbers that are a combination of letters, numbers, and Roman numerals. For example, assume you have been asked to research the issue of mobility rights under the *Canadian Charter of Rights and Freedoms* and you want to find some cases on that topic. If you browse through the Table of Classification in Volume 24 of the *Canadian Abridgment* (3d ed.) under the topic of "Constitutional Law," you will see the following breakdown:

Constitutional Law
XI.   *Charter of Rights and Freedoms*
   3.   Nature of rights and freedoms
      e.   Mobility rights
         i.   General principles

Figure 2.5
Sample Entry from Carswell's *Canadian Abridgment* on Westlaw Canada

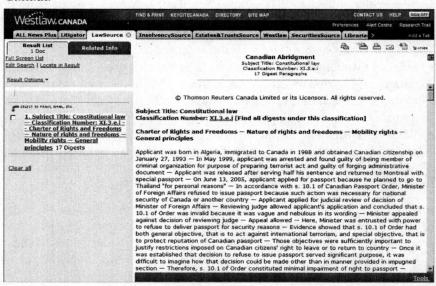

Figure 2.5 shows a sample entry from the online version of the *Canadian Abridgment*, 3d, for this topic, showing the first of seventeen digests.

For all future cases involving this topic, the editors of the *Canadian Abridgment* will continue to classify or group cases involving general principles of mobility rights under the *Charter* under this category, which can be summarized by its classification numbers derived from the Table of Classification: Constitutional Law XI.3.e.i.

The *Canadian Abridgment* on Westlaw Canada has several advantages over the print and CD-ROM versions. The Internet version is both browsable by topic and searchable by keyword using templates, natural language, or Boolean operators. With the Internet version, a case summary can be clicked on to launch the full text of most decisions (which then allows the researcher to click on the "note up" feature to note up the case).

Another extensive (online) case law digest is the Canada Digest from LexisNexis Quicklaw, developed in part to compete with Westlaw Canada's *Canadian Abridgment*. The content is organized according to the LexisNexis Classification System, with the summaries organized by court level, jurisdiction, and date. At the broadest level are (currently) fifty-three topics, ranging from Aboriginal to Wrongful Dismissal. Within each topic is a further breakdown. In the Canada Tort Law Digest, for example, there are twenty-five subheadings, one of which is "Invasion of Privacy — TOR1965,"under which are nine further subheadings, one of which is "Surveillance — TOR2000," under which are several cases that LexisNexis Quicklaw editors have assigned to this topic. The digests are browsable and keyword searchable.

In addition to the *Canadian Abridgment* and the Canada Digest database on Quicklaw, there are a number of other Canadian subject-specific case law digests in print, such as Maritime Law Book's *National Reporter Digest and Index*,[14] the *Charter of Rights Annotated*,[15] and the *Weekly Criminal Bulletin*,[16] to name a few.

A major British case law digest is *The Digest* (Butterworths), formerly the *English and Empire Digest*, which provides coverage of Commonwealth cases, with an emphasis on English cases, but includes limited coverage of Canadian cases. Access is also by legal topic or case name to the main volume; research is then updated by annual cumulative updates and then quarterly softcover updates (*The Digest Quarterly Survey*). Cross references are given to the relevant sections of *Halsbury's Laws of England*. Another important British case law digest is *Current Law* (Sweet & Maxwell), which appears as a monthly issue and is then

---

14   (Fredericton, NB: Maritime Law Book, 1974–).
15   Looseleaf (Aurora, ON: Canada Law Book, 1982).
16   (Aurora, ON: Canada Law Book, 1977–).

consolidated annually and thereafter periodically. Cases can be found using either the current Cumulative Index (for the current year) and the Cumulative Index in the *Current Law Yearbook* (covering 1947 to the year previous to the current year). *Current Law* also includes a case law and legislative citatory component to note up British case law and legislation.

The main American case law digest is found as part of *West's Digest System*, which is comprised of the *Decennial Digest* and the *General Digest*. The *Decennial Digest* is a series now published in increments of periods less than ten years (as implied by its name when series were published every decade), with the most recent series being the *Eleventh Decennial Digest* (2001–2004). Cases are organized alphabetically by topic and are classified by West's detailed "key-numbering" system, which assigns a unique key number to ever discrete sub-topics for each major legal topic. Cases in the *Decennial Digest* are then updated by using the *General Digest* of which every tenth volume consolidates cases from the previous ten volumes; once the topic and key number have been determined using the general index to the *Decennial Digest*, the updating in the *General Digest* can best be done by merely checking to see if the key number for that topic has any updates for that particular volume or volumes of the *General Digest*. The *General Digests* also contain a table of cases appealed, affirmed, or reversed.

In Australia, the case law digest system parallels the situation in Canada with their being "competing" services available from each of Thomson Reuters (Australia) and LexisNexis (Australia). Lawbook (Thomson Reuters) publishes the *Australian Digest*, currently in a third edition, that identifies Australian cases from 1825 to current, by topic. This service also references any articles discussing a specific case. It is available in print and via online subscription on Westlaw Australia. LexisNexis Australia, on the other hand, publishes a case law digest service called *Australian Current Law*, also available in print and online, that organizes case summaries by topic (among other things).

Case law digests are an effective finding tool to locate cases by topic within a particular jurisdiction. Print case law digests often require checking multiple volumes (an index, the main volume, and supplemental "updater" volumes) but are generally easy to use. Online case law digests, such as Westlaw Canada's "Canadian Case Digests" (the online equivalent of the *Canadian Abridgment*) or Quicklaw's Canada Digest database, provide a focused set of data that can effectively be searched by keyword, resulting in relatively precise search results.

F. GENERAL LEGAL REFERENCE RESOURCES

In addition to textbooks, law journals, encyclopedias, and case law digests, there are a number of general legal reference resources that are useful for legal research:

1) Legal Dictionaries

For first-time legal researchers, the use of reference tools such as legal dictionaries can help explain legal terms and provide useful information. Legal dictionaries usually define legal terms by citing how courts or legislatures have defined them. Some major legal dictionaries include

- Dukelow, Daphne. *The Dictionary of Canadian Law*. 3d ed. Scarborough, ON: Carswell, 2004.
- Penner, James E. *The Law Student's Dictionary*. 13th ed. London: Oxford University Press, 2008.
- Garner, Bryan A., ed. *Black's Law Dictionary*. 9th ed. St. Paul, MN: West, 2009.

Law students or other researchers on a budget may wish to consider buying any of the following "abridged" dictionaries which are condensed and cheaper but which still provide definitions and explanations of key legal terms and Latin phrases:

- Dukelow, Daphne & Betsy Nuse. *Pocket Dictionary of Canadian Law*. 4th ed. Toronto: Carswell, 2006.
- Martin, Elizabeth A. & Jonathan Law. *A Dictionary of Law*. 7th ed. Oxford: Oxford University Press, 2009.
- Yogis, John & Catherine Cotter. *Canadian Law Dictionary*. 6th ed. New York: Barrons Educational Series, 2009.

Word and phrases dictionaries also define legal terms but differ from legal dictionaries by attempting to provide a fairly exhaustive list of how a particular term has been defined by every court within a jurisdiction. Major words and phrases services include the following sources:

- *The Canadian Abridgment: Words and Phrases*. Scarborough, ON: Carswell, 1993. Supplemented periodically. Also available by subscription on Westlaw Canada.
- *Sanagan's Encyclopedia of Words and Phrases, Legal Maxims*, 5th ed. Toronto: Carswell, 2009. Looseleaf and available by subscription on Carswell's online reference library (www.carswellereference.com).

- Stroud, Frederick. *Judicial Dictionary of Words and Phrases*. 7th ed. London: Sweet & Maxwell, 2006. Supplemented annually.
- *Words and Phrases*. Permanent edition. St. Paul, MN: West, 2002. Supplemented periodically.

Abbreviation dictionaries, on the other hand, explain the meaning of acronyms often used in the legal profession for legal resources, such as the acronym "C.C.L.T.," which stands for the *"Canadian Cases on the Law of Torts."* Many law-related publications, such as the *Canadian Abridgment*, contain their own "List of Abbreviations" at the front or back of the publication. Alternatively, there are a number of other sources for abbreviations:

- *Bieber's Dictionary of Legal Abbreviations: A Reference Guide for Attorneys, Legal Secretaries, Paralegals and Law Students*. 6th ed. Mary Miles Prince, ed. Buffalo, NY: Hein, 2009.
- Noble, Scott. *Noble's Revised International Guide to the Law Reports*. 2002 ed. Etobicoke, ON: Nicol Island Publishing, 2002.
- Raistrick, Donald. *Index to Legal Citations and Abbreviations*. 3d ed. London: Sweet & Maxwell, 2008.
- *World Dictionary of Legal Abbreviations*. Looseleaf. Igor Kavass and Mary Price, eds. Buffalo, NY: Hein, 1991.

There are also several free online legal abbreviation guides:

- Cardiff Index to Legal Abbreviations
  www.legalabbrevs.cardiff.ac.uk
- Case Project, University of Leeds Library
  http://case.leeds.ac.uk/abbreviations.htm

2) Legal Citation Guides

Legal citation guides are also indispensable for legal research and writing since they explain the formats for how to cite case law, legislation, and secondary legal resources. In Canada, the leading style guide is the *Canadian Guide to Uniform Legal Citation* (6th ed.) (the "McGill Guide") (see Figure 2.6 for a sample entry from the McGill Guide), discussed in more detail in Chapter 1, Section D. Some of the basic citation patterns are relatively easy to learn, such as how to cite a typical Canadian case by italicizing the parties' names, followed by the date and the volume, case reporter, page number, and level of court: *Cole v. Hamilton* (2002), 58 O.R. (3d) 584 (S.C.J.). Other citation formats are more technical, hence the advantage of having your own copy of the McGill Guide if you can afford the cost.

Figure 2.6
Sample Entry from Rule 6.2.1 (Books—General Form) of Carswell's
Canadian Guide to Uniform Legal Citation (6th ed.) ("McGill Guide")

E-154   SECONDARY SOURCES AND OTHER MATERIALS

6.1.3 Title of Article

- Place the title of the article in quotation marks.

- Do not put a comma after the title.

- A colon separates a title from a subtitle.

> Suzanne A. Kim, "'Yellow' Skin, 'White' Masks: Asian American 'Impersonations' of Whiteness and the Feminist Critique of Liberal Equality" (2001) 8 Asian L. J. 89.
>
> Darcy L. MacPherson, "Extending Corporate Criminal Liability?: Some Thoughts on Bill C-45" (2005) 30 Man. L.J. 253.

- Capitalize the title according to the conventions of the language in which the title is written.

- For further rules on titles, see section 6.2.3.

6.1.4 Year of Publication

Journal organized by volumes	David M. Brown, "Freedom From or Freedom For?: Religion As a Case Study in Defining the Content of Charter Rights" **(2000)** 33 U.B.C. L. Rev. 551.	• If a journal is identified by volume numbers, indicate the year of publication in parentheses.
Journal organized by year	Frédéric Pollaud-Dulian, "À propos de la sécurité juridique" **[2001]** R.T.D. civ. 487.	• If a journal is not organized by volume numbers, provide the year (shown on the spine of the volume) in brackets.

6.1.5 Volume

- Place the volume number between the year of publication and the name of the journal.

- Where issues of a volume are not consecutively paginated (i.e. where each issue starts with page 1), place the issue number immediately after the volume number, separated by a colon.

Paginated consecutively	David Lametti, "Publish *and* Profit?: Justifying the Ownership of Copyright in the Academic Setting" (2001) **26** Queen's L.J. 497.
Not paginated consecutively	Gregory R. Hagen, "Personal Inviolability and Public Health Care: Chaoulli v. Quebec" (2005) **14:2** Health L. Rev. 34.

Reprinted by permission of Carswell, a division of Thomson Reuters.

3) Legal Directories

A number of Canadian legal directories provide listings of addresses and other contact information for lawyers, courthouses, and other law-related organizations. The difference between these various directories is often one of preference or cost. Some of the major legal directories include the following:

- *Canada Legal Directory*. Toronto: Carswell [annual].
- *Canadian Law List*. Aurora: Canada Law Book [annual]. Modified form available online at www.canadianlawlist.com. Also available on CD-ROM.
- Law Society of Upper Canada. *Law Society Directory: The Official List of Licensees of The Law Society of Upper Canada* [annual]. Markham, ON: LexisNexis Canada, 2008.
- *Martindale-Hubbell* [annual]. Modified form available online at www.martindale-hubbell.ca. The print multi-volume version also has a useful two-volume digest of the laws of countries throughout the world which provides a simplified overview of the laws of selected countries.
- *Ontario Legal Directory* (the "orange book"). Toronto: Distributed by University of Toronto Press [annual].

4) Forms and Precedents

Most lawyers learn quickly in their career to take advantage of a number of publications known as "forms and precedents" that provide sample wording for legal agreements, court pleadings, and other legal documents. There are a number of commercially available sources of these forms and precedents (discussed in more detail in Chapters 10 and 12):

- *Canadian Forms & Precedents*. 2d ed. Looseleaf, CD-ROM, and on-line by subscription. Markham, ON: LexisNexis Canada. This is a multi-volume red and blue set available from LexisNexis Canada in print, on CD-ROM, and by subscription on LexisNexis Quicklaw. The forms and precedents are edited by experts in their field and cover a number of areas of law, including wills, land development, debtor/creditor, estates administration, commercial real estate financing, banking and finance, and commercial transactions.
- *O'Brien's Encyclopedia of Forms*. 11th ed. Looseleaf. Aurora, ON: Canada Law Book, 1987. This is a multi-volume burgundy set from Canada Law Book, also available on CD-ROM and now through an Internet subscription (called *O'Brien's Internet*[17]). The volumes, divided into "Divisions," cover a wide range of topics, including Commercial and General, Corporations, Conveyancing and Mortgage, Leases, Wills and Trusts, Ontario—Family Law, Labour Relations and Employment, Ontario—Court Forms, Municipal Corporations, and Computers and Information Technology.

---

17   See online: www.obriensforms.com.

In addition, many lawyers and law firms start to compile their own internal sample forms and precedents and make them available within the firm through an Intranet or networked database. See Chapter 12, Section G, for more on drafting agreements and court documents using forms and precedents.

5) Court Rules

Court rules govern procedure in lawsuits. Litigation lawyers will ordinarily have "rules of court" publications for their jurisdiction. These publications are usually published annually, may be kept current with pocket parts, and are generally annotated, providing commentary, digests of cases interpreting particular provisions of the court rules, and setting out other information relevant for litigators, such as practice directions from the court. There are several publications that explain these court rules and discuss how the rules have been interpreted by the courts. See the listing of books under "Civil Procedure" in Chapter 8 for specific titles for these rules of court services.

6) Current Awareness Tools

There are a number of current awareness tools that are useful for legal research. One of the purposes of these resources is to provide current information on law-related topics. Current awareness tools tend to fall into the following categories:

- *Newspapers*: There are two major, national law-related newspapers in Canada: *The Lawyer's Weekly*[18] and the *Law Times*.[19] Both papers provide good coverage of current legal issues, important court cases, trends in the legal industry, and special topical columns.
- *Magazines*: There are a number of magazines that are more current and topical than the academic journals discussed in Section B, above in this chapter. One of the more popular "glossy" magazines is *Canadian Lawyer*.[20] The Canadian Bar Association also sends to its members its *National* magazine. The Vancouver Bar Association publishes *The Advocate*, a journal that combines scholarly articles with current awareness information.

---

18   (Markham, ON: LexisNexis Canada, 1986–).
19   (Aurora, ON: Canada Law Book, 1990–).
20   (Aurora, ON: Canada Law Book). Information is available online at www.canadianlawyermag.com.

- *NetLetters*: Quicklaw provides a number of excellent online "netLetters" by topic that are written by experts in their field and that provide regular updates (usually weekly) on developments for that area of the law. One of their more popular netLetters for criminal law lawyers, for example, is Alan Gold's Criminal Law *NetLetter*. NetLetters on Quicklaw are also provided for the following topics: aboriginal law, administrative law, advocacy and practice, bankruptcy and insolvency, civil procedure, commercial law, construction law, education law, environmental law, family law, health law, human rights, immigration law, insurance law, intellectual property law, labour and employment law, municipal law, natural resources, personal injury, professional responsibility, real property law, securities law, taxation, and transportation law. Carswell also provides online newsletters for subject-based Internet subscriptions (*CriminalSource, SecuritiesSource, InsolvencySource, FamilySource, IPSource,* and *Estates&TrustsSource*).
- *Ontario Reports*: Members of the Law Society of Upper Canada receive as part of their membership a weekly softcover copy of the *Ontario Reports*, which contains recent decisions of Ontario courts. Also included with these weekly softcover editions is a series of preliminary pages that include notices to the profession, upcoming legal conferences or seminars, new law-related publications, and job advertisements for law-related positions.
- *Law Society Websites*: Most of the Canadian law societies have websites that provide a variety of information to their members (and to the public), including "what's new?"–type information. Set out in Table 2.2 is a list of those Canadian law societies that have websites, along with the website of the Canadian Bar Association and other lawyer's groups.

Table 2.2
Law Society Websites

Law Society	Website Address
Barreau du Québec	www.barreau.qc.ca
Canadian Bar Association	www.cba.org
Chambre des notaires du Québec	www.cdnq.org
Federation of Law Societies of Canada	www.flsc.ca
Law Society of Alberta	www.lawsocietyalberta.com
Law Society of British Columbia	www.lawsociety.bc.ca
Law Society of Manitoba	www.lawsociety.mb.ca
Law Society of New Brunswick	www.lawsociety-barreau.nb.ca
Law Society of Newfoundland	www.lawsociety.nf.ca

Law Society	Website Address
Law Society of Northwest Territories	www.lawsociety.nt.ca
Law Society of Nunavut	www.lawsociety.nu.ca
Law Society of Prince Edward Island	www.lspei.pe.ca
Law Society of Saskatchewan	www.lawsociety.sk.ca
Law Society of Upper Canada (Ontario)	www.lsuc.on.ca
Law Society of Yukon	www.lawsocietyyukon.com
Nova Scotia Barristers Society	www.nsbs.ns.ca
Advocates Society	www.advocates.ca
Alberta Civil Trial Lawyers Association	www.actla.com
Ontario Trial Lawyers Association	www.criminallawyers.ca
Trial Lawyers Association of B.C.	www.tlabc.org

- **Online discussion groups**: Listservs—or online discussion groups—are an excellent way to share information and keep current on legal issues. Simply put, one can subscribe (usually for free) to any number of law-related online discussion groups. Any person subscribing to the group can send and receive messages to the group. One of the best listservs in Canada for legal research information is CALL-L, the listserv of the Canadian Association of Law Libraries. More details on online discussion groups are provided in Chapter 5, Section K.
- **Blogs**: Chapter 10, Section 10 lists some of the major law-related blogs in Canada, including a "master list" of these blogs at Lawblogs (www.lawblogs.ca). There are hundreds of law-related blogs, ranging from academic to scholarly and covering a wide range of legal topics. One advantage of blogs is the ease by which one can monitor blog posts by subscribing to the RRS feeds for your blogs of choice so that new posts automatically get sent to you.
- **Law firm newsletters**: Law firms regularly publish free online bulletins or newsletters discussing new case law or legislative developments or new legal issues. The following sites can be useful to either subscribe to or search for law firm bulletins:
  - » **Lexology**
    www.lexology.com
  - » **Linex Legal**
    www.linexlegal.com
  - » **Search Canadian Law Firms and Law-Related Blogs** (Tjaden)
    www.tinyurl.com/canadianlawfirms
  - » **Fee Fie Foe Firm**
    www.feefiefoefirm.com

7) Web Guides

Law schools, public interest organizations, law firms, and other organizations are publishing useful online Web guides that provide information or tips on finding law-related information by topic. Research on the Internet is discussed in more detail in Chapter 5. Set out below in alphabetical order are a few of the better online research guides for conducting Canadian legal research.

- **BC Courthouse Library**
  www.courthouselibrary.ca

  The British Columbia Courthouse library has a number of practice portals (including civil litigation and family law), along with a number of research guides (covering such topics as "Class Actions" and "Costs").

- **Best Guide to Canadian Legal Research**
  www.legalresearch.org

  Research lawyer Catherine Best has an excellent site covering such topics as research essentials, electronic research, and statutory research, along with legal research news and links to various other resources for conducting legal research.

- **Bibliothèque de droit Michel-Bastarache: Legal Research Guides**
  www.umoncton.ca/umcm-bibliotheque-droit/node/97

  The Bibliothèque de droit Michel-Bastarache at the Université de Moncton has a number of excellent research guides (in French) on both civil law and common law research.

- **Bora Laskin Law Library: Research Guides**
  www.law-lib.utoronto.ca/resources/locate/finding.htm

  The Bora Laskin Law Library at the University of Toronto has extensive online guides for conducting legal research, ranging from case law and legislation to topical guides from Administrative Law to Trusts & Estates.

- **Law Society of Upper Canada: Legal Research Guides**
  http://rc.lsuc.on.ca/library/research_guides.htm

  The Great Library staff have compiled a number of excellent legal research guides that include (for now) "portals" on detailed research on employment law, estates and trusts, family law, and real estate, along with legislative audio/video tutorials and various pathfinders and "how to" guides.

- **Lederman Law Library (Queen's): Legal Research Guides**
  http://library.queensu.ca/law/

  The Lederman Law Library at the Faculty of Law, Queen's University, has a number of research guides, including its Legal Research Manual (http://library.queensu.ca/law/lederman/index.htm) and other links.

- **Osgoode Hall Law School Library (York University)**
  http://library.osgoode.yorku.ca/res_guides.html

  The Osgoode Hall Law School reference librarians have prepared a number of excellent online research guides by topic and by jurisdiction, including some online presentations and some general guides (e.g., "Checklist of Periodical Indexes")

- **Ted Tjaden**, **"Researching Canadian Law"** (Globalex)
  www.nyulawglobal.org/globalex/canada.htm

  The Hauser Global Law School Program at NYU has developed Globalex, "an electronic legal publication dedicated to international and foreign law research." It has compiled guides for conducting legal research by country, including my guide on researching Canadian law.

G. CONCLUSIONS

Secondary legal resources such as textbooks, journal articles, seminar papers, and encyclopedias should be relatively familiar and comfortable to use for most legal researchers. Although case digests are relatively unique to legal research, they are also an excellent starting point to help identify relevant cases, as are the various references tools and Web guides discussed in this chapter. Due to the competition in the legal publishing industry, the quality and currency of most secondary legal resources is quite excellent, which make them a useful way to find primary sources of law such as legislation (discussed next in Chapter 3) and case law (discussed in Chapter 4).

RESEARCHING LEGISLATION

A. INTRODUCTION

Legislative materials, in the form of statutes, regulations, and statutory instruments, are an important source of law. While some citizens may not realize the power of judge-made case law to affect their rights, most citizens do realize that statutes and regulations have the power to legally affect them. Created by or through elected politicians, legislation consists of written rules that govern or prescribe the conduct of the citizens who elected the government officials. Despite the importance of legislation to our legal system and to legal research, very few people enjoy conducting legislative research.

There are several reasons why legislative research can be a challenge:

- Until recently, legislation was mired in 19th-century print technology, replete with publishing delays, poor consolidation of amended provisions, and awkward "Tables" for updating changes to legislative text.
- The legislative process is still somewhat mysterious to most people, involving a sense of back-room lobbying and various technical legislative rules, such as the need for bills to progress through three readings before becoming law.
- Legislation involves a fairly obscure vocabulary and literature unfamiliar to the uninitiated, including such concepts or terms as proroguement, Royal Assent, proclamations, and Orders-in-Council (these terms are explained below in this chapter).

Fortunately, legislators are improving access to legislation on their websites. Although some governments have been slow to make their online versions of legislation official, the federal,[1] Ontario,[2] and Québec[3] governments have done so, and it is reasonable to assume that the other Canadian jurisdictions will do so in the near future. The Canadian Legal Information Institute (CanLII) (www.canlii.org) is also an excellent central "clearing house" for recent federal and provincial legislation.

Although the emphasis in this chapter will be using online resources for legislative research, there will also be a brief review of print resources. There are several occasions when there is no choice but to use print resources: (i) since online legislative databases tend to emphasize current content, it will still be necessary in most situations to conduct print legislative research for historical research, such as needing to confirm the state of the law at a period of time in the past, and (ii) since not all Canadian provincial jurisdictions have moved as quickly in making the online versions of their legislation official, it may be necessary to obtain print copies of legislation when official copies are needed for court. In addition, learning how to conduct legislative research in print can provide valuable context for understanding the legislative process and what is being viewed online.

What, then, is the best way to learn how to research legislation? This chapter proposes that most legislative research can be successfully, and somewhat enjoyably, undertaken using the following five-step legislative research checklist:

Legislative Research Checklist

Step 1:   Identify which level of government has jurisdiction over the subject matter of your research.

Step 2:   Identify and consult relevant statutes. If conducting historical research, use print resources. If researching current law, prefer online to print resources.

---

1   By s. 31(1) of the *Legislation Revision and Consolidation Act*, R.S.C. 1985, c. S-20, all consolidated Acts and regulations on the Justice Laws website are official, as of 1 June 2009.

2   Section 35(1)(b) of the *Legislation Act, 2006*, S.O. 2006, c. 21, Sched. F, makes legislation on e-Laws (www.e-laws.gov.on.ca) official, effective 30 November 2008.

3   *An Act respecting the Compilation of Québec Laws and Regulations*, S.Q. 2009, c. 40, makes Québec statutes published in print and online by Publications du Québec official as of 1 January 2010, with Québec regulations to become official by 1 January 2012 at the latest.

Step 3:   Check to ensure there are no amendments to the provisions of your statute by consulting recent bills, Tables of Public Statutes, or commercial services.

Step 4:   Check for relevant regulations, if any.

Step 5:   Check for court decisions that have considered your legislation or check for statutory interpretation materials if the legislation is ambiguous.

B. IDENTIFYING THE RELEVANT JURISDICTION (STEP 1)

Step 1 in the legislative research checklist is to identify the level of government that has jurisdiction to legislate on the topic being researched. In Canada, there is a division of power between the federal and provincial governments. Another level of government and legislation in the form of bylaws exist at the municipal level. When researching a particular topic, it is important to know which level of government has the power to enact laws for that subject or whether power to legislate may be shared by more than one level of government.

For example, under section 91 of the *Constitution Act, 1867*,[4] the federal government of Canada is given exclusive power to "make Laws for the Peace, Order, and good Government of Canada, in relation to all Matters not coming within the Classes of Subjects by this Act assigned exclusively to the Legislatures of the Provinces." Some of these federal powers to legislate include such topics as the regulation of trade and commerce, unemployment insurance, the postal service, militia, military and naval service, defence, banking, and patents and copyright. Federal statutes were last published as an up-to-date consolidated set in the mid 1980s as the *Revised Statutes of Canada* (1985), a multi-volume bilingual set that was published over approximately four years that includes a number of supplemental volumes and an index.[5]

---

4   (U.K.), 30 & 31 Vict., c. 3, reprinted in R.S.C. 1985, App. II, No. 5.

5   Canadian federal statutes have been revised as a "set" in the following years: 1886, 1906, 1927, 1952, 1970, and 1985. There will not likely be any further revised consolidated sets given that federal legislation is now updated online. The revised sets are entitled *Revised Statutes of Canada*, abbreviated to "R.S.C.," whereas annual federal statutes are entitled *Statutes of Canada*, abbreviated to "S.C." (i.e., without an "R" for *Revised*). Thus, the *Old Age Security Act*, R.S.C. 1970, c. O-6, is Chapter O-6 found in the print *Revised Statutes of Canada* from 1970.

Under section 92 of the *Constitution Act, 1867,* the provincial governments have exclusive power over such areas as direct taxation within the province to raise revenue for provincial purposes, prisons (but not penitentiaries), the incorporation of companies with provincial objects, the solemnization of marriage in the province, property and civil rights in the province, and generally all matters of a merely local or private nature in the province. Ontario, for example, has recently published its statutes as up-to-date consolidated bilingual sets every decade, with the most recent set being the *Revised Statutes of Ontario* (1990).[6]

Power is shared between the federal Parliament and the provincial legislatures over agriculture, immigration, and over certain aspects of natural resources; but federal laws would prevail in the event of any conflict between federal and provincial laws over these subject areas.[7] Parliament and the provincial legislatures also have power over old age, disability, and survivors' pensions; but provincial laws would prevail if there were conflicts between federal and provincial laws over these subject areas.[8] Aside from these areas, there is a general rule that everything not listed in the *Constitution Act, 1867,* as belonging to the provincial legislatures comes under the powers of Parliament.[9]

Municipal governments are generally given power by provincial legislation (typically called the *Municipal Act*) to enact bylaws to provide rules to govern on matters of a local nature including such things as school taxes, local roads and highways, and rules governing building permits.

Knowing which level of government has jurisdiction over a particular matter is often a matter of experience. Alternatively, one can check the legislative index of the revised statutes for the jurisdiction in question to see if the index covers the topic. In addition, one can consult the listing of the division of powers in sections 91 and 92 of the *Constitution Act, 1867.* One of the easiest ways to identify relevant legislation, however, is to consult a good book on the topic since most authors of law-related textbooks will identify relevant legislation and will include

---

6   Ontario statutes have been revised as a "set" in the following years: 1877, 1887, 1897, 1914, 1927, 1937, 1950, 1960, 1970, 1980, and 1990. There was no *Revised Statutes of Ontario 2000* (or 2010) since the Ontario government now introduces new legislation (or updates existing legislation) online. The revised sets in Ontario are entitled *Revised Statutes of Ontario,* abbreviated to "R.S.O.," whereas annual Ontario statutes are entitled *Statutes of Ontario,* abbreviated to "S.O." (i.e., without an "R" for Revised). Thus, the *Child Welfare Act,* R.S.O. 1980, c. 66, is Chapter 66 from the *Revised Statutes of Ontario* from 1980.

7   Above note 4, ss. 92A and 95.

8   *Ibid.,* s. 94A.

9   *Ibid.,* s. 91.

a "Table of Legislation" at the start or end of the book identifying the legislation discussed in the book. See Chapter 8 for an extensive listing of Canadian law-related textbooks, set out by various legal topics.

Ultimately, there will be a definite trend towards conducting legislative research using online resources where one can simply search applicable legislative databases by keyword or concept to determine if any legislative provisions deal with the keyword or concept.

C. ACCESSING STATUTES (STEP 2)

Once you have determined the correct jurisdiction in Step 1 (federal, provincial, or municipal), the next step is to identify and then consult the relevant statute, which is simply an Act or law enacted by elected government officials. As mentioned above, researchers will sometimes have a choice between print and online resources for conducting legislative research. If the research being done is historical, there is often no choice but to follow the traditional print method of finding statutes, discussed below. If the goal is to find a current version of a statute (or regulation), then use of online resources can save time and avoid some of the multiple steps involved in using the traditional print method.

1) Finding Current Statutes (Online)

If you are looking for a current statute, using free online resources through CanLII or the applicable government website is your easiest starting point (as long as you then follow Step 3 below to verify that the online version of the statute you are looking at is current and has not been amended or repealed).

Finding an online statute is as simple as browsing for your statute alphabetically by title (see Table 5.10 for a list of Canadian online legislative websites). Most online versions of statutes indicate how current the Act is (see the example in Figure 3.1 showing the date of currency for the federal government's legislative website). Make note of this date since you will need to check (in Step 3) whether there were any amendments to your statute in the "gap" between the currency date indicated in your statute and the day you are conducting your research. In most situations, the online statute will be current to within a few weeks to a few days, depending on the jurisdiction (and it is reasonable to assume that governments in the near future will make their legislation current to the day, thereby eliminating the need in Step 3 to update your online statute).

Figure 3.1
Department of Justice Laws Website (showing date of currency)

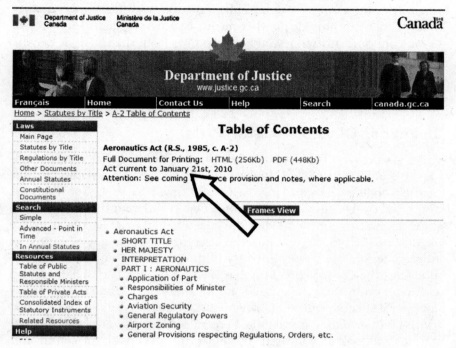

Another way to find current statutes online is to search by keyword on the applicable site. On CanLII, for example, you have an option to "Search all CanLII Databases" limited to legislation by using keywords in either the "full text" field or the "statute name field." This is a very powerful search if you are not entirely sure of which particular statute might be relevant or if you are looking for legislation in more than one jurisdiction. CanLII is also in the process of continually improving its databases. One recent feature is "point-in-time" legislation (also available on some of the commercial services). This feature allows you to select a date or date range in the recent past (on CanLII, currently you can go back in time about ten years, depending on the Act) and obtain a version of the Act that was in force for the specified period of time. The commercial online services also have full-text legislative databases, but for most researchers needing to know only the wording of a current statute or regulation, the free versions from the government website or CanLII are usually sufficient.[10]

---

10   However, as discussed in Step 5, below in this chapter, the commercial services have powerful citators that indicate which cases have considered a particular

Finally, another unofficial source for finding legislation is to consult commercially-published consolidated or annotated print or looseleaf versions of legislation.[11] Such publications often contain good quality indexes that can provide another means of accessing statutes by topic. If you cannot identify relevant access points from the Index, it may be that you made a mistake in Step 1 and you should try consulting legislation from a different jurisdiction in case the matter is one of federal (or provincial or municipal) jurisdiction, as the case may be.

2) Finding Older Statutes (in Print)

Using statutes in print is relatively easy to the extent that you have access to a law library. Legislation is usually shelved by jurisdiction and then chronologically, making it easy to browse by year. Consolidated or revised statutes are often offset in a colour different from the annual statutes, making it easy to spot the consolidated or revised statute set on the shelf. If you have a specific statutory or regulatory citation to older material, it is simply a matter of finding the applicable print volume (e.g., the *Construction Lien Act, 1983*, S.O. 1983, c. 6, will be found as Chapter 6 in the 1983 annual statute volume for Ontario). If you do not have a specific citation to the historical statute you are looking for, try the Index volume for the most recent set of revised or consolidated statutes and look up your issue by keyword, and consult the statute and section indicated in the Index. Expect to see an increasing amount of older Canadian legislation being digitized and made available online. The best example so far has been the Retrospective Law Collection that is part of the Alberta Heritage Digitization Project.[12] In addition, the federal government is in the process of digitizing the *Canada Gazette*,[13] and efforts are underway by a coalition of law libraries and others to

---

section of an Act; CanLII is also developing this feature for statutes and regulations on a "noteup" tab, but the free CanLII version is not yet as sophisticated or comprehensive in scope as the commercial services.

11   Consolidated statutes bring all relevant laws together in one publication, whereas annotated statutes provide summaries of cases that have considered particular sections of the legislation. Although consolidated or annotated print or looseleaf statute services are convenient, realize that they are "unofficial" and also risk being less current than online versions of legislation.

12   The Alberta Heritage Digitization Project's Retrospective Law Collection is available online at www.ourfutureourpast.ca/law/ where Alberta statutes have been digitized from 1906 to 1990 and made available online for free, with plans to digitize retrospective bills and Gazettes.

13   Library and Archives Canada, *A Nation's Chronicle: The Canada Gazette*, online: www.collectionscanada.gc.ca/canada-gazette/index-e.html.

make Ontario legislation available via the Canadian Libraries section of the Internet Archive.[14]

Print statutory materials are also usually required when you are tracing a particular section of a statute to see how its wording may have changed over time (you do this most often when researching the statutory interpretation of the section, discussed in more detail in Section F, below in this chapter). There is often two goals when doing this type of research: (i) tracing the section back to its origin or introduction or to look for any significant amendments to the section, or (ii) identifying previous section numbers of the section in question in order to find older cases that may have considered predecessor versions of the section (to do this, you need to know what the old section numbers are in order to use some of the "statutes judicially considered"–type services discussed in Section F(1), below in this chapter). To trace statutory sections, one can take advantage of the historical notes placed at the end of each section of the print statute by the Queen's Printer by using the information in the historical note to trace the section backwards (see Figure 3.2 showing the historical note from section 1 of the *Statutes Act*, R.S.O. 1980, c. 483, indicating that the wording of section 1 came *verbatim* from section 1 of the *Statutes Act*, R.S.O. 1970, c. 446, but had its wording changed in 1973 by section 4(3) of S.O. 1973, c. 2).

This sort of legislative history research is often used to help identify the date when the section in question was introduced by the legislature, which then allows the researcher to check the Hansard debates for any relevant debate or discussion about the statutory provisions (see Section F(3), below in this chapter, on statutory interpretation for more on researching Hansard debates).

3) Reading Legislation

When conducting legislative research, it is very important to carefully read any legislation. Statutes, for example, often have a particular structure, with definitions being at the start of the Act and "penalties and offences" and the power of the Lieutenant Governor or Governor General to make regulations being set out towards the end of the Act, along with any coming-into-force information. However, care must be taken since, for example, definitions can be found throughout the Act. Many online versions of statutes (and those in commercially published annotated or consolidated versions) will have a table of contents, which provides a good outline of how information in the Act is organized.

---

14   Internet Archive, "Canadian Libraries," online: www.archive.org/details/toronto.

D. BILLS: CHECKING FOR AMENDMENTS (STEP 3)

Once you have identified the correct jurisdiction (Step 1) and then identified and read the relevant statute (Step 2), it is essential in Step 3 to verify that the section in question has not been amended or repealed. There are two basic methods to note up statutory provisions: (i) print methods (rarely used nowadays), and (ii) online methods. Before these methods are discussed, it is important to understand the legislative process and the way in which legislation is amended or repealed.

Figure 3.2

Historical note from s. 1 of the *Statutes Act*, R.S.O. 1980, c. 483, showing that the wording of s. 1 came verbatim from s. 1 of the *Statutes Act*, R.S.O. 1970, c. 446, but had its wording changed in 1973 by s. 4(3) of S.O. 1973, c.2

CHAPTER 483

Statutes Act

1. An Act may be cited and referred to for all purposes   Citation of Acts
by its title, or by its short title, or by a reference to the
number of the particular chapter in the revised statutes or
in the annual volume of statutes printed by the Queen's
Printer.   R.S.O. 1970, c. 446, s. 1; 1973, c. 2, s. 4 (3).

2. The following words in an indicate the authority   Enacting clause
by virtue of which it is passed, Majesty, by and with
the advice and consent of the Legislative Assembly of the
Province of Ontario, enacts as follows".   R.S.O. 1970, c. 446,
s. 2.

3. Any Act may be amended, altered or repealed by an   Amendment or repeal
Act passed in the same session of the Legislature.   R.S.O.   during same session
1970, c. 446, s. 3.

4. The Clerk of the Assembly shall endorse on every Act,   Endorse-ments on Acts
immediately after the title of the Act, the day, month and
year when it was assented to, or reserved by the Lieutenant
Governor, and, where the Act is reserved, the Clerk shall also
endorse thereon the day, month and year when the Lieutenant
Governor has signified, either by speech or message to the
Assembly or by proclamation, that it was laid before the
Governor General in Council and that the Governor General
was pleased to assent thereto, and such endorsements shall
be taken to be a part of the Act.   R.S.O. 1970, c. 446, s. 4;
1974, c. 83, s. 1.

1) The Legislative Process

There is much written in the legal literature about how laws are made in Canada (see the resources in Section I, below in this chapter). To properly verify that a particular statute or section of a statute is current, it helps to review the legislative process to see how a bill (as draft legislation) becomes a binding "in force" statute.

As a starting point, the political party holding the highest number of seats controls the legislative process through its majority control of the legislature. As such, the party in power will introduce legislation that supports its political policies. Quite often, legislation and policies will be discussed by Cabinet and then the details of the legislation will be worked upon by the deputy minister and his staff for the relevant ministry most closely associated with the subject matter of the legislation.

Once the draft legislation has been prepared, it will be introduced into the legislature as a bill and must pass through three stages or "readings" before it can become law. The procedure below describes the typical process for provincial legislation.

First reading: The bill is introduced by the Minister responsible, who may also explain its objectives and make a motion for its formal introduction. If the members vote in favour of the bill, it is assigned a number, printed, given to each member of the legislative assembly, and scheduled for future debate (there is usually no debate on first reading). Provincial bills are assigned a (consecutive) number depending whether they are public bills (Bill 76) or private bills (Bill Pr 7).[15]

Second reading: The bill is debated in the Legislative Assembly. There is then a vote whether the bill will proceed to the committee stage (or directly to third reading stage, in some cases). If the bill is "sent to committee," this means it will be examined in detail by the committee for that subject matter or ministry (a "standing committee") or by a specially created committee (a "select" committee). The committee will usually be made up of members from all political parties but controlled by the party with majority power. The bill is usually discussed section by section (time permitting). This is the stage where changes are made, sometimes as a result of political compromise, sometimes because of a change in policy by the government, and sometimes simply to improve clarity.

The committee process may last a few days or a few months, depending on the bill. The committee will then debate whether to send

---

15   Federal bills are also assigned numbers in addition to a letter (C or S) signifying where the bill originated: Bill C-5 signifies the bill originated in the House of Commons; Bill S-11 signifies the bill originated in the Senate.

the bill to the Committee of the whole House (for more study by the entire legislature) or directly into final debate.

Third reading: This is the final debate on the bill. If the vote carries, the bill is sent to the Lieutenant Governor for approval or "Royal Assent." The bill is also given a chapter number at this time.

Federally, a bill must pass through three readings in both the House of Commons and the Senate. Alternatively, the Senate itself can introduce legislation (usually only so long as it does not relate to taxes or financial expenditures). In this case, the bill must pass three readings in the Senate and then pass three readings in the House of Commons.

Figure 3.3
"Status of the Bill" Page from the Federal LegisINFO

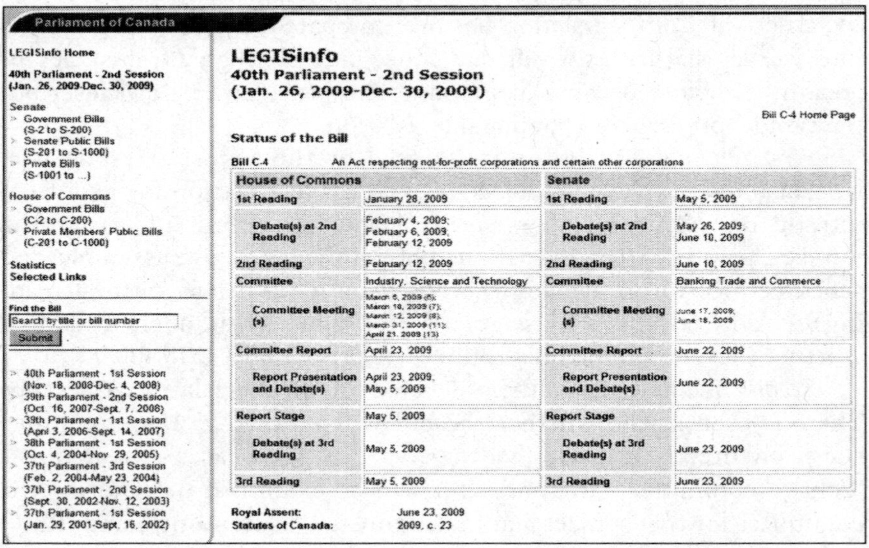
Parliament of Canada

LEGISinfo Home

40th Parliament - 2nd Session
(Jan. 26, 2009-Dec. 30, 2009)

Senate
- Government Bills (S-2 to S-200)
- Senate Public Bills (S-201 to S-1000)
- Private Bills (S-1001 to ...)

House of Commons
- Government Bills (C-2 to C-200)
- Private Members' Public Bills (C-201 to C-1000)

Statistics
Selected Links

Find the Bill
Search by title or bill number
Submit

- 40th Parliament - 1st Session (Nov. 18, 2008-Dec. 4, 2008)
- 39th Parliament - 2nd Session (Oct. 16, 2007-Sept. 7, 2008)
- 39th Parliament - 1st Session (April 3, 2006-Sept. 14, 2007)
- 38th Parliament - 1st Session (Oct. 4, 2004-Nov 29, 2005)
- 37th Parliament - 3rd Session (Feb. 2, 2004-May 23, 2004)
- 37th Parliament - 2nd Session (Sept. 30, 2002-Nov. 12, 2003)
- 37th Parliament - 1st Session (Jan. 29, 2001-Sept. 16, 2002)

LEGISinfo
40th Parliament - 2nd Session
(Jan. 26, 2009-Dec. 30, 2009)

Bill C-4 Home Page

Status of the Bill

Bill C-4 An Act respecting not-for-profit corporations and certain other corporations

House of Commons		Senate	
1st Reading	January 28, 2009	1st Reading	May 5, 2009
Debate(s) at 2nd Reading	February 4, 2009; February 6, 2009; February 12, 2009	Debate(s) at 2nd Reading	May 26, 2009; June 10, 2009
2nd Reading	February 12, 2009	2nd Reading	June 10, 2009
Committee	Industry, Science and Technology	Committee	Banking Trade and Commerce
Committee Meeting (s)	March 5, 2009 (5); March 10, 2009 (7); March 12, 2009 (8); March 31, 2009 (11); April 21, 2009 (13)	Committee Meeting (s)	June 17, 2009; June 18, 2009
Committee Report	April 23, 2009	Committee Report	June 22, 2009
Report Presentation and Debate(s)	April 23, 2009; May 5, 2009	Report Presentation and Debate(s)	June 22, 2009
Report Stage	May 5, 2009	Report Stage	
Debate(s) at 3rd Reading	May 5, 2009	Debate(s) at 3rd Reading	June 23, 2009
3rd Reading	May 5, 2009	3rd Reading	June 23, 2009

Royal Assent: June 23, 2009
Statutes of Canada: 2009, c. 23

The federal LegisINFO site[16] is an excellent way to track federal legislation. Figure 3.3 shows the "Status of the Bill" page for Bill C-4, *An Act respecting not-for-profit corporations and certain other corporations*,[17] from the federal LegisINFO site showing the progress of the bill through both the House of Commons and the Senate. Federal bills must also be published in the *Canada Gazette, Part III*, before they are official. If a legislative session ends (when it is "prorogued"), any bills not specific-

16 LegisINFO, online: www2.parl.gc.ca/Sites/LOP/LEGISINFO/.

17 Bill C-4, *An Act respecting not-for-profit corporations and certain other corporations*, 2nd Sess., 40th Parl., 2009.

ally brought forward to the next session of the legislative assembly are said to have "died on the Order paper" and will not come into force.

An excellent commercial service for tracking bills (and regulations) is CCH's *Canadian Legislative Pulse* (http://pulse.cch.ca). This product tracks the progress of bills and new or amended regulations with sophisticated alert features and the ability to produce custom reports.

2) Types of Bills

Most bills are public bills—these are typically introduced by a member of Cabinet and relate to laws of general application throughout the jurisdiction. Public bills will usually either introduce a new statute not yet in existence or amend (or repeal) an existing statute. In those situations where the government amends a large number of statutes in a new bill, such bills are called "omnibus bills" since they apply to a large number of statutes.[18] There are also private member bills—these can be introduced by any member and are often introduced by members of the opposition party. If they are too controversial, they often do not pass third reading.[19] In addition, there are private bills—these can be introduced by any member and are not of general application but typically relate to a particular organization or individual.[20]

3) Coming into Force

When does a bill turn into an "in force" statute or Act? Once a bill has received Royal Assent, it may not yet be in force. A statute may come into force in one or more of the following three ways:

- The statute will state when it comes into force (usually at the end of the statute).
- The statute will state it comes into force upon Royal Assent.

---

18   The Harris Conservative government in Ontario was notorious for their "red tape reduction" legislation (e.g., the *Red Tape Reduction Act, 2000*, S.O. 2000, c. 26) that contained numerous amendments to a wide variety of statutes, which sometimes made tracking the changes difficult.

19   For example, in 2002 in Ontario, the NDP introduced Bill 212, *The Man Who Wasn't There Act, 2002*, and the Liberal Party introduced Bill 219, *Consultants Boondoggle Freeze Act, 2002*, both aimed (in part) to embarrass the governing party or other politicians. Neither bill made it past first reading. And one wonders why the electorate has such a cynical view of politicians.

20   For example, Bill Pr13 2008, *2076467 Ontario Inc. Act, 2008*, was a bill to revive the named company, which had dissolved. It is "private" to the extent it will usually only affect the company or person named in the Act.

• The statute will state it comes into force upon "proclamation."

The date of proclamation is usually given in the applicable govern-ment *Gazette*, a publication used by the government to publish regu-lations and other notices. Section 11(3)(c) of the *Statutory Instruments Regulations*,[21] for example, requires federal proclamations to be pub-lished in Part II of the *Canada Gazette*. If a federal bill is silent on coming into force, the Act will come into force on the date of Royal Assent, as per sections 5 and 6 of the federal *Interpretation Act*.[22] The advantage to the government in having a law come into force upon "proclamation" is that it may not know at the time the bill passes third reading when it and the relevant ministry will be ready for the new legislation. Brochures may need to be printed, staff may need training, and so on. A proclamation date therefore provides flexibility since the government can cause the Lieutenant Governor (or Governor General, federally) to announce the proclamation date whenever it suits the needs of the government.

There are several online sources for proclamation dates and coming into force (CIF) information. Federally, the *Canada Gazette, Part III*, is the official master list of proclamation dates. You can also find CIF in-formation in the federal Table of Public Statutes (listed at the end of each listing for each Act) and in the "Proclamations of Canada" tables in the annual statute volumes. Carruthers.com (www.carruthers.com) is an excellent unofficial source for online federal governmental information, including its "Proclamation of Acts Page." Canada Law Book's *Canada Statute Citator* product (print and online) also provides federal proclam-ation dates (in addition to other value-added information). Provincially, the applicable *Gazette* is the official source for proclamation informa-tion, but there are also other options, depending on the province. In Ontario, for example, the Table of Proclamation on the e-Laws website is very convenient and the British Columbia government publishes its Pro-visions in Force online (www.leg.bc.ca/PROCS/list.htm). Canada Law Book also has statute citators for British Columbia and Ontario.

4) Confirming Your Statute Is Up to Date

Assume that on May 15th you located an online version of the statute relevant to your research. The online version is current to May 1st. Your next concern is to ensure that there were no bills brought into force during the fourteen-day period (the "gap") between May 1st (the currency date of the statute) and May 15th (the day of research) that

---

21   C.R.C. 1978, c. 1509
22   R.S.C. 1985, c. I-21.

could have amended or repealed your statute. In the near future, expect Canadian governments to have their online statutes current to the day. Until that time, however, there are several techniques to ensure your statute is up to date:

- *Table of Public Statutes*: The official method of checking for amendments to statutes is to consult the most recent Table of Public Statutes for the jurisdiction in question. Tables of Public Statutes are official alphabetical lists of statutes published by the Queen's Printer for the jurisdiction that show any amendments or repeals to specific statutory provisions or entire Acts up to the date indicated in the start of the Table. However, depending on the jurisdiction, the Table of Statutes will not necessarily be current to your day of research (May 15th, in the scenario above). If so, you must then check for recent bills.

- *Check for bills brought into force during the gap*: To check for amendments or repeals during the gap it is necessary to check the website for the legislature of the applicable jurisdiction for any recent bills that may have amended the statute in question, checking for both specific amendment bills (relating to only the Act you are researching) and omnibus bills (which may affect more than one piece of legislation). If there are no bills affecting your statute, you know that the online version current to May 1st is up to date. If there are bills affecting your statute, you must (i) check to see if the specific section in the Act you are researching is affected by the bill, and (ii) check to see if the bill or your section has come into force during the gap. In some situations, it may be necessary to phone the legislative counsel or Clerk of the House for the jurisdiction in question to confirm such information. One of the best commercial services for checking for recent bills that might affect your statute is the previously mentioned *Canadian Legislative Pulse* (CCH) Internet subscription service. This database makes tracking of federal and provincial bills extremely easy (in addition to providing links to the full text of the bills). It is continuously updated and the system keeps track of changes since you last logged in. The database is searchable and allows legislation to be sorted by bill number, bill title, or chapter number.

E. UNDERSTANDING AND RESEARCHING REGULATIONS (STEP 4)

Once you have identified the correct jurisdiction (Step 1) and identified and read the relevant statute (Step 2), and then checked to make sure the statute had not been amended or repealed (Step 3), it is often prudent to check for regulations enacted under the statute to determine if any regulations are relevant to the legal research problem (Step 4). To start with, it is important to realize that both statutes *and* regulations are considered to be legislation since they regulate the conduct of people and have the impact of law. There are, however, several basic distinctions between statutes and regulations. Simply put:

- Statutes are enacted by the legislative assembly after debate and vote of the entire house. Regulations, on the other hand, do not endure the same public scrutiny but are instead promulgated by the appropriate government ministry bureaucrats or other bodies after varying degrees of public consultation, and then most often enacted by the Lieutenant Governor or Governor General. As such, regulations are considered subordinate or delegated legislation.

- The phrase "statutory instrument" is broader than the term "regulation" and is defined under the federal *Statutory Instruments Act*[23] to include "any rule, order, regulation, ordinance, direction, form, tariff of costs or fees, letters patent . . . made . . . under an Act of Parliament . . . or under the authority of the Governor-in-Council" (the Governor-in-Council is just a fancy way of saying the Governor General acting on behalf of the federal Cabinet—the same applies at the provincial level with a "Lieutenant Governor-in-Council"). Thus, an "Order-in-Council" is an order made by the Governor General (or Lieutenant Governor at the provincial level) on behalf of Cabinet, usually under statutory authority, although the power to issue these orders can arise under royal prerogative.

- The government may not legislate by regulation. What this means is that the contents of the regulation are prescribed by the governing statute—the regulations must not exceed the powers given for making regulations in the main statute. This restriction prevents the government from attempting to do through regulation what would not have been allowed by statute. This is an important restriction since the regulatory process is often not subject to the same public scrutiny as the statutory process.

- Statutes tend to state broad principles or statements whereas regulations state the minute details that explain the broader principles or statements in the enacting statute. Thus, the *Highway Traffic Act*[24] provides that drivers must not speed and must yield to other drivers,

23   R.S.C. 1985, c. S-22, s. 2.
24   R.S.O. 1990, c. H.8.

while regulations to that Act will describe in very specific terms the size, shape, and colour of highway traffic signs, the safety features of school buses, and so on.

- One advantage of putting the details into regulations is that these details often change and it is—in theory—easier for the government to amend regulations than statutes since amendments to regulations are not debated in the legislative assembly.

The federal regulations were last consolidated in print in 1978 in the *Consolidated Regulations of Canada, 1978* (C.R.C. 1978) but are available online as official through the Department of Justice website and unofficially on CanLII and various other commercial services. Amendments to federal regulations and new regulations are published officially in the *Canada Gazette Part II* but are typically consolidated online with existing regulations by the government and the various commercial providers in a matter of a few days (if not sooner). Procedures for the publication of federal regulations are governed by the *Statutory Instruments Act*.[25] Provincial regulations are available on the applicable government's website, through CanLII, and through a number of commercial services. There is typically provincial legislation governing the publication of regulations in the form of a *Regulations Act* (in Ontario, it is the *Legislation Act, 2006*[26]).

There are no true subject indexes to assist in finding relevant information in a regulation. Instead, indexes to regulations tend to be alphabetical lists of the enabling statute showing which regulations have been promulgated under each statute.

For federal regulations, use the "Consolidated Index of Statutory Instruments," a quarterly publication of the *Canada Gazette Part II*, which updates the additions and revisions to the *Consolidated Regulations of Canada, 1978*, or simply browse regulations online. Provincially, there will also usually be Tables of Regulations, or you may simply browse for them online.

Realize that certain industries are heavily regulated and that in some situations regulations are frequently amended. It is often beneficial to consult a leading treatise on the area you are researching for a discussion of the applicable regulations, or consult the applicable government ministry's website to see if there is a discussion of the regulatory environment related to the subject matter being researched.

---

25   Above note 23.
26   Above note 2.

Figure 3.4
Screenshot from CanLII Showing Regulations Listed under Name of the Act

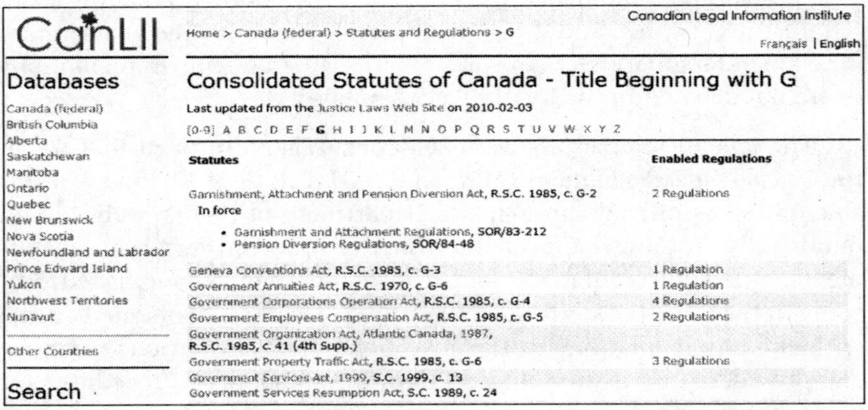

F. STATUTORY INTERPRETATION (STEP 5)

Finding and updating legislation are important skills. Equally important is understanding what the legislation says, and knowing the rules and principles that courts use to interpret legislation. Some people take for granted that legislation means what it says and is the law. What is not always appreciated, however, is the interplay between legislatures and courts and the role that judges can play in interpreting legislation—legislation may not always mean what it says: if it is unconstitutional, it can be struck down, and if it is ambiguous, there are special rules to guide how the legislation should be interpreted. What follows next is Step 5 of the Legislative Research Checklist—understanding the basic principles of statutory interpretation and how these principles can affect legal research. Readers wanting more in-depth treatment should consult any of the leading textbooks on statutory interpretation set out at the end of this chapter.

1) Statutes Judicially Considered

A useful starting point in legal research on statutory interpretation is to find cases in which courts have interpreted particular sections of statutes or regulations. There are two basic ways to find such cases:

- The traditional method is to use print-based services such as Carswell's *Canada Statute Citations* or tables called "Statutes Judicially Considered" found in the back of indexes to print case law reporters.

These services list statutes (and sometimes regulations and court rules) alphabetically by jurisdiction providing citations to cases that have considered particular sections of the legislation. Print and looseleaf annotated states are also another way of identifying cases that have considered particular sections of a statute.

Figure 3.5
Screenshot Showing the Results of KeyCiting s. 11 of B.C.'s *Evidence Act* on Westlaw Canada

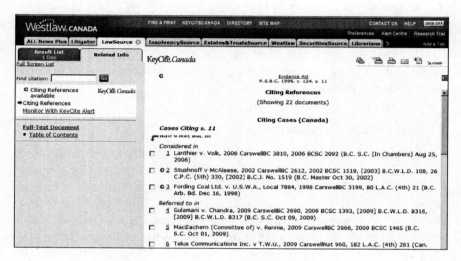

- A more modern technique is to use online citators since they are usually more current than print or looseleaf services. Two of the more comprehensive online legislative citators are QuickCITE Statute Citator (LexisNexis Quicklaw) and KeyCite (Westlaw Canada), the latter being a modified version of Carswell's print *Canadian Statute Citations*. Simply put, both services allow you to indicate a particular section of a statute and then to check which cases have considered that section. On LexisNexis Quicklaw, you simply type in the name of the Act and section number and the system generates a list of cases (and their treatment) that have considered the section (their scope of coverage is currently for Canadian court decisions since 1992 and 2005 for Québec). On Westlaw Canada, by way of comparison, there is a "citing references" link for federal and provincial statutes (and court rules). For example, if viewing section 16 of the *Criminal Code* on Westlaw Canada, it is possible to click on the "citing references" link to generate a list of all of the cases that have cited, discussed, mentioned, or applied that section, as decided by Carswell's editors (see Figure 3.5 for a screenshot of Westlaw Canada's KeyCite statute citator). CanLII is also developing a "noteup" feature that allows you to check for cases on CanLII that have considered particular statutes or regulations. Aside from online citators, another technique is to search on the keywords in or a phrase from the statutory section you are researching and to search across all available jurisdictions to see if courts from different jurisdictions have considered the specific (or similar) language.

As discussed above, it is important to remember when looking for cases that have considered a particular section of a statute that predecessor versions of the section may have had different section numbers in the past. It is therefore usually necessary, before looking for cases, to first trace the section historically to its origin to confirm the prior section numbers.

2) Interpretation Statutes

Those who conduct legal research regularly should bookmark copies of the federal and applicable provincial *Interpretation Act* for easy reference.[27] The contents of these Acts are relatively uniform across all jurisdictions. Topics covered by this legislation include how legislation is to be interpreted, the effect of amendments and repeals, rules of construction, and the calculation of time. These interpretation statutes also define important terms that apply to all legislation across the jurisdiction, definitions such as the meaning of "holiday." An example regarding one of the calculations of time in section 27(2) of the federal *Interpretation Act*[28] is as follows:

> Where there is a reference to a number of days, not expressed to be clear days, between two events, in calculating that number of days the day on which the first event happens is excluded and the day on which the second event happens is included.

These rules are not necessarily easy to memorize, despite their importance and application to legislation across the applicable jurisdiction; hence the value in being aware of these Acts and having a copy close at hand for frequent consultation.

---

27   In Ontario, there is a recent *Legislation Act, 2006, ibid.*, that repealed and replaced the former *Interpretation Act, Regulations Act, Statute and Regulation Revision Act, 1998*, and *Statutes Act*. See James L.H. Sprague & Michèle René de Cotret, *The 2008 Annotated Ontario Legislation Act* (Toronto: Thomson Carswell, 2007).

28   Above note 22.

3) Hansard Debates

Legal researchers should also be familiar with Hansard debates and other legislative documents and the role that they can play in legal research and statutory interpretation. The name "Hansard" comes from the family of "reporters" who first began to officially transcribe the debates of the British Parliament in the 19th century and is used in Canada to describe the reports of legislative debates of the federal and provincial legislatures. The traditional method of researching Hansard debates is to use annual or sessional print volumes of the debates using a print index to access information by topic, speaker, or bill name, depending on the jurisdiction involved. The modern method of researching Hansard debates is through the websites of the applicable legislative assembly (see Chapter 5, Table 5.10 for a list of these websites) and searching by keyword or by browsing through an online index. Another source of useful information can often be found in various legislative committee reports regarding questions raised by legislators when reviewing draft legislation. These are generally available in print and are increasingly available online through the various government websites. The reason to research Hansard debates or legislative committee reports is to gain a better understanding of the legislative purpose of a particular piece of legislation (discussed below under the "Purposive Analysis Rule"). Although courts are wary of placing too much weight on legislative history, it can provide useful context and help explain the purpose of the legislation.[29]

4) Traditional Approaches to Statutory Interpretation

In researching legislation that has been judicially considered, it is important to have an understanding of the various approaches that courts take to interpret legislation. The danger in trying to simply list the various rules of statutory interpretation, however, is to trivialize what should ordinarily be a complex balancing act by judges that takes into account a number of cultural, legal, and social factors that affect how we use language.[30] Nonetheless, it is hoped that the brief overview that

---

29   Ruth Sullivan, *Statutory Interpretation*, 2d ed. (Toronto: Irwin Law, 2007)
      [Sullivan] at 285–86. For a good history and comparative review on the use
      of Parliamentary materials in statutory interpretation, see Stéphane Beaulac,
      "Parliamentary Debates in Statutory Interpretation: A Question of Admissibility
      Or of Weight?" (1998) 43 McGill L.J. 287.
30   See Ruth Sullivan, *Sullivan on the Construction of Statutes*, 5th ed. (Markham,
      ON: LexisNexis Canada, 2008) at xi ("Foreword to the Third Edition").

follows can provide an introduction to statutory interpretation that identifies some basic issues that legal researchers face when they conduct legislative research.

There are several broad approaches to statutory interpretation identified in the literature that have been used by the courts over time:

a)   The Ordinary Meaning Rule

This rule, simply put, requires courts to interpret legislation using the ordinary meaning of its language unless there is a valid reason to reject the ordinary meaning in favour of another interpretation.[31] The ordinary meaning can be established by judicial notice or by reference to dictionary definitions, but is not always that simple a process since "ordinary meaning" usually would involve a textual analysis that requires looking at the words in their context. This analysis can be supported by other aids to statutory interpretation (such as looking to the purpose of the legislation).

b)   The Purposive Analysis Rule

This rule requires the court to infer the legislative purpose when interpreting legislative text. As explained by Professor Sullivan, "an interpretation that promotes the purpose is preferred over one that does not, while interpretations that would tend to defeat the purpose are avoided."[32] Legislative purpose can be inferred from the language of the statute itself (often from a preamble to the Act) or from sources outside of the legislation, such as Hansard debates and legislative committee reports. Other methods used by courts are to look at the "mischief" to be cured by the legislation or to look at the evolution of the legislation through amendments as a means to aiding interpretation of the legislation.

c)   The Contextual Analysis Rule

This rule requires the court to interpret legislative text not just in its immediate context but the entire Act as a whole and even other legislation and the social conditions in which the legislation operates.[33]

d)   The Consequential Analysis or Absurdity Rule

This rule takes into account the fact that particular interpretations will result in particular consequences and that courts will take into account the likely outcome or effect of a particular interpretation:

---

31   Sullivan, above note 29 at 49. See also *Thomson v. Canada (Deputy Minister of Agriculture)*, [1992] 1 S.C.R. 385.

32   Sullivan, *ibid.* at 194.

33   *Ibid.* at 128.

Consequences that are judged to be good are generally presumed to be intended and are regarded as part of the legislative purpose. Consequences that are judged to be absurd or otherwise unacceptable are presumed not to have been intended. As much as possible, interpretations that lead to unacceptable consequences are avoided.[34]

e) The Plausible Meaning Rule

This rule is used by courts when they wish to depart from the "ordinary meaning" of a statute in order to give the statute a more plausible interpretation. This is only allowed, however, where the "plausible meaning" is reasonable given the language of the legislative text; courts usually cannot add or delete text to the legislation or otherwise change the intent of the legislators.

f) The Original Meaning Rule

This is a special rule of statutory interpretation that most often applies to "ordinary" legislation as opposed to "constitutional" legislation (such as the *Charter of Rights and Freedoms*). The rule suggests that the meaning of words in ordinary legislation is relatively fixed at the time it was enacted and is hence imbued with its "original meaning," whereas constitutional text is "organic" and interpreted in light of changing times.

g) The Modern Principle

It can be seen that there is much overlap between the foregoing "rules" and there is no real sense of a hierarchy or systematic order by which a court will apply one rule over another. However, if there is one overriding principle of interpretation applied, it would be what is referred to as Driedger's "modern principle," a principle that has been fully endorsed by the Supreme Court of Canada:

> Today there is only one principle or approach, namely, the words of an Act are to be read in their entire context and in their grammatical and ordinary sense harmoniously with the scheme of the Act, the object of the Act, and the intention of Parliament.[35]

Sullivan sums up this approach in these terms:

> The words of the text must be read and analyzed in light of a purposive analysis, a scheme analysis, the larger context in which the legislation was written and operates and the intention of the legislature,

---

34 *Ibid.* at 209.
35 *Re Rizzo & Rizzo Shoes Ltd.*, [1998] 1 S.C.R. 27 at para. 21.

which includes implied intention and the presumptions of legislative intent.[36]

In addition to these broad "rules," there are a number of presumptions in the literature of statutory interpretation that courts rely upon as aids, presumptions that are too numerous to list here but that include such things as a presumption that legislators exhibit linguistic and drafting competence and have encyclopedic knowledge.[37] There are also special rules for interpreting bilingual legislation.[38]

There are also a number of Latin phrases or maxims that predominate in statutory interpretation with which every legal researcher should be familiar:

- *Ejusdem generis* ("of the same kind" or the "limited class" rule): this "rule" presumes that a general term following a list of specific terms will be limited to the more specific type or class of things that precede the general term.[39] Example: the phrase "other association" in the "list" of "a fraternal, trade, professional, or other association" would be defined by the more specific terms "fraternal, trade, professional" and would not include, for example, the Consumers' Association of Canada.[40]
- *Expressio unius est exclusio alternius* ("to express one thing is to exclude another" or the "implied exclusion" rule): this maxim suggests that if the legislature left something out, it intended to do so since if it had wanted to include something, it would have expressly set it out. Professor Sullivan refers to this as the "implied exclusion rule."[41]
- *Noscitur a sociis* ("one is known by one's associates" or the "associated words rule"): this maxim suggests that courts should look to the common features of words linked by "and" or "or" and limit the interpretation of those words to fit within the scope of those terms.[42] Example: the association of the word "conceals" with "removes" and "disposes" in "removes, conceals, or disposes of property" suggests the concealing would require a positive act of concealment since

---

36 Above note 29 at 42.
37 *Ibid.* at 164–67.
38 *Ibid.*, c. 5. See also Michel Bastarache, *The Law of Bilingual Interpretation* (Markham, ON: LexisNexis Canada, 2008).
39 See *National Bank of Greece (Canada) v. Katsikonouris* (1990), 74 D.L.R. (4th) 197 at 203 (S.C.C.). See also Sullivan, above note 29 at 178–82.
40 See *Consumers' Association of Canada v. Canada (Postmaster General)* (1975), 11 N.R. 181 (Fed. C.A.).
41 Sullivan, above note 29 at 193.
42 *Ibid.* at 175–78.

both removing and disposing require positive acts (as opposed to concealing being interpreted as a failure to disclose).[43]

• *Generalia specialibus non derogant* ("the general does not detract from the specific" or the "implied exception" rule): this maxim suggests that a court prefer specific provisions over provisions of general application where the provisions are in conflict.[44]

Being aware of the general rules of statutory interpretation and the more detailed resources that discuss statutory interpretation is important for legal researchers since legislation is a key primary resource. Thus, finding and updating legislation is one thing; knowing how to interpret the legislation can be an equally important component of legal research.

G. CITATION OF LEGISLATION

Statutes and regulations are ordinarily given a short title, the name by which you may refer to the statute. Use the short title plus the balance of the citation (year, chapter number, and source) when citing statutes or regulations. Similar rules are also applied to bills and other legislative documents. Refer to Chapter 2 of the McGill Guide for more information on citing legislation, or consider the following examples of selected federal legislative citations:

• **Consolidated Statute**: *National Anthem Act*, R.S.C. 1985, c. N-2
• **Annual Statute**: *Nuclear Fuel Waste Act*, S.C. 2002, c. 23
• **Consolidated Regulation**: *Hatchery Regulations*, C.R.C., c. 1023
• **Annual Regulation**: *Meat Inspection Regulations, 1990*, S.O.R./90-288
• **Bill**: Bill C-26, *An Act to establish the Canada Border Services Agency*, 1st Sess., 38th Parl., 2005 (as passed by the House of Commons 13 June 2005).

H. CONCLUSIONS

Much has changed in the last decade regarding legislative research with the advent of current online legislative databases. To date, however, this has not meant the death of print-based legislative research as most historical legislative data are not easily available in electronic format. It is likely that both government and commercial publishers will con-

---

43   *R. v. Goulis* (1981), 33 O.R. (2d) 55 (C.A.).
44   Sullivan, above note 29 at 310–11.

tinue to expand and improve upon electronic access to their legislation, so readers should monitor any developments regarding the publication and availability of legislative material in electronic format.

I. ADDITIONAL RESOURCES

Books and Guides

Appleby, Eric B. *Legal Research Guide to Statutes*. Fredericton, NB: Maritime Law Book, 2007. Available online: www.mlb.nb.ca/site/ffiles/statute.pdf.

Bastarache, Michel. *The Law of Bilingual Interpretation*. Markham. ON: LexisNexis Canada, 2008.

Beaulac, Stéphane. *Handbook on Statutory Interpretation: General Methodology, Canadian Charter and International Law*. Markham. ON: LexisNexis Canada, 2008.

Bédard, Michel. *Coming into Force of Federal Legislation* (15 May 2009). Ottawa: Library of Parliament, 2009. Available online: http://dsp-psd.pwgsc.gc.ca/collection_2010/bdp-lop/prb/prb0903-eng.pdf.

Côté, Pierré-Andre. *The Interpretation of Legislation in Canada*. 3d ed. Toronto: Carswell, 2000.

Fitzgerald, Patrick & Barry Wright. *Looking at Canada's Legal System*. 5th ed. Markham, ON: Butterworths Canada, 2000.

Forsey, Eugene. *How Canadians Govern Themselves*. 6th ed. Ottawa: Government of Canada, 2005. Available online: www.parl.gc.ca/information/library/idb/forsey/index-e.asp.

Gall, Gerald. *The Canadian Legal System*. 5th ed. Scarborough, ON: Carswell, 2004.

Graham, Randy N. *Statutory Interpretation: Cases, Text and Materials*. Toronto: Emond Montgomery, 2002.

Graham, Randy N. *Statutory Interpretation: Theory and Practice*. Toronto: Emond Montgomery, 2001.

Guide to Making Federal Acts and Regulations. 2d ed. Ottawa: Government of Canada, 2001. Available online: www.pco-bcp.gc.ca.

Jeffery, Michael I., Kenneth Harril Gifford, & Donald James Gifford. *How to Understand Statutes and By-Laws*. Toronto: Carswell, 1995.

Keeshan, M. David & Valerie M. Steeves. *The Annotated Federal and Ontario Interpretation Acts.* Scarborough, ON: Carswell, 1996.

Law Society of Upper Canada. *Canadian Legislation Online.* Online: http://rc.lsuc.on.ca/library/research_law_ca_legis.htm.

MacLean, M. Virginia & John R. Tomlinson. *A User's Guide to Municipal By-laws.* 2d ed. Markham, ON: LexisNexis Canada, 2008.

O'Brien, Audrey & Marc Bosc, eds. *House of Commons Procedure and Practice.* 2d ed. Ottawa: Government of Canada, 2009. Available online: www.parl.gc.ca.

Salembier, John Paul. *Legal and Legislative Drafting.* Markham, ON: LexisNexis Canada, 2009.

Sprague, James L.H. & Michèle René de Cotret. *The 2008 Annotated Ontario Legislation Act.* Toronto: Thomson Carswell, 2007.

Sullivan, Ruth. *Statutory Interpretation.* 2d ed. Toronto: Irwin Law, 2007.

Sullivan, Ruth. *Sullivan on the Construction of Statutes.* 5th ed. Markham, ON: LexisNexis Canada, 2008.

Online Resources
- *B.C. Citator Service* (Canada Law Book)
- *Canada Statute Service* (Canada Law Book)
- Canadian Legal Information Institute (CanLII).
- *CCH: Canadian Legislative Pulse* (CCH Canada)
- *Code civil du Québec annoté Baudouin Renaud* (SOQUIJ)
- Droit civil en ligne (Editions Yvon Blais)
- LexisNexis Quicklaw
- *Ontario Citator Service* (Canada Law Book)
- Westlaw Canada

Selected Articles

Bale, Gordon. "Parliamentary Debates and Statutory Interpretation: Switching on the Light or Rummaging in the Ashcans of the Legislative Process" (1995) 74 Can. Bar Rev. 1.

Beaulac, Stéphane. "International Treaty Norms and Driedger's 'Modern' Principle of Statutory Interpretation" (2004) Can. Council Int'l L. 141.

Beaulac, Stéphane. "Parliamentary Debates in Statutory Interpretation: A Question of Admissibility Or of Weight?" (1998) 43 McGill L.J. 287.

Beaulac, Stéphane. "Recent Developments at the Supreme Court of Canada on the Use of Parliamentary Debates" (2000) 63 Sask. L. Rev. 581.

Beaulac, Stéphane & Pierre-André Côté. "Driedger's 'Modern Principle' at the Supreme Court of Canada: Interpretation, Justification, Legitimization" (2006) 40 R.J.T. 131.

Binnie, Ian. "Constitutional Interpretation and Original Intent" (2004) 23 Sup. Ct. L. Rev. 345.

Eaton, John. "Creating a Model Act for Teaching Statutory Publication: Introducing the Federal Tea Cup Act" (1997) 22 Can. L. L. 13.

Gray, Wayne D. "Interpretation of Commercial Statutes in the Supreme Court of Canada: A Triumph of Pragmatism" (2004) 26 Sup. Ct. L. Rev. 593.

Hall, Geoff R. "Statutory Interpretation in the Supreme Court of Canada: The Triumph of a Common Law Methodology" (1998) 21 Advocates' Q. 38.

Hubley, Wendy & Micheline Beaulieu. "Locating Canadian Orders in Council" (2001) 26 Can. L. Libraries 83.

Kaye, Philip. "When Do Ontario Acts and Regulations Come into Force" (Research Paper B31, revised August 2007). Available online: www.ontla.on.ca.

Keyes, John Mark. "Judicial Review and the Interpretation of Legislation: Who gets the Last Word?" (2006) 19 Can. J. Admin. L. & Prac. 119.

Keyes, John Mark. "May the Force Be with You: The Netherworld of Unproclaimed Statutes" (2007) 20 Can. J. Admin. L. & Prac. 261.

Larsen, Norman. "Statute Revision and Consolidation: History, Process and Problems" (1987) 19 Ottawa L. Rev. 321.

Rhone, Christopher. "Accepting the Words of Parliament: Parliamentary History as a Means to Interpret Legislation" (2001) 59 Advocate 697.

Risk, Richard. "Here Be Cold and Tygers: A Map of Statutory Interpretation in Canada in the 1920s and 1930s" (2000) 63 Sask. L. Rev. 195.

Roach, Kent. "The Uses and Audiences of Preambles in Legislation" (2001) 47 McGill L.J. 129.

Ross, Stephen F. "Statutory Interpretation in the Courtroom, the Classroom, and Canadian Legal Literature" (1999–2000) 31 Ottawa L. Rev. 39.

Sullivan, Ruth. "Statutory Interpretation in the Supreme Court of Canada" (1998–99) 30 Ottawa L. Rev. 175.

Tjaden, Ted. "Finding and Updating Canadian Federal Private Acts." The SLAW Blog, comment posted 30 September 2009, online: www.slaw.ca/2009/09/30/finding-and-updating-canadian-federal-private-acts.

CHAPTER 4

RESEARCHING CASE LAW

A. INTRODUCTION

New law students and first-time legal researchers are sometimes surprised by how much judge-made law exists and how important it can be in determining legal rights. This judge-made law, made up of the decisions of judges and administrative tribunals, forms what is referred to as the "common law," a body of law that becomes the judicial precedents by which current judges are bound. Unfortunately, this body of law is not always well-organized or coherent, creating the challenge of researching case law to ensure that all relevant cases have been found and have not been overruled or questioned by subsequent court decisions. One of the goals of a lawyer or self-represented party in litigation in a common law system, therefore, is to find previous court decisions similar on the facts and favourable on the results so that the judge presently presiding over the current litigation will be obliged to follow the previous cases and rule in favour of the lawyer or self-represented litigant.

This chapter will discuss case law by first providing a brief overview of the judicial system, followed by an explanation of the role of "judicial precedent" (also known as *stare decisis*) and how case law is published. Techniques to find relevant cases will then be discussed, along with "noting up" case law, a technique to update or verify your research to ensure the cases you have found have not been overruled on appeal or negatively questioned by subsequent cases.[1]

B. THE JUDICIAL SYSTEM

There are a lot of similarities between the judicial systems in most common law countries, including but not limited to Canada, England, the United States, and Australia. Central to these systems is the rule of law, an idea that all persons are governed by a known set of rules and procedures that include agreed upon methods for parties to resolve their disputes. In reality, litigating disputes in the judicial systems of most modern countries can be unduly complex, time-consuming, and expensive. Fortunately, for the purpose of putting legal research in context, it is generally sufficient to have only a broad understanding of how the judicial system operates, an understanding that can be simplified to explain how legal research relates to the judicial process.

Judges are appointed by the state to resolve criminal and civil disputes and are given power to enforce laws and punish wrongdoers through imposing imprisonment and fines enforceable by the state in criminal matters or through awarding judgments enforceable by parties to the dispute in civil matters. The independence of judges is ensured in most modern countries through various means, including appointment procedures, security of tenure, high salaries, and institutional independence of the courts.[2] An important issue in recent years in the legal literature has been the topic of judicial activism, a notion held by some commentators that judges, as unelected officials, wield too much (political) power in their decision making, deciding matters that are more properly decided by elected politicians.[3]

---

1   Readers needing specific information on researching Québec legal materials should consult any of the following resources: Denis LeMay, Dominique Goubau, & Marie-Louise Pelletier, *La recherche documentaire en droit*, 6th ed. (Montreal: Wilson & Lafleur, 2008); Denis LeMay, "Researching Québec Law" in Douglass T. MacEllven et al., eds., *Legal Research Handbook*, 5th ed. (Toronto: Butterworths, 2003), c. 12; or the research web pages of the University of Montreal Law School (www.droit.umontreal.ca) and the University of Laval Law School (www.fd.ulaval.ca).

2   W.R. Lederman, "The Independence of the Judiciary" (1956) 34 Can. Bar Rev. 769; *R. v. Valente*, [1985] 2 S.C.R. 673.

3   Ian Greene, "Democracy, Judicial Independence, and Judicial Selection for Federally Appointed Judges" (2008) 58 U.N.B.L.J. 105; Beverley McLachlin, "Judicial Accountability" (2008) 1 Journal of Parliamentary and Political Law 293; Edward Bayda, "Judicial Activism" (2007) 70 Sask. L. Rev. 225; Sanjeev

When conducting case law research, it helps to have a basic under-standing of the judicial process, and the ways in which disputes begin in the legal system and proceed through to the appeal level. The chart set out in Table 4.1, albeit overly simplistic, represents a broad descrip-tion of the three levels that represent the judicial system in most com-mon law jurisdictions. In most judicial systems, there is an inverted pyramid court structure, with a single judge at the lowest trial level, typically three to five judges at the second appeal level, and seven to nine judges at the third and final national appeal court level. Appeal courts sit with an odd number of judges to avoid there being a tie or deadlock in the event the appeal judges disagree (i.e., an odd number of judges avoids a deadlock).

In reality, the structure of the court system is much more com-plicated than what is presented in Table 4.1. Many jurisdictions, for example, have several different trial courts, including a small claims court (for matters involving smaller amounts of money), a family court, and a provincial criminal court. Some jurisdictions may also have an intermediate appeal court between the trial court and the Court of Ap-peal to screen appeals and to decide other matters (in Ontario, such a court is called the Divisional Court).

In Canada, the power of the legislature over courts is set out in the *Constitution Act, 1867*[4] and is shared between the federal and provincial governments. Simply put, the federal government has power to appoint and pay for judges in the superior courts of the provinces and to estab-lish a federal court system (sections 96–105). The provinces have power under section 92, paragraph 14 for the "Administration of Justice in the Province, including the Constitution, Maintenance, and Organization of Provincial Courts, both of Civil and Criminal Jurisdiction, and in-cluding Procedure in Civil Matters in those Courts."

Anand, "The Truth about Canadian Judicial Activism" (2006) 15 Const. Forum Const. 87; Murray Mollard, "Delivering Democracy: The Challenge of Judicial Accountability" (2004) 62 Advocate 337; Robert Martin, *The Most Dangerous Branch: How the Supreme Court of Canada has Undermined Our Law and Our Democracy* (Montreal: McGill-Queen's University Press, 2003); F.L. Morton, ed., *Law, Politics and the Judicial Process in Canada*, 3d ed. (Calgary: University of Calgary Press, 2002); Kent Roach, *The Supreme Court on Trial: Judicial Activ-ism or Democratic Dialogue* (Toronto: Irwin Law, 2001); F.L. Morton & Rainer Knopff, eds., *The Charter Revolution and the Court Party* (Peterborough, ON Broadview Press, 2000); Christopher P. Manfredi & James B. Kelly, "Six Degrees of Dialogue: A Response to Hogg and Bushell" (1999) 37 Osgoode Hall L.J. 513; Peter W. Hogg & Allison A. Bushell, "The Charter Dialogue Between Courts and Legislatures" (1997) 35 Osgoode Hall L.J. 75.

4   30 & 31 Vict., c. 3, reprinted in R.S.C. 1985, App. II, No. 5.

Table 4.1
Simplified Overview of the Canadian Court System

First Level: Trial Court

- A single judge who usually hears "live" witnesses (or affidavit evidence) in court
- The judge's decisions are often unreported, available only in the court file or on commercial or free online legal databases
- It can be a superior court (with federally appointed judges), a provincial court (with provincially appointed judges), or a federal court
- Typical abbreviations for trial-level courts in Canada: Supreme Court (S.C.), Trial Division (T.D.), Queen's Bench (Q.B.), Superior Court of Justice (S.C.J.)

Second Level: Provincial/Federal Court of Appeal

- Usually three judges (sometimes five) sit as a panel; "majority" rules in the case of a split decision
- There are usually no "live" witnesses; appeal based on a written appeal record
- Decisions are more likely reported in print case reporters
- Court abbreviation: C.A.

Third Level: National Supreme Court

- Seven or nine judges sit as a panel in Ottawa
- The Court screens appeals by requiring that "leave to appeal" be obtained for most cases
- Because of the volume of appeals, the Court hears only the most important appeals, usually those involving national or constitutional issues, or those limited number of appeals—usually serious criminal charges—where leave to appeal is a right
- Decisions are reported in English and French through its website, in the Supreme Court Reports, and in various commercial print case reporters and commercial online databases

For most Canadian provinces, there is in essence only the first level and second level of courts described above, being a trial court and a provincial Court of Appeal. The third level of courts for the provinces is the national Supreme Court of Canada in Ottawa—the court of last resort since 1949 for civil appeals and since 1933 for criminal appeals[5]—where it is possible to appeal from a provincial Court of

---

5   It was possible to appeal from the Supreme Court of Canada to the Judicial Committee of the Privy Council (in England) but this avenue of appeal was abolished in 1933 for criminal appeals and in 1949 for civil appeals. Note, however, that civil appeals for cases begun before 1949 were allowed to appeal to the Privy Council, resulting in the final Canadian lawsuit being heard by the Privy Council in 1959, being *Ponoka-Calmar Oils v. Wakefield*, [1960] A.C. 18 (P.C.). See online: Wikipedia

Appeal in limited circumstances (with the Supreme Court of Canada determining which appeals it will hear).

In addition to the "three-level" system of courts in the provinces, there is the separate federal court system established by the federal government. The federal court system consists of a trial division and a Court of Appeal, with the third and final level of appeal being the Supreme Court of Canada in Ottawa (the Supreme Court of Canada also has special jurisdiction under section 53 of the *Supreme Court Act*[6] to directly hear "reference questions" posed to it by the federal government).[7] The federal courts have offices in all major cities across the country. A large number of litigation lawyers do not regularly appear in federal court since its jurisdiction is for special matters falling under limited federal jurisdiction, such as copyright actions, immigration, maritime law matters, and actions against the Crown.

Viewed in its most basic structure, it can be said that the court systems of other countries tend to follow the same three-level structure with a single trial judge, an intermediate court of appeal, and a national court of final appeal. Set out below is a brief review and comparison of the judicial systems for the United Kingdom, the United States, and Australia, those being the three most likely jurisdictions whose court decisions are cited—and sometimes considered persuasive—by Canadian courts. Because of our common heritage, British court decisions tend to be the most highly cited decisions from foreign courts. In the brief review that follows of the British, American, and Australian judicial systems, realize that, as with the Canadian judicial system, there is much potential complexity involved but that a simplified overview often suffices for conducting legal research.

1) United Kingdom

Compared to the other jurisdictions described in this chapter, the British court system is relatively simple, in part since Britain, as a unitary jurisdiction, has no direct equivalent of a federal court system.[8] Of

---

contributors, "Judicial Committee of the Privy Council," *Wikipedia, The Free Encyclopedia*, http://en.wikipedia.org/wiki/Judicial_Committee_of_the_Privy_Council.

6   R.S.C. 1985, c. S-26.

7   There have been a number of well-known reference question cases heard by the Supreme Court of Canada, including such cases as *Reference re Secession of Quebec*, [1998] 2 S.C.R. 217 and *Reference re Same-Sex Marriage*, [2004] 3 S.C.R. 698, 2004 SCC 79.

8   For a good overview of the legal system in the United Kingdom, see Sarah Carter, "A Guide to the UK Legal System" (May 2009), online: www.nyulaw-global.org/globalex/United_Kingdom1.htm.

the four countries comprising the United Kingdom—England, Wales, Scotland, and Northern Ireland—the decisions of England (and Wales) tend to be of most interest to Canadian legal researchers. Decisions from Scotland and Northern Ireland are less frequently cited (due, in part, to the relatively unique nature of the Scottish and Irish legal systems). As such, the discussion that follows focuses on the English court system. Since October 2009, the top court is the Supreme Court of the United Kingdom (replacing the long-established House of Lords). The Supreme Court of the United Kingdom is the court of last resort for England, Wales, Northern Ireland, and for Scottish civil cases. Decisions of the (former) House of Lords still remain relatively influential in Canada, due in part to our common heritage (and decisions of the new Supreme Court are also obviously expected to be of interest to Canadian legal researchers).

The next highest court in England is the Court of Appeal of England and Wales, where there is a Civil Division (that hears appeals from County Courts and the High Court of Justice) and a Criminal Division (that hears appeals from Magistrates' Court and Crown Courts). Although it is typically decisions from the House of Lords (now Supreme Court) and the Court of Appeal that are of the most interest to Canadian legal researchers, decisions of the High Court of Justice—beneath the Court of Appeal in the judicial hierarchy—are sometimes cited by Canadian courts (the High Court of Justice has three divisions, the decisions of which are easily recognized by most legal researchers: the Queen's Bench Division, the Chancery Division, and the Family Division). There are also other, lower trial courts in England but decisions from those lower courts tend to be of less interest to Canadian researchers.

2) United States

In the American judicial system, just as in Canada, there are both federal and (in their nomenclature) state courts. In the United States, their federal court system, however, is much more "active" than the relatively "sleepy" Canadian federal court system, due in part to a broader jurisdiction and a higher volume of work. Federal courts in the United States deal with cases involving federal laws, U.S. treaties, and international law; the constitutionality of a law; bankruptcy law; and admiralty law. One key area of difference in U.S. and Canadian federal jurisdiction is that in the United States, disputes between persons from two or more states fall under federal court "diversity" jurisdiction (involving claims by persons from "diverse" or different states or countries), a concept that is not applicable to the Canadian federal courts.

Like the Canadian federal court system, the United States federal court system mirrors the three-level pyramid structure:

- *U.S. federal trial courts*: There are many district (or federal trial) courts (including separate bankruptcy courts) spread across ninety-four judicial districts (with more populous regions having more than one district court).[9]
- *U.S. federal courts of appeal*: Appeals from district courts are made to a smaller number of federal courts of appeal, which are organized into thirteen circuit courts, including eleven numbered regional circuits[10] and the District of Columbia Circuit and a Federal Circuit (with the Court of Appeals for the Federal Circuit having special jurisdiction for appeals involving patent law or appeals from the Court of International Trade and the Court of Federal Claims).
- *U.S. Supreme Court*: The United States Supreme Court is comprised of the Chief Justice of the United States and eight associate judges. Like the Supreme Court of Canada, the U.S. Supreme Court is a court of last resort and it hears a limited number of cases, usually those involving questions of national importance or constitutional law.

The U.S. state court system also mirrors a multi-level structure, although it can vary from state to state how many levels of court are involved from trial to final appeal. For example, in Florida, there are potentially five levels of court, listed below from lowest to highest:

- County Court (akin to small claims courts in most Canadian provinces), of which there is one in each of the state's sixty-seven counties
- Circuit Court (in each of the state's twenty judicial circuits)
- District Court (in each of the state's five judicial districts)
- Florida Supreme Court (consisting of seven judges), the state's highest court
- U.S. Supreme Court

In most situations, the District Court will be the final appellate court in Florida, since appeals to the Florida Supreme Court and the U.S. Supreme Court are limited.[11] Due to the differences among state courts, any explanations of the U.S. state court system must, by necessity, be general. For the Canadian legal researcher faced with research-

---

9 For example, there are four districts in New York, being the Eastern District, Northern District, Southern District, and Western District.

10 The United States Court of Appeal for the Second Circuit, for example, has appellate jurisdiction over decisions from the district (or federal trial) courts within the judicial districts of Connecticut, New York, and Vermont.

11 Florida State Courts, online: www.flcourts.org.

ing American case law, it is important to understand the specific court hierarchy for the state in which case law is being researched. Fortunately, most state courts now have good websites explaining their jurisdictional powers and relevant appeal procedures.[12]

3) Australia

Australia—like Canada and the United States—has both a federal judicial system and state/territorial judicial systems.[13] The highest court is the High Court of Australia and is comprised of seven judges. Of all Australian judgments, it is the decisions of the High Court that are of the most interest to Canadian legal researchers. The High Court has original jurisdiction to hear cases directly to interpret and apply the laws of Australia (particularly involving cases involving interpretation of the Constitution), but the majority of cases it hears—by leave (or permission)—are appeals from the other courts in the federal system or from state or territorial courts. Also within the federal court system is the Federal Court of Australia and the Family Court of Australia (each of which has its own appeal courts) and the Federal Magistrates Court of Australia (where appeals are brought to the Federal Court or the Family Court).

Each of the six Australian states and two mainland territories have Superior Courts (which have appeals courts of their own), under which are a variety of district or magistrates courts, depending on the state or territory. Appeals from Superior Courts to the High Court of Australia are usually only by leave.

C. *STARE DECISIS* AND THE ROLE OF PRECEDENT

The doctrine of *stare decisis* ordinarily requires a judge to follow past court decisions from higher courts within that judge's jurisdiction. This requirement provides certainty and stability in the way in which the

---

12   See National Center for State Courts, online: www.ncsc.org. See also Gretchen Feltes, "A Guide to the U. S. Federal Legal System Web-based Public Accessible Sources" (December 2008), online: www.nyulawglobal.org/globalex/United_States1.htm.

13   For more detailed information on the Australian legal system, see: Petal Kinder, "A Guide to Online Research Resources for the Australian Federal Legal System with Some Reference to the State Level" (December 2008), online: www.nyulawglobal.org/Globalex/Australia1.htm.

common law develops since it restricts a judge from making completely ad hoc rulings depending on how she was feeling that day.

Because of this doctrine, which is also known as judicial precedent, it becomes important for lawyers and law librarians to find "like" cases, that is, cases from the past dealing with the client's issue that are similar on the facts and which result in a favourable ruling for the lawyer's client. Much of the lawyer's advocacy skills will be in convincing the judge that the cases that the lawyer is relying upon in support of his arguments are more similar and therefore more relevant than those of his opponent. In doing so, the lawyer "distinguishes" the cases of his opponent.

Because of *stare decisis*, an Ontario lawyer, for example, is less interested in a previous trial decision of a judge in Prince Edward Island than a previous decision of the Ontario Court of Appeal or the Supreme Court of Canada on the same facts and issues. This is because the decision of the judge in Prince Edward Island is of less precedential value and not necessarily binding on the Ontario judge, whereas the past decisions of the Ontario Court of Appeal or the Supreme Court of Canada on the same facts and issues are binding on the Ontario judge.

Thus, when researching case law, the researcher must always be sensitive to the desirability of finding court decisions from the appeal courts of his or her province or of the Supreme Court of Canada. Having said that, however, since some provincial laws do not differ much from province to province (such as securities legislation), decisions from other provinces may have relatively strong persuasive value (especially if the issue involved stems from federal statutes, such as the *Criminal Code*, where the statute applies across the entire country). Occasionally, it is not possible to find any relevant case law from the courts of the jurisdiction in which the matter is being tried. In such cases, it may be necessary to resort to case law from other provinces (or other countries—decisions of the high courts in the United Kingdom, the United States, and Australia are generally treated with much respect by Canadian courts).

D. HOW CASE LAW IS PUBLISHED

Unlike the legislative process, which involves a systematic, formalized method of rule-making, case law develops organically. At the court of first instance in a civil trial, legal issues are framed by the parties themselves (the plaintiff and the defendant), with the judge being a neutral arbitrator (unlike civil code jurisdictions, such as France, where the judge often takes a much more active role in the process). A trial judge in Canada is charged with hearing the evidence of the witnesses and then deciding the matter before her. Juries are decreasing in use in Canada, but where a jury is involved, it becomes the decider of fact, and therefore there is often less need or reason for a judge to issue written reasons.

A judge usually keeps notes during the trial of the argument and evidence he has heard. In most cases, the judge simply makes a decision at the end of the trial or hearing without giving detailed reasons or judgment (there is simply a notation in the court file called an endorsement in which the trial judge might say "case dismissed" and provide one or two handwritten or typed lines of "reasons"). In other cases, the judge will "reserve" her reasons, which means that the judge is going to think about how she will rule. In some cases, these reasons will be oral, a simple explanation in open court of how the judge has ruled. In other cases, however, where the reasons may be of interest to other parties (such as where there has been a complicated point of law argued) or where the case may likely be appealed, the judge will issue written reasons. Most civil trials rulings will typically be one of two types:

- **Interlocutory or pre-trial rulings**: One way case law develops is when a judge issues a written ruling based on an interlocutory or pre-trial dispute between the parties. These types of decisions are based largely on procedural disputes between the parties, such as whether a party is properly named, whether the pleadings (the court papers) disclose a proper cause of action, or whether a party must disclose certain documents to the other side. *Carswell's Practice Cases* (C.P.C.) is a good example of a case reporter series that publishes these types of decisions.
- **Trial or appeal rulings**: Another way case law develops is when a judge issues a written ruling after a trial (or an appeal) has finished. In these types of cases, the judge is deciding issues on their merits, and the judge's ruling—subject to an appeal—is binding on the parties and may affect their legal rights (such as whether they can collect damages or whether they must go to jail). The judge's reasons, once again subject to being appealed, can act as a precedent and affect the rights of subsequent litigants.

Where judges issue written reasons, those reasons will either be (i) published in print case law reporters or, more likely, (ii) made available online on the court's website or on another online database.

1) Published Print Case Law Reporters

Cases or judicial decisions can be found in print in books called "case reports" or "case reporters." Decisions are typically available in full text, with most publishers providing a "headnote" or summary of the case. It is important to remember, however, that not all written reasons of judges get reported in print. Editors of print case reporters will ordinarily choose only cases of interest or significance, not merely "run-of-the-mill" type decisions of interest only to the parties involved in the dispute[14] (contrast this with the situation described below where for the last decade or so, depending on the jurisdiction, most if not all recent court decisions are available online). In the old days, it would usually be one of the lawyers who would submit the reasons to a traditional print-based publisher of case law reporters for publication (presumably, some judges would also do the same). If the judgment raised an important point, the publisher would then publish the judgment, either in a topical reporter (such as the *Municipal & Planning Law Reports*, if the case involved an issue of municipal law) or a national reporter (such as the *Dominion Law Reports*). All of the decisions of the Supreme Court of Canada are published in the *Supreme Court Reports*. There is usually a publishing lag of at least several months for a full text case to appear in a print case law reporter from the time the decision has been released by the court (on some online databases, this publishing lag is reduced for important cases to a matter of a few days or less, slightly longer for "run-of-the-mill" cases).

In Canada, the well-known, national coverage print case reporters include the following:

- *Supreme Court Reports* (S.C.R.)
- *Federal Court Reports* (F.C.)
- *Dominion Law Reports* (D.L.R.)
- *Western Weekly Reports* (W.W.R.)

Other reports can be found by region. There are, for example, case law reporters for each of the Canadian provinces, ranging from the *British Columbia Law Reports* (Carswell) on the West coast to the *Newfoundland and Prince Edward Island Reports* (Maritime Law Book) on the East coast. To the extent that the rule of *stare decisis* or judicial precedence encourages lawyers to first look for decisions from within

---

14   See Paul Perell, "Selecting Cases for the *Ontario Reports*" (Dec. 1991) 4:1 Legal Research Update 1. Also see Martha L. Foote, ed., *Law Reporting and Legal Publishing in Canada: A History* (Kingston, ON: Canadian Association of Law Libraries, 1997).

their own jurisdiction, these provincial case law reporters are an important (albeit not complete) source of case law for lawyers. There are also regional case law reporters that report cases from a number of provinces. These regional case law reporters include, but are not limited to, the *Western Weekly Reports* (Carswell) and the *Atlantic Provinces Reports* (Maritime Law Book).

Decisions of administrative tribunals are reported in print by both commercial legal publishers, such as the *Administrative Law Reports* (Carswell), and directly by individual administrative tribunals, such as the decisions of the Canadian Radio-Television and Telecommunications Commission (CRTC).

In the United Kingdom, the leading case reporters are *The Law Reports*, the *All England Law Reports* (All E.R.), and the *Weekly Law Reports* (W.L.R.). There are also numerous print-based topical reporters for U.K. case law.

In the United States, West Publishing is the dominant case reporter publisher with its National Reporter System, which includes full text American court decisions organized into the following geographic areas:

- *Atlantic Reporter* (A. and A.2d): Connecticut, Delaware, District of Columbia, Maine, Maryland, New Hampshire, New Jersey, Pennsylvania, Rhode Island, and Vermont.
- *California Reporter* (Cal. Rptr., Cal. Rptr. 2d, and Cal. Rptr. 3d): California supreme and intermediate appellate courts.
- *New York Supplement* (N.Y.S., N.Y.S.2d): New York supreme and intermediate appellate courts.
- *Northeastern Reporter* (N.E. and N.E.2d): Illinois, Indiana, Massachusetts, New York (Court of Appeals), and Ohio.
- *Northwestern Reporter* (N.W. and N.W.2d): Iowa, Michigan, Minnesota, Nebraska, North Dakota, South Dakota, and Wisconsin.
- *Pacific Reporter* (P., P.2d, and P.3d): Alaska, Arizona, California (limited), Colorado, Hawaii, Idaho, Kansas, Montana, Nevada, New Mexico, Oklahoma, Oregon, Utah, Washington, and Wyoming.
- *Southeastern Reporter* (S.E. and S.E.2d): Georgia, North Carolina, South Carolina, Virginia, and West Virginia.
- *Southern Reporter* (So. and So. 2d): Alabama, Florida, Louisiana, and Mississippi.
- *Southwestern Reporter* (S.W., S.W.2d, and S.W.3d): Arkansas, Kentucky, Missouri, Tennessee, and Texas.

West also publishes selected federal U.S. District court cases in the *Federal Supplement* (F. Supp.) or the *Federal Rules Decisions* (F.R.D.), and

U.S. Court of Appeals decisions are published by West in the *Federal Reporter* (F., F. 2d and F. 3d).

In Australia, there are a number of privately published case law reporters in print, ranging from jurisdictional, type of court, or topic. The Australian *Commonwealth Law Reports*, for example, only publishes decisions of the Australian High Court. The Australian *Federal Law Reports*, on the other hand, publish selected decisions of various Australian courts that exercise federal jurisdiction. There are also various "state" reporters and a number of topical reporters.

Although major Canadian university or courthouse law libraries may maintain case law reporters in print from Canada, the United Kingdom, the United States, and Australia, many Canadian law firms are instead relying on electronic versions of case law.

2) Unpublished Cases

In Canada, aside from Supreme Court of Canada decisions, the large majority of judicial decisions are not published in print since there would be too many and most of them would be of interest to only the parties who had the dispute. Hence, most judicial decisions being handed down every day are not published in print. Access to some of these unpublished cases can be provided through digest services, such as the *All Canada Weekly Summaries*, which provide a basic digest of the case and offer to provide the full text of the decision for a fee or the various topical "caseAlerts" published by Canada Law Book (to name only two of many such services). Another way unpublished judgments may be accessed is through online databases, such as court websites or the Canadian Legal Information Institute (CanLII)—discussed in more detail in Chapter 5—or the various commercial online databases, including LexisNexis Quicklaw, Westlaw Canada, BestCase, Maritime Law Book, REJB, and SOQUIJ/Azimut.

Since most of the online databases publish all recent Canadian court decisions, realize that these online databases will also contain the select few number of cases that get published in case reporters, meaning that some decisions are published in both print and online. One can easily determine whether a decision is published or unpublished by "noting up" the decision (discussed in Section F, below in this chapter) to see where, if at all, the case has been reported. For example, when noting up the decision *Bank of Montreal v. Unified Homes Ltd.*, [1994] O.J. No. 875 (Gen. Div.) on Quicklaw, one learns from the "Reported at" field near the top of the screen that the decision is reported only at [1994] O.J. No. 875, meaning that it is only available on Quicklaw (or possibly other commercial online databases). On the other hand, when noting up *Nijjer v. Hildebrant*, [2000] B.C.J. No. 727 (C.A.), one learns from the "Reported at" field that the decision has also been reported at (2000), 75 B.C.L.R. (3d) 322 (in addition to other print-based reporters).

Court decisions from the United Kingdom are well represented online, both from the free British and Irish Legal Information Institute (www.bailii.org) — discussed in more detail in Chapter 5 — and from commercial databases, including LexisNexis and Westlaw, along with other specialized subscription services such as Justis.com (www.justis.com), which contains HTML and PDF decisions from the U.K. *Law Reports* and *Weekly Law Reports* (among other things), or Lawtel (www.lawtel.com).

For American federal and state court decisions there are many online options, too numerous to list individually. Court websites are often a good source of recent, free trial court decisions. The Cornell Legal Information Institute (www.law.cornell.edu) provides useful links to American court websites. In late 2009, Google Scholar (http://scholar.google.ca) allows free searching of American legal opinions that, at the time of implementation, includes U.S. state appellate and supreme court cases since 1950; U.S. federal district, appellate, tax, and bankruptcy courts since 1923; and U.S. Supreme Court cases since 1791. LexisOne (www.lexisone.com) also allows free searching on the last ten years of State and Federal Courts and on the U.S. Supreme Court from 1781 to the present. For lawyers and law students (and others) who have subscriptions to either LexisNexis or Westlaw, both databases have extensive coverage of American case law, including very powerful value-added features that include smart search engines, sophisticated noter-uppers and access to some of the briefs filed with the decision.

The two major commercial database providers in Australia (Westlaw Australia and LexisNexis Australia) both have good databases of Australian case law. But, as discussed in Chapter 5, the Australasian Legal Information Institute — AustLII — has an extensive, free website of Australian case law at www.austlii.org.

Case law is increasingly being published in electronic format, which brings with it the advantage of keyword searching, avoidance of publication delays, and savings in the space required by print materials.[15] Since the market in Canada for legal materials is so small and

---

15   For a discussion on the transformation (good and bad) of legal research by full-text searching, see Julie M. Jones, "Not Just Key Numbers and Keywords Anymore: How User Interface Design Affects Legal Research" (2009) 101 Law Library Journal 7; Lee F. Peoples, "The Death of the Digest and the Pitfalls of Electronic Research: What Is the Modern Legal Researcher to Do" (2005) 97

the cost of publishing small runs of print case law reports is so great, one can easily imagine that the publication of print case law reporters will diminish and the publication of case law in electronic format will continue to expand.

E. FINDING CASE LAW

There are a number of ways to find relevant cases. In the list that follows, note that searching by keyword on full-text case law databases is the last method listed since, although convenient and often powerful, searching full text by keyword is not always the best or most effective starting point to find cases. Here are some ways to find relevant cases:

- **Books and treatises:** Legal textbooks usually provide some access to case law since most authors provide footnoted citations to important cases that support the points they are making in the textbook. Textbooks are discussed in more detail in Chapter 2, Section A.
- **Journal articles and CLE papers:** Articles written by law students or law professors will often discuss important or leading cases and can be used to identify relevant cases. Law journals are discussed in more detail in Chapter 2, Section B. Likewise, papers presented at legal symposia will often discuss important court decisions. Continuing legal education and seminar papers are discussed in more detail in Chapter 2, Section C. In addition, searching on law firm bulletins on the Internet can also sometimes help identify relevant cases.[16]
- **Legal encyclopedias:** Legal encyclopedias are also a good way of finding cases, especially by topic, since the various articles or paragraphs in the encyclopedia on a particular topic are usually supported in the footnotes by citations to the cases that support the principles discussed in the main text. In Canada, the major legal encyclopedias are Carswell's *Canadian Encyclopedic Digest* and LexisNexis Canada's *Halsbury's Laws of Canada* and *JurisClasseur Québec*, discussed in more detail in Chapter 2, Section D.

Law Library Journal 661; and Allan F. Hanson, "From Key Numbers to Keywords: How Automation Has Transformed the Law" (2002) 94 Law Library Journal 563.

16   See my custom Google search of Canadian law firms and blogs, online: http://tinyurl.com/canadianlawfirms or try Fee Fie Foe Firm, online: www.feefiefoefirm.com.

- **Words and phrases services:** If you are researching the meaning of particular legal terminology, words and phrases services, discussed in more detail in Chapter 2, Section F, can help identify cases that have interpreted that particular legal terminology.
- **Case law digests:** Simply put, a digest in the context of legal literature is a summary (or digest) of case law, arranged by topic and by case name. In Canada, the leading print-based case law digest is the *Canadian Abridgment* (also available on Westlaw Canada), discussed in more detail in Chapter 2, Section E. Other well-known case digest systems in Canada include the *All Canada Weekly Summaries* (Canada Law Book) and a fairly recent online database called Canada Digests on LexisNexis Quicklaw.
- **Statutes or Regulations Judicially Considered:** If your issue involves a section of a statute or regulation, you can note up the section to see which, if any, cases have interpreted that section. In addition, there are numerous annotated statute services (identified by topic in Chapter 8) that also list cases by section of legislation for cases that have considered the particular legislative section.
- **Using a known case to find more cases:** If you have already found a relevant case, read it carefully for all of the decisions cited in it and then read those cases to see if they are relevant or lead to other cases. Perhaps more importantly, note up your known case to check not only for its judicial history but to also find any subsequent decisions that may have cited it, since the chances are good that any cases citing your known case raise either similar facts or issues.
- **Print indexes to case reporters:** Print publishers of case reporters provide indexes to their publications that allow access by subject and by case name. Thus, to find cases dealing with insurance law, one could search the indexes to the *Canadian Cases on the Law of Insurance* (C.C.L.I.) to get a relatively good overview of a limited number of cases on topic.
- **Newspapers and current awareness services:** The various newspapers and current awareness services discussed in more detail in Chapter 2, Section F, can be searched to help identify possibly relevant cases, especially recent or more controversial, newsworthy cases.
- **Online legal databases:** Online legal resources are of course an excellent way to find case law, using keyword searches by subject or by case name. Online databases allow searches across full-text case law databases to retrieve cases based on quite discrete criteria, such as individual keywords or combinations thereof, searches that are simply not possible if using only print resources.

F. NOTING UP CASE LAW

Once a case is published—whether in print or on an electronic data-base—it is important to realize that two things could happen: (i) the case could be appealed and possibly overturned; and (ii) the case could be used as a precedent or instead criticized in other subsequent court decisions. To speak of whether a case has been reversed or affirmed on appeal is to speak of its judicial history. To speak of how a case has been followed by subsequent courts is to speak of its judicial treatment.

The *judicial history* of a case is important since, if a case has been overturned on appeal, the lower court decision that has been overturned will be of little or no precedential value and a lawyer relying upon a case that is overturned stands to be greatly embarrassed in court. The *judicial treatment* of a case is equally important since the number of times a case may have been considered may indicate the strength of the case: if the case you are interested in has been mentioned and con-sidered by a large number of subsequent judges in other cases, it may likely be important. There is also the other possibility, however, that other subsequent courts may now look upon your case with disfavour, due to changes in the law (this is one way in which the common law evolves). Hence, it is extremely important to know the judicial treat-ment of a particular case (even if the case you are interested in has no judicial treatment, this does not mean your case is unimportant or of questionable precedential value—many relevant cases have no judicial treatment). Learning the judicial treatment of your case is also import-ant since it may lead you to other, more recent relevant cases on the topic of your research. To this extent, noting up for judicial treatment is a way of creating a "chain" of related cases. In this way, it is often possible to see how a particular legal principle has evolved over time through subsequent cases that have considered cases on point. The techniques to note up case law are relatively similar across Canada, the United Kingdom, the United States, and Australia.

Generally, there are several methods for noting up case law:

- **Tables of cases judicially considered**: Most print publishers of case law reporters have a section in the indexes to their reporters called "Table of Cases Judicially Considered," which is an alphabetical list of cases published in their reporters that have judicial histories or treatment.
- **Print citators**: There are print publications available in Canada (Car-swell's *Canadian Case Citations*) and the U.S. (*Shepards*) whose sole purpose is to provide the judicial history and judicial treatment of

case law (there is no equivalent British publication that provides exhaustive treatment; both *The Digest* and *Current Law* provide some print-based noting up of U.K. case law, as do Tables in the indexes to the *All England Law Reports*).

- **Online citators:** There is a definite move towards noting up case law using online noter-uppers. For decisions in its own database, CanLII has a noter-upper. However, it is not as extensive as the Canadian noter-uppers on LexisNexis Quicklaw or on Westlaw Canada's Key-Cite. In addition, both LexisNexis Quicklaw and Westlaw Canada have extensive noter-uppers for British, American, and Australian court decisions. A key feature of these online databases is the ability to click on the appropriate "link" to note up the case to get a list of the case's judicial history (i.e., whether it has been appealed or not) and a list of the case's judicial treatment (i.e., whether other courts have considered the case). When noting up cases with a lot of judicial treatment, these online citators have various features that allow you to "limit" the list of treating cases by jurisdiction or level of court, for example.

For additional resources on noting up, see the following:

- Dabney, Dan. "Another Response to Taylor's Comparison of KeyCite and Shepard's" (2000) 92 Law Library Journal 381.
- Gannage, Mark. "Noting-up Cases" (1999) 21 Advocates' Q. 489.
- McKenzie, Elizabeth M. "Comparing KeyCite with Shepard's Online" (1999) 17:3 Legal Ref. Serv. Q. 85.
- Mireau, Shaunna. "Noting Up: Best Practices or Overkill?" (2007) 31(4) LawNow No. 35.
- Morris, Jane W. "A Response to Taylor's Comparison of Shepard's and KeyCite" (2000) 92 Law Library Journal 143.
- Rintoul, Ruth, with contributions from Rosalie Fox. "Case Law in Canada" (2003) 28 Can. L.L. 166.
- Taylor, William L. "Comparing KeyCite and Shepard's for Completeness, Currency, and Accuracy (2000) 92 Law Library Journal 127.
- Wurzer, Greg, Aleksandra Zivanovic, & Rhonda O'Neill. "Canadian Electronic Citators: An Evaluation of their Accuracy and Efficiency" (2004) 29 Canadian Law Library Review 68.

G. CONCLUSIONS

Expect to see an ongoing increase in the availability of free case law in electronic format. The advantages of being able to search full text by keyword, the ability to store large amounts of data, and the ability to provide access to recent material are all reasons why case law in electronic format will flourish. Expect free sources of full-text cases law—such as those offered by the various Legal Information Institutes—to improve. For lawyers and law students who have access to the various commercial online services, there is usually the added advantage of powerful search engines and online noter-uppers to provide detailed information about a particular case, including its judicial history and how it has been treated by subsequent courts or academic commentary.

CHAPTER 5

LEGAL RESEARCH ON THE INTERNET

A. INTRODUCTION

The Internet continues to drastically change legal research. Traditionally, legal researchers used print materials in law libraries to find law-related information. This meant that one was limited to the amount of space and materials the print-based law library could afford, a limitation that often meant that the law library had a finite collection focusing on materials from within its own jurisdiction. While CD-ROMs and online commercial databases have brought legal research to the researcher's desktop (especially over the last fifteen to twenty years), it has been recent Internet technology that continues to revolutionize the way legal research is conducted. This chapter will focus on freely available Internet resources, while Chapter 6 will focus on commercial, fee-based online legal research databases.

The free Internet has several applications for legal research:

- as a source of information (searching the World Wide Web)
- as a means of communication (using e-mail)
- as a virtual community (using law-related discussion groups, blogs, and RSS feeds)

The usefulness of the Internet for legal research is reinforced by its wide availability throughout most jurisdictions in the world and its relative ease-of-use.[1] A particularly nice feature of the Internet is the ability to expand legal resources beyond the walls of one's own print law library to online international and foreign legal resources that would not have been easily accessible to most researchers through traditional means. While the Internet has a number of useful features, it is always necessary for the researcher to evaluate the quality of information that is being found, especially since not all material on the Internet has been subject to the same level of editorial control as most print or online fee-based publications.

B. EVALUATING WEB INFORMATION

There are standard criteria by which free websites should be evaluated.[2] These criteria include a number of things that evaluate the quality and reliability of the information to be found on the site:

- *Authorship*: Who authored the material? Is it clear who owns the website? Is the site affiliated with a reliable or known publisher or organization? Does the site provide a mailing address, phone number, and e-mail address? It is always important to consider authorship when using freely available websites—anyone can publish a website with relative ease with no objective editorial policies or control.
- *Accuracy and quality:* Is the site free of spelling and grammatical errors? Does the site contain broken links? Well-maintained websites tend to mean that the owner of the site is taking the time to keep the information current and accurate.

---

1   This chapter assumes the reader has some experience in using the Internet for research or basic searching. If not, the following two books, although now somewhat dated, are good introductory resources for lawyers or law students: Lewis S. Eisen's *Canadian Lawyer's Internet Guide*, 3d ed. (Thornhill, ON: Amicus Legal Publishing, 1997) (also available on LexisNexis Quicklaw) or Drew Jackson & Timothy Taylor, *The Internet Handbook for Canadian Lawyers*, 3d ed. (Toronto: Carswell, 2000).

2   See, for example, Genie Tyburski, "Evaluating the Quality of Information on the Internet," online: www.virtualchase.com/quality; American Association of Law Libraries, "General Website Evaluation Criteria," online: www.aallnet. org/committee/aelic/criteria.html; Sabrina I. Pacifici, "Getting It Right: Verifying Sources on the Net" (1 March 2002), online: www.llrx.com www.llrx.com/ features/verifying.htm; Mirela Roznovschi, "Update to Evaluating Foreign and International Legal Databases on the Internet" (30 September 2000), online: www.llrx.com www.llrx.com/features/evaluating2.htm.

- *Purpose*: Why does the website exist? Is it trying to sell a product or advocate a particular viewpoint? Print publications, like websites, can contain biased points of view. The one difference between print publications and websites, however, may be the ease with which one can access web pages and the speed by which one may scan the information without appreciating that the information may contain subtle biases.

- *Scope*: What is the scope or date range of the material on the website? How often is the site updated? Good websites will show when the page was last updated. This information is often on the bottom of the page (hold down the "Ctrl" key on your keyboard and then press the "End" or the "PgDn" key to get quickly to the bottom of the website page to check this information).

When evaluating websites, it helps to consider the different categories of websites that exist, including personal websites, business/marketing websites, advocacy websites, and university or government websites. Each of these different types of websites has a different reason for existing with differing goals and motivations that can affect the quality of information to be found on them. One major difference between free Internet sites and commercial online databases is often the amount of editorial and quality control (in addition to value-added features). In addition, one drawback of free Internet resources is the potential lack of permanency of information — linkrot is a serious issue that tends to be less of an issue with fee-based online resources.[3] However, it is sometimes possible to find older, unavailable web pages using the Internet Archive search engine (www.archive.org) to look

---

3   Linkrot even affects legal scholarship where one would like to think that references to Web sources would generally be reliable. However, in Mary Rumsey, "Runaway Train: Problems of Permanence, Accessibility, and Stability in the Use of Web Sources in Law Review Citations" (2002) 94 Library Law Journal 27 at 35, the author's study of citations to web pages in law review articles showed linkrot to be a problem with close to 40 percent of Web links cited being dead within about one and a half years with as many as 70 percent being dead within four and a half years. See also Carmine Sellitto, "The Impact of Impermanent Web-Located Citations: A Study of 123 Scholarly Conference Publications" (2005) 56 Journal of the American Society for Information Science & Technology 695; Judit Bar-Ilan & Bluma C. Peritz, "Evolution, Continuity, and Disappearance of Documents on a Specific Topic on the Web: A Longitudinal Study of 'Informetrics'" (2004) 55 Journal of the American Society for Information Science & Technology 980 at 986 and 988; Joel D. Kitchens & Pixey Anne Mosley, "Error 404: or, What is the Shelf-life of Printed Internet Guides?" (2000) 24 Library Collections, Acquisitions, and Technical Services 467; Wallace Koehler, "Keeping the Web Garden Weeded: Managing the Elusive URL" (2000) 8 Searcher 43.

for cached Web pages.[4] Likewise, some governments are starting to do a better job of archiving their older online material.[5] Basically, when using free websites, it is important to constantly evaluate the quality and permanency of information being found.

C. SEARCH ENGINES

A basic technique for finding information on the Internet is to search for material by keyword using search engines. Search engine companies, such as Google, deploy special Web crawler computer programs (sometime referred to as "robots" or "spiders") to periodically mine through or "scrape" the full text of web pages on the Internet to index or catalogue words and other information found on those pages. The company then stores this information in its databases. When the researcher types in keywords in the search engine, a search is done against the site's database (as opposed, typically, to a "live" search on actual web pages) to look for appropriate matches, leveraging any particular search algorithms applicable to the search engine. Although Google continues to dominate Internet search engines, there are an increasing number of new search engines that attempt to improve search results or that provide other features such as organizing your results to make them easier to review.

Table 5.1
Popular Internet Search Engines

Internet Search Engines	Address
Alta Vista	http://ca.altavista.com
Ask.com	www.ask.com
Bing	www.bing.com
Google	www.google.ca
Yahoo! Search	http://search.yahoo.com

4   Matthew Fagan, "Can You Do a Wayback on That? The Legal Community's Use of Cached Web Pages in and out of Trial" (2007) 13 B.U.J. Sci. & Tech. L. 46.

5   See, for example, ArchivesCanada.ca, online: www.archivescanada.ca/english/index.html, to search over 800 repositories from federal and provincial governments. In addition, Library and Archives Canada is in the process of digitizing the *Canada Gazette* back to 1841. See *A Nation's Chronicle: The Canada Gazette*, online: www.collectionscanada.gc.ca/canada-gazette/index-e.html.

Not all search engines are the same—differences between search engines usually relate to any or all of the following three major factors: (i) the number of pages "catalogued"; (ii) the frequency by which the search engine updates its database; and (iii) the level of sophistication of the different types of searches that can be run on the search engine. There are a number of useful websites that compare or rank search engines.[6] In addition, there are several basic techniques that apply to most search engines:[7]

- Know your search engine—get to know one or two search engines well and do not be afraid to click on the "help" or "advanced find" link of the search engine to learn more about the search engine, such as whether it allows Boolean searching, truncation of terms, or nested searches.
- If you are getting too many results for your search ("4,045,720 pages found"), consider having at least four or five search terms in your search using the "and" format (an "and" search is now the default form of search in most Internet search engines so you usually do not need to add the word "and"). Also try to use unique terms whenever possible.
- Use phrases—most search engines allow phrase searches ("To Kill a Mockingbird"); this will usually provide more precise results.

There are a number of useful features on Google's "advanced search" to make your Internet searches more precise:

- You can easily change the default results from "10 results" to "100 results" (this allows you to quickly scan more results on a single page).
- There are useful search templates for phrase searches or to exclude words from your search.
- Under the "Search within a site or domain" field, you can use Google to limit your search to a particular website (e.g., un.org).
- Under the field called "Where your keywords show up," you can limit your search to where the terms only appear in the title of the web page (this often results in more focused search results on the theory that the "title" of a web page likely means that the web page is about that topic).

---

6   See, for example, Diana Botluk, "Update to Search Engines Compared" (15 July 2000), online: LLRX.com, www.llrx.com/features/engine3.htm, and InfoPeople, "Best Search Tools Chart," online: http://infopeople.org/search/chart.html.

7   See, for example, "Web Searching Tips," online: SearchEngineWatch.com: http://searchenginewatch.com/facts, for practical tips and comparisons of how different search engines operate.

Google also allows researchers to create custom Google searches designed to search specific websites. Set out below are two such custom Google searches that target law firms and law-related blogs:

- **Search Canadian Law Firms and Law-Related Blogs (Tjaden)**
  www.tinyurl.com/canadianlawfirms
- **Fee Fie Foe Firm**
  www.feefiefoefirm.com

In addition, although free Web searches are not a replacement for proper journal index searches (discussed in Chapter 2, Section B), Google Scholar (http://scholar.google.ca) is a simple way to supplement legal research since the search will focus on more scholarly online resources or references.

Another type of search engine is a subject guide or "directory" that provides a means of browsing through a clickable directory of topics (see Table 5.2 for a list of subject directories). An example of a well-known Web directory is Yahoo! or Yahoo! Canada, whose editors have organized categories of information on the Internet by a hierarchical directory of topics. There are also a number of law-related Internet subject directories, such as Findlaw and Hieros Gamos, that organize links to online material by law-related topics.

Table 5.2
Popular Internet Subject Guides

Internet Subject Guides	Address
Findlaw	www.findlaw.com
Hieros Gamos	www.hg.org
Justia.com	www.justia.com
Law Guru	www.lawguru.com
Guide to Law Online	www.loc.gov/law/help/guide.php
Law Library Resource Xchange	www.llrx.com
Yahoo!	www.yahoo.com
Yahoo! Canada	http://ca.yahoo.com

Another variation of Internet search engines is the so-called meta or "all-in-one" search engine (see Table 5.3 for a list of meta search engines). Meta search engines run searches over more than one search engine and then organize the search results usually by search engine.

Table 5.3
Popular Meta Search Engines

Meta Search Engines	Address
Clusty.com	http://clusty.com
Dogpile	www.dogpile.com
Mamma	www.mamma.com
Metacrawler	www.metacrawler.com
Search.com	www.search.com
SurfWax	www.surfwax.com

A more recent phenomenon in Internet searching has been the need for strategies to deal with the so-called deep Web or invisible Web, being the online content not found by a typical search engine because the site blocks the search engine from crawling its site or the site is otherwise password-protected.[8] Statistics suggest that normal search engines catalogue only a small percentage of Web pages and that there is a large amount of information resident on proprietary servers or unindexed pages that form the "deep Web."[9] A website such as Completeplanet. com (www.completeplanet.com) purports to provide a comprehensive listing of over 70,000 searchable databases and specialty search engines. The reality is that much of the value-added online content of interest to legal researchers will not be found or accessible for free using basic search engines but instead be "invisible" or hidden within proprietary databases accessible and searchable only through password subscriptions (such as LexisNexis Quicklaw or Westlaw Canada). Increasingly, though, sites such as Google Scholar do "crawl" proprietary databases (such as HeinOnline) and present search results, giving the searcher the opportunity to purchase the content found in the search result. In the same way (sort of), Google Books allows the searching of millions

---

8   See, for example, Marcus P. Zillman, "Deep Web Research 2010" (13 December 2009), online: LLRX.com, www.llrx.com/features/deepweb2010.htm; Alex Wright, "Exploring a 'Deep Web' That Google Can't Grasp" *New York Times* (22 February 2009) B4; Diana Botluk, "Mining Deeper into the Invisible Web" (15 November 2000), online: LLRX.com, www.llrx.com/features/mining.htm.

9   Although it is difficult to know precisely how much online content remains invisible, a study in 2000 is frequently quoted for the suggestion that the deep Web contains 7,500 terabytes of information or 550 billion individual documents compared to only 19 terabytes or 1 billion documents on the surface web—see Michael K. Bergman, "The Deep Web: Surfacing Hidden Value" (July 2000), online: www.brightplanet.com.

of pages of text from books that would otherwise only be available in print, giving the searcher a glimpse at part of the text (where it is protected by copyright) with an opportunity to then purchase the material that was found.

D. FINDING PEOPLE

Although not directly related to pure legal research, finding information about people is an important part of lawyering, whether it be tracking down the phone number or address of a potential witness or party to a lawsuit, trying to find an expert, or trying to find another lawyer.[10] The Internet is extremely useful for this purpose given the large number of directories and phone books available online. Set out below in Table 5.4 is a list of some of the more useful Internet tools for finding information about people (realize that stricter privacy laws in Canada tend to make it more difficult to find information on Canadians, at least compared to the situation in the United States). Some of the sites, such as InfoSpace (listed below), provide such added-value features as the ability to look up people by phone number or mailing address in addition to looking up people by name. Legal directories are listed below in Table 5.5, and sites for finding experts are listed in Table 5.6. Prudence is warranted when using free online directories for finding lawyers or experts. Most lawyers or law librarians would take the extra step of checking for references, or, for example—in the situation of identifying a potential expert witness—search online case law databases to see if a particular expert has had her report considered by a judge.

Table 5.4
Online Directories and Phone Books

Websites	Address
Canada 411	www.canada411.ca
InfoSpace	www.infospace.com
Infobel.com	www.infobel.com
YellowPages.ca	www.yellowpages.ca

10   For finding legal experts, see Jim Robinson, "Finding and Researching Expert Witnesses on the Web" (1 October 2002), online: LLRX.com, www.llrx.com/features/findingexperts.htm.

Table 5.5
Online Legal Directories

Websites	Address
Canadian Law List	www.canadianlawlist.com
Lexpert.ca	www.lexpert.ca
Martindale.com	www.martindale.com
FindLaw—Find a Lawyer	http://lawyers.findlaw.com

Table 5.6
Websites for Finding Experts

Websites	Address
ExpertLaw	www.expertlaw.com
Expert Pages	http://expertpages.com
Internet Online Directory	http://national-experts.com
University of Toronto Blue Book	www.library.utoronto.ca/bluebook

E. FINDING COMPANIES AND PRIVATE ORGANIZATIONS

The Internet is also an excellent place to find information on companies. Two obvious starting points for companies that publicly trade their shares are the SEDAR (System for Electronic Document Analysis and Retrieval) website for Canadian companies and the EDGAR (Electronic Data-Gathering, Analysis, and Retrieval) website for American companies (both of these sites are listed below), since disclosure rules in both countries require public companies to post their documents on these sites. Other sources of corporate information include company home pages, investor websites, and newswire websites, which will include news releases and other public statements by corporations. Finding information on privately held corporations is much more difficult. A list of some of the more popular free websites for finding information on corporations is set out in Table 5.7 below.

Table 5.7
Websites for Finding Corporation Information

Websites	Address
Canada NewsWire	www.newswire.ca
Canadian Securities Administrators	www.securities-administrators.ca
Corporations Canada	www.corporationscanada.ic.gc.ca
EDGAR (U.S.)	www.sec.gov/edgar.shtml
Ontario Securities Commission	www.osc.gov.on.ca
SEDAR (Canada)	www.sedar.com
TMX Group	www.tmx.com

F. FINDING REFERENCE MATERIALS

In addition to the various directories already discussed above, there are a number of extremely useful reference materials freely available on the Internet that include dictionaries, encyclopedias, currency converters, translation services, and news sites. The biggest development in free online reference tools in the last five years is *Wikipedia, The Free Encyclopedia* (www.wikipedia.org). With more than 14 million articles in more than 260 languages, *Wikipedia* has developed into not only a convenient reference resource but also a reliable one, due in part to its open and collaborative editing.[11]

Table 5.8 sets out some general reference sites available on the Internet, along with several subject-specific reference sites.

Table 5.8
Online Reference Websites

Websites	Address
Currency Converter (Yahoo!)	http://finance.yahoo.com/currency-converter
Google Maps	http://maps.google.com
Law Dictionary (Nolo Press)	www.nolo.com/dictionary/

---

11 Wikipedia contributors, "Reliability of Wikipedia," *Wikipedia, The Free Encyclopedia*, online: http://en.wikipedia.org/wiki/Wikipedia_reliability. See also Hannah B. Murray & Jason C. Miller, "Wikipedia in Court: When and How Citing Wikipedia and Other Consensus Websites is Appropriate" (2010) 84 St. John's Law Review [forthcoming in 2010].

Websites	Address
Library Spot	www.libraryspot.com
Refdesk.com	www.refdesk.com
Statistics Canada	www.statcan.gc.ca
Translations	www.foreignword.com
Wikipedia	www.wikipedia.org
Your Dictionary	www.yourdictionary.com

G. FINDING GOVERNMENTS

In recent years, governments have taken advantage of Internet technology to publish useful information, forms, and pamphlets on the Internet that—in the past—would have only been published in print. Table 5.9 lists the home pages for the Canadian federal and provincial governments.

Table 5.9
Online Government Websites

Websites	Address
Federal Government (Canada)	www.canada.gc.ca
Alberta	www.gov.ab.ca
British Columbia	www.gov.bc.ca
Manitoba	www.gov.mb.ca
New Brunswick	www.gov.nb.ca
Newfoundland	www.gov.nf.ca
Northwest Territories	www.gov.nt.ca
Nova Scotia	www.gov.ns.ca
Nunavut	www.gov.nu.ca
Ontario	www.gov.on.ca
Prince Edward Island	www.gov.pe.ca
Québec	www.gouv.qc.ca
Saskatchewan	www.gov.sk.ca
Yukon Territory	www.gov.yk.ca

H. FINDING LEGISLATION

The Canadian federal, provincial, and territorial governments have greatly improved access to their statutes and regulations in the last several years, joined in part by the efforts of the Canadian Legal Information Institute (CanLII, www.canlii.org). Because of this, you can conduct good quality legislative research in Canada using free resources, either directly at the particular government's website (listed in Table 5.10) or via CanLII. One advantage of CanLII is the ability to search legislation across more than one jurisdiction. An excellent online guide for conducting Canadian legislative research is "Canadian Legislation Online" published by the Law Society of Upper Canada.[12]

Although some governments have been slow to make their online versions of legislation official, the federal,[13] Ontario,[14] and Québec,[15] governments have done so. In addition to statutes and regulations, individual government websites also usually include access to current (and some historical) legislative bills, Hansard debates, and other related documents. Most of the government websites have only the current or fairly recent versions of legislation, with little historical archives of older versions of statutes, regulations, or bills. One major exception, however, is the Alberta Heritage Digitization Project's Retrospective Law Collection,[16] where Alberta statutes have been digitized from 1906 to 1990 and made available online at this site for free, with plans to digitize retrospective bills and *Gazettes*. In addition, the federal government is in the process of digitizing the *Canada Gazette*,[17] and efforts are underway by a coalition of law libraries and others to make Ontario legislation available via the Canadian Libraries section of the Internet Archive.[18]

---

12   Law Society of Upper Canada, "Canadian Legislation Online," online: http://rc.lsuc.on.ca/library/research_law_ca_legis.htm.

13   By s. 31(1) of the *Legislation Revision and Consolidation Act*, R.S.C. 1985, c. S-20, all consolidated Acts and regulations on the Justice Laws website are "official," as of 1 June 2009.

14   Section 35(1)(b) of the *Legislation Act*, 2006, S.O. 2006, c. 21, Sch. F, makes legislation on e-Laws (www.e-laws.gov.on.ca) official, effective 30 November 2008.

15   *An Act respecting the Compilation of Québec Laws and Regulations*, S.Q. 2009, c. 40, makes Québec statutes published in print and online by Publications du Québec official as of 1 January 2010, with Québec regulations to become official by 1 January 2012 at the latest.

16   Online: The Alberta Heritage Digitization Project, www.ourfutureourpast.ca/home.htm.

17   See above note 5.

18   Internet Archive, "Canadian Libraries," online: www.archive.org/details/toronto.

Table 5.10
Online Government Legislative Websites

Websites	Address
Federal Government (Canada)	http://laws.justice.gc.ca www.parl.gc.ca
Alberta	www.qp.gov.ab.ca www.assembly.ab.ca
British Columbia	www.bclaws.ca www.leg.bc.ca
Manitoba	www.gov.mb.ca/legislature/ www.gov.mb.ca/laws
New Brunswick	www.gnb.ca/0062/acts/ www.gnb.ca/legis/
Newfoundland	www.assembly.nl.ca/legislation/ www.assembly.nl.ca
Northwest Territories	www.justice.gov.nt.ca/Legislation/SearchLeg&Reg.shtml www.assembly.gov.nt.ca
Nova Scotia	www.gov.ns.ca/legislature/legc/ www.gov.ns.ca/legislature/
Nunavut	www.assembly.nu.ca www.justice.gov.nu.ca
Ontario	www.e-laws.gov.on.ca www.ontla.on.ca
Prince Edward Island	www.gov.pe.ca/law/statutes/index.php3 www.assembly.pe.ca
Québec	www.publicationsduquebec.gouv.qc.ca www.assnat.qc.ca
Saskatchewan	www.qp.gov.sk.ca www.legassembly.sk.ca
Yukon Territory	www.gov.yk.ca/legislation/ www.legassembly.gov.yk.ca

The ease-of-use and the currency of information on these freely available government websites varies from province to province, as does the range of legislative information that is available.

There has been a move in several jurisdictions, including Canada, to establish online "Legal Information Institutes," which allow the researcher to search for case law and legislation of the jurisdiction in question using a single search engine/interface, thereby eliminating the need to visit individual case law or legislative websites (see Table 5.11 for a list of these sites).

Table 5.11
Legal Information Institute Websites

Websites	Address
Canada—CanLII	www.canlii.org
Commonwealth—CommonLII	www.commonlii.org
Australia—AustLII	www.austlii.edu.au
U.S.—Cornell's LII	www.law.cornell.edu/index.html
U.K./Ireland—BAILII	www.bailii.org
International—WorldLII	www.worldlii.org

I. FINDING CASE LAW

Just as the availability of free online legislation has greatly improved over the last five years, so has the availability of free case law. Once again, CanLII is the best "clearing house" for free online Canadian case law, although the websites of the federal and provincial courts also generally provide access to their recent judgments and other court-related information. Table 5.12 sets out a list of the website addresses for those Canadian court websites that release their judgments for free on the Internet, along with the Canadian Legal Information Institute. In most cases, using the CanLII website will be the preferred method of accessing free Canadian case law, although in some situations you may need or want to visit the actual court website as well.

Table 5.12
Canadian Court Websites

Court	Website address
CanLII	www.canlii.org
Supreme Court of Canada	http://scc.lexum.umontreal.ca/en/
Federal Court of Canada	http://decisions.fct-cf.gc.ca/en/index.html
Tax Court of Canada	www.tcc-cci.gc.ca
British Columbia	www.courts.gov.bc.ca
Alberta	www.albertacourts.ab.ca
Saskatchewan	www.sasklawcourts.ca
Manitoba	www.manitobacourts.mb.ca

Court	Website address
Ontario	www.ontariocourts.on.ca
Québec	www.jugements.qc.ca
Nova Scotia	www.courts.ns.ca
Prince Edward Island	www.gov.pe.ca/courts/supreme/index.php3
New Brunswick	www.gnb.ca/cour/
Newfoundland	www.court.nl.ca
Northwest Territories	www.justice.gov.nt.ca/dbtw-wpd/nwtjqbe.htm
Nunavut	www.nucj.ca
Yukon	www.yukoncourts.ca

Commercial online databases have a number of advantages over free worldwide court websites primarily as a result of their deeper scope of materials and their sophisticated search engines that allow one to search by judge's name, by party name, and by keywords using proximity connectors (searching on the name of a judge before whom one is arguing a case can be very strategic if you are able to find cases that can help you identify any particular viewpoints of that judge from cases he may have decided in the past). In addition, the commercial online databases have other valued-added features, such as extensive online citators that allow one to easily verify or note up a case's judicial history or treatment.

J. FINDING INTERNATIONAL AND FOREIGN LAW MATERIALS

As mentioned at the start of this chapter, the Internet has brought the world to the desktop of the legal researcher. International or foreign law materials that were once only available in print through inter-library loan are now available at the click of the mouse via the Internet. Material now widely available on the Internet includes primary sources of international law as treaties, conventions, and decisions of international courts and tribunals. Increasingly, foreign jurisdictions are making their own legislation and court decisions available on the Internet. Fortunately, a number of good websites exist that provide links to international and foreign law sites. Table 5.13 below lists some of the more popular international and foreign law sites on the Internet, along with a list of some excellent guides to conducting international legal research on the Internet, many of which contain additional links. In addition, Chapter 7 provides detailed information on researching international and foreign law.

Table 5.13
International and Foreign Law Websites and Research Guides

Internet Websites	Address
Canada Treaty Information	www.treaty-accord.gc.ca
Canado-American Treaties	www.lexum.umontreal.ca/ca_us/index_en.html
Foreign Affairs and International Trade Canada	www.international.gc.ca
JuriGlobe: World Legal Systems	www.juriglobe.ca
European Commission of Human Rights	www.coe.int/Commissioner/
European Court of Human Rights	www.echr.coe.int
Hague Conference on Private International Law	www.hcch.net
International Court of Justice	www.icj-cij.org
Project on International Courts and Tribunals	www.pict-pcti.org
UNCITRAL: United Nations Commission on International Trade Law	www.uncitral.org
UNIDROIT: International Institute for the Unification of Private Law	www.unidroit.org
United Nations	www.un.org
United Nations Treaty Collection	http://treaties.un.org/Pages/Home.aspx?lang=en
World Trade Organization	www.wto.org
Research Guides	**Address**
ASIL Guide to Electronic Resources for International Law	www.asil.org/resource/Home.htm
International Constitutional Law	www.servat.unibe.ch/law/icl/
GlobaLex (NYU Law)	http://nyulawglobal.org/Globalex/
LLRX.com International Law Guides	www.llrx.com/international_law.html
Max Planck Institute	www.mpil.de
Women's Human Rights Resources	www.law-lib.utoronto.ca/Diana

K. USING DISCUSSION GROUPS AND SOCIAL NETWORKS FOR LEGAL RESEARCH

Online discussion groups—also known as listservs—have been formed on almost any conceivable topic, from jazz music to figure-skating.[19] There are a huge number of law-related discussion groups that allow one to subscribe (usually for free) to be added to the group. When one subscribes to a discussion group, any e-mails sent to the group are sent to all subscribers. In many cases, what then happens is a discussion, or at least responses to the initial e-mail, that are sent to that discussion group by the subscribers. Every legal researcher should be aware of several things about discussion groups:[20]

- Some discussion groups are moderated, which means that questions to be posted to the group are first vetted by the moderator; most discussion groups are unmoderated, however, meaning that questions are not vetted in advance, which sometimes results in irrelevant or inappropriate questions being posted.
- The quality of the discussions or responses varies widely among different discussion groups. Fortunately, the quality of discussion for law-related discussion groups is generally quite good, but as can be imagined, it is prudent for subscribers to avoid giving legal advice (or even the appearance of giving legal advice).
- Some discussion groups provide archives of the entire history of all questions and responses for that particular group. Many of these archives are searchable and can sometimes provide valuable information. An example of a searchable archive is the discussion group of the Canadian Association of Law Libraries (discussed below), the archive of which is available at http://listserv.unb.ca/archives/call-l.html.

One of the better sites in Canada for getting information on legal research or issues affecting the world of legal researchers is the discussion group of the Canadian Association of Law Libraries (CALL-L)—see: www.callacbd.ca. There are also a number of American-based law library listservs, such as the Law-Lib discussion group hosted by the Law Library of the University of California, Davis. Information on

---

19   See online: CataList, www.lsoft.com/lists/listref.html, for a searchable and browsable list of over 70,000 publicly available online discussion groups.

20   See also Lewis S. Eisen, *Canadian Lawyer's Internet Guide*, 3d ed. (Thornhill, ON: Amicus Legal Publishing, 1997) c. 8 entitled "Mailing Lists" and Catherine J. Lanctot, "Attorney-Client Relationships in Cyberspace: The Peril and the Promise" (1999–2000) 49 Duke L.J. 147 for a useful overview of online discussion groups and listservs.

some of the major law library discussion groups is available through the following page of the American Association of Law Libraries: www. aallnet.org/discuss/list_other.asp.

L. LAW-RELATED CURRENT AWARENESS ON THE INTERNET

The immediacy of the Internet has made staying current with substantive changes in the law much easier. Law-related blogs—discussed in more detail in Chapter 10, Section J—are written by subject experts on a wide variety of legal topics. Blogs allow readers to subscribe via an RSS ("Real Simple Syndication") reader to blogs of interest and to be notified when new posts have been added to the blog. In addition, publishers of legal information are increasingly adding RSS feeds to which the researcher can subscribe to be notified of new developments. The Ontario Court of Appeal, for example, has an RSS feed that announces the release of their new judgments. By subscribing to the court's feed, one can get immediate notice of their new judgments. Set out below in Table 5.14 is a list of Internet sites that are useful for law-related current awareness.

Table 5.14
Current Awareness Tools on the Internet for Legal Researchers

Internet Websites	Address
Canadian Law Blogs List	www.lawblogs.ca
Fee Fie Foe Firm	www.feefiefoefirm.com
Law Times	www.lawtimesnews.com
Lexology	www.lexology.com
Linex Legal	www.linexlegal.com
Mondaq	www.mondaq.com
Search Canadian Law Firm Websites, Blogs & Journals	www.tinyurl.com/canadianlawfirms
SLAW	www.slaw.ca
The Lawyers Weekly	www.lawyersweekly.ca

M. CITING MATERIAL FOUND ON THE INTERNET

Chapter 1, Section D discusses citation of legal materials in depth, including the citation of online materials. Citing material on the Web can be more of a challenge than citing to an unreported decision on a commercial database since websites are not always stable and often do not provide numbered paragraphs for pinpoint citations. There is no single, uniform method for citing material on the Internet. The 6th edition of the McGill Guide provides several examples in different contexts of how to cite material found on the Internet: Rule 2.9 (legislation), Rule 4.8 (government documents), Rule 5.3 (international materials), and Rule 6.19 (electronic services, e-journals, and Internet sites). The recommended citation practice—generally speaking—is to cite the material as if it were from a traditional print source followed then by the designation "online," the name of the organization or website, and the URL in angle brackets. Set out below are some additional examples—including citing to a blog—that attempt to follow the spirit of McGill Guide style. Other style books are available, and since there is not yet a universal standard for citing Internet material, researchers should apply a consistent standard that provides the most helpful information to the user:[21]

- The Law Society of Upper Canada, "Home page," online: The Law Society of Upper Canada, www.lsuc.on.ca.
- Don Ford, "Canon Law Research Guide" (July 2007), online: GlobaLex NYU, nyulawglobal.org/globalex/Canon_Law.htm.
- Simon Fodden, "U.K. Report on Costs of Civil Litigation," SLAW Blog, comment on 18 January 2010, slaw.ca/2010/01/18/u-k-report-on-costs-of-civil-litigation/

As discussed in Chapter 1, Section D, the Canadian Citation Committee has developed neutral citation formats, which are being adopted by Canadian courts. These formats are expected to be more widely seen over the next few years and will greatly simplify the citation of online cases.[22] In addition, the Supreme Court of Canada has special

---

21 For citing general information from the Internet, see Janice R. Walker & Todd Taylor, *The Columbia Guide to Online Style*, 2d ed. (New York: Columbia University Press, 2006) or Kate L. Turabian, *A Manual for Writers of Research Papers, Theses, and Dissertations*, 7th ed. (Chicago: Chicago University Press, 2007) at paras. 15.4 and 19.7.

22 See the website of the Canadian Citation Committee, online: www.lexum.umontreal.ca/ccc-ccr/index_en.html.

rules governing the citation of electronic versions of decisions of the Supreme Court of Canada and other courts.[23]

N. USING E-MAIL AND SOLICITOR-CLIENT PRIVILEGE

Although e-mail has no direct application for hands-on legal research, it has revolutionized the ways in which lawyers communicate with each other and with clients. The advantages of e-mail are obvious: e-mail is inexpensive, easy to use, widely available, and instantaneous. E-mail also allows the sender to attach documents that can then be sent around the world to be retrieved, opened by the recipient, and sent back to the original sender with comments or amendments.

With these advantages comes a potential disadvantage: the very speed of e-mail raises the risk of the lawyer inadvertently (i) disclosing confidential information by accidentally sending the e-mail to an unintended recipient; or (ii) sending a message in haste that, if written in print, may have brought more thought and deliberation. Clearly, the risk exists that a lawyer could inadvertently waive a client's right to privilege by sending an e-mail message to an unintended recipient.[24] This may explain the increase in the use of standard "privileged and confidential" notices that are inserted in e-mails being sent by law firms (just in the same way that law firms include "privileged and confidential" notices as part of their fax cover sheets when sending faxes). In addition to using such notices, lawyers can consider using encryption software for e-mail communications or establishing office training and policies (including a policy not to use e-mail for highly sensitive matters).

O. CONFIDENTIALITY: AVOIDING ELECTRONIC FOOTPRINTS

Another potential risk of disclosure on the Internet is in inadvertently identifying one's self or a client's interest by leaving "electronic foot-

---

23   Supreme Court of Canada, *Bulletin* (6 October 2000), online: University of Montreal, scc.lexum.umontreal.ca/en/bulletin/2000/00-10-06.bul/00-10-06.bul.html.

24   See Paul Dodd & Daniel R. Bennett, "Waiver of Privilege and the Internet" (1995) 53 Advocate 365 and Jane Bailey, "Email's Impact on Lawyers and Litigation: Recent Developments in Ontario" (2002) 3 Internet & E-Commerce Law in Canada 9 for a discussion of this issue.

prints" on various websites being visited on behalf of a client. When you use a Web browser to find information on a website, your Internet Service Provider (ISP) has the technical capability of tracking the details of your visits (due to the volume of traffic, it is unlikely it would have the time to do this on a regular basis). In addition, the website you are visiting can gather basic information about you, including the time you visited the site, the identity of your ISP, and even your e-mail address (if you have provided this information). In addition, your browser has "cookie" technology, which—if enabled—leaves information in a "cookie" text file on your computer that provides information about you the next time you visit the same website. In addition, although the risk is likely extremely low, there is a potential opportunity for hackers to eavesdrop on your Internet activity. Since lawyers have strict professional obligations to protect a client's confidentiality, and although the risk of disclosure is likely extremely low, some legal researchers or law firms may wish to implement confidentiality policies to minimize these risks further. One thing to consider is the need to clear the "history" button of your Web browser (especially on public or shared computers). If this is not done, the next user can identify websites you have visited or even e-mails that you have sent (assuming you use Web-browser based e-mail software). Another solution is to obviously "disable" cookies in your Web browser by turning off this feature in the browser's "preferences." Alternatively, you may wish to conduct highly confidential Web searches (such as "due diligence" searches on possible target companies in a merger and acquisition) on a secure line or through an Internet service provider not connected with the law firm.

P. CONCLUSIONS

The Internet will continue to dramatically impact the way lawyers practise law and conduct legal research. Governments, courts, universities, and other institutions will continue to publish an increasing amount of law-related information on the Internet. New technologies will increase the speed and ease-of-use of the Internet and new applications of the Internet will flourish, such as the delivery of continuing legal education programs to lawyers and legal researchers. It is also reasonable to expect that governments will take steps in the future to publish historical legal materials on the Internet (older statutes, for example) as scanning technology improves.

Q. ADDITIONAL RESOURCES

There is plenty of print and online information available on legal research and the Internet. Set out below is a list of some of the more popular print publications that discuss the Internet and legal research:

Ambrogi, Robert J. *The Essential Guide to the Best (and Worst) of Legal Sites on the Web*. 2d ed. New York: ALM Publishing, 2004.

Botluk, Diana. *The Legal List: Research on the Internet*. St. Paul, MN: Thomson West, 2009 [annual].

DiGilio, John J. "Bridging the DiGital Divide: Custom Search Engines Put You in Control" (14 June 2009), online: www.llrx.com/columns/customsearch.htm.

Eisen, Lewis S. *Canadian Lawyer's Internet Guide*. 3d ed. Thornhill, ON: Amicus Legal Publishing, 1997. Also available on LexisNexis Quicklaw.

Fish, Bonnie. *You've Got the Whole World in Your Hands: Using the Internet to Expand the Boundaries of Legal Research*. Toronto: Ontario Bar Association, 2004.

Fullerton, Barbara & Sabrina Pacifici. "Beyond Google and Yahoo — New, Nifty Search Engines to Optimize Your Research" (6 June 2006), LLRX.com, online: www.llrx.com/features/supersearch.pdf.

Gordon, Stacey L. *Online Legal Research: A Guide to Legal Research Services and Other Internet Tools*. Buffalo, NY: W.S. Hein, 2003.

Halvorson, T.R. *Law of the Super Searchers: The Online Secrets of Top Legal Researchers*. Medford, NJ: CyberAge Books, 2000.

Jackson, Drew & Timothy L. Taylor. *The Internet Handbook for Canadian Lawyers*. 3d ed. Toronto: Carswell, 2000.

Kennedy, Dennis & Tom Mighell. *The Lawyer's Guide to Collaboration Tools and Technologies: Smart Ways to Work Together*. Chicago, IL: American Bar Association Law Practice Management Section, 2008.

Kozlowski, Ken. *The Internet Guide for the Legal Researcher*. 3d ed. Teaneck, NJ: Infosources Pub., 2001. Updated online.

Levitt, Carole & Mark Rosch. *The Cybersleuth's Guide to the Internet: Conducting Effective Investigative & Legal Research on the Web*. 8th ed. Culver City, CA: Internet for Lawyers, 2006.

Levitt, Carole & Mark Rosch. *The Lawyer's Guide to Fact Finding on the Internet*. 3d ed. Chicago, IL: American Bar Association, 2006.

Miller, Janine. "The Development of the Legal Information Institutes Around the World" (2005) 30 Canadian Law Library Review 8.

Mintz, Anne P., ed. *Web of Deception: Misinformation on the Internet*. Medford, NJ: CyberAge Books, 2002.

Mireau, Shaunna. "Family Law Sources on the Web" (2008) 32(5) LawNow 42.

Simonsen, Craig & Christian R. Andersen. *Computer-Aided Legal Research (CALR) on the Internet*. Upper Saddle River, NJ: Pearson/ Prentice Hall, 2006.

Tjaden, Ted. "The Impact of Web Technology on Law Librarianship" (2002) 27 Can. L. L. 8.

Tjaden, Ted. "Legal Issues in Using the Internet for Law-Related Work and Research" (1996) 21 Can. L. L. 180.

Whelan, David (Chair). *High Octane Internet Legal Research*. Columbus, OH: Ohio State Bar Association CLE, 2007.

Whelan, David (Chair). *Managing Information Overload: Internet Resources, Tips and Tools*. Toronto: Continuing Legal Education, Law Society of Upper Canada, 2008.

Zillman, Marcus P. "Deep Web Research 2010" (13 December 2009), Online: www.llrx.com/features/deepweb2010.htm.

CHAPTER 6

LEGAL RESEARCH DATABASES AND CD-ROMS

A. INTRODUCTION

The impact of computer technology on the practice of law has been huge. Its impact on legal research has been no less. With computers comes the capacity to store and search a large body of textual information, which has given researchers the ability to locate specific terms within that body of information. There are now a growing number of high quality, easy-to-use commercial databases for conducting online legal research. These subscription databases usually contain one or more of the following features: they have sophisticated search engines that allow a number of different ways of finding information; they contain a variety of law-related information, in most situations including case law, legislation, journal literature, and news; they are available only by subscription for a fee; they are increasingly made available to subscribers via the Internet; and their publishers are constantly making value-added improvements to these databases, including extra content and easier-to-use interfaces.

For law students, your law school has or can likely obtain passwords for you to use some of these databases for academic research. For lawyers and other professionals, the vendors of these online databases will negotiate access to their databases through one of several methods (usually hourly rates, flat-rate fees, or transactional fees, the recovery of which is discussed in Chapter 1, Section C). For members of the public, short-term access to these databases is more difficult, and it may be necessary to instead either hire a lawyer to conduct research on these databases on your behalf or conduct your own legal research using other resources discussed in this book.

This chapter will discuss the advantages and disadvantages of conducting legal research using online law-related commercial databases, followed by a brief review of some of the leading services, discussed alphabetically by resource in the following three categories:

- *Comprehensive services:*
  » LexisNexis Quicklaw
  » Westlaw Canada

LexisNexis Quicklaw and Westlaw Canada are included as comprehensive services due to the extent of their content for primary and secondary legal resources, news and other non-legal resources, and to their domestic and international scope.

- *Canadian and Civil Law services:*
  » CCH Online
  » Canada Law Book/BestCase
  » Droit civil en ligne (DCL)
  » Maritime Law Book
  » Répertoire électronique de jurisprudence du Barreau (REJB)
  » Société québécoise d'information juridique (SOQUIJ)

The strength of the foregoing services is their strong domestic content (Canadian and Québec), including both primary and secondary law-related resources, depending on the product.

- *Specialized services:*
  » Criminal Spectrum
  » DisclosureNet
  » HeinOnline
  » Justis.com
  » Kluwer Arbitration Online
  » Labour Spectrum
  » PrivaWorks
  » TaxnetPRO
  » Westlaw Business

The foregoing services offer specialized content for Canadian legal researchers, depending on the focus of the research being conducted.

Although CD-ROMs are now an old-fashioned technology (and gradually falling into disuse), legal publishers are still offering CD-ROMs for some of their products. As such, law-related CD-ROMs are briefly reviewed at the end of this chapter.

B. ADVANTAGES AND DISADVANTAGES OF ONLINE COMMERCIAL DATABASES

There are a number of fairly obvious advantages to using online law-related databases for legal research compared to using print resources:

- *Current information*: The delay that occurs in publishing law-related material in print or CD-ROM is ordinarily eliminated with online databases, which can be updated instantaneously. For example, rather than publishing annual or monthly cumulative supplements in print for updates to legislation, commercial publishers can update their legislative databases more often, providing the researcher with current, cumulative versions of legislation.
- *Scope of coverage*: Publishers of online legal databases are increasingly broadening the scope of their databases by adding more judgments and a wider variety of material, including full-text legal books, journals, and encyclopedias. In addition, the commercial online databases may in some situations be the only convenient source for unpublished case law.
- *Full-text searching*: Historically, print law-related material in Canada has not been well indexed, sometimes making it more difficult than it should be to find relevant material in print. Online legal research, however, allows the researcher to search for the single or multiple occurrence of a particular word or phrase within a case or statute, something that cannot be done using print resources. Since most information in online databases is in full text, and since most of these databases have relatively sophisticated search engines, it is possible to conduct both fairly exhaustive research and quite specific or narrow research on specific terms.
- *Noting up*: The major commercial legal databases provide sophisticated online citators that allow a legal researcher to note up cases quickly and accurately for judicial history and judicial treatment. Due to the volume of case law, it is becoming difficult, if not impossible, for legal publishers to publish their citators in print format. As such, expect to see a movement towards case law citators being available only in electronic format.
- *Reliability*: The vendors of online legal databases and sources of law-related information in electronic format retain very high levels of quality and editorial control, thereby making the content of their databases very reliable. This gives online legal databases an advantage over other material found for free on the Internet, although the trade-off in favour of reliability is the cost of online commercial

databases, a problem not generally associated with information on the Internet.

- *Availability/remote access/space savings*: The information in these online law-related databases is generally available twenty-four hours a day and can be accessed by multiple users, unlike a single copy of a volume of a print case law reporter. In addition, these online databases save large amounts of space by avoiding the need to store print materials in a library.

- *Time tracking*: For law libraries in the private sector, online legal databases are an excellent value for their cost since most of the cost of online searches can be passed on to the client as a disbursement (in appropriate circumstances, as discussed in Chapter 1, Section C). As such, a law firm law library could in theory not subscribe to any print publications yet still operate a high level of research service at a very low overhead, if the costs of online searches can be billed back to the firm's clients.

Although there are a number of advantages to electronic legal resources, there are a number of potential disadvantages:

- *Cost*: Some people find the cost of online legal databases or Internet subscription services to be expensive. To the casual researcher who cannot bill back this cost to a client, the cost may well be prohibitive.[1] Many firms, however, are moving to a fixed monthly fee price arrangement or a transactional charge arrangement with the online vendors, thereby stabilizing part of the cost of online searches. In addition, the fees paid to online vendors by the private sector help to subsidize the free or low-cost access that most online vendors provide to academics, law students, and law librarians.

- *Difficulty in use*: To an untrained user, some online legal databases may be difficult to use. These difficulties include vendor-specific search commands and knowing which databases within a particular

---

1   Although free Internet resources—such as the Canadian Legal Information Institute (www.canlii.org)—provide increasingly better access to the law, access to information remains a concern for those who cannot afford to access the value-added services on the subscription databases discussed in this chapter. See, for example, Olufunmilayo B. Arewa, "Open Access in a Closed Universe: Lexis, Westlaw, Law Schools, and the Legal Information Market" (2006) 10 Lewis & Clark Law Review 797; Ted Tjaden, *Access to Law-Related Information in Canada in The Digital Age* (LL.M. Thesis, 2005, University of Toronto, Faculty of Law), online: http://files. slaw.ca/TedTjadenLLMThesis.pdf; Teresa Scassa, "The Best Things in Law are Free? Towards Quality Free Public Access to Primary Legal Materials in Canada" (2000) 23 Dal. L.J. 301 at 328; and Robert Berring, "Chaos, Cyberspace and Tradition: Legal Information Transmogrified" (1997) 12 Berkeley Tech. L.J. 189.

vendor's database to choose. When these difficulties are combined with the cost of online charges, the average person may find it difficult to use online legal databases for legal research. Fortunately, improvements, such as online help guides and search templates, are constantly being made by publishers for their databases making it easier and more intuitive to use their products.

- *Limited material:* Most online legal databases emphasize current information, thereby making online access to older, historical, or archival material less available. To a certain extent, this problem is lessened with the court judgments of the higher courts for which online vendors usually carry a complete online set, but for lower courts and for older volumes of legal journals, there is no consistently good online historical coverage.
- *Lack of ownership*: One usually owns the books and other print materials in one's library, whereas a subscription to online commercial databases only provides access and use of data—there is no ownership. Thus, when one stops paying for or subscribing to an online service, one is left with no tangible materials with which to research.

Since technology is changing so quickly and since there appears to be a relatively healthy amount of competition among the vendors of online commercial law-related databases, it may well be that most of the disadvantages of these databases listed above will diminish or disappear over time.

What follows for the next few sections is a review of some of the major commercial online law-related databases of interest to Canadian legal researchers.

C. COMPREHENSIVE SERVICES

LexisNexis Quicklaw and Westlaw Canada can be considered "comprehensive" services because of the volume of their content, ranging from case law and legislation to secondary resources, including books, journals and journal indexes, encyclopedias, reference tools, and news content for Canada and major countries of the world (depending on the terms of your subscription).

1) LexisNexis Quicklaw (www.lexisnexis.ca)

The current LexisNexis Quicklaw service came about in 2002 as a result of a merger between LexisNexis Butterworths Canada and Quicklaw.

Prior to that merger, LexisNexis Canada was part of the LexisNexis group of companies owned by Reed Elsevier, one of the world's largest publishers. LexisNexis began in 1973 in Dayton, Ohio, as an American-based provider of online legal resources that initially emphasized American legal materials but grew to include news databases and law-related information from around the world. Also included within the Reed Elsevier group are such well known legal imprints as Matthew Bender, Martindale-Hubbell, and Butterworths.

Quicklaw, on the other hand, started in 1967 at Queen's University Faculty of Law by Professor Hugh Lawford as a joint research project between IBM and the University. In 1972, IBM was forced to withdraw from the project due to the policies of the Canadian federal government that require Canadian companies to control information systems. Since the government did not continue to fund the database, Professor Lawford and Richard von Briesen founded QL Systems Ltd. as a private company and took over the database.[2] Quicklaw grew over time, constantly expanding its content, with a focus on Canadian content and, prior to being taken over by LexisNexis Canada, was regarded by many at the time as one of the leading Canadian services.

Since the merger of the LexisNexis Canada and Quicklaw services in 2002, the resultant LexisNexis Quicklaw interface evolved into what is a LexisNexis (as opposed to Quicklaw) "look and feel," common to all LexisNexis services around the world (thus, Australian lawyers logging into LexisNexis Australia would see a similar interface but defaulting to Australian content). Figure 6.1 shows a typical "Start" page on LexisNexis Quicklaw, including a customized "Bookshelf" of frequently accessed databases.

Since there are thousands of databases on LexisNexis Quicklaw, it is impossible to list or discuss all available in this chapter. As such, users will find their online Source Directory to be the best starting point when unsure which database to choose. One method of finding information is to browse the Source Directory by topic or jurisdiction. When browsing by jurisdiction, there is typically a further subdivision on one or more of the following topics, depending on the jurisdiction involved (some jurisdictions, such as Canada or the United States, tend to have more content):

---

2   See Bill Rogers, "QuickLaw Founder a Trailblazer in Online Legal Research" *Lawyers Weekly* (30 October 1998) 18; Simon Chester, "Hugh Lawford 1933–2009," SLAW Blog, online: www.slaw.ca/2009/08/18/hugh-lawford-1933-2009/ (18 August 2009); Sandra Martin, "Prof's System Revolutionized Legal Practice; Witty and Hard-Working Entrepreneur Founded World's First Online Legal Data Base" *The Globe and Mail* (26 September 2009) S13.

- Administrative Boards &
  Tribunals
- Citators & Digests
- Companies & Organizations
- Forms & Precedents
- Legal Indices & Tables
- Legal News
- News
- Scientific Materials

- Cases
- Commentary
- Dictionaries
- Industries & Markets
- Legal Journals
- Legislation
- People
- Treaties & International
  Agreements

You can also search the Source Directory by keyword. Searching on "evidence" in the Source Directory, for example, resulted in nine hits (at the time this book was published), one of which was the online version of the third edition of the treatise *The Law of Evidence in Canada* (by Sopinka, Lederman, and Bryant), published by LexisNexis Canada. Their interface allows customization of your start page and the ability to create a virtual bookshelf of your frequently accessed databases. There is also the ability to track your history (of recent searches) and to set up "alerts" (to run saved searches on specified terms across specified databases). LexisNexis Canada offers a number of packages for licensed content, ranging from basic to comprehensive coverage. They have also started to package Practice Area libraries for such topics as criminal law, family law, immigration law, intellectual property and information technology, labour law, and litigation, with each licensed library containing specialized LexisNexis content for that topic.

Depending on individual subscriptions, LexisNexis Quicklaw has a number of unique databases that are useful for Canadian legal researchers (Chapter 8 lists some specific LexisNexis Quicklaw databases by topic):

- **Secondary Resources**
  - » **Treatises**: A number of LexisNexis Canada treatises are available on LexisNexis Quicklaw (e.g., Professor Janet Walker's *Canadian Conflict of Laws*—see Chapter 8 for actual titles).
  - » *Halsbury's Laws of Canada*: This recently developed legal encyclopedia is available in print and online, as is the British and Australian equivalent (depending on your subscription).
  - » **Canadian Law Symposia Index**: Although LexisNexis Quicklaw has the *Index to Canadian Legal Literature* (as does Westlaw Canada), an extremely useful database only available on LexisNexis Quicklaw is the *Canadian Law Symposia Index* (*CLSI*), which indexes the contents of papers presented at seminars, continuing legal education workshops, and other legal symposia since January 1986.

» *The Lawyers Weekly*: The full text of articles from *The Lawyers Weekly* newspaper are available online from November 1990 (as are case digests listed in the newspaper).

» **NetLetters**: There are over 100 NetLetters on a variety of topics that serve as current awareness tools for lawyers (e.g., LexisNexis Employment Law NetLetter).

Figure 6.1
Screenshot of LexisNexis Quicklaw "Start" Page, Showing Search Boxes and My Bookshelf

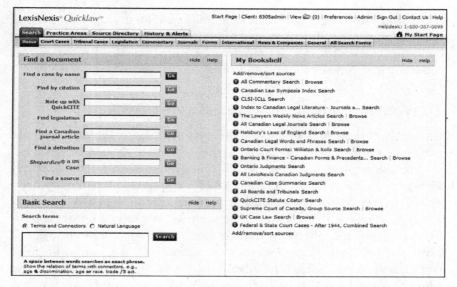

» *Canadian Forms & Precedents*: *Canadian Forms & Precedents*, although available in print and on CD-ROM, is also on LexisNexis Quicklaw (see Chapter 8 for specific titles).

» *The Canada Digest*: As a response to Westlaw Canada's *Canadian Abridgment* case digests, LexisNexis has recently developed *The Canada Digest*, organized into fifty-two topical titles and containing hundreds of thousands of case summaries.

» *Canadian Legal Words and Phrases*: In response to the *Words and Phrases* services on Westlaw Canada, LexisNexis developed the online *Canadian Legal Words and Phrases* database, which contains words and phrases judicially defined in Canadian court and tribunal decisions.

» **QuickCite Case and Statute Citator**: Noting up cases and legislation on LexisNexis Quicklaw is easy using their QuickCITE service.

- **Primary Sources**
  - » LexisNexis Quicklaw has very good legislative and case law databases for Canada (and in most situations, the differences in content for legislation and case law between LexisNexis Quicklaw and Westlaw Canada are minor). However, one area of strength for LexisNexis Quicklaw is its broad coverage of decisions from administrative tribunals, ranging (literally) from Administrative Tribunal of Québec, Economic Affairs Division Decisions to the Yukon Labour Arbitration Awards, decisions that are often otherwise not easily available elsewhere.

Aside from the foregoing unique content, LexisNexis Quicklaw has extensive international content as part of its international subscription, including good coverage for the United Kingdom, the United States, Australia and New Zealand, and France.

2) Westlaw Canada (http://canada.westlaw.com)

Currently part of the Thomson Reuters conglomerate, Westlaw Canada can trace its history back to 1864 when Robert Carswell first started selling law books in Toronto. From that early history—the Carswell Company Ltd. was incorporated in 1892—the Carswell name has been associated with legal publishing in Canada, including early ties with Sweet & Maxwell in the United Kingdom.[3] Currently, other legal publishers within the Thomson Reuters family include Carswell and Les Éditions Yvon Blais (Canada), Sweet & Maxwell (U.K.), Lawbook (Australia), and West (U.S.). One advantage that Carswell has had in the Canadian legal publishing industry was early development of a case digest service (the *Canadian Abridgment*) and legal encyclopedia (the *Canadian Encyclopedic Digest*), both of which are discussed in more detail in Chapter 2. These products have required strong editorial control by Carswell in developing a classification scheme for how legal content would be organized. Prior to the advent of online services, both of these services in their print format were sometimes a challenge to use for the first-time researcher. However, Carswell was able to leverage

---

3   For more on the history of Carswell, see Ken Barnett, "The Carswell Story 1864–2001" (2001) 26 Can. L.L. 49; Lisa Moran, "The Legal Publishing Industry in Canada, 2000: Challenges and Opportunities" (2000) 25 Can. L. L. 152; and Vivienne Denton, "A Look at the Development of the Legal Publishing Industry in Canada" in Martha L. Foote, ed., *Law Reporting and Legal Publishing in Canada: A History* (Kingston, ON: Canadian Association of Law Libraries, 1997).

these products—along with their ownership of the *Index to Canadian Legal Literature* and *Words & Phrases*—in their online products, particularly LawSource on Westlaw Canada.

The online directory on Westlaw Canada is a good starting point for researchers to find the applicable database to search. Otherwise, the service contains templates on the homepage for LawSource that give the user options to search or browse the key components of the service, including the *Canadian Encyclopedic Digest*, the Canadian Case Digests (the online name for the *Canadian Abridgment*), the *Index to Canadian Legal Literature*, *Words & Phrases*, and full-text case law or legislation. Westlaw Canada also allows researchers to customize the tabs available at the top of their screen to allow quick access to frequently used material (therefore, clicking on the InsolvencySource tab provides quick access to the various insolvency-related resources on Westlaw Canada, including, for example, Houlden & Morawetz analysis and Bulletins from the Office of the Superintendent of Bankruptcy). Figure 6.2 shows the Westlaw Canada interface, including selected topical "tabs" across the top of the screen. In addition to some of the specialized content described below, Westlaw Canada also offers tables of concordance that concord legislation across the provinces on selected topics. In addition, searches can be programmed to run on a regular basis and users can track a history of their past searches.

Figure 6.2
Screenshot of Westlaw Canada's LawSource Tab

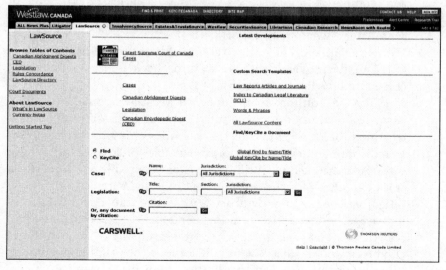

Depending on individual subscriptions, Westlaw Canada has a number of unique databases that are useful for Canadian legal researchers (Chapter 8 lists some specific Westlaw Canada databases by topic):

- **Secondary Resources**
  - » **Treatises**: There are a large number of Carswell-authored treatises available on Westlaw Canada, usually as part of a specific "Source" subscription (discussed below). Treatises available on Westlaw Canada are searchable and browsable and include such titles as Waters, *Laws of Trusts in Canada* (as part of *Estates&TrustsSource*) and Watt's *Manual of Criminal Evidence* (as part of CriminalSource), to name but two examples.
  - » *Canadian Encyclopedic Digest*: The online version of the *Canadian Encyclopedic Digest* (CED) is both browsable and searchable, organized by topics (see Chapter 2, Section D for a more detailed discussion). Recent improvements include the "chunking" paragraphs into larger groups (minimizing the need to scroll through screens on the computer) and providing links from the CED to the relevant sections of the *Canadian Abridgment*.
  - » *Canadian Abridgment*: The online version of the *Canadian Abridgment* is also both browsable and searchable, organized by topics (see Chapter 2, Section E for a more detailed discussion). Most digests have links to the full text of the version.
  - » *Index to Canadian Legal Literature*: The advantage of the online version of the *Index to Canadian Legal Literature* on Westlaw Canada (compared to LexisNexis Quicklaw) — at least at the time of publication of this book — is that the Westlaw Canada version is searchable by date restriction.
  - » *Words & Phrases*: The online version of *Words & Phrases* on Westlaw Canada provides an easy way to check for cases that have considered particular words or phrases.
  - » *KeyCite*: The online noter-upper on Westlaw Canada is called KeyCite. In addition to providing the judicial history and judicial treatment of a case, KeyCite also provides citing references to selected commentary (such as journal articles or treatises) that have discussed the case in question. It is also possible to "KeyCite" a statute to check for cases that have discussed the section.
  - » *Litigator*: The Litigator database is unique in Canada for the access it provides to court-filed pleadings and facta in selected Canadian court decisions. The documents are searchable by keyword and can be viewed in HTML or as a PDF file of the original document. More information is available online (www.litigatoronline.ca).

» **Source Products (topical coverage)**: In addition to the LawSource service described above, users can subscribe to the following Source products containing specialized content:

  › *CriminalSource*: a database of criminal law materials that includes relevant legislation, case law, newsletters, and criminal law textbooks.

  › *Estates&TrustsSource*: a database of materials related to estates, trusts, and wills, including relevant legislation, case law, textbooks, and estates, trusts, and wills precedents.

  › *FamilySource*: a database of family law materials that includes relevant legislation, case law, newsletters, and family law textbooks.

  › *InsolvencySource*: a database of bankruptcy and insolvency law materials that includes relevant legislation, case law, newsletters, and insolvency law textbooks.

  › *IPSource*: a database of intellectual property (IP) law materials that includes relevant legislation, case law, newsletters, and IP law textbooks.

  › *SecuritiesSource*: a database of securities law materials that includes relevant legislation, case law, precedents, newsletters, and securities law textbooks.

• **Primary Sources**
  » Westlaw Canada has extensive online case law and good coverage of current Canadian legislation.

Aside from its Canadian content, international subscriptions on Westlaw Canada provide excellent content for the major common law jurisdictions. American coverage, for example, includes the West "Key Number" system that organizes case law by topic, along with strong legislative coverage and extensive secondary commentary, including the West legal encyclopedias (*Corpus Juris Secundum* and *American Jurisprudence*, discussed in more detail in Chapter 2, Section D). There is also strong coverage for the United Kingdom and Australia, among other jurisdictions.

D. CANADIAN AND CIVIL LAW SERVICES

The following databases are of no less quality than LexisNexis Quicklaw or Westlaw Canada but are discussed separately in part because their focus tends to be narrower on Canadian content.

1) CCH Online (www.cch.ca)

CCH Canada is part of the Wolters Kluwer group, a large international publisher. Prior to the advent of online resources, CCH Canada was known for its black looseleaf binders on various legal topics containing relevant case law, legislation, and commentary. The content of these binders are also available on CCH Online, an Internet-based subscription service provided by CCH for many types of information, including tax, law, and human resources (this content is also available on DVD). The CCH Legal library includes coverage for alternative dispute resolution (ADR), business law, environmental law, family law, health law, estate law, insurance law, real estate law, securities law, and international law. The CCH Tax library includes various databases regarding federal and provincial income tax and the GST. The CCH Business library covers employment and labour law, health and safety law, and pension benefits.

CCH also provides excellent legislative and "bill-tracking" options for Canadian federal and provincial legislation through a separate CCH LegislativePulse database (which requires a subscription) at http://pulse.cch.ca.

2) Canada Law Book/*BestCase* (www.canadalawbook.ca)

Canada Law Book—the oldest legal publisher in Canada—has remained independent of the other three major Canadian legal publishers (Thomson Reuters, LexisNexis Canada, and CCH Canada). Although it has had a number of CD-ROM and Internet products for some time now (e.g., the *Canada Statute Service* and the *Dominion Law Reports Plus*), it is the recent launch of *BestCase* by Canada Law Book that has raised its profile as a potential third alternative to LexisNexis Quicklaw and Westlaw Canada. *BestCase* is an online subscription service containing the full text of the major Canada Law Book case law reporters, including *Canadian Criminal Cases* (1898 to present), *Dominion Law Reports* (1912 to present), *Labour Arbitration Cases* (1948 to present), *Land Compensation Reports* (1971 to present), and *Ontario Municipal Board Reports* (1972 to present). An online noter-upper is provided. One unique feature—for online Canadian case law—is that online versions of the case are available in both HTML and PDF.

3) Droit civil en ligne (DCL)
(www.dcl.editionsyvonblais.com)

Droit civil en ligne, published by Éditions Yvon Blais (part of the Thomson Reuters group), contains French language civil law content for Québec, including applicable treatises published by Éditions Yvon Blais, current awareness newsletters, dictionaries, and commentary on the *Civil Code of Québec*, along with legislation and case law.

4) Maritime Law Book (www.mlb.nb.ca)

Maritime Law Book, founded in 1969, is a publisher of Canadian case law and publishes the following case law reporters in print and now through an online Internet subscription: *Alberta Reports* (A.R.), *Atlantic Provinces Reports* (A.P.R.), *British Columbia Appeal Cases* (B.C.A.C.), *British Columbia Trial Cases* (B.C.T.C.), *Federal Trial Reports* (F.T.R.), *Manitoba Reports* (2d) (Man. R.(2d)), *National Reporter* (N.R.), *New Brunswick Reports* (2d) (N.B.R.(2d)), *Newfoundland and Prince Edward Island Reports* (Nfld. & P.E.I.R.), *Nova Scotia Reports* (2d) (N.S.R.(2d)), *Ontario Appeal Cases* (O.A.C.), *Ontario Trial Cases* (O.T.C.), *Saskatchewan Reports* (S.R.), and *Western Appeal Cases* (W.A.C.). Unique to Maritime Law is the development of a custom key number digest system ranging over 150 topics (from Actions to Workers' Compensation). Maritime Law Book has recently allowed free searching on its website of over 215,000 "raw" judgments (cases without any headnotes or key numbers).

5) Répertoire électronique de jurisprudence du Barreau (REJB) (www.rejb.editionsyvonblais.com)

The Répertoire électronique de jurisprudence du Barreau is an online service from Thomson Reuters containing doctrine, legislation, and summaries and full-text decisions of Québec courts and the Supreme Court of Canada. Commentary includes the Collection de droit (2006–2007) and articles from Développements récents (2002–2007) from the Barreau du Québec.

6) Société québécoise d'information juridique (SOQUIJ) (http://soquij.qc.ca)

La Société québécoise d'information juridique (SOQUIJ) was founded in 1976 and is a legal information society created for the purpose of making Québec law available and for promoting legal research in Québec. It publishes various sources of primary law in Québec, including legislation, the reports of the Québec courts, and various administrative tribunals within Québec. Decisions are available in summaries and full text.

E. SPECIALIZED SERVICES

The following Internet subscriptions have specialized content of interest to Canadian legal researchers, depending on the topic. More information about each service is available on the applicable company's website.

1) Criminal Spectrum (www.canadalawbook.ca)

This online service, depending on the scope of one's subscription, provides access to criminal law resources of interest to criminal lawyers, including the full-text of the *Canadian Criminal Cases* (1898 to current), *Weekly Criminal Bulletin* case summaries, *Martin's Annual Criminal Code* and *Martin's Related Criminal Statutes*, the *Criminal Law Quarterly* journal, and various criminal law treatises published by Canada Law Book (including, for example, *McWilliams' Canadian Criminal Evidence*, 4th ed.).

2) DisclosureNet (www.disclosurenet.com)

DisclosureNet provides access to the securities law filings of public companies (whose stocks are traded to the public). Coverage includes Canada, the U.S., and the U.K. Its strength over the free versions of such databases (e.g., SEDAR at www.sedar.com) is a more powerful search engine to make searches more precise. Many lawyers use these databases for sample precedents for prospectuses, contracts, or other merger and acquisition documents (in addition to monitoring corporate activities).

3) HeinOnline (www.heinonline.org)

HeinOnline, already mentioned in Chapter 2, Section B, is perhaps best known for its over 1,300 full-text law journals (in PDF and HTML), including over fifty Canadian law journals. However, it has other content of interest to Canadian legal researchers, including the full text of the *English Reports* (1220–1865), the *U.S. Reports*, the U.S. *Statutes at Large*, the American *Federal Register* and *Code of Federal Regulations*, a Treaties and Agreements Library, and a Legal Classics library containing over 1,400 classic legal treatises (mostly olders ones that are in the public domain).

4) Justis.com (www.justis.com)

Although this database, based in the United Kingdom, has a variety of international and EU databases, of most interest to Canadian legal researchers is its collection of U.K. caselaw in PDF and HTML, includ-ing the *English Reports*, the *Law Reports*, and the *Weekly Law Reports* (to name only a few).

5) Kluwer Arbitration Online (www.kluwerarbitration.com)

The content of Kluwer Arbitration Online is quite unique, specializing in resources on commercial arbitration. As stated on its website, content includes close to 1,700 bilateral investment treaties, over 5,000 court decisions and 1,750 arbitration awards, twenty-five multilateral treaties, legislation, model clauses, and over 400 rules from major arbitral institu-tions, along with eighty-eight books, five journals, and two looseleafs.

6) Labour Spectrum (www.canadalawbook.ca)

This online service, depending on the scope of one's subscription, pro-vides access to labour law resources published by Canada Law Book, including Brown and Beatty's *Canadian Labour Arbitration* (4th ed.), *Labour Arbitration Cases*, *Canadian Labour Arbitration Summaries*, *British Columbia Decisions, Labour Arbitration*, and other commentary, in-cluding Adams and Adams, *Canadian Labour Law* (2d ed.) and *Willis & Winkler on Leading Labour Cases*.

7) PrivaWorks (www.privaworks.com)

PrivaWorks is a database containing access to privacy law content for Canada, the U.S., the E.U., Asia-Pacific, and South America. A module called "Manage the Risks" helps to identify and manage privacy risks (e.g., cross-border transfers). Another section called "Find the Refer-ences" contains access to thousands of primary and secondary sources for privacy law, including decisions of the Canadian federal and prov-incial privacy commissioners (among many other sources). A third module called "Know the Rules" provides access to relevant privacy legislation.

8) TaxnetPRO (www.taxnetpro.com)

Although TaxnetPRO is published by Thomson Reuters, it is a separate subscription from Westlaw Canada. Its focus is on Canadian primary and secondary tax resources (including coverage of estate planning). It contains daily news alerts and a monthly newsletter (Tax Hyperion), commentary from various Carswell tax authors, various tax planning guides, government publications, case law, and provincial and federal tax and G.S.T. legislation.

9) Westlaw Business (http://business.westlaw.com)

This subscription service from Thomson Reuters contains a number of modules (depending on the particular subscription) relating to business law, including a securities law centre (providing access to SEDAR, EDGAR, and U.K. company filings and various securities law primary and secondary resources), a corporate finance module, a restructuring module, a private equity module (focusing on corporate and financial information related to private companies), and an Islamic finance module.

F. LAW-RELATED CD-ROMS

In the last two decades, CD-ROMs (and now DVDs) were an important storage medium for electronic information, used by software publishers for storing and publishing various forms of data. In the legal field, CD-ROMs have been popular because of the large amount of textual information they can contain. With the advent of the Internet, some have started to question whether these CD-ROMs will face extinction since large amounts of information can be easily stored and distributed via servers on the Internet.[4] One advantage of CD-ROMs was portability. However, given the ubiquity of wireless remote access to the Internet, and given the following disadvantages of CD-ROMs, it is reasonable to assume that CD-ROMs will be used less frequently in the future.

- **Disadvantages of CD-ROMs**
  - » *Maintenance*: When CD-ROMs have been licensed to be distributed to multiple users over a computer network, it can be very time-consuming (and sometimes difficult) for technical staff to be constantly reinstalling updated CD-ROMs.
  - » *Lack of ownership*: Some people are surprised when they are reminded that they generally do not own the CD-ROM or the infor-

---

4   See, for example, Elizabeth H. Klampert, "CD-ROM: An Interim Technology?" (1997) 466 Practising Law Institute/Patents, Copyrights, Trademarks, and Literary Property Course Handbook 67. See also Mary A. Sharaf, "Taking the Plunge: The Switch from Books to CD-ROMs: A Pessimist's View" (1997) 444 Practising Law Institute/Patents, Copyrights, Trademarks, and Literary Property Course Handbook 81; Barbara A. Bintliff, "Introducing CD-ROMs into a Law Library: Administrative Issues and Concerns" (1992) 84 Law Library Journal 725.

mation on it when they pay for it. What one is paying for is merely a licence to access the information on the CD-ROM. In addition, most law-related CD-ROMs published in Canada are "time-bombed," meaning that built into the software is a mechanism that denies access to the information on the CD-ROM once the licence period for which access has been paid for has expired.

» *Difficulty in use*: Many law-related CD-ROMs in Canada use search engines different from those on most Internet databases. As such, extra training is often needed to learn how to search CD-ROMs.

Whether the advantages of CD-ROMs outweigh the disadvantages depends on the needs of the individual legal researcher. CD-ROMs are ideal for lawyers who practise in a fairly narrow subject specialty (such as criminal law) who want to carry a wide body of relevant law on their laptops. CD-ROMs are also good for those law libraries willing to cancel print publications in favour of the CD-ROM equivalent as a space-saving measure (remembering, however, that this would result in a loss of ownership of the material). Chapter 8 provides a list of resources by topic, which includes some of the leading CD-ROMs by topic. More information on law-related CD-ROMs can be found on the respective web pages of legal publishers or by consulting the *Directory of Law-Related CD-ROMs*.[5] Increasingly, as discussed above, there is a move by Canadian legal publishers to publish their CD-ROMs through Internet subscriptions.

G. CONCLUSIONS

Given the wide choices of legal resources—ranging from print, CD-ROM, Internet, and commercial online services—under what circumstances would one choose commercial online services? There are several possible answers to this question:

- *Scope of material*: Some of the online commercial services provide access to materials, such as unreported court decisions, that are otherwise unavailable or extremely difficult or expensive to acquire directly from the court file. Most lawyers and legal researchers will therefore want to access these databases to ensure the widest possible scope of their searches.

---

5   Arlene Eis, ed., *Directory of Law-Related CD-ROMs* (Teaneck, NJ: Infosources Publishing, 1993) [annual].

- *Precision of searching*: Commercial online databases have sophisticated search engines that allow the user to limit keyword searches precisely to specific fields (the name of a party to the lawsuit or the name of opposing counsel), a feature not usually available on free Web resources.
- *Online noting up*: These commercial services also have current, easy-to-use note up abilities that allow the researcher to verify whether the case being researched is still good law. While noting up can still be done in print, the speed, currency, and accuracy of noting up online is far superior to print resources.
- *Bill back*: While a potential disadvantage of these commercial online services is their cost, this can also be a potential advantage since, in theory and in practice, it is usually possible to bill back the cost of many online search charges to the client (and to the losing party in a lawsuit) where the research was necessary and reasonable (see the cases discussed in Chapter 1, Section C). Thus, while many larger firms will maintain both a print and online law library collection, it may be that other firms can rationalize parts of their print collection (usually case law reporters and legislation) in favour of using online resources, especially where the firm has the resources of a larger academic, law society, or courthouse library nearby that can be relied upon for access to print materials not held by the firm. Advice on selecting and acquiring legal resources is found in Chapter 9.

INTERNATIONAL AND FOREIGN LEGAL RESEARCH

With increasing globalization, most Canadian lawyers will regularly be exposed to some aspect of international or foreign law. Despite its growing importance, however, many Canadian lawyers lack experience in researching in this area. Therefore, the goal of this chapter is to introduce international and foreign legal research and provide a good overview of relevant print and online resources for effectively conducting this type of research.[1] Material in this chapter is divided into the following sections:

A. The importance of international and foreign law
B. Tips for conducting international and foreign legal research
C. Researching conflict of laws
D. Print and online *secondary* sources of international law
E. Print and online *primary* sources of international law
F. Researching the domestic laws of foreign countries
G. Sample problems and suggested approaches

---

1   This chapter incorporates, with permission, material from Ted Tjaden, "The Best Online Sources for International and Foreign Law" in Bonnie Fish, ed., *You've Got the Whole World in Your Hands: Using the Internet to Expand the Boundaries of Legal Research* (Toronto: Ontario Bar Association, 2004).

A. THE IMPORTANCE OF INTERNATIONAL AND FOREIGN LAW

Canadian courts are increasingly looking to international treaties and conventions as an indication of standards and norms that should be used in interpreting and applying *Charter* standards in the Canadian context. In *Baker v. Canada (Minister of Citizenship and Immigration),*[2] for example, Madam Justice l'Heureux-Dubé wrote that "the values reflected in international human rights law may help inform the contextual approach to statutory interpretation and judicial review,"[3] even where, as in that decision, the Canadian Parliament had not yet implemented the Convention being considered. Likewise, in *Suresh v. Canada (Minister of Citizenship and Immigration),*[4] the Supreme Court of Canada looked to international treaties dealing with the prohibition of deporting persons to countries that allow torture in assessing whether the government was justified in deporting a Sri Lankan refugee to his home country where he might be tortured:

> International treaty norms are not, strictly speaking, binding in Canada unless they have been incorporated into Canadian law by enactment. However, in seeking the meaning of the Canadian Constitution, the courts may be informed by international law. Our concern is not with Canada's international obligations *qua* obligations; rather, our concern is with the principles of fundamental justice. We look to international law as evidence of these principles and not as controlling in itself.[5]

More recently, in *R. v. Hape,*[6] the Supreme Court of Canada had to determine whether the *Charter* applied to searches and seizures conducted in the Turks and Caicos in an investigation of a Canadian on charges of suspected money laundering. To answer this, the Court looked to principles of state jurisdiction under international law and the principle of the comity of nations. In dismissing the appeal of the accused and ruling that the *Charter* did not apply, Mr. Justice LeBel held "the principles of non-intervention and territorial sovereignty may be adopted into the common law of Canada in the absence of conflict-

---

2   [1999] 2 S.C.R. 817.
3   *Ibid.* at para. 70. See also Oonagh E. Fitzgerald, *The Globalized Rule of Law: Relationships between International and Domestic Law* (Toronto: Irwin Law, 2006).
4   [2002] 1 S.C.R. 3.
5   *Ibid.* at para. 60.
6   2007 SCC 26.

ing legislation."[7] He also confirmed the "well-established principle of statutory interpretation that legislation will be presumed to conform to international law" and that in "interpreting the scope of application of the *Charter*, the courts should seek to ensure compliance with Canada's binding obligations under international law where the express words are capable of supporting such a construction."[8]

Likewise, with the increase in global business and trade, most lawyers will be required to have some familiarity with international and foreign law, regardless of their area of practice. This can range from international trade issues governed by the World Trade Organization (WTO) or the North American Free Trade Agreement (NAFTA), international intellectual property laws governed by World Intellectual Property Organization (WIPO) conventions, international environmental treaties, and international child abduction conventions, to name but a few examples. Recent literature in Canada is rife with examples of the increasing domestic application of international and foreign law.[9]

There has also been a relatively strong tradition in Canada for our courts to rely on case law from individual countries outside of Canada, particularly from Commonwealth countries and the United States, depending on the issues or areas of law. A number of studies have been done to examine the extent to which the Supreme Court of Canada, for

---

7   *Ibid.* at para. 46.
8   *Ibid.* at paras. 53 and 56.
9   See, for example, Gib van Ert, "*Hape*: International Law Expands Reach into Formerly Domestic Areas of Law" *The Lawyers Weekly* (24 August 2007) 9; Myra J. Tawfik, "No Longer Living in Splendid Isolation: The Globalization of National Courts and the Internationalization of Intellectual Property Law" (2007) 32 Queen's L.J. 573; Lorraine E. Weinrib, "A Primer on International Law and the Canadian Charter" (2006–2007) 21 N.J.C.L. 313; Anne Warner La Forest, "Domestic Application of International Law in *Charter* Cases: Are We There Yet?" (2004) 37 U.B.C. L. Rev. 157; Reem Bahdi, "Truth and Method in the Domestic Application of International Law" (2002) 15 Can. J.L. & Jur. 255; Robert K. Goldman *et al.*, *The International Dimension of Human Rights: A Guide for Application in Domestic Law* (Washington, DC: Inter-American Development Bank: American University, 2001); Hugh M. Kindred *et al.*, *International Law, Chiefly as Interpreted and Applied in Canada*, 7th ed. (Toronto: Emond Montgomery, 2006); Karen Knop, "Here and There: International Law in Domestic Courts" (2000) 32 N.Y.J.J. Int'l L. & Pol. 501; William A. Schabas, "Twenty-five Years of Public International Law at the Supreme Court of Canada" (2000) 79 Can. Bar Rev. 174; Stephen J. Toope, "The Uses of Metaphor: International Law and the Supreme Court of Canada" (2001) 80 Can. Bar Rev. 534; Gibran van Ert, *Using International Law in Canadian Courts*, 2d ed. (Toronto: Irwin Law, 2008); Gérard V. La Forest, "The Expanding Role of the Supreme Court of Canada in International Law Issues" (1996) 34 Can. Y.B. Int'l Law 89; and Anne F. Bayefsky, *International Human Rights Law: Use in Canadian Charter of Rights and Freedoms Litigation* (Toronto: Butterworths, 1992).

example, has relied on British and American precedents or decisions from other countries.[10] As might be expected, in Canada's early history, there was a heavy reliance on British precedent, but over time, as Canadian courts developed their own bodies of decisions, dependence on British precedence has declined over time.[11] But given the similarities between our legal systems, Canadian judges still show a great deal of deference to the persuasive value of decisions from the House of Lords or the English Court of Appeal, especially in areas of common law or other areas of law where Canadian law has remained relatively consistent with English law, including such areas of law as contracts, torts, equity, partnership law, sale of goods, and land law.[12] With the introduction of the *Charter*, we have also seen an increase in the number of times the Supreme Court of Canada has relied upon American case law in helping it interpret constitutional provisions (and in other areas of private law as well), at least in the early days of the *Charter*.[13]

In addition to using international and foreign law materials as "tools of persuasion" to convince a Canadian judge to follow particular arguments or principles being espoused in international or foreign law, Canadian lawyers might also need to research international or foreign law to learn what the law actually is on a particular point in order to understand the context of a transaction a client might be entering into in the foreign jurisdiction (but lawyers must always be careful to not provide legal opinions on the law outside of the jurisdiction in which they are licensed to practise law).

One final area where international and comparative law is increasingly important is the research being done by legal academics on a variety of important and timely topics, ranging from terrorism to international environmental law to cross-border trade, to name but a few.

---

10   See, generally, Cynthia L. Ostberg, Matthew E. Wetstein, & Craig R. Ducat, "Attitudes, Precedents and Cultural Change: Explaining the Citation of Foreign Precedents by the Supreme Court of Canada" (2001) 34 Canadian Journal of Political Science 377; Peter McCormick, "The Supreme Court of Canada and American Citations 1945–1994: A Statistical Overview" (1997) 8 Sup. Ct. L. Rev. (2d) 527; Peter McCormick, "What Supreme Court Cases Does the Supreme Court Cite? Follow-up Citations on the Supreme Court of Canada, 1989–1993" (1996) 7 Sup. Ct. L. Rev. (2d) 451 ; Christopher Manfredi, "The Use of United States Decisions by the Supreme Court of Canada Under the *Charter of Rights and Freedoms*" (1990) 23 Canadian Journal of Political Science 499; and Ian Bushnell, "The Use of American Cases" (1986) 35 U.N.B.L.J. 157.

11   McCormick, "The Supreme Court of Canada," *ibid.* at 533.

12   See, for example, Simon Chester, "Is the Internet Ready for English Legal Research?" in Bonnie Fish, ed., above note 1.

13   Ostberg, Wetstein, & Ducat, above note 10 at 391–92; Manfredi, above note 10 at 505–6.

B. TIPS FOR CONDUCTING INTERNATIONAL AND FOREIGN LEGAL RESEARCH

Until recently, international and foreign law was a relatively isolated and specialized area of law practised by a select few; its literature was also highly specialized, organized, and taught by highly-trained international and foreign law librarians. In the last ten years, however, the Internet has transformed the way in which legal researchers access international and foreign legal materials. Prior to the Internet, only major academic law libraries could afford to maintain print collections of major international legal resources with selected print coverage of the domestic laws of foreign countries. Very often these collections would be incomplete or out-of-date and not easily accessible by researchers who did not live in major cities that had large academic law libraries. With the Internet, however, we see an explosion of intergovernmental organizations and foreign countries publishing both primary and secondary legal resources online. The tips in this section will discuss several ways to approach conducting international and foreign legal research, many of which take advantage of the Internet.

Tip #1. *Start with secondary resources before primary resources.* For researchers who do not regularly conduct international and foreign legal research, it can be a challenge to start a research project if you do not have a good overview of the area of law or the issues. The simplest way to get over any fear of doing international or foreign legal research is to apply the same techniques discussed in Chapter 1—start your international or foreign legal research project by using *secondary* resources (books, journals, or websites, for example) to help you identify, locate, and understand relevant *primary* resources (international case law, arbitral awards, treaties, and foreign case law or legislation). Secondary resources are usually written by experts in their field and provide a good overview or explanation of the law. The leading textbooks, journals, dictionaries, and websites for researching international law are discussed in Section D, below in this chapter. Those for researching the domestic laws of foreign countries are discussed in Section F, below in this chapter.

Tip #2. *Google it!* You can often easily locate international or foreign materials by simply typing in the name of a treaty, a U.N. Document Symbol (e.g., E/CN.4/Sub.2/1997/1) or the name of a case in a good Internet search engine. Legal research on the Internet is discussed in detail in Chapter 5; using the Internet specifically for international and foreign legal research is discussed below. As with any Internet research, care must be taken to evaluate the source of the information, and preference should be shown for information found on the official websites of foreign governments, intergovernmental organizations, non-governmental organizations, or other reliable sources, such as reputable law schools and other public interest organizations. For one of the better sites on evaluating international and foreign law Internet sources, see the excellent guide prepared by Mirela Roznovschi entitled "Update to Evaluating Foreign and International Legal Databases on the Internet"[14] in which she discusses the following eighteen criteria in evaluating online information: accuracy, archiving, author/publisher, completeness, copyright stipulations, cost over print format, coverage, currency, database definition, language, licensing, product description, search quality, source of data, stability, structural considerations, user interactivity, and workability.

Tip #3. *Know your definitions and acronyms.* With the increasing integration of international and foreign legal materials in general legal practice, legal researchers should become more familiar with some of the terminology of international and foreign law. Not too much rests on the strict definitions of some of the terms discussed below—lines between some of these categories are blurring every day. Despite this, for the sake of clarity, here are a few key definitions:

- *Public international law:* "Public International Law is composed of the laws, rules, and principles of general application that deal with the conduct of nation states and international organizations among themselves as well as the relationships between nation states and international organizations with persons, whether natural or juridical. Public International Law is sometimes called the "law of nations" or just simply International Law."[15] Example: The *United Nations Convention on the Law of the Sea.*[16]

- *IGO (Intergovernmental Organization):* "[A] permanent association of states with international legal rights and obligations distinct from those of its members and equipped with permanent organs or institutions; also international organization.[17] Examples: The United Nations[18] and the World Intellectual Property Organization (WIPO).[19]

---

14   Online: LLRX.com, www.llrx.com/features/evaluating2.htm.
15   Vicenç Feliú, "Introduction to Public International Law Research" (May/June 2008), online: Globalex, www.nyulawglobal.org/Globalex/Public_International_Law_Research.htm.
16   *United Nations Convention on the Law of the Sea,* Montego Bay, Dec.10, 1982, U.N. Doc. A/Conf.62/122, reprinted in 21 I.L.M. 1245 (1982). Online: www.un.org/Depts/los/convention_agreements/convention_overview_convention.htm.
17   John H. Currie, *Public International Law,* 2d ed. (Toronto: Irwin Law, 2008) at 582.
18   Online: United Nations, www.un.org.
19   Online: World Intellectual Property Organization, www.wipo.int.

- *NGO (Non-governmental Organization)*: "[A] legally constituted, non-business organization created by natural or legal persons with no participation or representation of any government. In the cases in which NGOs are funded totally or partially by governments, the NGO maintains its non-governmental status insofar as it excludes government representatives from membership in the organization."[20] Example: The International Chamber of Commerce.[21]

- *Private international law*: "Private international law is the body of conventions, model laws, national laws, legal guides, and other documents and instruments that regulate private relationships across national borders. Private international law has a dualistic character, balancing international consensus with domestic recognition and implementation, as well as balancing sovereign actions with those of the private sector."[22] Example: The *Hague Convention on the Service Abroad of Judicial and Extrajudicial Documents in Civil or Commercial Matters.*[23]

- *Treaties/conventions*: For the most part, there is no major difference in the generic meaning of the term "treaty" or "convention." The 1969 *Vienna Convention on the Law of Treaties* defines a treaty as "an international agreement concluded between States in written form and governed by international law, whether embodied in a single instrument or in two or more related instruments and whatever its particular designation." The 1986 *Vienna Convention* extends the definition of treaties to include international agreements involving international organizations as parties.[24]

- *Travaux préparatoires*: Literally the "preparatory works" of a treaty. Currie defines them as "early drafts and other documents relating to the negotiation of the text of a treaty."[25] Article 32 of the *Vienna Convention* allows travaux préparatoires to be used to help interpret treaties if the meaning of the treaty is ambiguous.[26]

---

20 Wikipedia, *s.v.* "Nongovernmental organization," online: http://en.wikipedia.org/wiki/Non-governmental_organization.
21 Online: International Chamber of Commerce, www.iccwbo.org.
22 Louise Tsang, "Private International Law," online: The American Society of International Law, www.asil.org/pil1.cfm.
23 *Hague Convention on the Service Abroad of Judicial and Extrajudicial Documents in Civil or Commercial Matters* (15 November 1965), online, www.hcch.net/index_en.php?act=conventions.text&cid=17.
24 See United Nations, "Treaty Reference Guide," online: United Nations, http://untreaty.un.org/English/guide.asp.
25 Currie, above note 17 at 591.
26 For a good overview of researching travaux préparatoires, see Jonathan Pratter, "À la Recherche des Travaux Préparatoires: An Approach to Researching the

- *Foreign law*: For Canadian legal researchers, "foreign law" represents the domestic law of countries outside of Canada. However, it would be strange to refer to the law of England or the law of other Commonwealth countries as "foreign" law, although it might be technically correct to do so. Some Canadians would instead be more comfortable referring to foreign law as the domestic law of countries outside of the Commonwealth, especially those countries based on civil law or Islamic law traditions.

Not much rests on the precise meanings of the foregoing definitions (but realize that these terms are sometimes used with some precision in the legal literature). As more countries incorporate international law into their domestic laws in a variety of ways, the entire "globalization" phenomena is truly blurring the boundaries between the terms defined above. For example, while the traditional definition of *public* international law incorporates the notion of "state-to-state" action, we have seen a shift (particularly in recent years) in public international laws being used for "state-to-individual" action, such as the various war crimes prosecutions, including the current prosecution of Bosnian Serb President Radovan Karadžić. Likewise, there are aspects of *private* international law involving a fair amount of state activity and coordination.

For those conducting treaty research (discussed in more detail in Section E, below in this chapter), it helps to be familiar with the following treaty-making terminology:[27]

- *adoption*: when the treaty was concluded or fixed
- *entry into force*: the date the treaty becomes effective
- *ratification*: indicates a country's consent to be bound by a treaty
- *accession*: where a state, not one of the original parties, later consents to be bound by the treaty
- *reservation*: where a state excludes part of the treaty

Abbreviations and acronyms are also common in international and foreign legal research. Be aware of the many abbreviation dictionaries available (discussed in more detail in Chapter 2) that can explain these terms. Often simply searching on the acronym or abbreviation in an In-

---

Drafting History of International Agreements," online: Globalex, www.nyulaw-global.org/globalex/Travaux_Preparatoires1.htm.

27   See, for example, United Nations, "Treaty Reference Guide" available online: United Nations, http://untreaty.un.org/English/guide.asp. These terms are also nicely explained in Jeanne Rehberg, "Finding Treaties and Other International Agreements" in Jeanne Rehberg & Radu Popa, eds., *Accidental Tourist on the New Frontier: An Introductory Guide to Global Legal Research* (Littleton, CO: F.B. Rothman, 1998) at 123–50.

ternet search engine will identify the term in the top ten search results or provide a link to the organization if the acronym is the name of a well-known NGO or IGO (for example, a Google search on "UNCTAD" results in the first result providing a link to www.unctad.org, the home page for the United Nations Conference on Trade and Development).

Tip #4. *Learn another language and understand civil law concepts.* Although English is one of several official languages of the United Nations, much international and foreign legal material will be in languages other than English. Knowledge of other languages can therefore be useful, especially when the free online translation tools are somewhat limited and not a substitute for an official translation, preferably by a qualified translator with legal experience. Equally important, especially for law students or lawyers trained in the common law tradition, is an understanding of civil law since most international law incorporates civilian concepts.

C. RESEARCHING CONFLICT OF LAWS

The body of law known as "conflict of laws" arises most often in private international legal transactions or situations involving parties from different jurisdictions, such as when two corporations from different countries transact business or a resident of one country negligently causes injuries to other persons in a motor vehicle accident that occurred in a different country. Which laws govern the parties and their legal issues?

Researching conflict of laws can be tricky and is beyond the scope of this chapter. In fact, entire books have been written on the topic and should be consulted for any in-depth research. The best resources for Canadian researchers are Professor Walker's looseleaf entitled *Castel & Walker: Canadian Conflict of Laws*, 6th ed. (Markham, ON: LexisNexis Canada, 2005) and Lawrence Collins *et al.*, eds., *Dicey and Morris on the Conflict of Laws*, 14th ed. (London: Sweet & Maxwell, 2006).[28] Both of these treatises, which are listed in Section D, below in this chapter, have extensive footnotes and are well-indexed. As such, the brief overview of conflict of laws that follows does not extensively cite primary sources or the applicable sections of the foregoing treatises since these points have been researched in depth in both of these treatises.

---

28   The Wikipedia entry for "Conflict of Laws" at http://en.wikipedia.org/wiki/Conflict_of_laws actually provides a good overview of the topic.

Researching conflict of laws typically involves needing to research a combination of legislation, the common law, and commentary.[29] Although it is difficult to attempt to simplify the complex area of conflict of laws, the breakdown by Professor Walker of "jurisdiction, judgments and applicable law" as the three main aspects of conflict of laws inquiry[30] provides a useful starting point for a broad overview of this area:

- *Jurisdiction*: Can and should a particular court take jurisdiction over a legal dispute to hear the parties and decide their issue? Simply put, a Canadian court will take jurisdiction over a matter where there is a "real and substantial connection" between the parties and the jurisdiction. In *Van Breda v. Village Resorts Ltd.*,[31] the Ontario Court of Appeal has recently reformulated its test for determining when an Ontario court should take jurisdiction over a non-resident defendant:

  1. *Should a real and substantial connection be presumed?* The court should presume a real and substantial connection if the plaintiff's claim is one that falls under rules for serving foreign defendants (Rule 17.02 in Ontario[32]), except there would be no presumption in the situation in which service is effected for a claim in respect of damage sustained in Ontario or where the claim is against a person outside Ontario who is a necessary or proper party (since these last two grounds are not necessarily reliable indicators of a real and substantial connection). The onus would be on the defendant to show that a real and substantial connection does not exist.

  2. *Has the plaintiff established a real and substantial connection?* At this stage, the core of the analysis is on the connection between the forum and the plaintiff's claim, and the connection between the forum and the defendant. Remaining considerations, which should not be treated as independent factors having more or less equal weight when determining whether there is a real and substantial connection but as general legal principles that bear upon the analysis, would include fairness to the parties if Ontario were to assume jurisdiction, and whether assuming jurisdiction is consistent with other principles of international law. An example of the latter principles would be reciprocity—if

---

29   In Québec, conflict of laws has been largely codified in Book X of the *Civil Code of Québec*, R.S.Q. 1991, c. 64, arts. 3134–54.

30   Janet Walker, ed., "Conflict of Laws" in *Halsbury's Laws of Canada* (Toronto: LexisNexis, 2006) at para. HCF-1 *et seq.*

31   2010 ONCA 84.

32   *Rules of Civil Procedure*, R.R.O. 1990, Reg. 194.

an Ontario judge would not be prepared to recognize and enforce an extra-provincial judgment against an Ontario defendant
rendered on the same jurisdictional basis, it should not assume
jurisdiction against the extra-provincial defendant.

3. *Forum non conveniens*: A consideration of whether Ontario is the
most appropriate forum is considered only after it has been determined that there is a real and substantial connection and that
jurisdiction *simpliciter* has been established.

Courts will also take jurisdiction over a matter where a party has
consented to the jurisdiction or has appeared in the jurisdiction
to defend the matter on its merits. Likewise, parties to a contract
may agree in their contract, on an exclusive or non-exclusive basis,
that they will resolve disputes in a specified jurisdiction. Since parties may sometimes sue in a jurisdiction for purely tactical reasons
(so-called forum shopping), courts can decline jurisdiction on the
grounds of *forum non conveniens*, that is, when they are not the convenient or appropriate forum. In Ontario, Rule 17 of the *Rules of
Civil Procedure* governs service of court documents on parties outside of Ontario. There is extensive jurisprudence and commentary
surrounding application of this rule.[33] Finally, realize that issues of
jurisdiction are sometimes impacted by legislation that creates immunity from prosecution for heads of state and diplomats.[34]

• *Judgments*: When will a Canadian court enforce a court judgment
from another jurisdiction? What types of judgment can be enforced?
The answers to these questions are becoming clearer with a series of recent Supreme Court of Canada decisions.[35] The trend, simply put, is for foreign judgments to be more easily enforceable in
Canadian courts where there is a "real and substantial connection"
between the issue being litigated and the foreign jurisdiction. The
principles of *comity* ("the deference and respect due by other states
to the actions of a state legitimately taken within its territory") and
reciprocity—combined with the constitutional requirements of the
principles of order and fairness—require Canadian courts to recognize such foreign judgments. The enforcement of foreign judgments

---

33   See, for example, "Commentary on Rule 17" in Garry D. Watson & Craig Perkins,
Holmested and Watson: Ontario Civil Procedure, looseleaf (Toronto: Carswell, 1984).

34   For example, section 3 of the *State Immunity Act*, R.S.C. 1985, c. S-18, states,
subject to exceptions in the Act, that a foreign state is immune from the jurisdiction of any court in Canada.

35   See *Morguard Investments Ltd. v. De Savoye*, [1990] 3 S.C.R. 1077; *Hunt v. T & N
plc*, [1993] 4 S.C.R. 289; *Beals v. Saldanha*, 2003 SCC 72; and *Pro Swing Inc. v.
Elta Golf Inc.*, 2006 SCC 52.

in fact is no longer necessarily restricted to money judgments.[36] Resisting enforcement of a foreign judgment has become more difficult, usually requiring a party to establish that the foreign judgment was obtained by fraud, that the foreign proceedings were contrary to natural justice, or that the recognition and enforcement of the foreign judgment would be contrary to public policy.

• *Applicable law*: Which jurisdiction's laws will govern a particular transaction or issue? In most court hearings, the law of the forum (*lex fori*) will govern the issues between the parties. However, in some situations, the governing law (*lex causae*) may be different from the law of the forum, and the court must then resort to a number of "choice of law" rules, many of which have been passed down over time as Latin maxims (e.g., whether to apply the law of the place where a contract is performed, or the *lex loci solutionis*). In other situations, the parties to a contract, for example, may agree that the laws of a particular jurisdiction govern any dispute that might arise in the future, thereby requiring the court to apply a foreign law. When a foreign law applies, the party relying on that foreign law is ordinarily required to "prove" the foreign law by providing expert evidence on what the foreign law is.

D. PRINT AND ONLINE SECONDARY SOURCES OF INTERNATIONAL LAW

This section will provide information on *secondary* sources of international law, focusing on the major books, journals, encyclopedias/dictionaries, and websites that provide commentary or overviews of international legal research. As mentioned above, the resources listed below should ordinarily be the first place you go to get an explanation or overview of a particular area of international law.

1) Books

You can safely assume that someone, somewhere, has written a book on an area of international law that you need to research. The titles

---

36   *Pro Swing Inc. v. Elta Golf Inc.*, *ibid.*, where the Court suggested a flexible approach was required and that foreign equitable judgments (such as an injunction issued by a foreign court) could be recognized and enforced in Canada where the judgment was rendered by a court of competent jurisdiction, was final, and was of the type that the principle of comity requires the domestic court to enforce (at para. 31).

below are only a selected list of fairly general titles on international law. If you need to find more specific or topical books, simply try a title keyword search in a major law library catalogue using the keywords "international" and "law" plus a keyword for the particular sub-topic, for example, "environmental" if you were looking for a book on international environmental law.

a) Selected Canadian Texts on Public International Law

- Alexandrowicz, George *et al. Dimensions of Law: Canadian and International Law in the 21st Century.* Toronto: Emond Montgomery, 2004.
- Currie, John H., Craig Forcese, & Valerie Oosterveld. *International Law: Doctrine, Practice, and Theory.* Toronto: Irwin Law, 2007.
- Currie, John H. *Public International Law.* 2d ed. Toronto: Irwin Law, 2008.
- Currie, Robert J. *International and Transnational Criminal Law.* Toronto: Irwin Law, 2010.
- Fitzgerald, Oonagh E., ed. *The Globalized Rule of Law: Relationships between International and Domestic Law.* Toronto: Irwin Law, 2006.
- Forcese, Craig. *National Security Law: Canadian Practice in International Perspective.* Toronto: Irwin Law, 2008.
- Freeman, Mark & Gib van Ert. *International Human Rights Law.* Toronto: Irwin Law, 2004.
- Holding, John D. *Canadian Manual of International Air Carriage.* Toronto: Irwin Law, 2005.
- Kindred, Hugh M. *et al. International Law, Chiefly as Interpreted and Applied in Canada.* 7th ed. Toronto: Emond Montgomery, 2006.
- Schabas, William A. & Stéphane Beaulac. *International Human Rights and Canadian Law: Legal Commitment, Implementation and the Charter.* 3d ed. Toronto: Thomson Carswell, 2007.
- Van Ert, Gibran. *Using International Law in Canadian Courts.* 2d ed. Toronto: Irwin Law, 2008.

b) Selected Canadian Texts on Private International Law

- Appleton, Barry. *Navigating NAFTA: A Concise User's Guide to the North American Free Trade Agreement.* Toronto: Carswell, 1994.
- Baer, Marvin. *Private International Law in Common Law Canada: Cases, Text, and Materials.* 2d ed. Toronto: Emond Montgomery, 2003.
- Barin, Babak. *Carswell's Handbook of International Dispute Resolution Rules.* Toronto: Carswell, 1999.
- Castel, Jean G. *Introduction to Conflict of Laws.* 4th ed. Markham, ON: Butterworths, 2002.

- Gold, Edgar *et al. Maritime Law.* Toronto: Irwin Law, 2004.
- Johnson, Jon R. *International Trade Law.* Toronto: Irwin Law, 1998.
- Krishna, Vern. *Canadian International Taxation.* Looseleaf. Scarborough, ON: Carswell, 1995.
- Lemieux, Denis & Ana Stuhec. *Review of Administrative Action under NAFTA.* Scarborough, ON: Carswell, 1999.
- Nicholson, Mary Jo. *Legal Aspects of International Business: A Canadian Perspective.* 2d ed. Toronto: Emond Montgomery, 2007.
- Pitel, Stephen G.A. & Nicholas Rafferty. *Conflict of Laws.* Toronto: Irwin Law, 2010.
- Thomas, Jeffrey S. & Michael A. Meyer. *The New Rules of Global Trade: A Guide to the World Trade Organization.* Scarborough, ON: Carswell, 1997.
- Walker, Janet. *Castel & Walker: Canadian Conflict of Laws.* Looseleaf. 6th ed. Markham, ON: LexisNexis Canada, 2005.

c) **Selected American and British Texts on Public and Private International Law**

- Brownlie, Ian. *Basic Documents in International Law.* 6th ed. London: Oxford University Press, 2008.
- Brownlie, Ian. *Principles of Public International Law.* 7th ed. London: Oxford University Press, 2008.
- Buergenthal, Thomas & Sean D. Murphy. *Buergenthal and Murphy's Public International Law in a Nutshell.* 4th ed. St. Paul, MN: West Group, 2007.
- Cassese, Antonio. *International Law.* 2d ed. London: Oxford University Press, 2005.
- Chuah, Jason. *Law of International Trade.* 4th ed. London: Sweet & Maxwell/Thomson Reuters, 2009.
- Collins, Lawrence *et al.*, eds. *Dicey and Morris on the Conflict of Laws.* 14th ed. London: Sweet & Maxwell, 2006.
- Hoffman, Marci & Robert C. Berring. *International Legal Research in a Nutshell.* St. Paul, MN: Thomson/West, 2008.
- Janis, Mark. *An Introduction to International Law.* 5th ed. Frederick, MD: Aspen Publishers, 2008.
- Koskenniemi, Martti. *Sources of International Law.* Burlington, VT: Ashgate/Dartmouth, 2000.
- Malanczuk, Peter. *Akehurst's Modern Introduction to International Law.* 8th ed. New York: Routledge, 2010 [forthcoming].
- Fawcett, James, Janeen Carruthers, & Peter North. *Cheshire and North's Private International Law.* 14th ed. London: Oxford University Press, 2008.

- Rehberg, Jeanne & Radu Popa, eds., *Accidental Tourist on the New Frontier: An Introductory Guide to Global Legal Research*. Littleton, CO: F.B. Rothman, 1998.
- Sands, Philippe & Pierre Klein. *Bowett's Law of International Institutions*. 6th ed. London: Sweet & Maxwell/Thomson Reuters, 2009.
- Shaw, Malcolm N. *International Law*. 6th ed. Cambridge: Cambridge University Press, 2008.
- Symeonides, Symeon. *American Private International Law*. Frederick, MD: Aspen Publishers, 2008
- Wallace, Rebecca. *International Law*. 6th ed. London: Sweet & Maxwell, 2009.

2) Journals

Increasingly, Canadian scholars and lawyers are writing articles on international legal issues. To find law journal articles dealing with international (or foreign) law, consider first checking any of the following print or online journal indexes:

- *Index to Canadian Legal Literature*. Toronto: Carswell, 1981– [updated quarterly]. Available in print (as part of Carswell's *Canadian Abridgment*) and online through Westlaw Canada or LexisNexis Quicklaw.
- *Index to Canadian Legal Periodical Literature*. Montreal: Canadian Association of Law Libraries, 1965– [updated irregularly]. Available in print only.
- *Index to Foreign Legal Periodicals*. Chicago: American Association of Law Libraries, 1960– [updated quarterly].

Law journal articles on international or foreign legal topics are also well-indexed in the *Index to Legal Periodicals & Books* and *LegalTrac*, available online at most major academic law libraries.

The following is a list of the major Canadian law journals with an international focus:[37]

- *Asper Review of International Business and Trade Law*. Asper Program, Faculty of Law, University of Manitoba, 2001– [updated annually]. Also available on LexisNexis Quicklaw.

---

37 There are too many American, British, and other international law journals to mention. The Bora Laskin Law Library has a fairly extensive list of law journals available online at www.law-lib.utoronto.ca/journals/search.asp, where you can search on the keyword "international" to generate a list of all international law journals available online, regardless of country of publication.

- *Bulletin.* Canadian Council on International Law, 1974– [published three times per year].
- *Canada–United States Law Journal.* Canada–United States Law Institute, 1978– [published annually]. Selected coverage also available on LexisNexis Quicklaw and Westlaw Canada.
- *Canadian Foreign Policy.* Canadian Foreign Policy Publishing Group, 1992– [published three times per year].
- *Canadian International Lawyer.* Canadian Bar Association, International Law Section, 1994– [published irregularly].
- *The Canadian Yearbook of International Law.* International Law Association, Canadian Branch. University of British Columbia Press, 1963– [published annually].
- *International Insights: A Dalhousie Journal of International Affairs.* John E. Reed International Law Society, Dalhousie Law School, 1985– [published annually].
- *Journal of International Law and International Relations.* University of Toronto, Faculty of Law and Munk Centre for International Studies, 2004– [published annually].

3) Encyclopedias/Dictionaries

The three major Canadian legal encyclopedias are discussed in more detail in Chapter 2. Each of these encyclopedias provides some commentary in this area, as follows:

- The *Canadian Encyclopedic Digest* (Thomson Carswell) (print, CD-ROM, and on Westlaw Canada) has the following titles:
  » Conflict of Laws
  » International Law
  » Trade and Commerce — Foreign Investment in Canada

- *Halsbury's Laws of Canada* (LexisNexis Canada) (print and on LexisNexis Quicklaw) has the following titles (titles marked with an asterisk had not yet been published at the time of the release of this book):
  » Competition and Foreign Investment*
  » Conflict of Laws
  » Extradition and Mutual Legal Assistance*
  » International Law*

- *JurisClasseur Québec*: Collection Droit civil (LexisNexis Canada) (print and will be added to LexisNexis Quicklaw in 2010)
  » Droit international privé

In addition, volume 8(3) of *Halsbury's Laws of England* (4th ed.) provides commentary on conflict of laws, and the American *Corpus Juris Secundum* includes the following titles related to international law: Ambassadors and Consuls; Conflict of Laws; Extradition; International Law; States, Territories and Dependencies; Treaties; and War and National Defence. The American encyclopedia *American Jurisprudence*, 2d ed., includes the following titles: Ambassadors, Diplomats and Consular Officials; Conflict of Laws; Extradition; International Law; States, Territories and Dependencies; Terrorism; Treaties; and War.

In addition to the foregoing comprehensive legal encyclopedias, there are a number of other encyclopedias or dictionaries relating to international and foreign law:

- Bernhardt, Rudolf, ed. (Max Planck Institute for Comparative Public Law and International Law) *Encyclopedia of Public International Law.* Amsterdam: North-Holland, 2003 [5 volumes consolidated library edition].
- Fox, James R. *Dictionary of International and Comparative Law.* 3d ed. Dobbs Ferry, NY: Oceana Publications, 2003.
- Gibson, John S. *Dictionary of International Human Rights Law.* Lanham, MD: Scarecrow Press, 1996.
- Grant, John P. & J. Craig Barker. *Parry and Grant Encyclopaedic Dictionary of International Law.* 2d ed. Dobbs Ferry, NY: Oceana Publications, 2003.
- Lindbergh, Ernst. *Modern Dictionary of International Legal Terms: English-French-German.* Boston: Little, Brown, 1993.

Another useful reference source for international and foreign law is Chapter 5 of the *Canadian Guide to Uniform Legal Citation* (6th ed.)(the "McGill Guide").[38] This chapter discusses in detail how to properly cite treaties and international case law and has other useful information on international and foreign legal materials.

4) Case Law Digests

The *Canadian Abridgment*, discussed in more detail in Chapter 2, Section E, has case digests on the following topics: Conflict of Laws, International Law, and International Trade and Customs.

---

38 Toronto: Carswell, 2006.

The West Key Digest System, which provides digests of American cases organized by topic (as discussed in Chapter 2, Section E) has the following title: International Law.

5) Websites

There are websites too numerous to list here that provide excellent overviews or explanations of international or foreign law. The main publishers of these websites are IGOs, NGOs, law schools, universities, and other public interest groups. The sites below — listed in no particular order — are included for their quality and comprehensiveness.

- **American Society for International Law (ASIL).** *ASIL Guide to Electronic Resources for International Law.*
  www.asil.org/resource/Home.htm

  Founded in 1906, ASIL is described as "the premier membership organization in the United States dedicated to advancing the study and use of international law." The online guide listed above, which is also available in print book format, provides free, excellent information, commentary, and links on international legal topics ranging from human rights, international commercial arbitration, international criminal law, international economic law, international environmental law, international intellectual property law, international organizations, treaties, and the United Nations.

- *GlobaLex.* **Published by the Hauser Global Law School Program at NYU School of Law and edited by Mirela Roznovschi.**
  www.nyulawglobal.org/Globalex

  This excellent free site is a warehouse of online guides in areas of international, foreign, and comparative law research. For example, the guide entitled "Introduction to Public International Law Research"[39] by librarian Vicenç Feliú provides an excellent overview on the topic of public international law research.

- **Law Library Resource Xchange (LLRX.com).** *International Law Guides.*
  www.llrx.com/international_law.html

  LLRX, established in 1996, describes itself as a "free, independent, one person produced Web journal dedicated to providing legal, library, IT/IS, marketing and administrative professionals with the

---

39   Feliú, above note 13.

most up-to-date information on a wide range of Internet research and technology-related issues, applications, resources and tools." The web page above provides free links to over forty customized guides prepared by leading law librarians and lawyers on various international legal topics.

- **Library and Archives Canada.** *International Organizations and Related Information.*
  www.collectionscanada.gc.ca/the-public/005-1121-e.html

This web page provides links to international organizations, constitutions of the world, and treaties and international covenants.

- **Foreign Affairs and International Trade Canada.**
  www.international.gc.ca

The mandate of the Department of Foreign Affairs and International Trade Canada—known by its acronym DFAIT—as stated on its website is:
  » ensuring that Canada's foreign policy reflects true Canadian values and advances Canada's national interests;
  » strengthening rules-based trading arrangements and expanding free and fair market access at bilateral, regional, and global levels; and
  » working with a range of partners inside and outside government to achieve increased economic opportunity and enhanced security for Canada and for Canadians at home and abroad.

Two areas of its website frequented by legal researchers include the section on Export and Import Controls and on Trade Negotiations and Agreements.

- **University of Ottawa. JuriGlobe—World Legal Systems.**
  www.juriglobe.ca

As stated on its website, JuriGlobe is "a research group formed by professors from the Faculty of Law of the University of Ottawa, which focuses on the development of a multilingual information data bank, accessible to all on the internet, containing general information relating to the different legal systems in the world, to the different official languages and to some of the most important international commercial conventions, as well as other multilateral commercial tools."

- **University of Michigan Documents Center.** *International and Related Organizations.*
  www.lib.umich.edu/govdocs/intl.html

This site provides extensive links to various IGOs, NGOs, and other international agencies and treaties.

- **Harvard Law School.** *Foreign & International Law Resources: An Annotated Guide to Web Sites Around the World.*
  www.law.harvard.edu/library/research/guides/int_foreign/web-resources/index.html

  Extensive links, with annotations.

- **Bora Laskin Law Library, University of Toronto, Faculty of Law.** *Women's Human Rights Resources.*
  www.law-lib.utoronto.ca/Diana

  The main goal of the Women's Human Rights Resources site is to assist individuals and organizations in using international women's human rights law to promote women's rights. Their database is organized into fourteen subject areas related to women's human rights, and within each subject area links are provided to scholarly literature, books, case law, and treaties, with full-text information being provided, wherever possible.

- **Louise Tsang.** *Private International Law.*
  www.asil.org/pil1.cfm

  On the website of The American Society of International Law (ASIL), this excellent online guide provides commentary on researching private international law on the Web, in addition to providing links to major sites, including UNCITRAL, UNIDROIT, and the Hague Conference on Private International Law, in addition to other topical sites relating to international trade and business.

- **Marci Hoffman.** *Revised Guide to International Trade Law Sources on the Internet.*
  www.llrx.com/features/trade3.htm

  International and foreign law librarian Marci Hoffman provides excellent commentary on researching international trade law, including providing links for finding WTO, GATT, and NAFTA decisions and other information.

- *INT-LAW: Foreign and International Law Librarians List.*
  http://listserver.ciesin.columbia.edu

  This is a fairly active listserv of foreign and international law librarians and other researchers interested in international and foreign legal research. To register for this listserv, go to http://listserver.ciesin.

columbia.edu and choose "INT-LAW." Archives of recent INT-LAW messages can be found online at the site. For members of the American Association of Law Libraries there is also the Foreign, Comparative and International Law SIS Listserv (see the "Online Discussion" link at www.aallnet.org).

E. PRINT AND ONLINE PRIMARY SOURCES OF INTERNATIONAL LAW

In the previous section, discussion focused on *secondary* sources of international law, such as leading books, law journals, dictionaries/encyclopedias, and websites that explain international law. In this section, the discussion will focus on print and online *primary* sources of international law in the form of treaties and international case law.

1) Treaties

Treaties — in their broad sense — are the means by which nation states enter into bilateral or multilateral agreements on subjects of mutual interest, ranging anywhere from postal services to the environment to extradition. In Canada, the Treaty Section of the Department of Foreign Affairs is responsible for the implementation and publication of treaties entered into by Canada. These treaties are officially published in the *Canada Treaty Series*, available at most major academic law libraries. The Canadian government also makes access to Canadian treaties accessible through their Canada Treaty Information website at www.treaty-accord.gc.ca. This website provides access to lists of treaties Canada has entered into, along with the full text of most treaties. Treaties are divided between bilateral and multilateral, and "word wheels" are provided to allow the searcher, if desired, to choose a treaty by subject, country, or IGO. Another important source of Canadian–American treaties is the Canado-american Treaties website available online at www.lexum.umontreal.ca/ca_us/index_en.html. This site provides free access to the text of all bilateral treaties established between the United States and Canada from 1783 to 1997.

Treaties entered into by other countries are also published in official treaty series in print but will not necessarily be widely held by law libraries in Canada. Fortunately, most countries now publish online versions of their treaty series. Here is a partial list of some of the international treaties sites most likely of interest to Canadian legal researchers:

- **U.K. Treaties:** www.fco.gov.uk/en/about-us/publications-and-documents/treaties
- **U.S. Treaties:** www.state.gov/s/l/treaty/index.htm
- **U.S. Treaties** (via Tufts): http://fletcher.tufts.edu/multi/multilaterals.html
- **E.U. Treaties:** http://europa.eu/abc/treaties/index_en.htm
- **France Treaties (*Base Pacte*):** www.doc.diplomatie.gouv.fr/pacte
- **Australia Treaties:** www.austlii.edu.au/au/other/dfat

However, one of the most prolific producers of international treaties and other primary sources of international law is the United Nations (www.un.org), which was established on 24 October 1945, when fifty-one original member countries, including France, the U.K., and the U.S., ratified the *UN Charter*. Today, nearly every nation in the world belongs to the UN, bringing its membership total to 192 countries. United Nations members are sovereign countries. As such, the UN is not a world government, and it does not make laws. It does, however, provide the means to help resolve international conflicts and formulate policies on matters affecting all of us. The United Nations has six main organs. Five of them — the General Assembly, the Security Council, the Economic and Social Council, the Trusteeship Council, and the Secretariat — are based at the UN Headquarters in New York. The sixth main organ is the International Court of Justice, located in The Hague.

Because the UN website is so massive, it helps to be aware of some online guides available on their site to help with research:

- **UN Documentations: Research Guide**:
  www.un.org/Depts/dhl/resguide/symbol.htm
  Among other things, this guide explains UN symbols (e.g., E/CN.4/Sub.2/AC.2/1987/WP.4/Add.1)

- **Official Web Site Locator of the United Nations Systems of Organizations**:
  www.unsystem.org

- **UN Organization Chart**:
  www.un.org/aboutun/chart.html

An excellent source of UN treaties is the UN Treaty Database available online at http://treaties.un.org. This database provides access to the full text of treaties from the *United Nations Treaty Series* as well as HTML versions of Treaties Deposited with the Secretary-General. There is a very current table indicating the location and status of each treaty, and full text of all declarations and reservations of parties up to the date indicated in the introductory section, usually within no more than two or three days.

In addition, the United Nations Official Document System (UN-ODS), available online at www.ods.un.org, is a full text, searchable subscription database of nearly all United Nations official documents from 1992 onwards. Searching may be performed by UN document number, keywords, author, and with date restriction. Documents display in PDF or TIFF format; appropriate plug-ins can be easily downloaded, and documents may be printed or saved to disk.

One final important source of treaty information—although unofficial—is the highly cited *International Legal Materials* (I.L.M.), published by the American Society for International Law (ASIL) since 1962. It is published bimonthly and includes the full text of new, important treaties in addition to other important legal materials, including selected international case law. This publication is also available as a full-text database on both LexisNexis Quicklaw and Westlaw Canada, as well as by subscription on HeinOnline.

Treaties or conventions relating to *private* international law are readily found online and will be the way most researchers access such materials. Set out below are some of the major primary sources of private international law available on the Internet:

- **Hague Conference on Private International Law**.
  www.hcch.net

  As stated on its website, The Hague Conference on Private International Law is an intergovernmental organization, the purpose of which is "to work for the progressive unification of the rules of private international law." There are seventy member States with a larger number of non-member States becoming parties to various Hague Conventions. There are thirty-eight Conventions entered into, ranging in topics from civil procedure, the international sale of goods, child support, to enforcement of judgments, to name a few. The fulltext of conventions is provided, along with full status information.

- **UNCITRAL—United Nations Commission on International Trade Law**.
  www.uncitral.org

  The mandate of UNCITRAL is "the progressive harmonization and unification of the law of international trade." UNCITRAL has produced a number of texts in fields of the international sale of goods, arbitration, insolvency, international payments, transport, and e-commerce, in the form of conventions, model laws, guides to enactment, legislative guides, legislative recommendations, and model contract rules, all available on the website.

- **UNIDROIT — International Institute for the Unification of Private Law.**
  www.unidroit.org

  UNIDROIT is an independent intergovernmental organization whose purpose is to study needs and methods for modernizing, harmonizing, and coordinating private and, in particular, commercial law as between States and groups of States. There are currently sixty-three member States, including Canada, the United Kingdom, and the United States. The website contains the full text of the UNIDROIT Conventions, including, for example, the *Convention relating to a Uniform Law on the International Sale of Goods* (The Hague, 1964). The site also contains, among other things, UNILEX, a database of international case law and bibliography on the *United Nations Convention on Contracts for the International Sale of Goods* (CISG) and on the *UNIDROIT Principles of International Commercial Contract*.

2) International Courts

There are a number of important international courts, the oldest continuing one being the International Court of Justice through the United Nations, whose decisions are available online at www.icj-cij.org. As explained on its website, the International Court of Justice has two main roles: (i) to settle in accordance with international law the legal disputes submitted to it by States, and (ii) to give advisory opinions on legal questions referred to it by duly authorized international organs and agencies. The court only hears decisions by party States who are members of the United Nations.

Rather than individually listing the websites for the other major international courts, readers are encouraged to consult the excellent Project on International Courts and Tribunals website at www.pict-pcti.org. This project, established in 1997, is now undertaken by the Centre on International Cooperation and the Centre for International Courts and Tribunals, University College London. Its purpose, according to its website, is to couple "academic research with concrete action aimed at facilitating the work of international courts and tribunals at developing the lawyering skills of potential actors, in particular, in developing countries and economies-in-transition." This site, among other things, provides academic research, bibliographies, and links to all of the major international courts and tribunals, including the following:

- International Court of Justice (ICJ)
- International Tribunal for the Law of the Sea (ITLOS)
- Dispute Settlement System of the World Trade Organization (WTO)
- International Criminal Tribunal for the former Yugoslavia (ICTY)
- International Criminal Tribunal for Rwanda (ICTR)
- International Criminal Court (ICC)
- Internationalized criminal tribunals in Sierra Leone, East Timor, Kosovo, and Cambodia
- European Court of Human Rights (ECHR)
- European Court of Justice and the Court of First Instance (ECJ/CFI)
- European Free Trade Association Court (EFTA)
- Benelux Court of Justice (BeneluxCJ)
- Inter-American Court of Human Rights (IACHR)
- Andean Court of Justice (TJAC)
- Central American Court of Justice (CACJ)
- Caribbean Court of Justice (CCJ)
- Common Court of Justice and Arbitration of the Organization for the Harmonization of Corporate Law in Africa (OHADA)
- Court of Justice of the Common Market for Eastern and Southern Africa (COMESA)
- African Commission and Court of Human and Peoples' Rights (ACHPR)
- Permanent Court of Arbitration (PCA)
- International Centre for Settlement of Investment Disputes (ICSID)
- Arbitral decisions under the North American Free Trade Agreement (NAFTA)

The international courts or tribunals have fairly extensive information on their individual websites that explain the procedures for that court or tribunal in addition to providing access to their decisions.

F. RESEARCHING THE DOMESTIC LAWS OF FOREIGN COUNTRIES

Governments around the world are increasingly publishing their legislation and case law for free on the Internet. The scope and depth of such material is variable from country to country. Equally important is the notion that it is rare for countries whose official languages are not English to publish their primary sources of law in English. Therefore, do not expect to get Italian case law in English for free on the Internet. Most primary sources of law are published in the vernacular or "native" tongue. It also goes without saying that lawyers should not provide legal advice outside of the jurisdiction in which they are licensed to practise law. Nonetheless, access to foreign laws still plays an important role for lawyers in getting a sense of what foreign law might be with the goal of getting an understanding of the foreign law and assessing when it might be necessary to retain counsel from that foreign jurisdiction to provide a formal legal opinion.

There are a number of excellent print and online sources for finding the domestic laws of foreign countries (set out below in no particular order):[40]

- **Reynolds, Thomas H. & Arturo A. Flores.** *Foreign Law: Current Sources of Codes and Basic Legislation in Jurisdictions of the World.* Littleton, CO: F.B. Rothman, 1989. Also available online via subscription is the *Foreign Law Guide*: www.foreignlawguide.com

  As described in the online version of this product, the *Foreign Law Guide* "is designed for the practitioner, scholar, and researcher and provides essential information on primary and secondary sources of foreign law—what it is, where to find it, and how to use it. It contains information on more than 170 jurisdictions from major nations to crown colonies, semi-independent states and supra-national regional organizations. The work is comprehensive in content and global in scope and contains exhaustive links within the work and to many URLs on the world level."

- **LexisNexis Martindale-Hubbell.** *International Law Digest* (3 volumes). Also available online on LexisNexis Quicklaw by subscription.

  This three-volume set, often included in the multi-volume legal directory published by Martindale-Hubbell, provides digests of the laws of the fifty states, the District of Columbia, Puerto Rico, and the U.S. Virgin Islands, and provides summaries of the laws of over sixty countries, in addition to the complete texts of over fifty Uniform and Model Acts and International Conventions.

- **Redden, Kenneth Robert, ed.** *Modern Legal Systems Cyclopedia* (10 volumes). Buffalo, NY: W.S. Hein, 1984– [updated periodically].

  This multi-volume (red) set is organized by regions of the world and provides detailed information about the legal systems of individual countries within those regions.

---

40   In this section, I use the term "foreign law" to not necessarily include British, American, or Australian law. To conduct British, American, or Australian legal research, see the relevant sections of Chapters 2 & 3.

- **Germain, Claire M.** *Germain's Transnational Law Research: A Guide for Attorneys.* Ardsley-on-Hudson, NY: Transnational Juris Publishing, Inc., 1991– [updated periodically].

  This practical text by Cornell Law Librarian and Professor Claire Germain provides an excellent overview of cross-jurisdictional legal research, particularly from an American point of view.

- **Blanpain, Roger, ed.** *International Encyclopaedia of Laws.* Deventer, Netherlands: Kluwer Law and Taxation Publishers, 1994– [updated periodically].

  This multi-volume encyclopedia is organized in the following broad topics: civil procedure, commercial and economic law, constitutional law, contracts, corporation and partnership law, criminal law, environmental law, family and succession law, insurance law, intellectual property law, intergovernmental organizations, medical law, social security law, and transport law. Within each topic, information is provided on primary and secondary sources of law for about sixty different countries.

- *GlobaLex.* Published by the Hauser Global Law School Program at NYU School of Law and edited by Mirela Roznovschi. Online: www. nyulawglobal.org/Globalex

  This website, mentioned in Section D(5), above in this chapter, has separate guides for each of well over 100 countries, providing advice on how to conduct legal research in each country, ranging from Afghanistan to Zimbabwe.

- **Law Library Resource Xchange (LLRX.com).** *Comparative and Foreign Law Guides.*
  www.llrx.com/comparative_and_foreign_law.html

  This resource is an excellent starting point when conducting research on the domestic laws of foreign countries. The goal of the LLRX editors is to eventually have a "Guide to Doing Legal Research in . . ." for every country of the world. There are currently over fifty countries or regions represented by these online guides.

- **GLIN — Nations of the World**
  www.loc.gov/law/help/guide/nations.php

  This web page, from the Law Library of Congress Global Legal Information Network, provides an alphabetical list of links to countries of the world. At each country link are a series of well-organized, "standardized" links to the following sources of law for each country:

constitution, executive, judicial, legislative, legal guides and miscellaneous, and general sources.

- **AustLII's World Law**
  www.worldlii.org

  This web page, from the Australasian Legal Information Institute, provides an alphabetical list of links for countries of the world. At each country link are further links to both primary sources of law (legislation and cases) and other background material for each country, where available.

- **Findlaw List of Countries**
  www.findlaw.com/12international/countries/index.html

  This is Findlaw's alphabetical list of countries (currently about ninety, from Afghanistan to Zimbabwe). You will find that the quality of information for each country is quite variable and often contains links only to other pages that provide links. The page for Turkey, for example, ranges from useful links to the Turkish Grand National Assembly to the Ankara University Faculty of Law.

In addition to the print materials and websites listed above on foreign law, each of LexisNexis Quicklaw and Westlaw Canada are substantially adding legal materials to their databases from jurisdictions outside of Canada (primarily British, Australian, and European). Note that LexisNexis Quicklaw has some unique Caribbean and African content. There are also a number of other commercial online services that provide access to foreign laws; a few examples of these commercial databases include, but are not limited to, the following:[41]

- **Africa**: Jutastat: www.jutastat.com. This commercial site provides Internet access (for a fee) to various African legislation and case law for various countries, including South Africa, Botswana, Zimbabwe, Namibia, and Tanzania. Juta also publishes print and CD-ROM African-related legal publications.
- **Africa**: LawAfrica.com: www.lawafrica.com. This commercial site provides limited free information on African legal matters but also provides an online (and print) subscription to the *East Africa Law Reports* and the *LawAfrica Law Reports*.
- **Caribbean**: CariLaw: http://carilaw.cavehill.uwi.edu. This commercial database is provided by the University of West Indies Faculty of

---

41   For more websites, see the NYU GlobaLex link, mentioned above in this section, where information is provided under each country's listing on the commercial database providers available for the particular country, where applicable.

Law Library and provides online access (by subscription). The database has over 30,000 Caribbean decisions, including:

- » Decisions of the Judicial Committee of the Privy Council (PC) and present-day Supreme/High Courts and Courts of Appeal of major Caribbean islands
- » The West Indian Court of Appeal (1920–1958)
- » Windward Islands and Leeward Islands Court of Appeal (1940–1967)
- » The Federal Supreme Court (1958–62)
- » The British Caribbean Court of Appeal (1962–1966)
- » West Indies Associated States Supreme Court (Court of Appeal and High Court) (1967–1980)
- » Eastern Caribbean Court of Appeal (1980 to present)
- » Eastern Caribbean Supreme Court (1980 to present)
- » Decisions from special courts such as the industrial Courts of Antigua and Barbados and Trinidad and Tobago, the industrial Disputes Tribunal of Jamaica, the Tax Appeal Board of Trinidad and Tobago, and the Revenue Court of Jamaica.

- **China**: LawInfo China: www.lawinfochina.com. Laws, regulations, and cases of the People's Republic of China are provided by subscription. These include basic laws of the National People's Congress and regulations of the State Council from 1949 to present, and selected cases of the Supreme People's Court and Supreme People's Procurate. There is full text in English translation and original Chinese.
- **France**: JurisClasseur (Lexis): www.juris-classeur.com. This subscription database provides extensive treatment of searchable and browsable French legislation and case law in addition to French legal periodicals dating back to the 1970s.
- **Germany**: Beck.de: www.beck.de. Beck Online provides access to German case law, legislation, and commentary (by subscription).
- **Singapore**: Singapore Lawnet Legal Workbench: www.lawnet.com. sg. This commercial database for the law of Singapore provides access to fully searchable, comprehensive databases of statutes, subsidiary legislation, case law (all cases in the *Singapore Law Reports* and the *Malayan Law Journal*), as well as treaties and secondary sources.

G. SAMPLE QUESTIONS AND SUGGESTED APPROACHES

Set out in this section are three hypothetical questions that a Canadian legal researcher might have, along with suggested approaches to answering these questions, with an emphasis on using free Internet resources, where feasible.

How do I serve Ontario court papers on a Swedish company?

There are several possible approaches to answering this question. Ontario litigators might think of checking Rule 17 (Service outside of Ontario) from one of the annotated versions of the *Ontario Rules of Civil Procedure* where the Rule itself mentions the *Hague Convention on the Service Abroad of Judicial and Extrajudicial Documents in Civil or Commercial Matters* (the annotated versions of the Rules in print provide added commentary).

Simply "Googling" the name of this Convention results in finding it on the first hit. The full text of the Convention is available online, and by clicking on the "Full Status" there is a link for Sweden that explains who the "contact" is within Sweden for the purpose of accepting foreign court documents under the Convention.

Alternative approaches: The *International Law Digests* (in print) from Martindale-Hubbell (part of its multi-volume Directory) has a listing for Sweden that mentions that Sweden is a party to this Convention. That might be enough to trigger one to search online for the Convention.

I have a citation to E/CN.4/Sub.2/1997/1. What is it and how can I get it?

Even if one is not certain this is a United Nations document symbol, simply Googling the citation retrieves the document on the first hit. The document turns out to be a 1997 Provisional Agenda from the Sub Commission on Prevention of Discrimination and Protection of Minorities of the Commission on Human Rights. The symbol/citation translates as follows:

E   = Economic and Social Council
CN.4   = Commission on Human Rights
Sub.2 = Sub Commission on Prevention of Discrimination and Protection of Minorities
1997   = year
1   = document #

I heard about the *Waldman* decision at the "United Nations" dealing with the lack of funding for Jewish schooling in Ontario; I think he was represented by Toronto lawyer, Raj Anand. Where can I get a copy of this decision?

Once again, Googling the words (without quotations) — waldman catholic school anand — brings a number of hits, albeit none of the first 10 results are official URLs from the UN. However, the first result appears to be an unofficial version of the decision from the Human Rights Library at the University of Minnesota. Looking at that document reveals a UN document symbol of CCPR/C/67/D/694/1996.

Googling that symbol brings up the official page from within the UN site for that decision. Alternatively, if one knew it was likely a decision from the Human Rights Committee, one could browse through the UN website for the document.

LEGAL RESEARCH BY TOPIC

This chapter provides information on Canadian legal resources, broken down into the following forty-five law-related topics:

A. Aboriginal law
B. Administrative law
C. Alternative dispute resolution (ADR)
D. Banking law
E. Bankruptcy and insolvency law
F. Charities and not-for-profit law
G. Civil procedure
H. Communications law
I. Competition and antitrust law
J. Constitutional and human rights law
K. Construction law
L. Contract and agency law
M. Corporate and partnership law
N. Criminal law
O. Crown law
P. Damages and remedies law
Q. Debtor/creditor law
R. Education law
S. Employment law
T. Environmental and natural resources law
U. Evidence law

V.   Family law
W.   Health and medical law
X.   Immigration and refugee law
Y.   Insurance law
Z.   Intellectual property law/e-commerce law
AA. International and foreign law
BB. Introduction to law/legal systems
CC. Labour law
DD. Landlord and tenant law/commercial leasing
EE. Legal practice
FF. Media law/defamation
GG. Motor vehicle and transportation law
HH. Municipal and planning law
II.   Occupational health and safety
JJ.   Pension law
KK. Personal property security law
LL.   Privacy law
MM. Property law (real and personal)
NN. Securities law
OO. Sports and entertainment law
PP.   Taxation law
QQ. Tort law
RR.   Trusts, wills, and estates law
SS.   Workers' compensation law

Included for each topic is a list of the following information:

- Short scope note for the topic
- Library of Congress Subject Headings
- Leading treatises
- Journals, if any
- Encyclopedia titles, as applicable[1]
- Case digests, as applicable
- Print case law reporters (full-text), if any
- Relevant online databases or CD-ROMs
- Relevant websites, if any

---

1   References to titles for the *Canadian Encyclopedic Digest* (CED) were taken from the
    online version on Westlaw Canada. Where there is both an Ontario and Western
    version of the CED available, this is indicated. There are both print and online
    versions for each of the CED and *Halsbury's Laws of Canada*. At the time of publica-
    tion of this book there were a number of titles from *Halsbury's Laws of Canada* that
    were scheduled for publication but that were not yet published. Those yet-to-be
    published titles have been marked with an asterisk (*) in the list below.

Readers should use this chapter when they are starting a new legal research project. Once the applicable broad area of law has been identified for the problem (e.g., "evidence law"), consult that particular section of this chapter to gain a quick overview of relevant resources for that topic to help reduce the risk of missing any obvious possible sources of information.

Due to lack of space, the following categories of law-related material were not included in the lists below:

- *Annual "desk copies" of consolidated legislation*: The major legal publishers have a number of softcover books published annually of consolidated legislation (e.g., Carswell's *Consolidated Bank Act and Regulations*). While these are convenient for some lawyers, they are not included below since they are often only a reprint of statutes and regulations that you can otherwise find online.
- *Casebooks intended for law school courses*: A number of law school professors have published "casebooks" intended primarily for teaching the particular area of law under consideration (e.g., Marvin Baer's *Private International Law in Common Law Canada: Cases, Text, and Materials*, 2d ed., published by Emond Montgomery). Since the main purpose of these casebooks is to teach the topic, they tend to raise more questions than they answer. As such, they tend to be less useful for legal research and are therefore not included below.
- *Canadian law-related blogs*: Chapter 10 discusses law-related blogs (there are hundreds of them). To find law-related blogs by topic, go to *Lawblogs* (www.lawblogs.ca) or the American Bar Association Journal Blawg Directory (www.abajournal.com/blawgs/).

In addition, not every possible online "library" or "database" of the major online publishers (discussed in Chapter 6) is included in the materials below (since there are hundreds of such databases for each publisher). As such, always check the source directory provided by these online publishers to check for additional material.

Every effort has been made in the list below to include the most recent editions of books listed at the time of publication of this book.[2] Inevitably, publishers will issue new editions or publish previously unpublished titles. To check for newer materials, consult one of the online library catalogues listed in Chapter 2 or visit the websites of the major Canadian legal publishers (listed in Table 9.1 in Chapter 9).

---

2   Some of the books published in 2010 listed in this chapter were not available for review at the time of publication of this book. Double-check the listing on the publisher's website to verify that the book was actually published.

A. ABORIGINAL LAW

Scope	Aboriginal law in Canada is governed largely by federal legislation such as the *Indian Act*, R.S.C. 1985, c. I-5, an Act administered by Indian and Northern Affairs Canada. Case law is highly relevant and often involves issues of constitutional law and fiduciary law.
Subject headings	Native Peoples—Canada—Legal status, laws, etc. Indians of North America—Canada—Legal status, laws, etc. Indigenous peoples—Canada—Legal status, laws, etc.
Books	Canada. Royal Commission on Aboriginal Peoples. *Report of the Royal Commission on Aboriginal Peoples.* Ottawa, ON: The Commission, 1996. Also available on CD-ROM and online: www.ainc-inac.gc.ca/ap/rrc-eng.asp.

Crane, Brian, Robert Mainville, & Martin W. Mason. *First Nations Governance Law.* 2d ed. Markham, ON: LexisNexis Canada, 2008.

Elliott, David W., ed. *Law and Aboriginal Peoples of Canada.* 5th ed. North York, ON: Captus Press, 2005.

Flatters, Michael J. *The Taxation and Financing of Aboriginal Businesses in Canada.* Looseleaf. Toronto: Carswell, 1998.

Gilbert, Larry. *Entitlement to Indian Status and Membership Codes in Canada.* Scarborough, ON: Carswell, 1996.

Henderson, James (Sákéj) Youngblood. *Treaty Rights in the Constitution of Canada.* Toronto: Thomson Carswell, 2007.

Henderson, James (Sákéj) Youngblood, Marjorie Benson, & Isobel H. Findlay. *Aboriginal Tenure in the Constitution of Canada.* Scarborough, ON: Carswell, 2000.

Imai, Shin. *The 2010 Annotated Indian Act and Aboriginal Constitutional Provisions.* Toronto: Carswell, 2009 [annual].

Law Commission of Canada & the Association of Iroquois and Allied Indians. *In Whom We Trust: A Forum on Fiduciary Relationships.* Toronto: Irwin Law, 2002.

Macaulay, Mary Locke. *Aboriginal & Treaty Rights Practice.* Looseleaf. Toronto: Carswell, 2000.

Magnet, Joseph & Dwight Dorey, eds. *Aboriginal Rights Litigation.* Toronto: LexisNexis Canada, 2003.

Magnet, Joseph & Dwight Dorey, eds. *Legal Aspects of Aboriginal Business Development.* Markham, ON: LexisNexis Butterworths, 2005.

Magnet, Joseph. *Litigating Aboriginal Culture.* Edmonton: Juriliber, 2005.

McCabe, J. Timothy S. *The Honour of the Crown and its Fiduciary Duties to Aboriginal Peoples.* Markham, ON: LexisNexis Canada, 2008.

Books	Morellato, Maria. *Aboriginal Law: Developments Since Delga-muukw*. Aurora, ON: Canada Law Book, 2009. Olthuis, John *et al.*, eds. *Aboriginal Law Handbook*. 3d ed. Toronto: Carswell, 2008. Reiter, Robert Alan. *The Law of First Nations*. Edmonton, AB: Juris Analytica Publishing, 1996. Salembier, J. Paul *et al.*, eds. *Modern First Nations Legislation Annotated*. Toronto: LexisNexis Canada, 2010 [annual]. Woodward, Jack. *Native Law*. Looseleaf. Toronto: Carswell, 1989.
Journals	*Indigenous Law Journal* (University of Toronto, Faculty of Law). Some content available online: www.indigenouslawjournal. org. Also available on LexisNexis Quicklaw and HeinOnline.
Encyclopedias	*Canadian Encyclopedic Digest*: Aboriginal Law *Halsbury's Laws of Canada*: Aboriginal Law*
Case digests	Canada Aboriginal Law Digest (LexisNexis Quicklaw) *Canadian Abridgment* (Carswell): Aboriginal law caseAlert — Aboriginal Law (Canada Law Book)
Case law reporters	*Canadian Native Law Reporter* (University of Saskatchewan, Native Law Centre)
Databases and CD-ROMs	LexisNexis Quicklaw: Aboriginal Law Cases — Topical LexisNexis Quicklaw: *Canadian Native Law Reporter*
Websites	Aboriginal Canada Portal: www.aboriginalcanada.gc.ca Assembly of First Nations: www.afn.ca Indian and Northern Affairs Canada: www.ainc-inac.gc.ca Indigenous Bar Association: www.indigenousbar.ca Royal Commission Report on Aboriginal Peoples: www.ainc-inac.gc.ca/ap/rrc-eng.asp UBC Library, "First Nations Law" (Research Guide): www.library.ubc.ca/xwi7xwa/law.htm University of Saskatchewan, "Canadian Native Law Cases": http://library2.usask.ca/native/cnlch.html

B. ADMINISTRATIVE LAW

Scope	Administrative law in Canada is a well-defined area of law due to the proliferation of government regulatory bodies in the past half-decade. Most administrative law arises through decisions of both provincial and federal courts and administrative tribunals, although many regulatory bodies, and the procedures they must follow, are governed by legislation. In addition, most jurisdictions have legislation, such as the *Judicial Review Procedure Act*, R.S.B.C. 1996, c. 241, specifically governing procedure to appear before or appeal from regulatory bodies.
Subject headings	Administrative law — Canada Judicial review of administrative acts — Canada
Books	Blais, Marie-Hélène *et al. Standards of Review of Federal Administrative Tribunals, 2007 edition*. Markham, ON: LexisNexis Canada, 2007. Blake, Sara. *Administrative Law in Canada*. 4th ed. Markham, ON: LexisNexis Butterworths, 2006. Also available by subscription on LexisNexis Quicklaw. Braverman, Lisa S. *Administrative Tribunals: A Legal Handbook*. Aurora, ON: Canada Law Book, 2002. Brown, Donald J.M. *Judicial Review of Administrative Action in Canada*. Looseleaf. Toronto: Canvasback Publishing, 1998. Dussault, René & Louis Borgeat. *Administrative Law: A Treatise*. 2d ed. Toronto: Carswell, 1988. Elliott, David W. *Administrative Law and Process*. Rev. 3d ed. Concord, ON: Captus Press, 2003. Elliott, David W. *Judicial Control of Administrative Action*. 4th ed. Concord, ON: Captus Press, 2005. Garant, Patrice. *Droit administratif*. 5e éd. Cowansville, QC: Éditions Y. Blais, 2004. Huscroft, Grant & Michael Taggart. *Inside and Outside Canadian Administrative Law: Essays in Honour of David Mullan*. Toronto: University of Toronto Press, 2006. Jones, David Phillip & Anne S. de Villars. *Principles of Administrative Law*. 5th ed. Toronto: Carswell, 2009. Jones, Gareth. *Conducting Administrative, Oversight & Ombudsman Investigations*. Aurora, ON: Canada Law Book, 2009. Kavanagh, John. *A Guide to Judicial Review*. 2d ed. Toronto: Carswell, 1984. Kligman, Robert. *Bias*. Toronto: LexisNexis Canada, 1998.

Books	Law Society of Upper Canada. *Special Lectures 2001: Constitutional and Administrative Law.* Toronto: Irwin Law, 2001.
	Swaigen, John. *Administrative Law: Principles and Advocacy.* 2d ed. Toronto: Emond Montgomery, 2010.
	Macaulay, Robert W. & James L.H. Sprague. *Hearings Before Administrative Tribunals.* 3d ed. Toronto: Thomson Carswell, 2007.
	Manuel, William J. & H. Christina Donszelmann. *Law of Administrative Investigations and Prosecutions.* Aurora, ON: Canada Law Book, 1999.
	Moskoff, Franklin R. *Administrative Tribunals: A Practice Handbook for Legal Counsel.* Aurora, ON: Canada Law Book, 1989.
	Mullan, David. *Administrative Law.* Toronto: Irwin Law, 2001.
	Ratushny, Ed. *The Conduct of Public Inquiries: Law, Policy, and Practice.* Toronto: Irwin Law, 2009
	Régimbald, Guy. *Canadian Administrative Law.* Markham, ON: LexisNexis Canada, 2008.
	Ruel, Simon. *The Law of Public Inquiries.* Toronto: Carswell, 2010.
	Salembier, Paul. *Regulatory Law and Practice in Canada.* Markham, ON: LexisNexis Butterworths, 2004.
	Sossin, Lorne. *Boundaries of Judicial Review: The Law of Justiciability in Canada.* Toronto: Carswell, 1999.
	Sossin, Lorne M. & Colleen Flood, *Administrative Law in Context.* Toronto: Emond Montgomery, 2008.
	Sprague, James L.H. *The Annotated British Columbia Administrative Tribunals Act.* Toronto: Thomson/Carswell, 2005 [annual].
Journals	*Canadian Journal of Administrative Law & Practice* (Carswell). Available on Westlaw Canada (database: CJALP) from v. 11, 1997–98.
Encyclopedias	*Canadian Encyclopedic Digest:* • Administrative Law • Public Inquiries • Public Utilities (Ontario and Western) • References and Inquiries (Ontario and Western) *Halsbury's Laws of Canada:* • Administrative Law • Public Inquiries* *JurisClasseur Québec:* Collection Droit public (Droit administratif)
Case digests	Canada Administrative Law Digest (LexisNexis Quicklaw) *Canadian Abridgment* (Carswell): Administrative law caseAlert—Administrative Law (Canada Law Book)

Case digests	Hamilton, Keith R. *Self-Governing Professions: Digests of Court Decisions.* Looseleaf. Aurora, ON: Canada Law Book, 1995. Harper Grey Administrative Law NetLetter — Digests (November 2006) (LexisNexis Quicklaw)
Case law reporters	*Administrative Law Reports* (Carswell) *Reid's Administrative Law* (Administrative Law Publishing, 1992–2000)
Databases and CD-ROMs	CanLII (www.canlii.org). CanLII is developing extensive databases of decisions of Canadian federal and provincial administrative tribunals and boards. Federal tribunal and board decision coverage, for example, includes decisions from the Canada Industrial Relations Board, Canadian Human Rights Tribunal, Canadian International Trade Tribunal, Competition Tribunal, Immigration and Refugee Board of Canada, Privacy Commissioner of Canada, Public Service Labour Relations Board, and Public Service Staffing Tribunal (scope varies by board or tribunal). Provincial coverage is also very good. LexisNexis Quicklaw: Administrative Law Cases — Topical LexisNexis Quicklaw: There are numerous databases of decisions from federal and provincial tribunals. Select "Administrative Procedure & Litigation" under "Topics" in the Source Directory.

C. ALTERNATIVE DISPUTE RESOLUTION (ADR)

Scope	Alternative dispute resolution — or ADR — has developed into its own discipline and practice area, in part because of the delays inherent in the traditional litigation system: individuals and companies need a fast, effective method to resolve disputes. ADR includes arbitration (where parties submit their dispute to one or more impartial persons for a final and binding ruling) and mediation (where a neutral person tries to mediate a settlement between the parties but does not have the power to make a binding ruling on the parties). ADR involves a combination of legislation (i.e., Ontario's *Arbitration Act, 1991*, S.O. 1991, c. 17), the possible adoption of arbitration rules or procedures from various organizations (such as the American Arbitration Association), contract law, and advocacy skills.
Subject headings	Dispute resolution (Law) — Canada

Books	Adams, George W. *Mediating Justice: Legal Dispute Negotiations*. Toronto: CCH Canadian, 2003.
	Barin, Babak. *Carswell's Handbook of International Dispute Resolution Rules*. Toronto: Carswell, 1999.
	Casey, Brian & Janet Mills. *Arbitration Law of Canada: Practice and Procedure*. Huntington, NY: Juris, 2005.
	Chornenki, Genevieve A. & Christine E. Hart. *Bypass Court: A Dispute Resolution Handbook*. 3d ed. Markham, ON: LexisNexis Butterworths, 2005.
	Corry, David J. & Courtenay Mercier. *Negotiation: The Art of Mutual Gains Bargaining*. 2d ed. Aurora, ON: Canada Law Book, 2009.
	Earle, Wendy J. *Drafting ADR and Arbitration Clauses for Commercial Contracts: A Solicitor's Manual*. Looseleaf. Toronto: Carswell, 2001.
	McEwan, J. Kenneth & Ludmila Barbara Herbst. *Commercial Arbitration in Canada: A Guide to Domestic and International Arbitrations*. Looseleaf. Aurora, ON: Canada Law Book, 2004.
	McLaren, Richard H. & John P. Sanderson. *Innovative Dispute Resolution: The Alternative*. Looseleaf. Toronto: Carswell, 1994.
	Nelson, Robert M. *Nelson on ADR*. Toronto: Carswell, 2003.
	Picard, Cheryl Ann *et al*. *The Art and Science of Mediation*. Toronto: Emond Montgomery, 2004.
	Pirie, Andrew J. *Alternative Dispute Resolution*. Toronto: Irwin Law, 2000.
	Silver, Michael P. (with the assistance of Peter G. Barton). *Mediation and Negotiation: Representing Your Clients*. Toronto: Butterworths, 2001.
	Stitt, Allan J. *Mediating Commercial Disputes*. Aurora, ON: Canada Law Book, 2003.
	Stitt, Allan J. & Ginette Fisher, eds. *Alternative Dispute Resolution Practice Manual*. Looseleaf. Toronto: CCH Canadian, 1996.
Journals	*ADR Forum* (CCH Canadian)
Encyclopedias	*Canadian Encyclopedic Digest*: Arbitration
Case digests	Canada Alternative Dispute Resolution Digest (LexisNexis Quicklaw)
	Canadian Abridgment (Carswell): Alternative dispute resolution
Databases and CD-ROMs	Kluwer Arbitration Online (Kluwer Law International). Available online by subscription: www.kluwerarbitration.com

Websites   ADR Institute of Canada: www.adrcanada.ca
                  B.C. International Commercial Arbitration Centre: www.
                  bcicac.com

D. BANKING LAW

Scope   Banking law in Canada is largely governed by federal legisla-
                  tion under the *Bank Act*, S.C. 1991, c. 46 and the *Trust and
                  Loan Companies Act*, S.C. 1991, c. 45. Federal banks fall
                  under the jurisdiction of the federal Department of Finance.
                  Additional legislation can also apply, and credit unions are
                  often governed by provincial legislation, such as the *Credit
                  Union Act*, S.N.S. 1994, c. 4.

Subject   Banking law — Canada
headings   Banks and banking — Canada

Books   Aster, Leora & Lazar Sarna. *The Annotated Bills of Exchange
                       Act*. Looseleaf. Markham, ON: LexisNexis Canada, 1999.
                  Baxter, Ian. F.G. *Law of Banking*. 4th ed. Toronto: Carswell,
                       1992.
                  Crawford, Bradley. *Law of Banking and Payment in Canada*.
                       Looseleaf. Aurora, ON: Canada Law Book, 2008.
                  Crawford, Bradley. *Payment, Clearing and Settlement in Can-
                       ada*. Aurora, ON: Canada Law Book, 2002.
                  David, Guy & Louise S. Pelly. *The 2000 Annotated Bank Act*.
                       Scarborough, ON: Carswell, 2000.
                  Dunn, William G. & Wayne S. Gray. *Marriott and Dunn
                       Practice in Mortgage Remedies in Ontario*. 5th ed. Looseleaf.
                       Scarborough, ON: Thomson Professional, 1991.
                  Gozlan, Audi. *Bankers' Acceptances*. Looseleaf. Montreal:
                       Jewel Publications, 2006.
                  Hendrickson, Barbara. *Canadian Institutional Investment
                       Rules*. Toronto: CCH Canadian, 2003.
                  L'Heureux, Nicole, Édith Fortin, & Marc Lacoursière. *Droit
                       bancaire*. 4th ed. Cowansville, QC: Editions Y. Blais, 2004.
                  Manzer, Alison R. & Howard Ruda. *Asset Based Lending in
                       Canada:Canadian Primer on Asset Based Financing*. Mark-
                       ham, ON: LexisNexis Canada, 2008.
                  Manzer, Alison R. & Jordan Bernamoff. *The Corporate Coun-
                       sel Guide to Banking and Credit Relationships*. Aurora, ON:
                       Canada Law Book, 1999.
                  McGuinness, Kevin P. *The Law of Guarantee*. 2d ed. Scarbor-
                       ough, ON: Carswell, 1996.

Books	Nicholls, Christopher C. *Corporate Finance and Canadian Law*. Scarborough, ON: Carswell, 2001.
	Nicholls, Christopher C. *Financial Institutions: The Regulatory Framework*. Markham, ON: LexisNexis Canada, 2008.
	Ogilvie, Margaret H. *Bank and Customer Law in Canada*. Toronto: Irwin Law, 2007.
	Ogilvie, Margaret H. *Canadian Banking Law*. 2d ed. Scarborough, ON: Carswell, 1998.
	Roach, Joseph E. *The Canadian Law of Mortgages of Land*. Toronto: Butterworths, 1993.
	Sarna, Lazar. *Letters of Credit: The Law and Current Practice*. 3d ed. Looseleaf. Toronto: Carswell, 1989.
	Sarna, Lazar & Leora Aster. *Annotated Bills of Exchange Act*. Markham, ON: LexisNexis Butterworths, 2004 [annual].
	Subic, Thomas L. *et al. Canadian Forms & Precedents: Banking & Finance*. Looseleaf. Markham, ON: LexisNexis Canada, 1991. Available on CD-ROM and on LexisNexis Quicklaw.
	Teolis, John W. & C. Dawn Jetten. *Bank Act: Legislation and Commentary*. Looseleaf. Toronto: Butterworths, 1998.
	Traub, Walter M. *Falconbridge on Mortgages*. 5th ed. Looseleaf. Aurora, ON: Canada Law Book, 2003.
	Waldron, Mary Anne. *The Law of Interest in Canada*. Scarborough, ON: Carswell, 1992.
Journals	*Banking & Finance Law Review* (Carswell). Available on Westlaw Canada (database: BFLR-CAN) from v. 13, 1997–1998).
	National Banking Law Review (LexisNexis Canada).
Encyclopedias	*Canadian Encyclopedic Digest*: • Banking • Bills of Exchange • Guarantee, Indemnity and Standby Letters of Credit *Halbsury's Laws of Canada*: • Banking and Finance* • Bills of Exchange and Negotiable Instruments* • Guarantee and Indemnity* *JurisClasseur Québec*: Collection Droit des affaires (Droit bancaire et financement de l'entreprise)
Case digests	Canada Banking and Finance Law Digest (LexisNexis Quicklaw) *Canadian Abridgment* (Carswell): Bills of exchange and negotiable instruments
Databases and CD-ROMs	LexisNexis Quicklaw: • Alan D. Gold's Money Laundering Update — Digests

Databases and CD-ROMs	LexisNexis Quicklaw (continued): • Investment Dealers Association of Canada Discipline Decisions • Ontario Financial Services Commission Insurance Decisions
Websites	Bank of Canada: www.bankof canada.ca Canadian Bankers Association: www.cba.ca Department of Finance: www.fin.gc.ca Office of the Superintendent of Financial Institutions: www.osfi-bsif.gc.ca

E. BANKRUPTCY AND INSOLVENCY LAW

Scope	Bankruptcy and insolvency law is generally governed by federal legislation, including the *Bankruptcy and Insolvency Act*, R.S.C. 1985, c. B-3 and the *Companies' Creditors Arrangement Act*, R.S.C. 1985, c. C-36. Provincial law also affects issues of bankruptcy and insolvency in various corporate legislation and laws governing preferences.
Subject headings	Bankruptcy—Canada Corporate reorganizations—Canada
Books	Ben-Ishai, Stephanie & Anthony Duggan. *Canadian Bankruptcy and Insolvency Law: Bill C-55, Statute c. 47 and Beyond*. Markham, ON: LexisNexis Canada, 2007. Bennett, Frank. *Bennett on Bankruptcy*. 12th ed. Toronto: CCH Canadian, 2010. Bennett, Frank. *Bennett on Bankruptcy Precedents*. 2d ed. Toronto: CCH Canadian, 2009. Bennett, Frank. *Bennett on Receiverships*. 2d ed. Scarborough, ON: Carswell, 1999. Bennett, Frank. *Bennett's A-Z Guide to Bankruptcy: A Professional's Handbook*. Toronto: CCH Canadian, 2001. Boucher, Bernard & Jean-Yves Fortin. *Faillite et insolvabilité: Une perspective québécoise de la jurisprudence canadienne*. Looseleaf. Toronto: Carswell, 1997. Honsberger, John D. *Debt Restructuring: Principles and Practice*. Looseleaf. Aurora, ON: Canada Law Book, 1990. Honsberger, John D. & Vern W. DaRe. *Bankruptcy in Canada*. 4th ed. Aurora, ON: Canada Law Book, 2009. Houlden, Lloyd W. & C.H. Morawetz. *Bankruptcy and Insolvency Law of Canada*. 4th ed. Looseleaf. Toronto: Carswell, 2009. Also available on CD-ROM and by·subscription on *InsolvencySource* on Westlaw Canada.

Books

Houlden, Lloyd W., C.H. Morawetz, & Janis P. Sarra. *Annotated Bankruptcy and Insolvency Act*. Toronto: Scarborough, ON, 1990 [annual].

Kershman, Stanley J. *Credit Solutions: Kershman on Advising Secured and Unsecured Creditors*. 2d ed. Scarborough, ON: Thomson Carswell, 2007.

Klotz, Robert A. *Bankruptcy, Insolvency and Family Law*. 2d ed. Scarborough, ON: Carswell, 2001.

Lamer, Francis L. *Priority of Crown Claims in Insolvency*. Looseleaf. Scarborough, ON: Carswell, 1996.

McElcheran, Kevin. *Commercial Insolvency in Canada*. Markham, ON: LexisNexis Butterworths, 2005.

McLaren, Richard H. *Canadian Commercial Reorganization: Preventing Bankruptcy*. Looseleaf. Aurora, ON: Canada Law Book, 1994.

Sarna, Lazar. *Bankruptcy of Corporations*. Looseleaf. Markham, ON: LexisNexis Butterworths, 2005.

Sarna, Lazar. *The Law of Bankruptcy and Insolvency in Canada*. Rev. ed. Looseleaf. Markham, ON: LexisNexis Butterworths, 2004.

Sarna, Lazar & Audi Gozlan. *Rank of Creditors' Rights in Canada*. Looseleaf. Markham, ON: LexisNexis Butterworths, 1995.

Sarra, Janis P. *Creditor Rights and the Public Interest: Restructuring Insolvent Corporations*. Toronto: University of Toronto Press, 2003.

Sarra, Janis P. *Rescue! The Companies' Creditors Arrangement Act*. Scarborough, ON: Thomson Carswell, 2007.

Sarra, Janis P. & Ronald B. Davis. *Director and Officer Liability in Corporate Insolvency: A Comprehensive Guide to Rights and Obligations*. Markham, ON:Butterworths, 2002.

Shea, E. Patrick. *Bankruptcy & Insolvency Act, Companies' Creditors Arrangement Act Bill C-55 & Commentary*. Markham, ON: LexisNexis Butterworths, 2006.

Shea, E. Patrick. *BIA, CCAA & WEPPA: A Guide to the New Bankruptcy & Insolvency Regime*. Markham, ON: LexisNexis Canada, 2009.

Tessis, Kenneth M. & Jerrard B. Gaertner. *Canadian Guide to Troubled Businesses and Bankruptcies*. Looseleaf. Scarborough, ON: Carswell, 2001.

van Kessel, Robert J. *Interim Receivers and Monitors*. Markham, ON: LexisNexis Butterworths, 2006.

Wood, Roderick. *Bankruptcy and Insolvency Law*. Toronto: Irwin Law, 2009.

Journals	*Annual Review of Insolvency Law* (Carswell) *Commercial Insolvency Reporter* (Butterworths). Available on LexisNexis Quicklaw from 1994. *National Insolvency Review* (LexisNexis Canada, 1983)
Encyclopedias	*Canadian Encyclopedic Digest*: • Bankruptcy and Insolvency • *Companies' Creditors Arrangement Act* • Receivers *Halbsury's Laws of Canada*: • Bankruptcy and Insolvency* • Receivers* *JurisClasseur Québec*: Collection Droit des affaires (Faillite, insolvabilité et restructuration)
Case digests	Canada Bankruptcy and Insolvency Law Digest (LexisNexis Quicklaw) *Canadian Abridgment* (Carswell): Bankruptcy and insolvency caseAlert — Bankruptcy & Insolvency (Canada Law Book)
Case law reporters	*Canadian Bankruptcy Reports* (Carswell)
Databases and CD-ROMs	*Bankruptcy Partner* [CD-ROM]. Scarborough, ON: Carswell. Updated four times per year. Contains bankruptcy-related legislation, case law, and full-text. Available in an expanded version as *InsolvencySource* by subscription on Westlaw Canada. LexisNexis Quicklaw: Insolvency Law Cases — Topical
Websites	Insolvency Institute of Canada: www.insolvency.ca Office of the Superintendent of Bankruptcy: http://osb-bsf.ic.gc.ca

F. CHARITIES AND NOT-FOR-PROFIT LAW

Scope	Charities and not-for-profit law in Canada tends to centre on non-share capital corporations incorporated under the federal *Canada Not-for-profit Corporations Act*, S.C. 2009, c. 23 or under equivalent provincial legislation.
Subject headings	Charity laws and legislation — Canada Non-profit organizations — Canada
Books	Bourgeois, Donald J. *Charities and Not-for-Profit Fundraising Handbook*. 2d ed. Markham, ON: LexisNexis Butterworths, 2006.

Books	Bourgeois, Donald J. *The Law of Charitable and Casino Gaming.* Toronto: Butterworths, 1999.
	Bourgeois, Donald J. *The Law of Charitable and Not-for-Profit Administration and Governance Handbook.* 2d ed. Markham, ON: LexisNexis Canada, 2009.
	Bourgeois, Donald J. *The Law of Charitable and Not-for-Profit Organizations.* 3d ed. Markham, ON: LexisNexis Canada, 2002.
	Burke-Robertson, R. Jane & Arthur Drache. *Non-Share Capital Corporations.* Looseleaf. Scarborough, ON: Carswell, 1992.
	Carter, Terence, Maria Elena Hoffstein, & Adam M. Parachin. *Charities Legislation & Commentary.* Markham, ON: LexisNexis Canada, 2003 [annual].
	Drache, Arthur B.C. *Canadian Not-for-Profit News: The Insider's Edge On Current Developments in Canadian Non-Profit Organizations.* Looseleaf. Scarborough, ON: Carswell, 2009.
	Drache, Arthur *et al. Charities Taxation, Policy and Practice.* Looseleaf. Toronto: Carswell, 2007.
	Hoffstein, Maria Elena *et al. Charities Law.* Looseleaf. Markham, ON: LexisNexis Butterworths, 2003.
	Murray, Vic. *Management of Nonprofit and Charitable Organizations in Canada.* 2d ed. Toronto: LexisNexis Butterworths, 2009.
	Saxe, Stewart D. & Jean A. Brough. *Charities and Not-for-Profit Employment Law Handbook.* Markham, ON: Butterworths, 2002.
	Sweatman, Jasmine M. *Bequest Management for Charitable Organizations.* Markham, ON: LexisNexis Butterworths, 2003.
	Wainberg, J.M. & Mark I. Wainberg. *Wainberg's Society Meetings Including Rules of Order.* 2d ed. Toronto: CCH Canadian, 2001.
Encyclopedias	*Canadian Encyclopedic Digest*: • Associations and Non-Profit Corporations • Charities (Ontario and Western) • Co-operatives • Religious Institutions *Halsbury's Laws of Canada*: • Charities, Associations and Not-for-Profit Organizations • Religious Institutions
Case digests	*Canadian Abridgment* (Carswell): Estates and trusts—Charities
Websites	Canada Revenue Agency—Charities and Giving: www.cra-arc.gc.ca/charities/ Corporations Canada: http://strategis.ic.gc.ca/eic/site/cd-dgc.nsf/eng/home

G. CIVIL PROCEDURE

Scope   Civil procedure in Canada is generally governed by rules of court applicable to the jurisdiction in question. Thus, there are rules of court for both provincial and superior courts and for the Federal Court of Canada and the Supreme Court of Canada. Judicial interpretation of rules of court is highly relevant. Included below are also materials on limitation periods.

Subject   Civil procedure— [jurisdiction]
headings   Court rules— [jurisdiction]

Books   **Selected texts on civil procedure:**

Abrams, Linda S. & Kevin P. McGuinness. *Canadian Civil Procedure Law*. Markham, ON: LexisNexis Canada, 2008.

Archibald, Todd, Gordon Killeen, & James C. Morton. *Ontario Superior Court Practice*. Markham, ON: Butterworths Canada, 2000 [annual].

Archibald, Todd, James C. Morton, & Corey D. Steinberg. *Discovery: Principles and Practice in Canadian Common Law*. 2d ed. Toronto: CCH Canadian, 2009.

Béliveau, Nathalie-Anne. *LegisPratique: Code de procédure civile annoté*. Montreal: LexisNexis, 2009.

Bennett, Daniel R. & William E. Cascadden. *Procedural Strategies for Litigators in British Columbia and Alberta*. Toronto: Butterworths, 2001.

Bouck, John C., Janice R. Dillon, & Gordon Turriff. *British Columbia Annual Practice*. Aurora, ON: Canada Law Book, 1987 [annual].

Branch, Ward. *Class Actions in Canada*. Looseleaf. Aurora, ON: Canada Law Book, 1996.

Burke, Todd *et al. E-Discovery in Canada*. Markham, ON: LexisNexis Canada, 2008.

Busby, Karen. *Manitoba Queen's Bench Rules*. Scarborough, ON: Carswell, 1992 [annual].

Carthy, James J., W.A. Derry Millar, & Jeff G. Cowan. *Ontario Annual Practice*. Aurora, ON: Canada Law Book, 1942 [annual].

Canada Law Book. *O'Brien's Encyclopedia of Forms: Division VIII, Ontario—Court Forms*. 11th ed. Aurora, ON: Canada Law Book, 1987. Also available on CD-ROM and by subscription on O'Brien's Internet

Cass, Fred D. *The Law of Releases in Canada*. Aurora, ON: Canada Law Book, 2006.

Crane, Brian A. & Henry S. Brown. *Supreme Court of Canada Practice*. Looseleaf. Toronto: Thomson/Carswell, 2008. Also available by subscription on Litigator (Westlaw Canada).

Books

Cromwell, Thomas A. *Effective Written Advocacy*. Aurora, ON: Canada Law Book, 2008.

Cudmore, Gordon D. *Choate on Discovery*. 2d ed. Looseleaf. Scarborough, ON: Carswell, 1993.

Cudmore, Gordon D. *Civil Evidence Handbook*. Looseleaf. Toronto: Carswell, 1987.

Ehrlich, David S. *Nova Scotia Annotated Rules of Practice*. Looseleaf. Toronto: Carswell, 1987.

Eizenga, Michael *et al. Class Actions Law and Practice*. 2d ed. Looseleaf. Markham, ON: LexisNexis Canada, 2008.

Ferguson, Dan. *Ontario Courtroom Procedure*. Markham, ON: LexisNexis Canada, 2007 [biennial]. Also available by subscription on LexisNexis Quicklaw.

Finlay, Bryan *et al. Electronic Documents: Records Management, e-Discovery and Trial*. Looseleaf. Aurora, ON: Canada Law Book, 2010.

Fradsham, Allan. *Alberta Rules of Court Annotated*. Scarborough, ON: Carswell, 1993 [annual]. Also available by subscription on Litigator (Westlaw Canada).

Fraser, Peter, John W. Horn, & Susan A. Griffin. *The Conduct of Civil Litigation in British Columbia*. 2d ed. Looseleaf. Markham, ON: LexisNexis Canada, 2007.

Guide to Civil Litigation — British Columbia Edition. Looseleaf. Toronto: Carswell, 1981.

Holder, William D. & John C. Fiddick. *Annotated British Columbia Court Order Enforcement Act*. Looseleaf. Aurora, ON: Canada Law Book, 2003.

Hrycko, Oleh. *Electronic Discovery in Canada: Best Practices and Guidelines*. Toronto: CCH Canadian, 2007.

Hughes, Roger T., Arthur B. Renaud, & L. E. Trent Horne. *Federal Courts of Canada Service*. 2d ed. Looseleaf. Markham, ON: LexisNexis Canada, 2008. Also available by subscription on LexisNexis Quicklaw.

Irvine, Frederick, ed. *British Columbia Practice*. 3d ed. Looseleaf. Markham, ON: LexisNexis Canada, 2006. Available on CD-ROM and LexisNexis Quicklaw.

Jones, Craig. *Theory of Class Actions*. Toronto: Irwin Law, 2003.

Jones, Craig & Jamie Cassels. *The Law of Large-Scale Claims: Product Liability, Mass Torts, and Complex Litigation in Canada*. Toronto: Irwin Law, 2005.

Kenkel, Joseph F. & William S. Chalmers. *Small Claims and Simplified Procedure Litigation*. 4th ed. Markham, ON: Butterworths, 2002.

Kerans, Roger & Kim Willey. *Standards of Review Employed by Appellate Courts*. 2d ed. Edmonton: Juriliber, 2006.

Books

Killeen, Gordon P. & Morton C. James. *A Guide to Costs in Ontario*. Toronto: CCH Canadian, 2002.

Lang Michener. *Settlement Procedure and Precedents in Ontario*. Markham, ON: Butterworths, 1998.

Lubet, Steven. Adapted for Canada by Sheila Block & Cynthia Tape. *Modern Trial Advocacy: Analysis and Practice* (Canadian edition). 2d ed. Notre Dame, IN: National Institute for Trial Advocacy, 2000. Also available by subscription on LexisNexis Quicklaw.

MacDonald, Kenneth. *Cross-Border Litigation: Inter-Jurisdictional Practice and Procedure*. Aurora, ON: Canada Law Book, 2009.

McCarthy Tetrault. *Defending Class Actions in Canada*. 2d ed. Toronto: CCH Canadian, 2007.

McHugh, Karen & Ira Nishisato. *Alberta Litigator's Pocket Reference*, Markham, ON: Butterworths Canada, 2008 [annual].

Meehan, Eugene *et al. Supreme Court of Canada Practice Manual: Practice and Advocacy*. Looseleaf. Aurora, ON: Canada Law Book, 1996.

Miller, Jeffrey. *The Law of Contempt*. Scarborough, ON: Carswell, 1997.

Morton, James C., Michael J. Iacovelli, & Corey D. Steinberg. *Procedural Strategies for Litigators*. 2d ed. Markham, ON: LexisNexis Canada, 2007.

Muldoon, Paul R. *Law of Intervention: Status and Practice*. Aurora, ON: Canada Law Book, 1989.

Nishisato, Ira. *Ontario Litigator's Pocket Reference*. Markham, ON: Butterworths Canada, 2001 [annual].

Oatley, Roger G. *Addressing the Jury: Achieving Fair Verdicts in Personal Injury Cases*. 2d ed. Aurora, ON: Canada Law Book, 2006.

Orkin, Mark M. *Law of Costs*. 2d ed. Looseleaf. Aurora, ON: Canada Law Book, 1987.

Page, S. John & Timothy Pinos. *Summary Judgment*. Aurora, ON: Canada Law Book, 1998.

Polster, Philip C. & Lisa Mendlowicz. *Ontario Litigation Procedures*. 4th ed. Toronto: Thomson Carswell, 2005.

Salhany, Roger E. *The Preparation and Presentation of a Civil Action*. Toronto: Butterworths, 2000.

Saunders, Brian J. *Federal Courts Practice*. Toronto: Carswell: 1987 [annual]. Also available by subscription on Litigator (Westlaw Canada).

Seckel, Allan, James MacInnis, & Leanne Berry. *British Columbia Supreme Court Rules Annotated*. Scarborough, ON: Carswell, 1997 [annual].

Books   Sopinka, John & Mark A. Gelowitz. *The Conduct of an Appeal*. 2d ed. Toronto: Butterworths, 2000.

Stockwood, David. *Civil Litigation: A Handbook*. 5th ed. Scaroborough, ON: Carswell, 2004.

Thomson, D.A. Rollie. *Nova Scotia Civil Procedure Rules*. 2d ed. Looseleaf. Markham, ON: LexisNexis, 2008.

Upenieks, Ed & Robert van Kessel. *Enforcing Judgments and Orders*. Markham, ON: Butterworths Canada, 2002.

Van Kessel, Robert J. *Dispositions without Trial*. 2d ed. Markham, ON: LexisNexis, 2007.

Walker, Janet & Lorne Sossin. *Civil Litigation*. Toronto: Irwin Law, 2010.

Watson, Garry D. & Craig Perkins. *Holmested and Watson: Ontario Civil Procedure*. Looseleaf. Toronto: Carswell, 1984. Also available by subscription on Litigator (Westlaw Canada).

Watson, Garry D. & Michael McGowan. *Ontario Civil Practice*. Toronto: Carswell, 1984 [annual].

White, Robert & Joseph Stratton. *The Appeal Book*. Aurora, ON: Canada Law Book, 1999.

Williston and Rolls' Court Forms. Looseleaf. Toronto: Butterworths, 1981. Also available on CD-ROM and LexisNexis Quicklaw.

Wirth, Christopher. *Interlocutory Proceedings*. Looseleaf. Aurora, ON: Canada Law Book, 2004.

Zuker, Marvin A. *Ontario Small Claims Court Practice*. Toronto: Carswell, 1991 [annual]. Also available by subscription on *Litigator* (Westlaw Canada).

Selected texts on limitation periods:

Alberta Limitations Manual. 2d ed. Looseleaf. Markham, ON: LexisNexis Canada, 2007.

British Columbia Limitations Manual. Looseleaf. Markham, ON: LexisNexis Canada, 2005.

Dukelow, Daphne A. *Guide to Ontario and Federal Limitation Periods*. Looseleaf. Scarborough, ON: Carswell, 1998.

Federal Limitations Manual. 2d ed. Looseleaf. Markham, ON: LexisNexis Canada, 2006.

Mew, Graeme. *The Law of Limitations*. 2d ed. Toronto: LexisNexis Butterworths, 2004. Also available by subscription on LexisNexis Quicklaw.

Ontario Limitations Manual. 3d ed. Looseleaf. Markham, ON: LexisNexis Canada, 2006.

Williams, Jeremy S. *Limitations of Actions in Canada*. 2d ed. Toronto: Butterworths, 1980.

Journals	*Advocate's Quarterly* (Canada Law Book) *Annual Review of Civil Litigation* (Carswell) *Canadian Class Action Review* (Irwin Law) *Class Action Defence Quarterly* (LexisNexis Canada) *Commercial Litigation Review* (LexisNexis Canada)
Encyclopedias	*Canadian Encyclopedic Digest*: • Actions (Ontario and Western) • Costs • Courts (Ontario and Western) • Discovery (Ontario and Western) • Injunctions • Interpleader • Judgments and Orders (Ontario and Western) • Limitations of Actions • Parties (Ontario and Western) • Pleadings (Ontario and Western) • Practice (Ontario and Western) • References and Inquiries (Ontario and Western) • Time • Trials (Ontario and Western) *Halsbury's Laws of Canada*: • Civil Procedure I and Civil Procedure II • Interim Preservation of Property Rights • Judges and Courts • Limitation of Actions* *JurisClasseur Québec*: Collection Droit civil (Obligations et responsabilité civile, Preuve et prescription, Procédure civile) Stevenson, W.A. & Jean E. Côté. *Civil Procedure Encyclopedia.* Edmonton: Juriliber, 2003.
Case digests	*All Canada Weekly Summaries* (Canada Law Book) *Canadian Abridgment* (Carswell): Civil practice and procedure caseAlert — Civil Litigation (Canada Law Book) LexisNexis Quicklaw: Canada Civil Procedure Digest
Case law reporters	*Carswell's Practice Cases* (Carswell)
Databases and CD-ROMs	*Civil Practice Partner* [CD-ROM]. Scarborough, ON: Carswell. Updated four times per year. Contains Ontario, Federal, and Supreme Court of Canada Rules of Court and *Carswell's Practice Cases*, along with other publications. LexisNexis Quicklaw: Civil Procedure Cases — Topical Litigation*Practice* (LexisNexis Quicklaw)

Databases and CD-ROMs	*Rules Concordance and Case Locator* [CD-ROM]. Toronto: Carswell, 1999. Contains full-text rules of court from all common law provinces, along with a concordance and links to full-text court decisions. The "data" from this CD-ROM is available in a modified format on *LawSource* by subscription on Westlaw Canada.

H. COMMUNICATIONS LAW

Scope	Communications law in Canada tends to be heavily regulated by the federal government through such government agencies as the Canadian Radio-television and Telecommunications Commission (CRTC) and by the federal *Broadcasting Act*, S.C. 1991, c. 11 and *Telecommunications Act*, S.C. 1993, c. 38. Media law (and the law of defamation) is discussed in a separate category below in this chapter (under Media Law).
Subject headings	Telecommunication—Law and legislation—Canada
Books	Biron, Dorthee & Philippe Vaillant. *Canadian Legislation on Telecommunications 1997*. Scarborough, ON: Carswell, 1997. Grant, Peter *et al. Canadian Broadcasting Regulatory Handbook*. 9th ed. Toronto: McCarthy Tétrault, 2009. Handa, Sunny *et al. Communications Law in Canada*. Looseleaf. Markham, ON: Butterworths, 2000. Ryan, Michael H. *Canadian Telecommunications Law and Regulation*. Looseleaf. Scarborough, ON: Carswell, 1993. Salter, Liora & Felix Nii Lantei Odartey-Wellington. *The CRTC and Broadcasting Regulation in Canada*. Toronto: Thomson Carswell, 2008.
Encyclopedias	*Canadian Encyclopedic Digest*: • Public Utilities (Ontario and Western) • Radio and Television • Telecommunications *Halsbury's Laws of Canada*: • Communications • Media and Postal • Public Utilities
Case digests	*Canadian Abridgment* (Carswell): Communications law LexisNexis Quicklaw: Canada Media and Communications Law Digest

Databases and
CD-ROMs
	LexisNexis Quicklaw:
	• Canadian Broadcast Standards Council Decisions
	• Canadian Radio-television & Telecommunications
	  Commission Broadcast Decisions
	• Canadian Radio-television & Telecommunications
	  Commission Telecom Decisions

Websites	Canadian Radio-television and Telecommunications Commission (CRTC): www.crtc.gc.ca

I. COMPETITION AND ANTITRUST LAW

Scope	Competition and antitrust law in Canada regulates mergers and acquisitions between businesses with the policy goal of ensuring adequate competition and a healthy economy for consumers and businesses. The major competition "watchdog" in Canada is the Competition Bureau which administers four major statutes: the *Competition Act*, R.S.C. 1985, c. C-34, the *Consumer Packaging and Labelling Act*, R.S.C. 1985, c. C-38, the *Textile Labelling Act*, R.S.C. 1985, c. T-10, and the *Precious Metals Marking Act*, R.S.C. 1985, c. P-19. Also included below are resources on unfair advertising, which is also regulated by the Competition Bureau.
Subject *headings*	Competition, Unfair— Canada Antitrust law— Canada Advertising laws— Canada
Books	Addy, George N. & William L. Vanveen. *Competition Law Service.* Looseleaf. Aurora, ON: Canada Law Book, 1988. Affleck, Don & Wayne McCracken. *Canadian Competition Law.* Looseleaf. Scarborough, ON: Carswell, 1990. Boyer, Marcel, Michael Trebilcock, & David Vaver. *Competition Policy and Intellectual Property.* Toronto: Irwin Law, 2009. Campbell, Neil. *Merger Law and Practice: The Regulation of Mergers under the Competition Act.* Scarborough, ON: Carswell, 1997. Facey, Brian A. & Dany H. Assaf. *Competition and Antitrust Law: Canada and the United States.* 3d ed. Markham, ON: LexisNexis Butterworths, 2006. Flavell, C.J. Michael & Christopher J. Kent. *The Canadian Competition Law Handbook.* Scarborough, ON: Carswell, 1997. Goldman, Calvin S. & Bodrug, John D., eds. *Competition Law of Canada.* Looseleaf. Yonkers, NY: Juris, 1988.

Books	Gourley, Albert C. *Merger Notification and Clearance in Canada*. Looseleaf. Toronto: CCH Canadian, 2003–2004.
	Musgrove, James. *Fundamentals of Canadian Competition Law*. Toronto: Thomson Carswell, 2007.
	Pitel, Stephen G.A., ed. *Litigating Conspiracy: An Analysis of Competition Class Actions*. Toronto: Irwin Law, 2006.
	Pritchard, Brenda & Susan Vogt. *Advertising and Marketing Law in Canada*. 3d ed. Markham, ON: LexisNexis Butterworths, 2009.
	Reiter, Barry J. & Melanie Shisler. *Joint Ventures: Legal and Business Perspectives*. Toronto: Irwin Law, 1999.
	Rowley, J. William & Donald I. Baker. *International Mergers: The Antitrust Process*. 3d ed. Looseleaf. London: Sweet & Maxwell, 2001.
	Stikeman Elliott LLP. *Competition Act and Commentary*. Markham, ON: LexisNexis Butterworths, 1999 [annual].
	Trebilcock, Michael J. *et al. The Law and Economics of Canadian Competition Policy*. Toronto: University of Toronto Press, 2002.
	Wakil, Omar, ed. *The Annotated Competition Act*. Scarborough, ON: Carswell, 1987 [annual].
	Young, David & Brian Fraser. *Canadian Advertising and Marketing Law*. Looseleaf. Scarborough, ON: Carswell, 1990.
Journals	*Canadian Business Law Journal* (Canada Law Book). Also available as an e-journal.
	Canadian Competition Record (Fraser Milner Casgrain LLP)
Encyclopedias	*Canadian Encyclopedic Digest*: Trade and Commerce
	Halsbury's Laws of Canada: Competition and Foreign Investment*
	JurisClasseur Québec: Collection Droit des affaires (Concurrence, consommation et distribution)
Case digests	*Canadian Abridgment* (Carswell): Commercial law—Trade and commerce
Databases and CD-ROMs	LexisNexis Quicklaw: Canada Competition Tribunal Decisions
Websites	Canadian Competition Policy Page (UBC): http://csgb.ubc.ca/ccpp
	Competition Bureau (Canada): www.cb-bc.gc.ca
	Competition Tribunal (Canada): www.ct-tc.gc.ca

J. CONSTITUTIONAL AND HUMAN RIGHTS LAW

Scope
The implementation of the Canadian *Charter of Rights and Freedoms* (the "*Charter*") in 1982 has increased the profile of constitutional law in Canada due to a number of high profile human rights cases being decided by the Supreme Court of Canada. Constitutional law involves a combination of the application of various federal legislation (including the *Charter* and the *Constitution Act, 1867*), provincial legislation, and case law.

Subject headings
Constitutional law — Canada
Civil rights — Canada

Books
Barrett, Joan. *Balancing Charter Interests: Victims' Rights and Third Party Remedies*. Looseleaf. Scarborough, ON: Carswell, 2001.

Bateman, Thomas *et al*. *The Court and the Charter: Leading Cases*. Toronto: Emond Montgomery Publications, 2008.

Beaudoin, Gerald A. & Errol Mendes. *Canadian Charter of Rights and Freedoms*. 4th ed. Markham, ON: LexisNexis Butterworths, 2005.

Boucher, Susanne & Kenneth Landa. *Understanding Section 8: Search, Seizure and the Canadian Constitution*. Toronto: Irwin Law, 2005.

Braha, W. Anita. *Annotated British Columbia Human Rights Code*. Looseleaf. Aurora, ON: Canada Law Book, 1998.

Brun, Henri, Guy Tremblay, & Eugénie Brouillet. *Droit constitutionnel*. 5e éd. Cowansville, QC: Éditions Y. Blais, 2008.

Bryant, Michael J. & Lorne Sossin. *Public Law: An Overview of Aboriginal, Administrative, Constitutional and International Law in Canada*. Toronto: Carswell, 2002.

Carswell. *The Annotated Charter of Rights and Freedoms*. Toronto: Carswell, 1994 [annual].

Carswell. *Canadian Charter of Rights Annotated*. 6 vol. Looseleaf. Scarborough, ON: Carswell, 1982.

Cooper-Stephenson, Kenneth. *Charter Damages Claims*. Toronto: Carswell, 1990.

Corbett, Stanley M. *Canadian Human Rights Law & Commentary*. Markham, ON: LexisNexis, 2007.

Cornish, Mary *et al*. *Enforcing Human Rights in Ontario*. Aurora, ON: Canada Law Book, 2009.

Faraday, Fay, Margaret Denike, & M. Kate Stephenson. *Making Equality Rights Real: Securing Substantive Equality under the Charter*. Toronto: Irwin Law, 2009.

Books

Forcese, Craig & Aaron Freeman. *The Laws of Government: The Legal Foundations of Canadian Democracy*. Toronto: Irwin Law, 2005.

Funston, Bernard & Eugene Meehan. *Canada's Constitutional Law in a Nutshell*. 3d ed. Toronto: Carswell, 2003.

Hogg, Peter W. *Constitutional Law of Canada*. 5th ed. Looseleaf. Toronto: Carswell, 2007.

Huscroft, Grant & Ian Brodie. *Constitutionalism in the Charter Era*. Toronto: LexisNexis Canada, 2004.

Jamal, Mahmud & Matthew Taylor. *Charter of Rights in Litigation: The Direction from the Supreme Court of Canada*. Looseleaf. Aurora, ON: Canada Law Book, 1991. Also available as a subscription online.

Laskin, John B. *The Canadian Charter of Rights Annotated*. Looseleaf. Aurora, ON: Canada Law Book, 1982.

Law Society of Upper Canada. *Special Lectures 2001: Constitutional and Administrative Law*. Toronto: Irwin Law, 2001.

Lokan, Andrew K. & Christopher M. Dassios. *Constitutional Litigation in Canada*. Looseleaf. Toronto: Carswell, 2006.

Magnet, Joseph E. *Constitutional Law of Canada*. 9th ed. Edmonton: Juriliber, 2007. Also available by subscription on LexisNexis Quicklaw.

Magnet, Joseph E. *Modern Constitutionalism: Equality, Identity and Democracy*. Toronto: LexisNexis Canada, 2004. Also available by subscription on LexisNexis Quicklaw.

McIntyre, Sheila & Sanda Rodgers. *Diminishing Returns: Inequality and the Canadian Charter of Rights and Freedoms*. Toronto: LexisNexis Canada, 2006.

McLeod, R.M. *et al. Canadian Charter of Rights: The Prosecution and Defence of Criminal and Other Statutory Offences*. Looseleaf. Toronto: Carswell, 2008.

Monahan, Patrick. *Constitutional Law*. 3d ed. Toronto: Irwin Law, 2006.

Morin, Alexandre. *Constitution, fédéralisme et droits fondamentaux: Commentaires et documents*. Toronto: LexisNexis Canada, 2008.

Morin, Alexandre (with Véronique Ardouin). *Le droit à l'égalité au Canada*. Toronto: LexisNexis Canada, 2008.

Pentney, William. *Discrimination and the Law*. Looseleaf. Toronto: Carswell, 1990.

Roach, Kent. *Constitutional Remedies in Canada*. Looseleaf. Aurora, ON: Canada Law Book, 1994.

Roach, Kent. *The Supreme Court on Trial: Judicial Activism or Democractic Dialogue*. Toronto: Irwin Law, 2001.

Books	Russell, Peter *et al. The Court and the Constitution.* Toronto: Emond Montgomery, 2008.
	Schabas, William & Stéphane Beaulac. *International Human Rights and Canadian Law: Legal Commitment, Implementation and the Charter.* 3d ed. Toronto: Thomson Carswell, 2007.
	Sharpe, Robert J. & Kent Roach. *The Charter of Rights and Freedoms.* 4th ed. Toronto: Irwin Law, 2009.
	Zinn, Russel W. & Patricia P. Brethour. *The Law of Human Rights in Canada: Practice and Procedure.* Looseleaf. Aurora, ON: Canada Law Book, 1996.
Journals	*Charter of Rights Newsletter* (Canada Law Book)
	Constitutional Forum (Centre for Constitutional Studies)
	National Journal of Constitutional Law (Carswell). Available on Westlaw Canada (database: NJCL) from v. 9 (1997–1998).
	Review of Constitutional Studies (Centre for Constitutional Studies)
	Supreme Court Law Review (LexisNexis Canada)
Encyclopedias	*Canadian Encyclopedic Digest*: • Constitutional Law • Human Rights (Ontario and Western) *Halsbury's Laws of Canada*: • Constitutional Law — Charter • Constitutional Law — Division of Powers* • Discrimination and Human Rights* *JurisClasseur Québec*: Collection Droit public (Droit constitutionnel)
Case digests	*Canadian Abridgment* (Carswell): • Constitutional law • Human rights *Canadian Charter of Rights Annotated* (Canada Law Book) caseAlert — Constitutional Law LexisNexis Quicklaw: Canada Constitutional Law Digest
Case law reporters	*Canadian Rights Reporter* (LexisNexis Canada)
Databases and CD-ROMs	LexisNexis Quicklaw: Constitutional Law Cases — Topical

K. CONSTRUCTION LAW

Scope	Construction law in Canada is governed by legislation, largely in the form of provincial builders or mechanics lien legislation, contract law, and case law.
Subject headings	Construction liens — [jurisdiction] Construction contracts — [jurisdiction] Mechanics' liens — [jurisdiction]
Books	Audet, Maurice. *Insuring the Construction Project*. Toronto: Carswell, 2006. Coulson, David. *Guide to Builders' Liens in British Columbia*. Looseleaf. Toronto: Carswell, 1992. Bristow, David I. *et al. Construction Builders' and Mechanics' Liens in Canada*. 7th ed. Looseleaf. Toronto: Carswell, 2005. Glaholt, Duncan W. *Conduct of a Lien Action*. Toronto: Carswell, 2004 [annual]. Glaholt, Duncan W. *Construction Trusts*. Toronto: Carswell, 1999. Glaholt, Duncan W. & M. David Keeshan. *Annotated Ontario Construction Lien Act*. Toronto: Carswell, 1995 [annual]. Goldsmith, Immanuel & Thomas Heintzman. *Goldsmith on Canadian Building Contracts*. 4th ed. Toronto: Carswell, 1995 [supplemented annually] Kirsh, Harvey J. *Kirsh's Construction Law Lien Finder*. Looseleaf. Toronto: LexisNexis Canada, 1992. Kirsh, Harvey J. *Kirsh's Guide to Construction Liens in Ontario*. 2d ed. Toronto: Butterworths, 1995. Kirsh, Harvey J. *Kirsh's Index to Canadian Construction Law Literature*. Toronto: Carswell, 2006. Kirsh, Harvey J. & Paul A. Ivanoff. *The Canadian Construction Law Dictionary*. Toronto: LexisNexis Canada, 2006. Kirsh, Harvey J. & Lori A. Roth. *Kirsh and Roth: The Annotated Construction Contract (CCDC 2-1994)*. Aurora, ON: Canada Law Book, 1997. Marston, Donald L. *Law for Professional Engineers: Canadian and Global Insights*. 4th ed. Toronto: McGraw-Hill Ryerson, 2008. McGuinness, Kevin P. *Construction Lien Remedies in Ontario*. 2d ed. Toronto: Carswell, 1997. McLachlin, Beverley M. *et al. The Canadian Law of Architecture and Engineering*. 2d ed. Toronto: LexisNexis Canada, 1994. Sandori, Paul & William M. Pigott. *Bidding and Tendering: What is the Law?* 4th ed. Toronto: LexisNexis Canada, 2009. Scott, Kenneth W. & R. Bruce Reynolds. *Scott and Reynolds on Surety Bonds*. Looseleaf. Toronto: Carswell, 1993.

Books	Silver, Robert & Gary Furlong. *Construction Dispute Resolution Handbook*. Toronto: LexisNexis Canada, 2004. Wise, Howard M. *The Manual of Construction Law*. Looseleaf. Toronto: Carswell, 1994.
Journals	*Construction Law Letter* (LexisNexis Canada) *Daily Commercial News and Construction Record* (Reed Construction Data), online: www.dcnonl.com *Journal of the Canadian College of Construction Lawyers* (Carswell). Available on Westlaw Canada from 2009.
Encyclopedias	*Canadian Encyclopedic Digest*: • Builders' Liens (Western) • Building Contracts • Construction Liens (Ontario) • Liens (Ontario and Western) *Halsbury's Laws of Canada*: Construction Law
Case digests	*Canadian Abridgment* (Carswell): Construction law LexisNexis Quicklaw: Canada Construction Law Digest
Case law reporters	*Construction Law Reports* (Carswell)
Databases and CD-ROMs	LexisNexis Quicklaw: Construction Law Cases — Topical
Websites	Canadian College of Construction Lawyers: www.cccl.org Papadopoulos, John. *Construction Law Research Guide*: www.law-lib.utoronto.ca/construction/

L. CONTRACT AND AGENCY LAW

Scope	Contract and agency law in Canada is governed largely by judge-made common law, although there is some legislation that affects contracts, including fraud legislation, consumer protection legislation, and sales of goods legislation (usually provincial legislation). Some regard is still granted to classic English textbooks on contract law in Canada, but there is now a large body of Canadian law on point to lessen the need to consult English authorities.
Subject headings	Contracts — Canada Agency (Law) — Canada
Books	Fitzgerald, Jean. *Fundamentals of Contract Law*. 2d ed. Toronto: Emond Montgomery, 2005. Fridman, Gerald. *Canadian Agency Law*. Markham, ON: Butterworths Canada, 2009.

Books	Fridman, Gerald. *The Law of Contract in Canada*. 5th ed. Toronto: Thomson Carswell, 2006.
	Fridman, Gerald. *Sale of Goods in Canada*. 5th ed. Toronto: Thomson Carswell, 2004.
	Hall, Geoff R. *Canadian Contractual Interpretation Law*. Markham, ON: LexisNexis, 2007.
	Harris, Gregory & Paul LeBreaux. *Annotated Business Agreements*. Looseleaf. Scarborough, ON: Carswell, 1993.
	Harvey, Cameron & Darcy MacPherson. *Agency Law Primer*. 4th ed. Scarborough, ON: Carswell, 2009.
	Klotz, James M. *International Sales Agreements: An Annotated Drafting and Negotiation Guide*. Aurora, ON: Canada Law Book, 1997.
	MacDougall, Bruce. *Introduction to Contracts*. Markham, ON: LexisNexis Canada, 2007.
	McCamus, John. *The Law of Contracts*. Toronto: Irwin Law, 2005.
	McGuinness, Kevin B. *Sale and Supply of Goods*. 2d ed. Markham, ON: Butterworths, 2010.
	Snyder, Ronald M. & Harvin D. Pitch. *Damages for Breach of Contract*. 2d ed. Looseleaf. Toronto: Carswell, 1989.
	Swan, Angela. *Canadian Contract Law*. 2d ed. Markham, ON: LexisNexis, 2009. Also available by subscription on LexisNexis Quicklaw.
	Waddams, Stephen M. *The Law of Contracts*. 6th ed. Aurora, ON: Canada Law Book, 2010.

Encyclopedias	*Canadian Encyclopedic Digest*:
	• Agency
	• Auctions
	• Bulk Sales (Ontario)
	• Contracts
	• Deeds and Documents
	• Sale of Goods
	Halsbury's Laws of Canada:
	• Auctions*
	• Consumer Protection*
	• Contracts
	JurisClasseur Québec: Collection Droit civil (Biens et publicité des droits, Contrats nommés, Obligations et responsabilité civile)

Case digests	*Canadian Abridgment* (Carswell):
	• Commercial law (for agency, bulk sales, sale of goods)
	• Contracts

Case digests	LexisNexis Quicklaw: • Canada Contracts Digest • Abrégé de jurisprudence—Congédiement injustifié (Québec) • Abrégé de jurisprudence—Rapports individuels de travail (Québec)
Case law reporters	*Business Law Reports* (Carswell)
Databases and CD-ROMs	LexisNexis Quicklaw: Canada Breach of Contract Quantums

M. CORPORATE AND PARTNERSHIP LAW

Scope	Corporate law in Canada is governed by both federal legislation (such as the *Canada Business Corporations Act*, R.S.C. 1985, c. C-44) and applicable provincial legislation (such as the *Company Act*, R.S.B.C. 1996, c. 62, for British Columbia companies), depending on whether the company is incorporated or does business federally or provincially. Partnership law in Canada is closely modelled on English law as reflected in various provincial partnership statutes. Corporate and partnership law often involve issues of commercial law, which includes aspects of contract law and competition law (each discussed above in this chapter as a separate topic) and personal property security law (discussed below as a separate topic). Charities and not-for-profit corporations are discussed above as a separate topic.
Subject headings	Corporation law—Canada Corporations—Canada Stockholders—Legal status, laws, etc.—Canada Directors of corporations—Legal status, laws, etc.—Canada
Books	Abraham, John & Jennifer Babe. *Canadian Forms & Precedents: Sale and Operation of a Business*. Looseleaf. 2d ed. Markham, ON: LexisNexis, 2007. Available on CD-ROM and on LexisNexis Quicklaw. Adams, Stephen N. *Annotated Ontario Business Corporations Act*. Looseleaf. Aurora, ON: Canada Law Book, 1990. Aird & Berlis LLP. *Shareholders Agreements: An Annotated Guide*. 2d ed. Aurora, ON: Canada Law Book, 2009. Archibald, Todd L., Kenneth E. Jull & Kent W. Roach. *Regulatory and Corporate Liability: From Due Diligence to Risk Management*. Looseleaf. Aurora, ON: Canada Law Book, 2004.

Books   Baker, Ash. *Extra-provincial Corporate Registrations in Canada*. Markham, ON: LexisNexis Canada, 2005 [annual].

Beaudin, Patrice & Anne-Marie Laberge, eds. Looseleaf. *Recueil des conventions commerciales*. Montreal: LexisNexis, 2008.

Borden Ladner Gervais LLP. *British Columbia Corporation Manual*. Looseleaf. Toronto: Thomson Carswell, 2004.

Canada Law Book. *O'Brien's Encyclopedia of Forms: Division II, Corporations*. 11th ed. Aurora, ON: Canada Law Book, 1987. Also available on CD-ROM and by subscription on O'Brien's Internet.

CCH Canadian Limited. *Alberta Corporations Law Guide*. Looseleaf. North York, ON: CCH Canadian, 1983. Available in print, on CD-ROM, and by online subscription.

CCH Canadian Limited. *British Columbia Corporations Law Guide*. Looseleaf. North York, ON: CCH Canadian, 1974. Available in print, on CD-ROM, and by online subscription.

CCH Canadian Limited. *Canadian Corporate Secretary's Guide*. Looseleaf. North York, ON: CCH Canadian, 1978. Available in print, on CD-ROM, and by online subscription.

CCH Canadian Limited. *Canadian Corporations Law Reporter*. Looseleaf. North York, ON: CCH Canadian, 1995. Available in print, on CD-ROM, and by online subscription.

CCH Canadian Limited. *The Directors Manual*. Looseleaf. North York, ON: CCH Canadian, 1994. Available in print, on CD-ROM, and by online subscription.

CCH Canadian Limited. *Ontario Corporations Law Guide*. Looseleaf. North York, ON: CCH Canadian, 1995. Available in print, on CD-ROM, and by online subscription.

CCH Canadian Limited. *Ultimate Corporate Counsel Guide*. Looseleaf. North York, ON: CCH Canadian, 2006.

Currie, Brenda-Jean. *The Annotated Business Corporations Act of Alberta*. 3d ed. Looseleaf. Scarborough, ON: Carswell, 1988.

Day, Midge (edited by Bernie Aron). *Ontario Corporate Procedures*. 4th ed. Scarborough, ON: Carswell, 2001.

Debenham. David. *Executive Liability and the Law*. Scarborough, ON: Thomson Carswell, 2006.

Ellis, Mark Vincent. *Corporate and Commercial Fiduciary Duties*. Scarborough, ON: Carswell, 1995.

Estey, Wilfred. *Legal Opinions in Commercial Transactions*. 2d ed. Markham, ON: Butterworths, 1997.

Books   Ewasiuk, Rick W. *A Guide to Drafting Shareholder's Agreements*. Scarborough, ON: Carswell, 1998.

Fasken Martineau DuMoulin LLP. *Annotated British Columbia Corporations Act*. Looseleaf. Aurora, ON: Canada Law Book, 2005.

Gillis, Elizabeth. *Advanced Corporate Legal Procedures*. Toronto: Emond Montgomery, 2004.

Gray, Wayne D. *The Annotated Canada Business Corporations Act*. 2d ed. Looseleaf. Toronto: Carswell, 2002.

Gray, Wayne D. *The Annotated Ontario Business Corporations Act*. 2d ed. Looseleaf. Toronto: Carswell, 2003.

Grover, Warren M. *Canada Corporation Manual*. Looseleaf. Toronto: Carswell, 1990.

Grover, Warren M. *Ontario Corporation Manual*. Looseleaf. Toronto: Carswell, 1990.

Halpern, Robert *et al.*, eds. *Advising the Family-Owned Business*. Looseleaf. Aurora, ON: Canada Law Book, 1999.

Hansell, Carol. *Directors and Officers in Canada: Law and Practice*. Looseleaf. Toronto: Carswell, 1999.

Hansell, Carol. *What Directors Need to Know: Corporate Governance*. Toronto: Carswell, 2003.

Hepburn, Lyle & William J. Strain. *Limited Partnerships*. Looseleaf. Toronto: Carswell, 1990.

Hutchinson, Allan. *The Companies We Keep: Corporate Governance for a Democratic Society*. Toronto: Irwin Law, 2005.

Iacovelli, Michael & Gil Lan. *Counselling Corporations and Advising Businesses*. Toronto: Butterworths, 2000.

Kerr, Michael *et al*. *Corporate Social Responsibility: A Legal Analysis*. Markham, ON: LexisNexis, 2009.

Kidd, Sandra, ed. *Canadian Corporate Counsel: A Practical Reference for Corporate, Municipal and Crown Counsel*. Looseleaf. Aurora, ON: Canada Law Book, 1991.

Koehnen, Markus. *Oppression and Related Remedies*. Toronto: Carswell, 2004.

Kwaw, Edmund. *The Law of Corporate Finance in Canada*. Toronto: Butterworths, 1997.

Law Society of Upper Canada. *Special Lectures 2004: Corporate & Commercial Law*. Toronto: Irwin Law, 2005.

Lipson, Barry D. *The Art of the Corporate Deal*. Toronto: Carswell, 2000.

Macleod Dixon LLP. *Alberta Corporation Manual*. Looseleaf. Toronto: Carswell, 1990.

Mahaffy, Paul A. *Business Succession Guide*. Toronto: Thomson Carswell, 2008.

Books

Manzer, Alison R. *et al. Canadian Commercial Law Guide.* Looseleaf. North York, ON: CCH Canadian, 1967. Available in print, CD-ROM and by online subscription.

Manzer, Alison R. *et al. A Practical Guide to Canadian Partnership Law.* Looseleaf. Aurora, ON: Canada Law Book, 1994.

Martel, Paul. *Business Corporations in Canada: Legal and Practical Aspects.* Looseleaf. Toronto: Carswell, 2004.

McCarthy Tetrault. *Directors' and Officers' Duties and Liabilities in Canada.* Toronto: Butterworths, 1997.

McGuiness, Kevin P. *Canadian Business Corporations Law.* 2d ed. Markham, ON: LexisNexis Canada, 2007.

McGuiness, Kevin P., ed. *Canadian Forms and Precedents: Corporations.* Looseleaf. Markham, ON: LexisNexis Canada, 2005. Available on CD-ROM and on LexisNexis Quicklaw.

McLeod, Andrew J. & Ian N. MacIntosh, eds. *British Columbia Business Corporations Act & Commentary.* Markham, ON: LexisNexis Canada, 2004 [annual].

Morritt, David, Sonia Bjorkquist, & Allan Coleman. *The Oppression Remedy.* Looseleaf. Aurora, ON: Canada Law Book, 2004.

Nathan, Hartley R. *Nathan's Company Meetings Including Rules of Order.* 8th ed. Toronto: CCH Canadian, 2009.

Nathan, Hartley R. *et al. Canadian Corporate Secretary's Guide.* Looseleaf. Toronto: CCH Canadian, 1978. Available in print, on CD-ROM, and by online subscription.

Nathan, Hartley R. & Mihkel E. Voore. *Corporate Meetings: Law and Practice.* Looseleaf. Toronto: Carswell, 1995.

Nicholls, Christopher C. *Mergers, Acquisitions, and Other Changes of Corporate Control.* Toronto: Irwin Law, 2007.

Peterson, Dennis H. *Shareholder Remedies in Canada.* 2d ed. Looseleaf. Markham, ON: LexisNexis Canada, 2009.

Phillips, Gordon. *Personal Remedies for Corporate Injuries.* Toronto: Carswell, 1992.

Reiter, Barry J. *Directors' Duties in Canada.* 4th ed. Toronto: CCH Canadian, 2009.

Reiter, Barry J. & Melanie Shisler. *Joint Ventures: Legal and Business Perspectives.* Toronto: Irwin Law, 1999.

Rousseau, Stéphane. *Droit des sociétés par actions au Québec.* Markham, ON: LexisNexis Butterworths, 2004 [annual].

Sarna, Lazar & Petra Alince. *Mergers and Acquisitions: A Canadian Legal Manual.* Rev. ed. Looseleaf. Markham, ON: LexisNexis Butterworths, 2005.

Books	Sarna, Lazar & Hillel Neuer. *Directors and Officers: A Canadian Legal Manual*. Rev. ed. Looseleaf. Markham, ON: LexisNexis Canada, 2005. VanDuzer, J. Anthony. *The Law of Partnerships and Corporations*. 3d ed. Toronto: Irwin Law, 2009. Welling, Bruce L. *Corporate Law in Canada: The Governing Principles*. 2d ed. Toronto: Butterworths, 1991. Yalden, Robert *et al. Business Organizations: Principles, Policies and Practice*. Toronto: Emond Montgomery, 2008. Zaid, Frank. *Canadian Franchise Guide*. Looseleaf. Toronto: Carswell, 1990. Zaid, Frank. *Franchise Law*. Toronto: Irwin Law, 2005.
Journals	*Bulletin de jurisprudence—compagnies et sociétés* (LexisNexis Canada) *Corporate Brief* (CCH Canadian) *Corporate Governance Report* (LexisNexis Canada) *Directors Briefing* (CCH Canadian)
Encyclopedias	*Canadian Encyclopedic Digest*: • Business Corporations (Ontario and Western) • Partnership (Ontario and Western) *Halsbury's Laws of Canada*: • Business Corporations I and II • Commercial Law* • Partnerships and Joint Ventures *JurisClasseur Québec*: Collection Droit des affaires (Droit des sociétés)
Case digests	*Canadian Abridgment* (Carswell): Business associations caseAlert—Corporate and Commercial (Canada Law Book) LexisNexis Quicklaw: Canada Corporations, Partnerships and Associations Digest
Case law reporters	*Business Law Reports* (Carswell)
Databases and CD-ROMs	*Corporate Law Partner (Federal and Ontario)* [CD-ROM]. Toronto: Carswell. Updated regularly. Contains relevant legislation, case law, and Carswell-published textbooks on federal and Ontario corporate law. LexisNexis Quicklaw: Corporations and Associations Law Cases—Topical

N. CRIMINAL LAW

Scope	Criminal law in Canada is generally governed by federal law, most often the *Criminal Code*, R.S.C. 1985, c. C-46, the *Youth Criminal Justice Act*, S.C. 2002, c. 1, and the *Controlled Drugs and Substances Act*, S.C. 1996, c. 19. Offences under provincial statutes also exist. Case law is highly relevant. Young offenders law is also included in this section.
Subject headings	Criminal law — Canada Criminal procedure — Canada
Books	Armstrong, Simon *et al. Sentencing Drug Offenders.* Looseleaf. Aurora, ON: Canada Law Book, 2004. Atrens, Jerome T. & Donald Egleston. *Criminal Procedure: Canadian Law & Practice.* Looseleaf. Toronto: Butterworths, 1981. Backhouse, Constance. *Carnal Crimes: Sexual Assault Law in Canada, 1900–1975.* Toronto: Irwin Law, 2008. Bala, Nicholas & Sanjeev Anand. *Youth Criminal Justice Law.* 2d. ed. Toronto: Irwin Law, 2009. Bentley, Christopher A.W. *Criminal Practice Manual: A Practical Guide to Handling Criminal Case.* Looseleaf. Toronto: Carswell, 2000. Bolton, Michael B. *Defending Drug Cases.* 3d ed. Toronto: Thomson/Carswell, 2006. Bouck, John C. *et al. British Columbia Annual Criminal Practice.* Toronto: Emond Montgomery, 1997 [annual]. Brauti, Peter M. & Brian G. Puddington. *Prosecuting and Defending Drug Offences.* Aurora, ON: Canada Law Book, 2003. Brucker, Theresa. *The Practical Guide to the Controlled Drugs and Substances Act.* 4th ed. Toronto: Carswell, 2008. Cameron, Jamie & James Stribopoulos. *The Charter and Criminal Justice: Twenty-five Years Later.* Markham, ON: LexisNexis, 2008. Castel, Jacqueline R. *Gaming Control Law in Ontario.* Looseleaf. Aurora, ON: Canada Law Book, 2001. Clewley, Gary R. & Paul G. McDermott. *Sentencing: The Practitioner's Guide.* Looseleaf. Aurora, ON: Canada Law Book, 1995. Available as an e-book on *Criminal Spectrum.* Colvin, Eric & Sanjeev Anand. *Principles of Criminal Law.* 3d ed. Toronto: Thomson Carswell, 2007. Coughlan, Stephen. *Criminal Procedure.* Toronto: Irwin Law, 2008. Cox, Harold J., Gregory Lafontaine, & Vincenzo Rondinelli. *Criminal Evidence Handbook.* Aurora, ON: Canada Law Book, 1988 [annual].

Books   Dadour, François. *De la détermination de la peine: principes et applications.* Markham, ON: LexisNexis, 2007.

Debenham, David. *The Law of Fraud and the Forensic Investigator.* Toronto: Thomson Carswell, 2006.

Delisle, Ron & Don Stuart. *Learning Canadian Criminal Procedure.* 7th ed. Toronto: Carswell, 2003.

Der, Balfour. *The Jury: A Handbook of Law and Procedure.* Looseleaf. Toronto: Butterworths, 1989.

Desjardins, Tristan. *L'appel en droit criminel et pénal.* Markham, ON: LexisNexis Canada, 2008.

Desjardins, Tristan. *Les infractions d'ordre moral en droit criminel canadien.* Markham, ON: LexisNexis Canada, 2007.

DesRosiers, Nathalie & Louise Langevin. *Representing Victims of Sexual and Spousal Abuse.* Toronto: Irwin Law, 2002.

Ewaschuk, Eugene G. *Criminal Pleadings & Practice in Canada.* 2d ed. Looseleaf. Aurora, ON: Canada Law Book, 1987. Available as an e-book on *Criminal Spectrum.*

Ferris, Thomas. *Sentencing: Practical Approaches.* Markham, ON: LexisNexis Canada, 2005.

Fontana, James & M. David Keeshan. *The Law of Search and Seizure in Canada.* 7th ed. Markham, ON: LexisNexis Canada, 2007.

Frater, Robert J. *Prosecutorial Misconduct.* Aurora, ON: Canada Law Book, 2009.

Gibson, John L. *Canadian Criminal Code Offences.* Looseleaf. Toronto: Carswell, 1988. Available by subscription on *CriminalSource* on Westlaw Canada.

Gibson, John L. & Henry Waldcock. *Criminal Law: Evidence, Practice and Procedure.* Looseleaf. Toronto: Carswell, 1988. Available by subscription on *CriminalSource* on Westlaw Canada.

Gold, Alan D. *Drinking & Driving Law.* Looseleaf. Toronto: Carswell, 2010.

Gold, Alan D. *Expert Evidence in Criminal Law: The Scientific Approach.* 2d ed. Toronto: Irwin Law, 2009.

Gold, Alan D. *Practitioner's Criminal Code.* Markham, ON: LexisNexis Butterworths, 2006 [annual].

Gold, Alan D. *Practitioner's Criminal Precedents.* Markham, ON: LexisNexis, 2007 [annual].

Granger, Christoper. *The Criminal Jury Trial in Canada.* 2d ed. Toronto: Carswell, 1996.

Greenspan, Edward L., ed. *Counsel for the Defence: The Bernard Cohn Memorial Lectures in Criminal Law.* Toronto: Irwin Law, 2005.

Books

Greenspan, Edward L. & Marc Rosenberg. *Martin's Annual Criminal Code*. Aurora, ON: Canada Law Book, 1955 [annual]. See also *Martin's Related Criminal Statutes*. Also available as an online subscription as *Martin's Online*.

Hageman, Cecilia *et al*. *DNA Handbook*. 2d ed. Markham, ON: LexisNexis, 2008.

Hall, Terence D. *A Guide to Canadian Money Laundering Legislation*. Markham, ON: LexisNexis, 2008 [annual].

Hamilton, Keith R. *Judicial Interim Release: A Bail Manual*. Looseleaf. 4th ed. Toronto: Butterworths, 1983.

Harris, Peter & Miriam H. Blommenfeld. *Youth Criminal Justice Act Manual*. Looseleaf. Aurora, ON: Canada Law Book, 2003. Available as an e-book on *Criminal Spectrum*.

Harris, Peter J. & Miriam H. Bloomenfeld. *Weapons Offences Manual*. Looseleaf. Aurora, ON: Canada Law Book, 1990.

Hill, S. Casey. *McWilliam's Canadian Criminal Evidence*. Looseleaf. 4th ed. Aurora, ON: Canada Law Book, 2003. Available as an e-book on *Criminal Spectrum*.

Hubbard, Robert W. *et al*. *Money Laundering and Proceeds of Crime*. Toronto: Irwin Law, 2004.

Hubbard, Robert W. *et al*. *Wiretapping and Other Electronic Surveillance: Law and Procedure*. Looseleaf. Aurora, ON: Canada Law Book, 2000.

Hutchison, Scott C. *Search and Seizure Law in Canada*. Looseleaf. Toronto: Carswell, 1991.

Jackman, Barbara L. *et al*. *Canadian Public Security Law Guide*. Looseleaf. Toronto: CCH Canadian, 2003. Available in print, on CD-ROM, and by online subscription.

Kenkel, Joseph F. *Impaired Driving in Canada*. Markham, ON: LexisNexis Canada, 2006 [biennial].

Levy, Earl J. *Examination of Witnesses in Criminal Cases*. 5th ed. Toronto: Carswell, 2004.

MacFarlane, Bruce, Robert J. Frater, & Chantal Proulx. *Drug Offences in Canada*. Looseleaf. 3d ed. Aurora, ON: Canada Law Book, 1996. Available as an e-book on *Criminal Spectrum*.

Maleszyk, Anna. *Crimes Against Children: Prosecution and Defence*. Aurora, ON: Canada Law Book, 2001.

Manning. Morris & Peter Sankoff. *Manning, Mewett & Sankoff: Criminal Law*. 4th ed. Markham, ON: LexisNexis, 2009.

Manson, Allan. *The Law of Sentencing*. Toronto: Irwin Law, 2001.

McLeod, R.M. *et al*. *Canadian Charter of Rights: the Prosecution and Defence of Criminal and other Statutory Offences*. Looseleaf. Toronto: Carswell, 1988. Also available by subscription online (Carswell eReference Library).

Books	Mewett, Alan & Shaun Nakatsuru. *An Introduction to the Criminal Process.* 4th ed. Toronto: Carswell, 2000.

Paciocco, David M. *Getting Away with Murder: The Canadian Criminal Justice System.* Toronto: Irwin Law, 2000.

Pink, Joel E. & David Perrier. *From Crime to Punishment: An Introduction to the Criminal Law System.* 6th ed. Toronto: Carswell, 2007.

Platt, Priscilla. *Young Offenders Service.* Looseleaf. Scarborough, ON: Butterworths, 1984.

Proulx, Michel & David Layton. *Ethics and Canadian Criminal Law.* Toronto: Irwin Law, 2001.

Renaud, Gilles. *The Sentencing Code of Canada: Principles and Objectives.* Markham, ON: LexisNexis, 2009.

Roach, Kent. *Criminal Law.* 4th. Toronto: Irwin Law, 2009.

Rodrigues, Gary P. *Crankshaw's Criminal Code.* 8th ed. Looseleaf. Toronto: Carswell, 1993. Available on *CriminalSource* on Westlaw Canada.

Ruby, Clayton C. *et al. Sentencing.* 7th ed. Markham, ON: LexisNexis Canada, 2008.

Salhany, Roger E. *Canadian Criminal Procedure.* 6th ed. Looseleaf. Aurora, ON: Canada Law Book, 1994. Available as an e-book on *Criminal Spectrum.*

Salhany, Roger E. *Police Manual of Arrest, Seizure and Interrogation.* 9th ed. Toronto: Carswell, 2009

Segal, Murray D. *Disclosure and Production in Criminal Cases.* Looseleaf. Toronto: Carswell, 1996. Available on *CriminalSource* on Westlaw Canada.

Stewart, Hamish (with John Norris). *Sexual Offences in Canadian Law.* Looseleaf. Aurora, ON: Canada Law Book, 2004.

Stuart, Don. *Canadian Criminal Law: A Treatise.* 5th ed. Scarborough, ON: Carswell, 2007.

Stuart, Don. *Charter Justice in Canadian Criminal Law.* 4th ed. Toronto: Thomson Carswell, 2005.

Stuart, Don, Ron Delisle, & Steve Coughlan. *Learning Canadian Criminal Law.* 11th ed. Toronto: Carswell, 2009.

Stuart, Don, Ron Delisle, & Tim Quigley. *Learning Canadian Criminal Procedure.* 9th ed. Toronto: Thomson Carswell, 2008.

Tanovich, David M. *The Colour of Justice: Policing Race in Canada.* Toronto: Irwin Law, 2006.

Tanovich, David M. *et al. Jury Selection in Criminal Trials: Skills, Science, and the Law.* Toronto: Irwin Law, 1997.

Trotter, Gary T. *The Law of Bail in Canada.* 2d ed. Toronto: Carswell, 1999.

Books	Tuck-Jackson, Andrea E.E. *et al.*, eds. *Annotated Youth Criminal Justice Act.* Looseleaf. Markham, ON: LexisNexis Canada, 2003.
	Watt, David. *Carswell's Forms and Precedent Collection: Criminal Law Precedents.* 2d ed. Looseleaf. Toronto: Carswell, 2007.
	Watt, David. *Watt's Manual of Criminal Evidence.* Toronto: Carswell, 1998 [annual]. Available by subscription on *CriminalSource* on Westlaw Canada.
	Watt, David & Michelle K. Fuerst. *Annotated Tremeear's Criminal Code.* Toronto: Carswell, 1964 [annual]. Available by subscription on *CriminalSource* on Westlaw Canada.
Journals	*Annual Review of Criminal Law* (Carswell)
	Bulletin de jurisprudence: Détermination de la peine (LexisNexis Canada)
	Canadian Criminal Law Review (Carswell). Available on Westlaw Canada
	Criminal Law Quarterly (Canada Law Book). Also available on *Criminal Spectrum.*
	For the Defence (LexisNexis Canada for the Ontario Criminal Lawyers Association)
Encyclopedias	*Canadian Encyclopedic Digest*:

- Conspiracy
- Criminal Law—Defences
- Criminal Law—Offences
- Criminal Law—Procedure
- Firearms, Weapons and Explosives
- Fraud and Misrepresentation
- Gaming
- Liquor Control (Ontario and Western)
- Narcotic Control
- Police
- Prisons
- Sentencing
- Sheriffs and Bailiffs (Ontario and Western)
- Victims of Crime—Compensation
- War and Emergency
- Youth Criminal Justice

Halsbury's Laws of Canada:
- Betting, Gaming and Lotteries*
- Criminal Offences and Defences
- Criminal Procedure
- Drugs and Controlled Substances*
- Firearms, Weapons and Dangerous Goods

Encyclopedias	*Halsbury's Laws of Canada* (continued):
	• Liquor Control*
	• Misrepresentation and Fraud*
	• Penitentiaries, Jails and Prisoners
	• Police, Security and Emergency Services
	JurisClasseur Québec: Collection Droit penal
Case digests	Canada Law Book:
	• caseAlert—Criminal Law
	• *Weekly Criminal Bulletin*
	Canadian Abridgment (Carswell):
	• Criminal law
	• Public law—Gaming
	• Public law—Liquor Control
	Criminal Law Digest, 3d ed. (Carswell)
	LexisNexis Canada:
	• *Canada Criminal Sentencing Digest*
	• *Criminal Lawyers' Trial Book*
	• *Impaired Driving and Breathalyzer Law: Recent Case Law*
	LexisNexis Quicklaw:
	• Abrégé de jurisprudence—Droit criminal
	• Canada Criminal Digest
	• Résumés de jurisprudence en droit criminel et pénal by Schneider & Dubois
Case law reporters	*Canadian Criminal Cases* (Canada Law Book). Also on BestCase.
	Criminal Reports (Carswell)
Databases and CD-ROMs	*Criminal Law Partner* [CD-ROM]. Toronto: Carswell. Updated regularly. Contains relevant legislation, case law, and Carswell-published textbooks on criminal law. Available in an expanded version as *CriminalSource* by subscription on Westlaw Canada.
	Criminal Spectrum (Canada Law Book)
	Criminal*Practice* (LexisNexis Quicklaw)
	LexisNexis Quicklaw:
	• Criminal Law Cases—Topical
	• Proceeds of Crime Cases—Topical

O. CROWN LAW

Scope	Crown law in Canada is still influenced by British law, although the law has developed on its own in Canada, partly as a result of federal legislation, such as the *Crown Liability and Proceedings Act*, R.S.C. 1985, c. C-50, and various provincial statutes, such as Ontario's *Public Authorities Protection Act*, R.S.O. 1990, c. P.38. The government—whether federal, provincial, or municipal—may often have the benefit of special limitation periods when being sued. Care should always be taken to check for applicable limitation periods when suing the government (limitation periods are discussed in the section above in this chapter on civil procedure).
Subject headings	Government liability—Canada Privileges and immunities—Canada
Books	Attwater, David M. *Procurement Review: A Practitioner's Guide*. Looseleaf. Scarborough, ON: Carswell, 2001. Cooper, Terrance G. *Crown Privilege*. Aurora, ON: Canada Law Book, 1990. Emanuelli, Paul. *Government Procurement*. 2d ed. Markham, ON: LexisNexis Canada, 2008. Hogg, Peter W. & Patrick J. Monahan. *Liability of the Crown*. 3d ed. Toronto: Carswell, 2000. Horsman, Karen & Gareth Morley. *Government Liability: Law and Practice*. Aurora, ON: Canada Law Book, 2007. Klein, Kris & Denis Kratchanov. *Government Information: The Right to Information and the Protection of Privacy*. 2d ed. Looseleaf. Toronto: Carswell, 2009. Létourneau, Gilles & Michel W. Drapeau. *Canadian Military Law Annotated*. Toronto: Thomson Carswell, 2006. Madsen, Chris. *Military Law and Operations*. Looseleaf. Aurora, ON: Canada Law Book, 2008. McGuinness, Kevin Patrick *et al. Municipal Procurement Handbook*. Markham, ON: Butterworths, 2002. Meunier, Pierre B. *Lobbying in Canada*. Looseleaf. Toronto: Thomson Carswell, 2003. Noonan, Peter W. *The Crown and Constitutional Law in Canada*. Calgary: Sripnoon Publications, 1998. Ratushny, Ed. *The Conduct of Public Inquiries: Law, Policy, and Practice*. Toronto: Irwin Law, 2009. Sgayias, David *et al. The 1995 Annotated Crown Liability and Proceedings Act*. Scarborough, ON: Carswell, 1995. Tarfi, Gregory. *The Law of Democratic Governing: Principles and The Law of Democratic Governing—Jurisprudence* (2 vol.). Toronto: Thomson Carswell, 2004.

Journals	The Hill Times (www.thehilltimes.ca) Journal of Parliamentary and Political Law (Carswell) Ottawa Letter (CCH Canadian)
Encyclopedias	Canadian Encyclopedic Digest: • Crown • Elections • Military Law • Prerogative Remedies • Public Authorities and Public Officers (Ontario and Western) • War and Emergency Halsbury's Laws of Canada: • Crown and Public Authorities* • Defence and Armed Forces* • Elections and Legislatures*
Case digests	Canadian Abridgment (Carswell): Public law
Case law reporters	Federal Court Reports

P. DAMAGES AND REMEDIES LAW

Scope	Damages law is governed by a combination of case law and (largely) provincial legislation too numerous to list here.
Subject headings	Damages—Canada Injunctions—Canada Remedies (law)—Canada Restitution—Canada Specific performance—Canada
Books	Apportionment of Liability in British Columbia. Looseleaf. Toronto: LexisNexis Butterworths, 1983. Berryman, Jeffrey. The Law of Equitable Remedies. Toronto: Irwin Law, 2000. Brown, Cara. Damages: Estimating Pecuniary Loss. Looseleaf. Aurora, ON: Canada Law Book, 2001. Bruce, Christopher J. Assessment of Personal Injury Damages. 4th ed. Toronto: LexisNexis Butterworths, 2004. Carlson, John & Karen D.P. Carlson. Personal Injury Damages. Markham, ON: LexisNexis Butterworths, 2004 [annual]. Cassels, Jamie & Elizabeth Adjin-Tettey. Remedies: The Law of Damages. 2d ed. Toronto: Irwin Law, 2008. Cooper-Stephenson, Ken. Personal Injury Damages in Canada. 2d ed. Scarborough, ON: Carswell, 1996.

Books

Feldthusen, Bruce. *Economic Negligence: The Recovery of Pure Economic Loss*. 5th ed. Scarborough, ON: Thomson Carswell, 2008.

Fitzgerald, Oonagh E. *Understanding Charter Remedies: A Practitioner's Guide*. Looseleaf. Scarborough, ON: Carswell, 1994.

Flaherty, James M. & Catherine H. Zingg. *Accident Benefits in Ontario*. Looseleaf. Aurora, ON: Canada Law Book, 2005. Online subscription also available.

Fridman, Gerald. *Restitution*. 2d ed. Toronto: Carswell, 1992.

Goldsmith, Immanuel. *Damages for Personal Injury and Death in Canada*. Toronto: Carswell, 1959 [annual supplements]. Available by subscription in modified form on Litigator on Westlaw Canada.

Klar, Lewis N. *Remedies in Tort*. Looseleaf. Toronto: Carswell, 1987.

Law Society of Upper Canada. *Special Lectures 2005: The Modern Law of Damages*. Toronto: Irwin Law, 2006.

Law Society of Upper Canada. *Special Lectures 2008: Personal Injury Law*. Toronto: Irwin Law, 2009.

Maddaugh, Peter D. & John D. McCamus. *The Law of Restitution*. 2d ed. Aurora, ON: Canada Law Book, 2004. Also available in a looseleaf edition.

Miller, Jeffrey. *The Law of Contempt in Canada*. Toronto: Carswell, 1997.

Oatley, Roger G. & John A. McLeish. *The Oatley-McLeish Guide to Anatomy and Impairment*. Markham, ON: LexisNexis, 2009.

Oatley, Roger G. & John A. McLeish. *The Oatley-McLeish Guide to Brain Injury Litigation*. Markham, ON: LexisNexis Butterworths, 2005.

Oatley, Roger G. & John A. McLeish. *The Oatley-McLeish Guide to Personal Injury Practice in Motor Vehicle Cases*. Looseleaf. Aurora, ON: Canada Law Book, 2002.

Perell, Paul M. & Bruce H. Engell. *Remedies and the Sale of Land*. 2d ed. Toronto: LexisNexis Canada, 1998.

Roach, Kent. *Constitutional Remedies in Canada*. Looseleaf. Aurora, ON: Canada Law Book, 1994.

Sarna, Lazar. *The Law of Declaratory Judgments*. 3d ed. Toronto: Thomson Carswell, 2007.

Sharpe, Robert J. *Injunctions and Specific Performance*. 3d ed. Aurora, ON: Canada Law Book, 2002. Also available in a looseleaf edition.

Snyder, Ronald M. & Harvin D. Pitch. *Damages for Breach of Contract*. 2d ed. Looseleaf. Toronto: Carswell, 1989.

Spry, Ian. *Equitable Remedies*. 6th ed. Toronto: Carswell, 2004.

Books	Waddams, Stephen M. *The Law of Damages*. 4th ed. Aurora, ON: Canada Law Book, 2004.

Encyclopedias	*Canadian Encyclopedic Digest*:

- Contempt of Court
- Damages
- Equity
- Estoppel
- Injunctions
- Restitution
- Specific Performance

Halsbury's Laws of Canada:
- Damages*
- Interim Preservation of Property Rights
- Equitable Remedies*
- Unjust Enrichment and Restitution*

Case digests	*Canadian Abridgment* (Carswell):

- Equity
- Estoppel
- Remedies
- Restitution and unjust enrichment

Databases and CD-ROMs	LexisNexis Quicklaw:

- Canada Medical Negligence Quantums
- Canada Property-Related Torts Quantums
- Canada Wrongful Dismissal Quantums

Litigator: Various Quantum Databases (currently covering breach of contract, child support, defamation, dependants' relief, personal injury, spousal support, and wrongful dismissal) (Westlaw Canada)

Personal Injury Damages Calculator and Partner [CD-ROMs]. Carswell.

Q. DEBTOR/CREDITOR LAW

Scope	Debtor/creditor law is affected by both case law and provincial (and federal) legislation too numerous to list here. In addition, in enforcing or defending a debt, it is often useful to have a good understanding of civil procedure, discussed above in this chapter. Bankruptcy and insolvency is also discussed above as a separate topic.
Subject headings	Debtor and creditor — Canada Fraudulent conveyances — Canada

Books	Babe, Jennifer. *Canadian Forms & Precedents: Debtor/Creditor.* Looseleaf. 2d ed. Markham, ON: LexisNexis, 2008. Available on CD-ROM and on LexisNexis Quicklaw.
	Bennett, Frank. *Bennett on Collections.* 5th ed. Scarborough, ON: Carswell, 2003.
	Bennett, Frank. *Bennett on Creditors' and Debtors' Rights and Remedies.* 5th ed. Toronto: Carswell, 2006.
	Doyle, Kelly R. *Asset Protection.* Markham, ON: LexisNexis Butterworths, 2005.
	Dunlop, Charles R.B. *Creditor-Debtor Law in Canada.* 2d ed. Scarborough, ON: Carswell, 1995.
	Edmunds, Ross. *The Canadian Credit and Collection Guide.* 2d ed. Looseleaf. Toronto: Carswell, 1996.
	Fraser, Marcia J. *Debt Collection: A Step-by-Step Guide.* Looseleaf. Aurora, ON: Canada Law Book, 1989.
	Kershman, Stanley J. *Credit Solutions: Kershman on Advising Secured and Unsecured Creditors.* 2d ed. Toronto: Thomson Carswell, 2008.
	McConnell, H. Rose. *A Guide to Collection Procedures in Ontario.* Toronto: CCH Canadian, 2002.
	Meehan, Eugene *et al. Creditors' Remedies in Ontario.* 2d ed. Markham, ON: LexisNexis, 2009.
	Olivo, Laurence M. & DeeAnn Gonsalves. *Debtor-Creditor Law and Procedure.* 3d ed. Toronto: Emond Montgomery, 2008.
	Petraglia, Philip & Lazar Sarna. *Annotated Creditors & Debtors Laws of Ontario.* Looseleaf. Markham, ON: LexisNexis Canada, 2002.
	Robinson, Lyman R. & R.C. Di Bella. *British Columbia Debtor-Creditor Law and Precedents.* Looseleaf. Scarborough, ON: Carswell, 1993.
	Springman, Melvin A. *Fraudulent Conveyances and Preferences.* Looseleaf. Scarborough, ON: Carswell, 1994.
	Tweedie, Michael G. *Debt Litigation.* Looseleaf. Aurora, ON: Canada Law Book, 2004.
Journals	*National Creditor-Debtor Review* (LexisNexis Canada). Available on LexisNexisQuicklaw.
Encyclopedias	*Canadian Encyclopedic Digest*: • Debtor and Creditor • Execution (Ontario and Western) • Fraudulent Conveyances and Preferences • Sheriffs and Bailiffs (Ontario and Western) *Halsbury's Laws of Canada*: Debtors and Creditors*
Case digests	*Canadian Abridgment* (Carswell): Debtors and creditors

R. EDUCATION LAW

Scope	Education law is governed by both legislation (largely provincial) and case law. It encompasses other areas of law including constitutional law and employment law.
Subject headings	Educational law and legislation— Canada Teachers—Legal status, laws, etc.— Canada
Books	Bowers, Grant & Rena Knox (Marvin A. Zuker, consulting editor). *Sexual Misconduct in Education: Prevention, Reporting and Discipline.* 2d ed. Markham, ON: LexisNexis Butterworths, 2006.

Bowlby, Brenda *et al. An Educator's Guide to Special Education Law.* Aurora, ON: Aurora Professional Press, 2001.

Brown, Anthony F. *Legal Handbook for Educators.* 5th Toronto: Carswell, 2004.

Brown, Anthony F. & Marvin A. Zuker. *Education Law.* 4th ed. Toronto: Thomson Carswell, 2007.

Brown, David M. *An Educator's Guide to Independent Schools.* Aurora, ON: Aurora Professional Press, 1998.

Hurlbert, Earl Leroy & Margot Ann Hurlbert. *School Law under the Charter of Rights and Freedoms.* 2d ed. Calgary: University of Calgary Press, 1992.

Keel, Robert G. *Student Rights and Responsibilities: Attendance and Discipline.* Toronto: Emond Montgomery, 1998.

Keel, Robert G. & Nadya Tymochenko. *An Educator's Guide to Managing Sexual Misconduct in School.* Aurora, ON: Aurora Professional Press, 2003.

Mackay, Wayne. *Education Law in Canada.* Toronto: Emond Montgomery, 1984.

Mackay, Wayne & Gregory M. Dickinson. *Beyond the "Careful Parent": Tort Liability in Education.* Toronto: Emond Montgomery, 1998.

Mackay, Wayne & Lyle I. Sutherland. *Teachers and the Law: A Practical Guide for Educators.* 2d ed. Toronto: Emond Montgomery, 2006.

McIntyre, Elizabeth J. & David I. Bloom. *An Educator's Guide to the Ontario College of Teachers.* Aurora, ON: Aurora Professional Press, 2002.

Phibbs, Douglas E.G., ed. *Annotated Ontario Education Act.* Toronto: Carswell, 1998 [annual].

Roher, Eric M. & Simon A. Wormwell. *An Educator's Guide to the Role of the Principal.* 2d ed. Aurora, ON: Canada Law Book, 2008.

Roher, Eric M. *An Educator's Guide to Violence in Schools.* Aurora, ON: Aurora Professional Press, 2000.

Books	Sarna, Lazar & Noah Sarna. *The Law of Schools and Universities.* Markham, ON: LexisNexis Canada, 2007. Shilton, Elizabeth J. & Karen Schucher. *Education Labour and Employment Law in Ontario.* 2d ed. Looseleaf. Aurora, ON: Canada Law Book, 2001. Sussel, Terri A. *Canada's Legal Revolution: Public Education, The Charter and Human Rights.* Toronto: Emond Montgomery, 1995. Trépanier, Jennifer E. *Student Discipline: A Guide to the Education Amendment Act, 2007.* 2d ed. Markham, ON: LexisNexis Canada, 2008.
Journals	*Education & Law Journal* (Carswell). Available on Westlaw Canada *Education Law Reporter* (Education Law Infosource) *Risk Management in Canadian Education* (LexisNexis Canada)
Encyclopedias	*Canadian Encyclopedic Digest*: Education (Ontario and Western) *Halsbury's Laws of Canada*: Education Law*
Case digests	*Canadian Abridgment* (Carswell): Education law LexisNexis Quicklaw: • Canada Education Law Digest • Shibley Righton Education Law NetLetter digests
Databases and CD-ROMs	LexisNexis Quicklaw: • Education Law Cases — Topical • Ontario College of Teachers Discipline Decisions (1988 to current)

S. EMPLOYMENT LAW

Scope	Employment law in Canada is governed by both common law principles (what constitutes just cause for dismissal of a senior employee?) and legislation (both provincial and federal, depending on whether the employment is governed by federal or provincial laws). Typical of a provincial statute is the Ontario *Employment Standards Act, 2000*, S.O. 2000, c. 41. Employment law tends to cover only non-unionized employees, whereas labour law (discussed below in this chapter) covers unionized employees.
Subject headings	Employees — Dismissal of — Law and legislation — Canada Labor laws and legislation — Canada
Books	Aggarwal, Arjun P. & Madhu M. Gupta. *Sexual Harassment in the Workplace.* 3d ed. Toronto: Butterworths, 2000.

Books

Ball, Stacey Reginald. *Canadian Employment Law.* Looseleaf. Aurora, ON: Canada Law Book, 1996. Also available by online subscription.

Bernardi, Lauren M. *Powerful Employment Policies.* Looseleaf. Aurora, ON: Canada Law Book, 2001.

Bolland, Joan & Ellen Mole. *Best Practices: Employment Policies that Work.* Looseleaf. Toronto: Carswell, 1995. Also available by subscription online (Carswell eReference Library).

Canada Law Book. *O'Brien's Encyclopedia of Forms: Division VII, Labour Relations and Employment.* 11th ed. Aurora, ON: Canada Law Book, 1987. Also available on CD-ROM and by subscription on O'Brien's Internet.

Chauvin, Peter F. *et al. Canadian Employment Law Factbook.* Looseleaf. Scarborough, ON: Carswell, 1992.

Corry, David J. & James M. Petrie. *Conducting a Wrongful Dismissal Action.* Scarborough, ON: Carswell, 1997.

D'Andrea, James A. *Employee Obligations in Canada.* Looseleaf. Aurora, ON: Canada Law Book, 2003.

Echlin, Randall Scott & Matthew L.O. Certosimo. *Just Cause: The Law of Summary Dismissal in Canada.* Looseleaf. Aurora, ON: Canada Law Book, 2000.

Echlin, Randall Scott *et al. Quitting for Good Reason: The Law Of Constructive Dismissal in Canada.* Aurora, ON: Canada Law Book, 2001.

England, Geoffrey. *Individual Employment Law.* 2d ed. Toronto: Irwin Law, 2008.

England, Geoffrey *et al. Employment Law in Canada.* 4th ed. Looseleaf. Markham, ON: LexisNexis Butterworths, 2005.

Harris, David. *Wrongful Dismissal.* 3d ed. Looseleaf. Scarborough, ON: Carswell, 1984. Also available by subscription online (Carswell eReference Library).

Heenan Blaikie LLP. *Québec Labour and Employment Law: Frequently Asked Questions.* Toronto: Carswell, 2002.

Klein, Kris *et al. Privacy in Employment: Control of Personal Information in the Workplace.* 2d ed. Toronto: Thomson Carswell, 2009.

Knight, James G. *et al. Employment Litigation Manual.* 2d ed. Looseleaf. Markham, ON: LexisNexis Canada, 2007.

Law Society of Upper Canada. *Special Lectures 2007: Employment Law.* Toronto: Irwin Law, 2007.

Levitt, Howard A. *The Law of Dismissal in Canada.* 3d ed. Looseleaf. Aurora, ON: Canada Law Book, 2003.

Litherland, Geoffrey J. & Kirsten Hume. *An Employer's Guide to Dismissal.* 2d ed. Aurora, ON: Canada Law Book, 2007.

Books	MacKillop Malcolm J., James G. Knight & Kerry D. Williams. *Damage Control: An Employer's Guide to Just Cause Termination*. Aurora, ON: Canada Law Book, 2005.
	Manning, Melanie. *Pregnancy, Workplace and the Law*. Aurora, ON: Canada Law Book, 2003.
	Milne, Catherine. *Canadian Forms & Precedents: Employment*. Looseleaf. Markham, ON: LexisNexis Canada, 2005. Available on CD-ROM and on LexisNexis Quicklaw.
	Mole, Ellen E. *The Wrongful Dismissal Practice Manual*. 2d ed. Looseleaf. Toronto: LexisNexis Canada, 2005.
	Mole, Ellen E. & Marion J. Stendon. *The Wrongful Dismissal Handbook*. 3d ed. Markham, ON: LexisNexis Butterworths, 2004.
	Ontario Ministry of Labour, Employment Standards Branch. *Employment Standards Act 2000: Policy and Interpretation Manual*. Looseleaf. Scarborough, ON: Carswell, 2001. Also available on CD-ROM.
	O'Reilly, John C. *An Employer's Guide to Surveillance, Searches and Medical Examinations*. Toronto: Thomson Carswell, 2003.
	Parry, Kimberly A. & David A. Ryan. *Employment Standards Handbook*. 3d ed. Looseleaf. Aurora, ON: Canada Law Book, 2002.
	Sproat, John R. *Wrongful Dismissal Handbook*. 4th ed. Toronto: Thomson Carswell, 2006.
	Steele, Gregory K. & Kenneth W. Thornicroft. *Employment Covenants and Confidential Information*. Markham, ON:Butterworths, 2002.
Journals	*Canadian Labour & Employment Law Journal* (Lancaster House)
	Employment and Labour Law Reporter (LexisNexis Canada). Available on LexisNexis Quicklaw from 1994.
	Employment Bulletin: Legal Issues in the Workplace (Canada Law Book)
	The Canadian Employer (Newsletter) (Carswell)
Encyclopedias	*Canadian Encyclopedic Digest*:
	• Employment Insurance
	• Employment (Ontario and Western)
	• Occupational Health and Safety (Ontario)
	• Workers' Compensation (Ontario and Western)
	• Wrongful Dismissal (Western)
	Halsbury's Laws of Canada:
	• Employment
	• Holidays
	• Trade and Professions*

Case digests	*Canadian Abridgment* (Carswell): Labour and employment law LexisNexis Quicklaw: Canada Employment Digest
Case law reporters	*Canadian Cases on Employment Law* (Carswell)
Databases and CD-ROMs	*Employment Law Partner* [CD-ROM]. Toronto: Carswell. Updated regularly. Contains relevant legislation, case law, and Carswell-published textbooks on employment law. Employment*Practice* (LexisNexis Quicklaw) LexisNexis Canada: • Numerous databases of decisions from various federal and provincial employment tribunals • *Wrongful Dismissal Notice Searcher* (Ellen Mole, LexisNexis Canada). Available on LexisNexis Quicklaw (1980 to current). *Wrongful Dismissal Database* (Fisher and Benaroche, Carswell)

T. ENVIRONMENTAL AND NATURAL RESOURCES LAW

Scope	Environmental law is governed by federal and provincial legislation. Examples include the federal *Canadian Environmental Assessment Act*, S.C. 1992, c. 37, the *Canadian Environmental Protection Act, 1999*, S.C. 1999, c. 33, and the *Environmental Protection and Enhancement Act*, R.S.A. 2000, c. E-12. Environmental law is heavily regulated in Canada and first-time researchers should ensure they have not overlooked any applicable statute or regulation. Included below are materials that cover natural resources and oil and gas law.
Subject headings	Environmental law — Canada Environmental policy — Canada
	Abdel-Aziz, Ahab *et al. The Canadian Brownfields Manual*. Looseleaf. Markham, ON: LexisNexis Butterworths, 2004. Benidickson, Jamie. *Environmental Law*. 3d ed. Toronto: Irwin Law, 2008. Berger, Stanley D. *Prosecution and Defence of Environmental Offences*. Looseleaf. Aurora, ON: Canada Law Book, 1993. A Sentencing Database is also available by online subscription. Boyd, David R. *Unnatural Law: Rethinking Canadian Environmental Law and Policy*. Vancouver: UBC Press, 2003.

Books   Canadian Institute of Resources Law. *Canada Energy Law
              Service*. Looseleaf. Toronto: Carswell, 1990. There is a
              two-volume federal component and a one-volume Alberta
              component of this service.

              Cameron, Duncan *et al. Annotated Guide to the Canadian En-
              vironmental Protection Act*. Looseleaf. Aurora, ON: Canada
              Law Book, 2004.

              Canadian Oil and Gas Law. Looseleaf. 2d ed. Toronto: Butter-
              worths, 1954.

              Coburn, Frederick & Garth Manning. *Toxic Real Estate
              Manual*. Looseleaf. Aurora, ON: Canada Law Book, 1994.

              Doelle, Meinhard. *Federal Environmental Process: A Guide and
              Critique*. Markham, ON: LexisNexis Canada, 2008.

              Estrin, David. *Business Guide to Environmental Law*. Loose-
              leaf. Scarborough, ON: Carswell, 1992.

              Estrin, David & John Swaigen. *Environment on Trial: A Guide
              to Ontario Environmental Law and Policy*. 3d ed. Toronto:
              Emond Montgomery, 1993.

              Faieta, Mario D. *et al. Environmental Harm: Civil Actions and
              Compensation*. Toronto: Butterworths, 1996.

              Ferguson, Reg. *WHMIS Compliance Manual*. Looseleaf. To-
              ronto: Carswell, 1989.

              Hobby, Beverly *et al. Canadian Environmental Assessment Act:
              An Annotated Guide*. Looseleaf. Aurora, ON: Canada Law
              Book, 1997.

              Hughes, Elaine L. *et al.*, eds. *Environmental Law and Policy*.
              3d ed. Toronto: Emond Montgomery, 2003.

              Jeffery, Michael. *Environmental Approvals in Canada: Practice
              and Procedure*. Looseleaf. Toronto: Butterworths, 1989.

              Lucas, Alastair & Roger Cotton. *Canadian Environmental Law*.
              Looseleaf. 2d ed. Markham, ON: LexisNexis Canada, 1991.

              Mahoney, Dennis, ed. *The Law of Climate Change in Canada*.
              Looseleaf. Aurora, ON: Canada Law Book, 2010.

              Mancell, Garry E. & Brian D. Gilfillan. *Davis & Company's
              British Columbia Forestry Law: An Annotated Guide to the
              Forest Practices Code & Forest Act*. Looseleaf. Aurora, ON:
              Canada Law Book, 1997.

              Muldoon, Paul & Richard Lindgren. *The Environmental Bill
              of Rights: A Practical Guide*. Toronto: Emond Montgomery,
              1995.

              Northey, Rod. *The Annotated Canadian Environmental Assess-
              ment Act and EARP Guidelines Order*. Scarborough, ON:
              Carswell, 1994.

              Pardy, Bruce. *Environmental Law: A Guide to Concepts*. To-
              ronto: Butterworths, 1996.

Books	Saxe, Dianne. *Environmental Offences: Corporate Responsibility and Executive Liability.* Aurora, ON: Canada Law Book, 1990.
	Saxe, Dianne. *Ontario Environmental Protection Act Annotated.* Looseleaf. Aurora, ON: Canada Law Book, 1990.
	Swaigen, John. *Regulatory Offences in Canada: Liability & Defences.* Scarborough, ON: Carswell, 1992.
	Theisen, Eric J. *Guide and Explanation to the Canadian Transportation of Dangerous Goods Act and Regulations.* Looseleaf. Scarborough, ON: Carswell, 1992.
	Wilson, Paul C., ed. *Canadian Environmental Law Guide.* Looseleaf. Vancouver STP Specialty Technical Publishers, 1996.
Journals	*Canadian Environmental Regulation & Compliance News* (CanadianEnvironmental.com)
	Canadian Journal of Environmental Law & Practice (Carswell). Available on Westlaw Canada
	Environment Policy & Law (Environment Policy & Law)
	Canadian Water Treatment (We Communications)
	Carbon & Climate Law Review (Lexxion)
	Dangerous Goods Newsletter. Available online from Transport Canada (www.tc.gc.ca)
	Mining & Exploration Company Financings (Gamah)
	Mining Journal (Aspermont)
	Northern Miner (Business Information Group)
Encyclopedias	*Canadian Encyclopedic Digest*:
	• Agriculture (Ontario and Western)
	• Animals
	• Environmental Law (Ontario and Western)
	• Fires (Ontario and Western)
	• Fish and Wildlife (Ontario)
	• Fish and Game (Western)
	• Mines and Minerals (Ontario and Western)
	• Oil and Gas
	• Timber
	• Waters and Watercourses (Ontario and Western)
	Halsbury's Laws of Canada:
	• Animals*
	• Environment
	• Fires, Hunting and Fishing
	• Mines and Minerals*
	• Oil and Gas
Case digests	*Canadian Abridgment* (Carswell):
	• Environmental law
	• Natural resources

Case law reporters	*Canadian Environmental Law Reports* (Carswell)
Databases and CD-ROMs	*EcoLog.com Legislation* (EcoLog Environmental Resources Group)
Websites	Canadian Environmental Law Association: www.cela.ca

U. EVIDENCE LAW

Scope	Evidence law governs the rules by which courts and other adjudicate bodies are governed regarding the admission of evidence before them. There is a federal *Evidence Act* in addition to provincial evidence Acts; this area of law is also strongly influenced by case law.
Subject headings	Evidence (law) — Canada
Books	Anderson, Glenn R. *Expert Evidence*. 2d ed. Markham, ON: LexisNexis Butterworths, 2009.
	Carswell. *Annotated Canadian Evidence Acts*. Scarborough, ON: Carswell, 1991 [annual].
	Chayko, Garry, ed. *Forensic Evidence in Canada*. 2d ed. Aurora, ON: Canada Law Book, 1999.
	Corbin, Ruth M. *et al. Trial by Survey: Survey Evidence & the Law*. Scarborough, ON: Carswell, 2000.
	Cudmore, Gordon. *Civil Evidence Handbook*. Looseleaf. Toronto: Carswell, 1987.
	Delisle, Ronald J. & Lisa Dufraimont. *Canadian Evidence Law in a Nutshell*. 3d ed. Toronto: Carswell, 2009.
	Deutscher, David & Heather Leonoff. *Identification Evidence*. Toronto: Carswell, 1991.
	Doherty, Michael P. *The Portable Guide to Evidence*. 3d ed. Toronto: Carswell, 2009.
	Gahtan, Alan M. *Electronic Evidence*. Scarborough, ON: Carswell, 1999.
	Gold, Alan D. *Expert Evidence in Criminal Law*. 2d ed. Toronto: Irwin Law, 2009.
	Goldstein, Elliott. *Visual Evidence: A Practitioner's Manual*. Looseleaf. Toronto: Carswell, 1991.
	Hageman, Cecilia *et al. DNA Handbook*. 2d ed. Markham, ON: LexisNexis, 2008.
	Hill, S. Casey. *McWilliam's Canadian Criminal Evidence*. Looseleaf. 4th ed. Aurora, ON: Canada Law Book, 2003.

Books	Hubbard, Robert *et al. The Law of Privilege in Canada*. Loose-leaf. Aurora, ON: Canada Law Book, 2006.
	Law Society of Upper Canada. *Special Lectures 2003: The Law of Evidence*. Toronto: Irwin Law, 2004.
	· Mewett, Alan W. *Witnesses*. Looseleaf. Scarborough, ON: Carswell, 1991.
	Morton, James C. *Ontario Litigator's Pocket Guide to Evidence*. 5th ed. Markham, ON: LexisNexis Canada, 2010. Also available in versions for British Columbia, Alberta, and Nova Scotia.
	O'Shea, Michael. *Records Retention: Law and Practice*. Loose-leaf. Toronto: Carswell, 1989. Also available by subscription online (Carswell eReference Library).
	Paciocco, David M & Lee Stuesser. *The Law of Evidence*. 5th ed. Toronto: Irwin Law, 2008.
	Rose, David & Lisa Goos. *DNA: A Practical Guide*. Looseleaf. Toronto: Thomson Carswell, 2004.
	Salhany, Roger E. *The Practical Guide to Evidence in Criminal Cases*. 6th ed. Scarborough, ON: Carswell, 2002.
	Sopinka, John *et al. The Law of Evidence in Canada*. 3d ed. Markham, ON: LexisNexis, 2009. Also available by subscription on LexisNexis Quicklaw.
	Underwood, Graham & Jonathan Penner. *Electronic Evidence in Canada*. Toronto: Carswell, 2010.
	White, Robert B. *The Art of Using Expert Evidence*. Aurora, ON: Canada Law Book, 1997.
Journals	*Advocate's Quarterly* (Canada Law Book)
	Annual Review of Civil Litigation (Carswell)
Encyclopedias	*Canadian Encyclopedic Digest*:
	• Evidence
	• References and Inquiries (Ontario and Western)
	Halsbury's Laws of Canada: Evidence*
	JurisClasseur Québec: Collection Droit civil (Preuve et prescription)
Case digests	*Canadian Abridgment* (Carswell): Evidence
	LexisNexis Quicklaw: Canada Civil Evidence Digest
Databases and CD-ROMs	LexisNexis Quicklaw: Civil Evidence Cases — Topical

V. FAMILY LAW

Scope	Family law is split between federal jurisdiction over divorce law under the *Divorce Act*, R.S.C. 1985 (2d Supp.), c. 3 and various provincial laws governing marriage, separation, and custody that are too numerous to list here.
Subject headings	Divorce — Law and legislation — Canada Domestic relations — [jurisdiction]
Books	Benotto, Mary Lou & Williams & Partners. *Income Tax and Family Law Handbook*. Looseleaf. Toronto: Butterworths, 1988. Bernstein, Marvin M. *et al. Child Protection Law in Canada*. Looseleaf. Toronto: Carswell, 1990. Available by subscription on *FamilySource* on Westlaw Canada. Bourassa, Luce. *La parole de l'enfant en matière de garde*. Markham, ON: LexisNexis Canada, 2007. Brodeur, Marie-Josée & Catherine La Rosa. *Loi sur le divorce annotée*. 2e éd. Scarborough, ON: Thomson Carswell, 2004. Canada Law Book. *O'Brien's Encyclopedia of Forms: Division VI, Ontario — Family Law*. 11th ed. Aurora, ON: Canada Law Book, 1987. Also available on CD-ROM and by subscription on O'Brien's Internet. CCH Canadian Limited. *Canadian Family Law Guide*. Looseleaf. Toronto: CCH Canadian, 1976. Also available on CD-ROM and on *CCH Online* (by subscription). Christopher, T. Catherine. *The Law of Domestic Conflict in Canada*. Looseleaf. Scarborough, ON: Carswell, 2002. Cochrane, Michael G. *Family Law in Ontario: A Practical Guide for Lawyers and Law Clerks*. Looseleaf. Aurora, ON: Canada Law Book, 1990. Côté, Christine *et al. LegisPratique — Droit de la famille — Jurisprudence en tableaux*. Montreal: LexisNexis, 2009 [annual]. Fodden, Simon. *Family Law*. Toronto: Irwin Law, 1999. Freedman, Andrew J. *et al. Financial Principles of Family Law*. Looseleaf. Scarborough, ON: Carswell, 2001. Hainsworth, Terry W. *Child Support Guidelines Service*. Looseleaf. Aurora, ON: Canada Law Book, 1998. Also available on CD-ROM or by online subscription. Hainsworth, Terry W. *Divorce Act Manual*. Looseleaf. Aurora, ON: Canada Law Book, 1994. Hainsworth, Terry W. *Ontario Family Law Act Manual*. Looseleaf. 2d ed. Aurora, ON: Canada Law Book, 1992. Also available on CD-ROM or by online subscription.

Books Harvey, Cameron & Linda Vincent. *The Law of Dependants' Relief in Canada*. 2d ed. Toronto: Thomson Carswell, 2006.

Holland, Winifred & Barbro Stalbecker-Pountney. *Cohabitation: The Law in Canada*. Looseleaf. Toronto: Carswell, 1990.

Klotz, Robert A. *Bankruptcy, Insolvency and Family Law*. 2d ed. Scarborough, ON: Carswell, 2002.

Landau, Barbara *et al. Family Mediation, Arbitration and Collaborative Practice Handbook*. 5th ed. Markham, ON: LexisNexis, 2009.

Law Society of Upper Canada. *Special Lectures 2006: Family Law*. Toronto: Irwin Law, 2007.

LexisNexis Canada. *Alberta Family Service*. Looseleaf. Vancouver, BC: LexisNexis Canada, 1982. Also available for British Columbia and Ontario.

MacDonald, James C. & Lee K. Ferrier. *Canadian Divorce Law and Practice*. Looseleaf. 2d ed. Toronto: Carswell, 1986. Available on *FamilySource* on Westlaw Canada (by subscription).

MacDonald, James C. & Ann C. Wilton. *The Annotated Divorce Act*. Toronto: Carswell, 1991 [annual]. Carswell also publishes annotated legislation titles for family law legislation in Ontario.

MacDonald, James C. & Ann C. Wilton. *Child Support Guidelines: Law and Practice*. Looseleaf. 2d ed. Toronto: Thomson Professional, 1998. Available on *FamilySource* on Westlaw Canada (by subscription).

MacDonald, James C. & Ann C. Wilton. *Law and Practice under the Family Law Act of Ontario*. Looseleaf. Revised ed. Toronto: Carswell, 1998. Available on *FamilySource* on Westlaw Canada (by subscription).

McLeod, James G. *Child Custody Law and Practice*. Looseleaf. Scarborough, ON: Carswell, 1992. Available by subscription on *FamilySource* on Westlaw Canada.

McLeod, James G. & Alfred A. Mamo. *Matrimonial Property Law in Canada*. Looseleaf. Toronto: 1980. Available by subscription on *FamilySource* on Westlaw Canada.

Ontario Annotated Family Law Service. Looseleaf. Toronto: Butterworths, 1978.

Payne, Julien D. & Marilyn A. Payne. *Canadian Family Law*. 3d ed. Toronto: Irwin Law, 2008.

Payne, Julien D. & Marilyn A. Payne. *Child Support Guidelines in Canada, 2009*. Toronto: Irwin Law, 2009.

Payne, Julien D. *Payne on Divorce*. 4th ed. Scarborough, ON: Carswell, 1996.

Books	Self-Counsel Press. Various titles aimed at non-lawyers on doing your own divorce or separation agreement: www. self-counsel.com.
	Shields, Richard W. *Collaborative Family Law: Another Way to Resolve Family Law Disputes.* Toronto: Carswell, 2003.
	Stark, Hugh G. & Kirstie J. Maclise. *Domestic Contracts.* Looseleaf. 2d ed. Scarborough, ON: Thomson Carswell, 2004. Available by subscription on *FamilySource* on Westlaw Canada.
	Steinberg, David M. *et al. Ontario Family Law Practice.* Scarborough, ON: LexisNexis Canada, 2009 [annual].
	Whaley, Kimberly *et al. Capacity to Marry and the Estate Plan.* Aurora, ON: Canada Law Book, 2010.
	Wilson, Jeffrey. *Wilson on Children and the Law.* Looseleaf. 3d ed. Toronto: Butterworths, 1994.
	Wilton, Ann C. & Judy Miyauchi. *Enforcement of Family Law Orders and Agreements: Law and Practice.* Looseleaf. Toronto: Carswell, 1989. Available by subscription on *FamilySource* on Westlaw Canada.
Journals	*Annual Review of Family Law* (Carswell)
	Canadian Family Law Matters (CCH Canadian)
	Canadian Family Law Quarterly: A Journal for Practitioners (Carswell). Available on Westlaw Canada from 1998.
	Canadian Journal of Family Law (Carswell). Available on LexisNexis Quicklaw from 1996 and Westlaw Canada from 1991.
	Money & Family Law (Carswell)
	Ontario Family Law Reporter Newsletter (LexisNexis Canada)
Encyclopedias	*Canadian Encyclopedic Digest:* • Children • Family Law—Divorce • Family Law—General (Ontario) • Family Law—Property • Family Law—General (Western) • Vital Statistics *Halsbury's Laws of Canada:* • Family Law* • Infants and Children • Vital Statistics* *JurisClasseur Québec:* Collection Droit civil (Personnes et famille)
Case digests	*Canadian Abridgment* (Carswell): Family law caseAlert—Family Law (Canada Law Book)

Case digests	LexisNexis Quicklaw: • Bulletin LexisNexis Droit de la famille — Résumés • Canada Family Law Digest
Case law reporters	*Reports of Family Law* (Carswell)
Databases and CD-ROMs	*Canadian Family Law Guide* (CCH Canadian). Also available by subscription on *CCHOnline*. *Family Law Library* (Canada Law Book). Also available by online subscription *Family Law Partner* [CD-ROM]. Toronto: Carswell. Updated regularly. Contains relevant legislation, case law, and Carswell-published textbooks on family law. Available in an expanded version as *FamilySource* by subscription on Westlaw Canada. Family*Practice* (LexisNexis Quicklaw) LexisNexis Quicklaw: Family Law Cases — Topical

W. HEALTH AND MEDICAL LAW

Scope	Health law in Canada is governed by a variety of federal and provincial legislation, policy, and case law.
Subject headings	Medical laws and legislation — Canada Medical jurisprudence — Canada Mental health laws — Canada Physicians — Malpractice — Canada Tort liability of hospitals — Canada
Books	Berry, Marie. *Canadian Pharmacy Law.* Looseleaf. Aurora, ON: Canada Law Book, 1995. Bloom, Hy & Michael Bay. *A Practical Guide to Mental Health, Capacity and Consent Law of Ontario.* Scarborough, ON: Carswell, 1996. Downie, Jocelyn *et al. Canadian Health Law and Policy.* 3d ed. Toronto: LexisNexis Canada, 2007. Downie, Jocelyn *et al. Dental Law in Canada.* Toronto: LexisNexis Butterworths, 2004. Downie, Jocelyn & Elaine Gibson. *Health Law at the Supreme Court of Canada.* Toronto: Irwin Law, 2007. Dykeman, Mary Jane. *Canadian Health Law Practice Manual.* Looseleaf. Markham, ON: LexisNexis Canada, 2000. Emson, Harry. *The Doctor and the Law: A Practical Guide for the Canadian Physician.* 3d ed. Toronto: Butterworths, 1995.

Books	Grant, Anne & Aileen Ashman. *Nurse's Practical Guide to the Law*. Aurora, ON: Canada Law Book, 1997.
	Gray, John E. *et al. Canadian Mental Health Law and Policy*. 2d ed. Markham, ON: LexisNexis Canada, 2008.
	Knoopers, Bartha Maria *et al. Legal Rights and Human Genetic Material*. Toronto: Emond Montgomery, 1996.
	Marshall, T. David. *Canadian Law of Inquests: a Handbook for Coroners, Medical Examiners, Counsel and the Police*. 3d ed. Toronto: Thomson Carswell, 2008.
	Marshall, T. David. *The Law of Human Experimentation*. Toronto: Butterworths, 2000.
	McPhedran, Marilou & Wendy Sutton. *Preventing Sexual Abuse of Patients: A Legal Guide for Health Care Professionals*. Markham, ON: LexisNexis Butterworths, 2004.
	McTeer, Maureen. *Tough Choices: Living and Dying in the 21st Century*. Toronto: Irwin Law, 1999.
	Morris, John. *Canadian Nurses and the Law*. 2d ed. Toronto: Butterworths, 1999.
	Morris, John. *Law for Canadian Health Care Administrators*. Toronto: Butterworths, 1996.
	Robertson, Gerald B. *Mental Disability and the Law in Canada*. 2d ed. Toronto: Carswell, 1994.
	Robertson, Gerald B. & Ellen I. Picard. *Legal Liability of Doctors and Hospitals*. 4th ed. Toronto: Thomson Carswell, 2007.
	Rozovsky, Lorne E. *Canadian Law of Consent to Treatment*. 3d ed. Toronto: LexisNexis Butterworths, 2003.
	Rozovsky, Lorne E. & Noela Inions. *Canadian Health Information: A Practical Legal and Risk Management Guide*. 3d ed. Markham, ON: Butterworths, 2002.
	Sneiderman, Barney *et al. Canadian Medical Law: An Introduction for Physicians, Nurses and Other Health Care Professionals*. 3d ed. Scarborough, ON: Thomson Carswell, 2003.
	Speakman, Jane *et al. Public Health Law and Practice in Ontario: The Health Protection and Promotion Act*. Toronto: Thomson Carswell, 2008.
	Steinecke, Richard. *A Complete Guide to the Regulated Health Professions Act*. Looseleaf. Aurora, ON: Canada Law Book, 1995.
Journals	*Health Law in Canada* (LexisNexis Canada). Available on LexisNexis Quicklaw from 1994.
	Health Law Journal (Health Law Institute). Available on LexisNexis Quicklaw from 1993.
	Health Law Review (Health Law Institute). Available on LexisNexis Quicklaw from 1991.
	Legal Medical Quarterly (Jonah Publications)

Journals	*McGill Journal of Law & Health* (McGill University). Also available on Westlaw Canada from 2007. *Risk Management in Canadian Health Care Newsletter* (LexisNexis Canada) *Telehealth Law Newsletter* (LexisNexis Canada)
Encyclopedias	*Canadian Encyclopedic Digest:* • Hospitals and Health Care (Ontario) • Hospitals (Western) • Medicine (Western) • Mental Incompetency (Ontario and Western) • Professions and Occupations (Ontario and Western) • Public Health and Welfare (Ontario and Western) *Halsbury's Laws of Canada:* • Medicine and Health Law* • Public Health* • Trade and Professions*
Case digests	*Canadian Abridgment* (Carswell): Health law caseAlert—Health Law (Canada Law Book) LexisNexis Quicklaw: • Abrégé de jurisprudence—Santé et sécurité du travail et maladies professionnelles (Québec) • Canada Health Law Digest • Canada Medical Negligence Quantums
Databases and CD-ROMs	LexisNexis Quicklaw: Health Law Cases—Topical
Websites	Health Law Institute (University of Alberta): www.law.ualberta.ca/centres/hli/ Health Law Institute (Dalhousie University): http://hli.law.dal.ca

X. IMMIGRATION AND REFUGEE LAW

Scope	Immigration and refugee law is governed primarily by federal law, including the *Immigration and Refugee Protection Act*, S.C. 2001, c. 27 and the *Citizenship Act*, R.S.C. 1985, c. C-29.
Subject headings	Citizenship—Canada Refugees—Legal status, laws, etc.—Canada Emigration and immigration law—Canada
Books	Bagley, Sasha & Martin Jones. *Refugee Law*. Toronto: Irwin Law, 2007.

Books	Bart, Jacqueline & Austin T. Fragomen. *Canada/U.S. Relocation Manual: Immigration, Customs, Employment and Taxation*. Looseleaf. Scarborough, ON: Carswell, 1998.
	Botting, Gary. *Canadian Extradition Law Practice, 2009*. Markham, ON: LexisNexis, 2009.
	Galloway, Donald. *Immigration Law*. Concord, ON: Irwin Law, 1997.
	Gaudet, Lynn & Camilla Jones. *Immigration Practitioner's Handbook, 2010*. Toronto: Thomson Carswell, 2009.
	Kranc, Benjamin. *North American Relocation Law*. Looseleaf. Aurora, ON: Canada Law Book, 2007.
	Krivel, Elaine *et al. A Practical Guide to Canadian Extradition*. Toronto: Carswell, 2002.
	Goslett, Henry & Barbara J. Caruso. *The 2009 Annotated Citizenship Act*. Toronto: Carswell, 2009 [annual] (includes CD-ROM).
	Goslett, Henry & Barbara J. Caruso. *The 2010 Annotated Immigration and Refugee Protection Act of Canada*. Toronto: Carswell, 2009 [annual] (includes CD-ROM).
	Schweitzer, Tony. *Canada-U.S. Work Permits: Issues for Human Resources Professionals*. Looseleaf. Toronto: Thomson Carswell, 2004.
	Waldman, Lorne. *Canadian Immigration and Refugee Law and Practice, 2010*. Markham, ON: LexisNexis, 2009 [annual].
	Waldman, Lorne. *The Definition of Convention Refugee*. Toronto: Butterworths, 2001.
	Waldman, Lorne. *Immigration Law and Practice*. 2d ed. Markham, ON: LexisNexis Butterworths, 2005.
	Zambelli, Pia. *Annotated Refugee Convention: Fifty Years of North American Jurisprudence*. Toronto: Thomson Carswell, 2004.
	Zambelli, Pia. *Annotated Refugee Convention 2005*. Toronto: Carswell, 2006.
Journals	*Canada's Immigration and Citizenship Bulletin* (Canada Law Book)
	ImmQuest (Carswell)
Encyclopedias	*Canadian Encyclopedic Digest*:
	• Extradition
	• Immigration and Refugees
	Halsbury's Laws of Canada:
	• Immigration and Citizenship
Case digests	*Canadian Abridgment* (Carswell): Immigration and citizenship caseAlert — Immigration Law

Case digests	LexisNexis Quicklaw: • Abrégé de jurisprudence — Immigration • Canada Immigration Digest
Case law reporters	*Immigration Law Reporter* (Carswell).
Databases and CD-ROMs	Immigration*Practice* (LexisNexis Quicklaw) LexisNexis Quicklaw: Immigration Law Cases — Topical
Websites	Citizenship and Immigration Canada: www.cic.gc.ca Immigration and Refugee Board of Canada: www.cisr-irb.gc.ca

Y. INSURANCE LAW

Scope	Insurance law in Canada is governed largely by provincial legislation (such as British Columbia's *Insurance Act*, R.S.B.C. 1996, c. 226), while insurance companies are governed by federal legislation (such as the *Insurance Companies Act*, S.C. 1991, c. 47).
Subject headings	Insurance law — Canada Insurance, liability — Canada
Books	Billingsley, Barbara. *General Principles of Canadian Insurance Law.* Markham, ON: LexisNexis Canada, 2008. Boivin, Denis. *Le droit des assurances dans les provinces de common law.* Markham, ON: LexisNexis, 2006. Brown, Craig. *Introduction to Canadian Insurance Law.* 2d ed. Toronto: LexisNexis Butterworths, 2006. Brown, Craig & Thomas Donnelly. *Insurance Law in Canada.* Looseleaf. Scarborough, ON: Carswell, 1999. Also available by subscription online (Carswell eReference Library). Gosnell, Sean, Bruce Webster, & John Seigel. *Business Interruption Insurance.* Aurora, ON: Canada Law Book, 2006. Grant, Anne E. *Dispute Resolution in the Insurance Industry: A Practical Guide.* Aurora, ON: Canada Law Book, 2000. Hayles, Richard. *Disability Insurance: Canadian Law and Business Practice.* Scarborough, ON: Carswell, 1998. Hilliker, Gordon G. *Insurance Bad Faith.* 2d ed. Markham, ON: LexisNexis, 2009. Hilliker, Gordon G. *Liability Insurance Law in Canada.* 4th ed. Markham, ON: LexisNexis Butterworths, 2006. Lanctôt, Sébastien & Paul A. Melançon. *Commentaires sur le droit des assurances et textes législatifs et réglementaires.* Montréal: LexisNexis, 2008.

Books	Leckie, Ann & Manjit Grewal *et al. Disability Claims Management*. 2d ed. Markham, ON: Butterworths, 2002.
	Lichty, Mark G. & Marcus B. Snowden. *Annotated Commercial General Liability Policy*. Looseleaf. Aurora, ON: Canada Law Book, 1997.
	Norwood, David & John P. Weir. *Norwood on Life Insurance Law in Canada*. 3d ed. Toronto: Carswell, 2002.
	Strathy, George R. & George C. Moore. *The Law and Practice of Marine Insurance in Canada*. Markkham, ON: LexisNexis Butterworths, 2003.
	Weir, John P. *The Annotated Insurance Act of Ontario*. Looseleaf (with additional CD-ROM content). Toronto: Carswell, 1988.
	Winsor, Roderick S.W. *Good Faith in Canadian Insurance Law*. Looseleaf. Aurora, ON: Canada Law Book, 2007.
Journals	*Canadian Insurance Law Review* (Carswell, 1988–1996)
	Canadian Insurance Regulation Reporter (LexisNexis Canada)
	Canadian Journal of Insurance Law (LexisNexis Canada)
Encyclopedias	*Canadian Encyclopedic Digest*: Insurance
	Halsbury's Laws of Canada: Insurance
Case digests	Canada Law Book: British Columbia Decisions, Insurance Law Cases
	Canadian Abridgment (Carswell): Insurance
	Insurance Case Law Digest: Property and Casualty (LexisNexis Quicklaw, 1985 to current)
	LexisNexis Quicklaw: Canada Insurance Law Digest
Case law reporters	*Canadian Cases on the Law of Insurance* (Carswell)
	Canadian Insurance Law Reporter (CCH Canadian)
	Ontario Accident Benefit Case Summaries (CCH Canadian)
Databases and CD-ROMs	LexisNexis Quicklaw:
	• Insurance Law Cases — Topical
	• Ontario Financial Services Commission Insurance Decisions

Z. INTELLECTUAL PROPERTY LAW/ E-COMMERCE

Scope	Intellectual property laws in Canada generally fall under federal jurisdiction and are regulated by such Acts as the *Copyright Act*, R.S.C. 1985, c. C-42, the *Trade-Marks Act*, R.S.C. 1985, c. T-13, and the *Patent Act*, R.S.C. 1985, c. P-4.

Subject *headings*	Copyright—Canada Trademarks—Canada Patent laws and legislation—Canada Intellectual property—Canada
Books	Abe, Lisa. *Internet and E-Commerce Agreements: Drafting and Negotiating Tips.* 2d ed. Toronto: LexisNexis Butterworths, 2004. Ashton, Toni. *Canadian Forms & Precedents: Intellectual Property Forms.* Looseleaf. Markham, ON: LexisNexis, 2007. Available on CD-ROM and on LexisNexis Quicklaw. Blanchard, Adrienne. *Life Sciences Law in Canada.* Looseleaf. Toronto: Thomson Carswell, 2006. Also available on *IPSource* by subscription on Westlaw Canada. Burshtein, Sheldon. *The Corporate Counsel Guide to Intellectual Property Law.* Aurora, ON: Canada Law Book, 2000. Canada Law Book. *Intellectual Property Statutes: Legislative History.* Looseleaf. Aurora, ON: Canada Law Book, 1999. Canada Law Book. *O'Brien's Encyclopedia of Forms: Division X, Computers and Information Technology.* 11th ed. Aurora, ON: Canada Law Book, 1987. Also available on CD-ROM and by subscription on O'Brien's Internet. Card, Duncan. *Information Technology Transactions: Business, Management and Legal Strategies.* 2d ed. Toronto: Thomson Carswell, 2007. Cornish, Diane E. *Licensing Intellectual Property.* Scarborough, ON: Carswell, 1995. Deturbide, Michael & Teresa Scassa. *Electronic Commerce and Internet Law.* Toronto: CCH Canadian, 2004. Dimock, Ronald E. *Intellectual Property Disputes: Resolutions and Remedies.* Looseleaf. Toronto: Carswell, 2002. Also available by subscription on *IPSource* on Westlaw Canada. Fecenko, Mark J. *Biotechnology Law: Corporate-Commercial Practice.* Markham, ON: Butterworths, 2002. Gahtan, Alan M. *Electronic Commerce: A Practitioner's Guide.* Looseleaf. Toronto: Carswell, 2003. Gahtan, Alan M. *Internet Law: A Practical Guide for Legal and Business Professionals.* Scarborough, ON: Carswell, 1998. Gratton, Eloise. *Internet and Wireless Privacy: A Legal Guide to Global Business Practices.* Toronto: CCH Canadian, 2003. Handa, Sunny. *Copyright Law in Canada.* Markham, ON: Butterworths, 2002. Harris, Lesley-Ellen. *Canadian Copyright Law.* 3d ed. Toronto: McGraw-Hill Ryerson, 2001.

Books   Hatzikiriakos, Kiriakoula. *Secured Transactions in Intel-lectual Property: Software as Collateral*. Markham, ON: LexisNexis Butterworths, 2006.

Henderson, Gordon. *Patent Law of Canada*. Scarborough, ON: Carswell, 1994.

Hughes, Roger. *Hughes on Copyright and Industrial Design*. Looseleaf. 2d ed. Markham, ON: LexisNexis Butter-worths, 2005.

Hughes, Roger. *Hughes on Trade Marks*. Looseleaf. 2d ed. Markham, ON: LexisNexis Butterworths, 2005.

Hughes, Roger & John H. Woodley. *Hughes and Woodley on Patents*. Looseleaf. 2d ed. Markham, ON: LexisNexis Butterworths, 2005.

Hughes, Roger T. *et al. Canadian Forms & Precedents: Licens-ing*. Looseleaf. 2d ed. Markham, ON: LexisNexis, 2007. Available on CD-ROM and on LexisNexis Quicklaw.

Joliffe, R. Scott & A. Kelly Gill. *Fox on Canadian Law of Trade-Marks and Unfair Competition*. Looseleaf. 4th ed. Toronto: Carswell, 2002. Also available by subscription on *IPSource* on Westlaw Canada.

Knopf, Howard P. *Security Interests in Intellectual Property*. Toronto: Thomson Carswell, 2002.

Kratz, Martin P.J. *Obtaining Patents*. 2d ed. Scarborough, ON: Carswell, 1999.

Kratz, Martin P.J. *Protecting Copyright and Industrial Design*. 2d ed. Scarborough, ON: Carswell, 1999.

Leger, Robic. *Canadian Copyright Act Annotated*. Looseleaf. Scarborough, ON: Carswell, 1993. Also available by sub-scription on *IPSource* on Westlaw Canada.

Leger, Robic. *Canadian Trade-Marks Act Annotated*. Looseleaf. Don Mills, ON: R. DeBoo, 1984. Also available by sub-scription on *IPSource* on Westlaw Canada.

Limpert, Brad. *Technology Contracting: Law, Precedents and Commentary*. Looseleaf. Toronto: Thomson Carswell, 2005. Also available by subscription on *IPSource* on West-law Canada.

Mann, Fraser J. *Information and Technology Law: Recent De-velopments for Professionals*. Scarborough, ON: Carswell, 1996 [five times per year].

McKeown, John. *Brand Management in Canadian Law*. 2d ed. Toronto: Thomson Carswell, 2006.

McKeown, John S. *Fox on Canadian Law of Copyright and Industrial Designs*. Looseleaf. 4th ed. Toronto: Carswell, 2003. Also available by subscription on *IPSource* on West-law Canada.

Books	Odutola, Bayo & Sylvie-Émanuelle Bourbonnais. *Odutola on Canadian Trade-Mark Practice*. Looseleaf. Toronto: Thomson Carswell, 2004. Also available by subscription on *IPSource* on Westlaw Canada.

Ramsay, John T. *Ramsay on Technology Transfers and Licensing*. 2d ed. Markham, ON: Butterworths, 2002.

Richard, Hugues G. *Canadian Trade-Marks Act: Annotated*. Looseleaf. Toronto: Carswell, 1990.

Richard, Hugues G. & Laurent Carrière. *Canadian Copyright Act: Annotated*. Looseleaf. Toronto: Carswell, 1992.

Sookman, Barry B. *Computer, Internet and Electronic Commerce Terms: Judicial, Legislative and Technical Definitions*. Toronto: Carswell, 2001 [annual].

Sookman, Barry B. *Sookman: Computer, Internet and Electronic Commerce Law*. Toronto: Carswell, 1989.

Takach, George S. *Computer Law*. 2d ed. Toronto: Irwin Law, 2003.

Tamaro, Normand. *Annotated Copyright Act*. Toronto: Carswell, 2005 [annual].

Tamaro, Normand. *Loi sur le droit d'auteur, texte annoté*. 6th ed. Toronto: Carswell, 2003.

Thorburn, Julie A. & Keith G. Fairburn. *Law of Confidential Business Information*. Looseleaf. Aurora, ON: Canada Law Book, 1998.

Vaver, David. *Copyright Law*. Concord, ON: Irwin Law, 2000.

Vaver, David. *Intellectual Property Law: Copyright, Patents, Trademarks*. Concord, ON: Irwin Law, 1997.

Journals	*Canadian Intellectual Property Review* (Patent and Trademark Institute of Canada).

Canadian Journal of Law and Technology (CCH Canadian). Available in print and on *CCHOnline* (by subscription).

Copyright & New Media Law Newsletter (Lesley Ellen Harris)

Intellectual Property Journal (Carswell). Available on Westlaw Canada

Encyclopedias	*Canadian Encyclopedic Digest*:

- Copyright
- Internet Law
- Patents
- Trade Marks and Industrial Designs

Halsbury's Laws of Canada:
- Copyright*
- Information Technology Law*
- Patents, Trade Secrets and Industrial Designs
- Trade-marks, Passing Off and Unfair Competition

Encyclopedias	*JurisClasseur Québec*: Collection Droit des affaires (Propriété intellectuelle)
Case digests	*Canadian Abridgment* (Carswell): Intellectual property caseAlert — Intellectual Property Law (Canada Law Book)
	LexisNexis Quicklaw:
	• Abrégé de jurisprudence — Brevets
	• Abrégé de jurisprudence — Droit d'auteur
	• Abrégé de jurisprudence — Marques de commerce
	• Abrégé de jurisprudence — Technologies de l'information
	• Canada Copyright Digest
	• Canada Patent Digest
	• Canada Trade-marks Digest
Case law reporters	*Canadian Patent Reporter* (Canada Law Book). Also available by online subscription.
Databases and CD-ROMs	*IP&ITPractice* (LexisNexis Quicklaw)
	IPSource (Westlaw Canada)
	LexisNexis Quicklaw:
	• Canada Copyright Board Decisions
	• Canada Patent Appeal Board and Commissioner of Patents Decisions
	• Canada Trade Marks Opposition Board Decisions
	• Canadian Internet Registration Authority Decisions
	• Intellectual Property Law Cases — Topical
Websites	Canadian Intellectual Property Office (CIPO): http://cipo.gc.ca

AA. INTERNATIONAL AND FOREIGN LAW

Scope	International law in Canada encompasses various international treaties and conventions Canada has entered into governing its relationships with other countries and between Canadians and citizens of other countries. Foreign law involves the domestic laws of countries outside of Canada. International and foreign legal resources are discussed in detail in chapter 7 (the books listed below are only a small sample).
Subject headings	International law — Canada
Books	Appleton, Barry. *Navigating NAFTA: A Concise User's Guide to the North American Free Trade Agreement*. Scarborough, ON: Carswell, 1994.
	Barin, Babak. *Carswell's Handbook of International Dispute Resolution Rules*. Scarborough, ON: Carswell, 1999.

Books *Books*	Bayefsky, Anne F. *International Human Rights Law: Use in Canadian Charter of Rights and Freedoms Litigation.* Toronto: Butterworths, 1992.

Castel, Jean G. *Introduction to Conflict of Laws.* 4th ed. Markham, ON: Butterworths, 2002.

Currie, John H. *Public International Law.* 2d ed. Toronto: Irwin Law, 2008.

Freeman, Mark & Gib van Ert. *International Human Rights Law.* Toronto: Irwin Law, 2004.

Gold, Edgar *et al. Maritime Law.* Toronto: Irwin Law, 2004.

Hayden, Peter & Jeffrey R. Burns. *Foreign Investment in Canada: A Guide to the Law.* Looseleaf. Toronto: Thomson Carswell, 1996.

Herman, Lawrence. *Export Controls & Economic Sanctions: A Guide to Canadian Trade Restrictions.* Looseleaf. Toronto: Carswell, 2010.

Johnson, Jon R. *International Trade Law.* Toronto: Irwin Law, 1998.

Kindred, Hugh M. *International Law, Chiefly as Interpreted and Applied in Canada.* 7th ed. Toronto: Emond Montgomery, 2006.

LaViolette, Nicole & Craig Forcese. *Human Rights of Anti-Terrorism.* Toronto: Irwin Law, 2008.

Lemieux, Denis & Ana Stuhec. *Review of Administrative Action under NAFTA.* Scarborough, ON: Carswell, 1999.

Nicholson, Mary Jo. *Legal Aspects of International Business: A Canadian Perspective.* 2d ed. Toronto: Emond Montgomery, 2007.

Schabas, William A. *International Human Rights Law and the Canadian Charter.* 2d ed. Scarborough, ON: Carswell, 1996.

Thomas, Jeffrey & Michael A. Meyer. *The New Rules of Global Trade: A Guide to the World Trade Organization.* Scarborough, ON: Carswell, 1997.

van Ert, Gibran. *Using International Law in Canadian Courts.* 2d ed. Toronto: Irwin Law, 2008.

Walker, Janet. *Castel & Walker: Canadian Conflict of Laws.* Looseleaf. 6th ed. Markham, ON: LexisNexis Butterworths, 2005. Also available by subscription on LexisNexis Quicklaw.

Journals	*Asper Review of International Business and Trade Law* (Faculty of Law, University of Manitoba)

Bulletin (Canadian Council on International Law)

Canada–United States Law Journal (Canada–United States Law Institute)

Journals	*Canadian International Lawyer* (Canadian Bar Association) *Canadian Yearbook of International Law* (International Law Association, Canadian Branch. University of British Columbia Press) *International Insights: A Dalhousie Journal of International Affairs* (John E. Reed International Law Society, Dalhousie Law School) *Journal of International Law and International Relations* (University of Toronto, Faculty of Law and Munk Centre for International Studies). Available on Westlaw Canada *Revue québécoise de droit international* (Éditions Thémis). Available on LexisNexis Quicklaw
Encyclopedias	*Canadian Encyclopedic Digest*: • Conflict of Laws • International Law • Trade and Commerce—Foreign Investment in Canada *Halsbury's Laws of Canada*: • Competition and Foreign Investment* • Conflicts of Laws • Extradition and Mutual Legal Assistance* • International Law* *JurisClasseur Québec*: Collection Droit civil (Droit international privé)
Case digests	*Canadian Abridgment* (Carswell): • International law • International trade and customs LexisNexis Quicklaw: • Canada Conflict of Laws Digest • Canada International Law Digest
Databases and CD-ROMs	LexisNexis Quicklaw: • Conflict of Laws Cases—Topical • International Treaties
Websites	Foreign Affairs and International Trade Canada: www.international.gc.ca Womens' Human Rights Resources: www.law-lib.utoronto.ca/diana

BB. INTRODUCTION TO LAW/ LEGAL SYSTEMS

Scope	This section provides information for first-time law students or persons interested in studying law. Some of the texts below are American but apply, for the most part, equally well to the study of law in any jurisdiction.
Subject headings	Justice, Administration of—Canada Law—Canada Law—Studying and teaching—Canada Law examinations— [jurisdiction] Law students—Canada
Books	Ali, Ramsey *et al. The ABC's of Law School: A Practical Guide to Success without Sacrifice.* Toronto: Irwin Law, 2002. Civiletto Carey, Christian & Kristen David Adams. *The Practice of Law School: Getting In and Making the Most of Your Legal Education.* New York: ALM, 2003. Dernbach, John. *Writing Essay Exams to Succeed (Not just to Survive).* 2d ed. New York: Aspen, 2007. Fischl, Richard. & Jeremy Paul. *Getting to Maybe: How to Excel on Law School Exams.* Durham, NC: Carolina Academic Press, 1999. Fitzgerald, Patrick & Barry Wright. *Looking at Law: Canada's Legal System.* 5th ed. Toronto: Butterworths, 2000. Gader-Shafran, Rachel. *The International Student's Survival Guide to Law School in the United States: Everything you Need to Succeed.* New York: iUniverse, 2003. Gall, Gerald L. *The Canadian Legal System.* 5th ed. Scarborough, ON: Carswell, 2004. Hegland, Kenney. *Introduction to the Study and Practice of Law in a Nutshell.* 5th ed. St. Paul, MN: Thomson/West, 2008. Hutchinson, Allan C. *The Law School Book: Succeeding at Law School.* 3d ed. Toronto: Irwin Law, 2009. Kissam, Philip C. *The Discipline of Law Schools: The Making of Modern Lawyers.* Durham, NC: Carolina Academic Press, 2003. Miller, Robert H. *Law School Confidential: A Complete Guide to the Law School Experience: By Students, For Students.* Rev. ed. New York: St. Martin's Griffin, 2004. Noyes, Shana Connell & Henry S. Noyles. *Acing Your First Year of Law School: The Ten Steps to Success You Won't Learn in Class.* 2d ed. Buffalo, NY: William S. Hein, 2008.

Books	Shapo, Helene & Marshall Shapo. *Law School Without Fear: Strategies for Success.* 3d ed. New York, NY: Foundation Press, 2009. Waddams, Stephen M. *Introduction to the Study of Law.* 6th ed. Scarborough, ON: Carswell, 2004.
Journals	*Canadian Lawyer* (Canada Law Book) *National* (Canadian Bar Association) *Precedent: The New Rules of Law and Style* (Law and Style Media)
Encyclopedias	*Canadian Encyclopedic Digest*: • Barristers and Solicitors (Ontario and Western) • Parliament and Legislature • Statutes *Halsbury's Laws of Canada*: • Judges and Courts • Legal Profession
Case digests	*Canadian Abridgment* (Carswell): • Judges and courts • Statutes

CC. LABOUR LAW

Scope	Labour law in Canada can fall under federal jurisdiction for employees working for the federal government or in the federal sector, and under provincial jurisdiction for all other unionized employees. Labour law tends to cover unionized employees, whereas employment law (discussed above in this chapter) tends to cover non-unionized employees. An example of typical provincial legislation would be Ontario's *Labour Relations Act*, S.O. 1995, c. 1, Sch. A.
Subject headings	Arbitration, industrial—Canada Collective labour agreements—Canada Grievance arbitration—Canada Labour laws and legislation—Canada Trade unions—Law and legislation—Canada
Books	Adams, George W. & Sandra Adams. *Canadian Labour Law.* Looseleaf. 2d ed. Aurora, ON: Canada Law Book, 1993. Andrew, Jeffrey M. *Labour Relations Board Remedies in Canada.* Jeffrey M. Andrew. Looseleaf. 2d ed. Aurora, ON: Canada Law Book, 2009. *Annotated British Columbia Labour Relations Code.* Looseleaf. Vancouver, BC: Butterworths, 1993.

Books

Brown, Donald J.M. & David M. Beatty. *Canadian Labour Arbitration*. Looseleaf. 4th ed. Aurora, ON: Canada Law Book, 2006. Also available on CD-ROM and as an e-book on *Labour Spectrum*.

Canada Law Book. *O'Brien's Encyclopedia of Forms: Division VII, Labour Relations and Employment*. 11th ed. Aurora, ON: Canada Law Book, 1987. Also available on CD-ROM and by subscription on O'Brien's Internet.

Carter, Don. *et al. Labour Law in Canada*. 5th ed. Markham, ON: Butterworths, 2002.

Casey, James & Ayla Akgungor. *Remedies in Labour, Employment and Human Rights Law*. Looseleaf. Scarborough, ON: Thomson, 1999. Also available by subscription online (Carswell eReference Library).

CCH Canadian Limited. *Canadian Master Labour Guide*. 24th ed. Toronto: CCH Canadian, 2009 [annual].

Certosimo, Matthew. *Federal Employment and Labour Law and Commentary*. 2008 ed. Markham, ON: LexisNexis, 2008.

Charney, Richard J. & Thomas E.F. Brady. *Judicial Review in Labour Law*. Looseleaf. Aurora, ON: Canada Law Book, 1997.

Clarke, Graham J. *Clarke's Canadian Industrial Relations Board*. Looseleaf. Aurora, ON: Canada Law Book, 1999.

Corry, David J. *Collective Bargaining and Agreement*. Looseleaf. Aurora, ON: Canada Law Book, 1997.

Faraday, Fay, Victoria Réaume & Sheilagh Turkington. *Education Labour and Employment Law in Ontario*. Looseleaf. 2d ed. Aurora, ON: Canada Law Book, 2001.

Geddie, Janine & Rita Mason. *Canadian Labour Law Reporter*. Looseleaf. Toronto: CCH Canadian, 1946.

Gorsky, Morley *et al. Evidence and Procedure in Canadian Labour Arbitration*. Looseleaf. Rev. ed. Scarborough, ON: Carswell, 1991.

Hadwen, Timothy *et al. Ontario Public Service Employment and Labour Law*. Toronto: Irwin Law, 2005.

Harnden, Emond. *Employment in the Federal Public Service*. Looseleaf. Aurora, ON: Canada Law Book, 2001.

Heenan Blaikie LLP. *Quebec Labour & Employment Law: Frequently Asked Questions*. Toronto: Carswell, 2002.

MacNeil, Michael *et al. Trade Union Law in Canada*. Looseleaf. Aurora, ON: Canada Law Book, 1994.

Martel, Nancy & Pierre E. Moreau. *Le devoir de juste representation*. Montreal: LexisNexis, 2009.

Mitchnick, Morton & Brian Etherington. *Labour Arbitration in Canada*. Toronto: Lancaster House, 2006.

Books	Poskanzer, Ethan & Jeffrey Sack. *Labour Law Terms: A Dictionary.* Toronto: Lancaster House, 1984.
	Rayner, Wesley. *Canadian Collective Bargaining Law.* 2d ed. Markham, ON: LexisNexis, 2007. Also available by subscription on LexisNexis Quicklaw.
	Rootham, Christopher. *Labour and Employment Law in the Federal Public Service.* Toronto: Irwin Law, 2007.
	Sack, Jeffrey & Ethan Poskanzer. *Contract Clauses: Collective Agreement Language in Canada.* Looseleaf. 3d ed. Toronto: Lancaster House, 1996.
	Sack, Jeffrey. *Winning Cases at Grievance Arbitration.* Toronto: Lancaster House, 1993.
	Sack, Jeffrey *et al. Ontario Labour Relations Board Law and Practice.* 3d ed. Looseleaf. Markham, ON: LexisNexis, 1997.
	Sanderson, John P. *The Art of Collective Bargaining.* 2d ed. Aurora, ON: Canada Law Book, 1989.
	Saxe, Stewart D. & Brian C. McLean. *Collective Agreement Handbook: A Guide for Employers and Employees.* 3d ed. Aurora, ON: Canada Law Book, 2010.
	Snyder, Ronald. *Collective Agreement Arbitration in Canada.* 4th ed. Markham, ON: LexisNexis, 2009. Also available by subscription on LexisNexis Quicklaw.
	Sommer, Neal B. & Stewart D. Saxe. *Understanding the Labour Relations Act.* 2d ed. Aurora, ON: Canada Law Book, 2001.
Journals	*Canadian Labour & Employment Law Journal* (Lancaster House)
	CLV Reports (Canada Labour Views Reports) (Carswell)
	College and University Employment Law Service (Lancaster House)
	Employment and Labour Law Reporter (LexisNexis Canada)
	Federal Labour & Employment Law Service (Lancaster House)
	IMPACT: Labour Law & Management Practices (Canada Law Book)
	Labour Arbitration Yearbook (Lancaster House)
	Willis & Winkler on Leading Labour Cases (Canada Law Book)
Encyclopedias	*Canadian Encyclopedic Digest*:
	• Labour Law—Federal
	• Labour Law—Alberta
	• Labour Law—British Columbia
	• Labour Law—Manitoba
	• Labour Law—Ontario
	• Labour Law—Saskatchewan
	Halsbury's Laws of Canada: Labour Law

Encyclopedias	*JurisClasseur Québec*: Collection Droit du travail (Droit des rapports individuels et collectifs du travail)
Case digests	*Canadian Abridgment*: Labour and employment law *Canadian Labour Arbitration Summaries* (Canada Law Book, 1986 to current) caseAlert — Labour Law (Canada Law Book) LexisNexis Quicklaw: *Labour Arbitration Xpress*
Case law reporters	*Canadian Labour Law Reporter* (CCH Canadian) *Canadian Labour Relations Boards Reports* (LexisNexis Canada) *Labour Arbitration Cases* (Canada Law Book) *Leading Cases on Labour Arbitration* (LexisNexis Canada)
Databases and CD-ROMs	LabourPractice (LexisNexis Quicklaw) *Labour Spectrum* (Canada Law Book) *LabourSource* (Carswell) LexisNexis Quicklaw: Various labour arbitration and tribunal databases

DD. LANDLORD AND TENANT LAW/ COMMERCIAL LEASING

Scope	Landlord and tenant law is governed largely by provincial legislation, which is often then interpreted by courts or provincial tribunals. Many landlord and tenant decisions are unpublished; hence, a good source for them is on LexisNexis Quicklaw.
Subject headings	Landlord and tenant — [jurisdiction] Rental housing — Law and legislation — [jurisdiction]
Books	Bentley, Christoper A.W. *et al. Williams and Rhodes' Canadian Law of Landlord and Tenant*. Looseleaf. 6th ed. Toronto: Carswell, 1988. Butkus, Mavis J. *Annotated Ontario Landlord and Tenant Statutes*. Toronto: Carswell, 1986 [annual]. Canada Law Book. *O'Brien's Encyclopedia of Forms: Division IV, Leases*. 11th ed. Aurora, ON: Canada Law Book, 1987. Also available on CD-ROM and by subscription on O'Brien's Internet. CCH Canadian. *Ontario Residential Tenancies*. 2d ed. Toronto: CCH Canadian, 2002. Feldman, Richard. *Residential Tenancies*. 9th ed. Toronto: Carswell, 2009.

Books	Ferguson, Jane & Rose H. McConnell. *Evictions: A Practical Guide to Residential Evictions in Ontario.* Toronto: CCH Canadian, 2001. Fleming, Jack. *Residential Tenancies in Ontario.* 2d ed. Markham, ON: LexisNexis Canada, 2010 [forthcoming]. Fraser, James D.M. & Lawrence H. Iron. *Canadian Forms & Precedents: Commercial Tenancies.* Looseleaf. 2d ed. Markham, ON: LexisNexis, 2007. Available on CD-ROM and on LexisNexis Quicklaw. Haber, Harvey M., ed. *Assignment, Subletting and Change of Control in a Commercial Lease: A Practical Guide.* Aurora, ON: Canada Law Book, 2002. Haber, Harvey M. *The Commercial Lease: A Practical Guide.* 4th ed. Aurora, ON: Canada Law Book, 2004. Haber, Harvey M., ed. *Distress: A Commercial Landlord's Remedy.* Aurora, ON: Canada Law Book, 2001. Haber, Harvey M. *Landlord's Rights and Remedies in a Commercial Lease: A Practical Guide.* Aurora, ON: Canada Law Book, 1996. Haber, Harvey M., ed. *Shopping Centre Leases.* 2d ed. Aurora, ON: Canada Law Book, 2008. Haber, Harvey M. *Tenant's Rights and Remedies in a Commercial Lease: A Practical Guide.* Aurora, ON: Canada Law Book, 1998. Haber, Harvey M. *Understanding the Commercial Agreement to Lease.* 2d ed. Aurora, ON: Canada Law Book, 2006. Hall, Daniel D. *How to Win at the Ontario Rental Housing Tribunal.* Toronto: Butterworths, 2000. Lamont, Donald H.L. *Residential Tenancies.* 6th ed. Scarborough, ON: Carswell, 2000. Lang Michener LLP. *O'Brien's Encyclopedia of Forms: Division IV, Leases.* Looseleaf. Aurora, ON: Canada Law Book, 1987. Michaeloff, Dawn. *Insurance and Risk Management in Commercial Leasing.* Aurora, ON: Canada Law Book, 2009. Olson, Richard. *A Commercial Tenancy Handbook.* Looseleaf. Toronto: Carswell, 2004. Overtveld, Joy, ed. *Ontario Residential Tenancies Law.* Looseleaf. 2d ed. Toronto: Thomson Carswell, 2007.
Encyclopedias	*Canadian Encyclopedic Digest*: • Distress (Ontario and Western) • Landlord and Tenant (Ontario and Western) *Halsbury's Laws of Canada*: Landlord and Tenant*
Case digests	*Canadian Abridgment* (Carswell): Real property—Landlord and tenant

Case digests	LexisNexis Quicklaw: Canada Landlord and Tenant Law Digest
Databases and CD-ROMs	LexisNexis Quicklaw: • Landlord & Tenant Law Cases—Topical • Ontario Landlord and Tenant Board Decisions

EE. LEGAL PRACTICE

Scope	This section sets out resources relating to the practice of law, including legal ethics, conflicts of interest, and law practice management.
Subject headings	Attorney and client—Canada Conflict of interests—Canada Lawyers—Malpractice—Canada Legal ethics—Canada Practice of law—Canada
Books	Adamski, Jakub. *Legal Profession*. Markham, ON: LexisNexis Canada, 2007. Backhouse, Constance & W. Wesley Pue. *The Promise and Perils of Law: Lawyers in Canadian History*. Toronto: Irwin Law, 2009. Canadian Bar Association. *CBA Code of Professional Conduct*. Online: www.cba.org/CBA/activities/code/. Chang, Henry J. *The Canadian Lawyer's Guide to Advanced Internet Marketing*. Scarborough, ON: Carswell, 1998. Dodek, Adam M. & Jeffrey G. Hoskins. *Canadian Legal Practice: A Guide for the 21st Century*. Looseleaf. Markham, ON: LexisNexis, 2009. Eaton, John & Denis Le May. *Essential Sources of Canadian Law / Les références essentielles en droit canadien*. Toronto: Irwin Law, 2009. Graham, Randy N. *Legal Ethics: Theories, Cases, and Professional Regulation*. Toronto: Emond Montgomery, 2004. Grant, Stephen M. & Linda Rothstein. *Lawyers' Professional Liability*. 2d ed. Toronto: Butterworths, 1998. Griesdorf, Wendy. *Law Firm Recruitment in Canada: Job Search Advice for Law Students and Associates*. Toronto: Irwin Law, 2004. Hardie, Robert. *A Practical Guide to Successful Law Firm Management*. Markham, ON: LexisNexis Butterworths, 2006. Hutchinson, Allan. *Legal Ethics and Professional Responsibility*. 2d ed. Toronto: Irwin Law, 2006.

Books	Jollimore, Mary. *A Lawyer's Guide to Managing the Media.* Aurora, ON: Canada Law Book, 2000.
	Knight, S. Patricia. *Ethics and Professional Practice for Paralegals.* 2d ed. Toronto: Emond Montgomery Publications, 2010.
	MacKenzie, Gavin. *Lawyers & Ethics: Professional Responsibility and Discipline.* Looseleaf. Toronto: Thomson Carswell, 1993.
	MacNair, M. Deborah. *Conflicts of Interest: Principles for the Legal Profession.* Looseleaf. Aurora, ON: Canada Law Book, 2005.
	Manes, Ronald D. & Michael Silver. *The Law of Confidential Communications in Canada.* Toronto: LexisNexis Canada, 1996.
	Manes, Ronald D. & Michael Silver. *Solicitor-Client Privilege in Canada.* Toronto: Butterworths, 1993.
	Oughtred, Wendy E. *Going it Alone: A Start Up Guide for the Sole Practitioner.* Aurora, ON: Canada Law Book, 1995.
	Perrell, Paul M. *Conflicts of Interest in the Legal Profession.* Toronto: Butterworths, 1995.
	Plant, Albert C. *Making Money: The Business of Law.* Aurora, ON: Canada Law Book, 1993.
	Smith, Beverley G. *Professional Conduct for Lawyers and Judges.* Looseleaf. 3d ed. Fredericton, NB: Maritime Law Book, 2007.
	Tjaden, Ted. *The Law of Independent Legal Advice.* Scarborough, ON: Carswell, 2000.
	Woolley, Alice *et al. Lawyers' Ethics and Professional Regulation.* Markham, ON: LexisNexis, 2008.
	Zwicker, Milton W. *Developing and Managing a Successful Law Firm.* Scarborough, ON: Carswell, 1995.
Journals	*Appeal: Review of Current Law and Law Reform* (UVIC). Available on LexisNexis Quicklaw from 1995.
	Canadian Bar Review (Canadian Bar Association)
	Canadian Lawyer (Canada Law Book)
	National (Canadian Bar Association)
Encyclopedias	*Canadian Encyclopedic Digest*: Barristers and Solicitors (Ontario and Western)
	Halsbury's Laws of Canada: Legal Profession
Case digests	*Canadian Abridgment* (Carswell): Professions and occupations
Databases and CD-ROMs	CanLII (www.canlii.org) has databases of decisions from a number of provincial law society discipline tribunals.
Websites	Canadian Bar Association: www.cba.org

FF. MEDIA LAW/DEFAMATION

Scope	This section discusses media law and the law of defamation, a topic (largely) governed by various provincial legislation and case law. See also Communications Law, discussed above in this chapter.
Subject headings	Freedom of the press—Canada Libel and slander—Canada Mass media—Law and legislation—Canada Press law—Canada
Books	Brown, Raymond. *Defamation Law: A Primer.* Toronto: Thomson Carswell, 2003. Brown, Raymond. *The Law of Defamation in Canada.* Looseleaf. 2d ed. Scarborough, ON: Carswell, 1994. Crawford, Michael G. *The Journalist's Legal Guide,* 5th ed. Scarborough, ON: Thomson Carswell, 2008. Downard, Peter A. *Libel.* Markham, ON: LexisNexis Butterworths, 2003. Duarte, Tony. *Canadian Film & Television Business & Legal Practice.* Looseleaf. Aurora, ON: Canada Law Book, 2000. Jobb, Dean. *The Fine Print: A Writer's Guide to Canadian Media Law.* Toronto: Emond Montgomery, 2004. Jollimore, Mary. *A Lawyer's Guide to Managing the Media.* Aurora, ON: Canada Law Book, 2000. Martin, Robert, ed. *Speaking Freely: Expression and the Law in the Commonwealth.* Toronto: Irwin Law, 1999. McConchie, Roger D. & David A. Potts. *Canadian Libel and Slander Actions.* Toronto: Irwin Law, 2004. Porter, Julian. *Canadian Libel Practice.* Scarborough, ON: Butterworths, 1986.
Encyclopedias	*Canadian Encyclopedic Digest:* Defamation *Halsbury's Laws of Canada:* • Defamation • Media and Postal Communications
Case digests	*Canadian Abridgment* (Carswell): Torts—Defamation
Databases and CD-ROMs	LexisNexis Quicklaw: Canada Defamation Quantums

GG. MOTOR VEHICLE AND TRANSPORTATION LAW

Scope	Motor vehicle law is governed largely by provincial legislation (with the exception of such matters as federal *Criminal Code* driving offences). Case law interpreting legislation is highly relevant. Also included below are resources on air transportation and on shipping and maritime law.
Subject headings	Insurance, No-fault automobile — Law and legislation — [jurisdiction] Motor vehicles — Law and legislation — [jurisdiction] Liability for traffic accidents — [jurisdiction] Traffic regulations — [jurisdiction]
Books	Fernandes, Rui. *Transportation Law.* Looseleaf. Scarborough, ON: Carswell, 1991. Flaherty, James M. *Financial Services Commission of Ontario (Motor Vehicle Insurance): Law and Practice.* Looseleaf. Aurora, ON: Canada Law Book, 1998. Gold, Alan D. *Defending Drinking and Driving Cases.* Toronto: Carswell, 1993 [annual]. Gold, Alan D. *Drinking & Driving Law.* Looseleaf. Toronto: Carswell, 2010. Gold, Edgar *et al. Maritime Law.* Toronto: Irwin Law, 2004. Gregory, Eleanor A. & George F.T. Gregory. *The Annotated British Columbia Insurance (Motor Vehicle) Act.* Looseleaf. 2d ed. Toronto: Carswell, 1990. Holding, John. *Canadian Manual of International Air Carriage.* Toronto: Irwin Law, 2005. Holding, John & Harvey Crush. *The British Manual of International Air Carriage.* Toronto: Irwin Law, 2009. Holding, John & John Huff. *The US Manual of International Air Carriage.* Toronto: Irwin Law, 2009. Hutchison, Scott C. *et al. The Law of Traffic Offences.* 3d ed. Toronto: Carswell, 2009. Levitt, Edward (Ned), Kevin McGuinness, & Catherine A. Pawluch. *Canadian Forms & Precedents: Sale, Distribution & Transport of Goods.* Looseleaf. 2d ed. Markham, ON: LexisNexis, 2007. Available on CD-ROM and on LexisNexis Quicklaw. Linden, Allen M. & Stephen Eric Firestone. *Butterworths Ontario Motor Vehicle Insurance Practice Manual.* Looseleaf. Toronto: Butterworths, 1995.

Books	McLeod, R.M. *et al. Breathalyzer Law in Canada: The Prosecution and Defence of Drinking and Driving Offences.* Looseleaf. 4th ed. Toronto: Carswell, 2009.
	McNeil, John S. *Motor Carrier Cargo Claims.* 5th ed. Toronto: Thomson Carswell, 2007.
	Muir, Douglas B. & Michael Libby. *Annotated British Columbia Motor Vehicle Act.* Looseleaf. Aurora, ON: Canada Law Book, 2000.
	Oatley, Roger G. & John McLeish. *The Oatley-McLeish Guide to Personal Injury Practice in Motor Vehicle Cases.* Looseleaf. Aurora, ON: Canada Law Book, 2002.
	Russell, W.D. (Rusty). *Russell on Roads.* 2d ed. Toronto: Thomson Carswell, 2008.
	Segal, Murray D. *The Annotated Ontario Highway Traffic Act.* Scarborough, ON: Carswell, 1992 [annual].
	Segal, Murray D. *Manual of Motor Vehicle Law.* Looseleaf. 3d ed. Toronto: Carswell, 1982.
Journals	*Journal of Motor Vehicle Law* (Carswell)
Encyclopedias	*Canadian Encyclopedic Digest:* • Aviation • Carriers • Highways and Streets (Ontario and Western) • Motor Vehicles (Ontario and Western) • Railways • Shipping *Halsbury's Laws of Canada:* • Aviation • Carriage of Goods* • Maritime Law* • Motor Vehicles* • Railways* • Roads, Highways and Bridges
Case digests	*Canadian Abridgment* (Carswell): • Maritime and admiralty law • Motor vehicles • Transportation caseAlert—Transportation (Canada Law Book)
Case law reporters	*Motor Vehicle Reports* (Carswell) *Ontario Accident Benefit Case Summaries* (CCH Canadian)
Databases and CD-ROMs	LexisNexis Quicklaw: Transportation Law Cases—Topical

HH. MUNICIPAL AND PLANNING LAW

Scope	Municipal and planning law is governed almost exclusively by provincial legislation but is affected by case law and the decisions of provincial municipal boards (e.g., the Ontario Municipal Board) and municipal planning boards that have statutory jurisdiction to rule on matters of municipal or planning law. Be aware that municipalities and their employees are often entitled to the benefit of shorter limitation periods.
Subject headings	Eminent domain—Canada Municipal corporations—Canada Zoning law—Canada
Books	Annibale, Quinto M. *Municipal Lands: Acquisition, Management and Disposal*. Aurora, ON: Canada Law Book, 2005. Auerback, Stephen & John Mascarin. *The Annotated Municipal Act*. 2d ed. Toronto: Carswell, 2004. Boghosian, David G. & J. Murray Davison. *The Law of Municipal Liability in Canada*. Looseleaf. Markham, ON: LexisNexis Butterworths, 1999. Buholzer, William. *British Columbia Planning Law and Practice*. Looseleaf. 2d ed. Markham, ON: LexisNexis, 2001. Canada Law Book. *O'Brien's Encyclopedia of Forms: Division IX, Municipal Corporations*. 11th ed. Aurora, ON: Canada Law Book, 1987. Also available on CD-ROM and by subscription. Chipman, John. *The Ontario Municipal Act: A Comprehensive Guide*. Looseleaf. Aurora, ON: Canada Law Book, 2003. Coates, John A. & Stephen F. Waqué. *New Law of Expropriation*. Looseleaf. Toronto: Carswell, 1990. Costello, Eileen. *Ontario Heritage Act and Commentary*. Markham, ON: LexisNexis Canada, 2010. Gill, David. *Annotated British Columbia Assessment Act*. Looseleaf. Aurora, ON: Canada Law Book, 1997. Gregory, Eleanor *et al*. *Annotated British Columbia Local Government Act and Community Charter*. Looseleaf. Aurora, ON: Canada Law Book, 2001. Johnson, Patrice Noé & Allan C. Ross (with the assistance of T.A. Bradbury). *The Law of Municipal Finance*. Markham, ON: LexisNexis Butterworths, 2004. Krushelnicki, Bruce. *A Practical Guide to the Ontario Municipal Board*. 2d ed. Toronto: LexisNexis, 2007. Laux, Frederick. *Planning Law and Practice in Alberta*. 3d ed. Edmonton: Juriliber, 2002. Longo, Leo & John Mascarin. *A Comprehensive Guide to the City of Toronto Act, 2006* (2008 edition). Markham, ON: LexisNexis Canada, 2008.

Books	MacLean, Virginia. *Canadian Forms & Precedents: Land Development.* Looseleaf. Markham, ON: LexisNexis, 1998. Available on CD-ROM and on LexisNexis Quicklaw.
	MacLean, Virginia & Thomas Richardson. *A User's Guide to Municipal By-Laws.* 2d ed. Markham, ON: LexisNexis Canada, 2008.
	Makuch, Stanley *et al. Canadian Forms & Precedents: Municpal Law.* Looseleaf. Markham, ON: LexisNexis Canada, 2010.
	Makuch, Stanley M. *et al. Canadian Municipal and Planning Law,* 2d ed. Toronto: Thomson Carswell, 2004.
	Mascarin, John & Paul De Francesca. *Annotated Land Development Agreements.* Looseleaf. Scarborough, ON: Carswell, 2000.
	McGuinness, Kevin P. & Stephen W. Bauld. *Municipal Procurement.* 2d ed. Markham, ON: LexisNexis, 2009.
	O'Connor, Michael Richard. *Conduct Handbook for Municipal Employees and Officials.* 2d ed. Toronto: Butterworths, 2003.
	Rogers, Ian M. *Canadian Law of Planning and Zoning.* Looseleaf. 2d ed. Toronto: Carswell, 2005.
	Rogers, Ian M. *The Law of Canadian Municipal Corporations.* Looseleaf. 2d ed. Toronto: Carswell, 1988.
	Rust-D'Eye, George. *The Ontario Municipal Act: A User's Manual.* Toronto: Carswell, 2008 [annual].
	Todd, Eric. *The Law of Expropriation and Compensation in Canada.* 2d ed. Scarborough, ON: Carswell, 1992.
	Troister, Sidney H. *The Law of Subdivision Control in Ontario: A Practical Guide to Section 50 of the Planning Act.* 2d ed. Scarborough, ON: Carswell, 1994.
	Walker, Jack & Jerry Grad. *Ontario Property Tax Assessment Handbook.* Looseleaf. 2d ed. Aurora, ON: Canada Law Book, 1998.
	Weir Foulds LLP. *Ontario Planning Practice: Annotated Statutes and Regulations.* Looseleaf. Aurora, ON: Canada Law Book, 1989.
	Whicher, Gordon James. *Ontario Planning Law & Practice.* Markham, ON: LexisNexis Butterworths, 2005.
	Wood, Dennis H. *The Planning Act: A Sourcebook.* 6th ed. Toronto: Thomson Carswell, 2008.
Journals	*Municipal Liability Risk Management Newsletter* (LexisNexis Canada)
Encyclopedias	*Canadian Encyclopedic Digest*: • Highways and Streets (Ontario and Western) • Hotels (Ontario and Western) • Municipal and School Taxation (Ontario and Western) • Municipal Corporations (Ontario and Western) • Planning and Zoning (Ontario and Western) • Public Authorities and Public Officers (Ontario and Western)

Encyclopedias	*Halsbury's Laws of Canada*: • Municipal Law* • Planning and Zoning *JurisClasseur Québec:* Collection Droit public (Droit municipal)
Case digests	*Canadian Abridgment* (Carswell): • Municipal law • Public law—Public authorities • Real property—Expropriation caseAlert—Municipal and Planning Law (Canada Law Book) *Digest of Municipal and Planning Law*, 2d ed. (Carswell)
Case law reporters	*Land Compensation Reports* (Canada Law Book) *Municipal and Planning Law Reports* (Carswell) *Ontario Municipal Board Reports* (Canada Law Book)
Databases and CD-ROMs	LexisNexis Quicklaw: • Municipal Law Cases—Topical • Municipal Law Tribunal Decisions—Topical • Ontario Municipal Board Decisions

II. OCCUPATIONAL HEALTH AND SAFETY

Scope	Occupational health and safety is a special subset of employment law that is (largely) governed by provincial legislation (such as Ontario's *Occupational Health and Safety Act*, R.S.O. 1990, c. O.1) aimed at ensuring safe work environments.
Subject headings	Industrial hygiene—Law and legislation—[jurisdiction] Industrial safety—Law and legislation—[jurisdiction]
Books	Arnott, Bruce *et al. Annotated Occupational Health and Safety Act*. Looseleaf. Aurora, ON: Canada Law Book, 1998. CCH Canadian. *Canadian Employment Safety and Health Guide*. Looseleaf. Toronto: CCH Canadian, 1980. Conlin, Ryan & Charles Humphrey. *The Employer's Health and Safety Manual, Ontario*. Looseleaf. 2d ed. Toronto: Thomson Carswell, 1995. Dee, Garth & Gary Newhouse. *Butterworths Workers' Compensation in Ontario Service*. Looseleaf. 2d ed. Toronto: Butterworths, 1993. Edwards, Cheryl & Ryan Conlin. *Employer Liability for Contractors under the Occupational Health and Safety Act*. 2d ed. Toronto: Thomson Carswell, 2007. Ferguson, Reg. *WHMIS Compliance Manual*. Looseleaf. Toronto: Carswell, 1989.

Books	Glasbeek, Sandra & Fred Campbell. *Occupational Health and Safety in Ontario Education: A Risk and Compliance Manual.* Looseleaf. Markham, ON: LexisNexis, 2001.
	Humphrey, Charles E. & Cheryl A. Edwards. *The Employer's Health and Safety Manual — Ontario Edition.* Looseleaf. 2d ed. Aurora, ON: Carswell, 1995.
	Keith, Norman. *Canadian Health and Safety Law: A Comprehensive Guide to the Statutes, Policies and Case Law.* Looseleaf. Aurora, ON: Canada Law Book, 1997.
	Keith, Norman. *Ontario Health and Safety Law: A Complete Guide to the Law and Procedures, with a Digest of Cases.* Looseleaf. Aurora, ON: Canada Law Book, 1989.
	Keith, Norman. *A Practical Guide to Occupational Health and Safety Compliance in Ontario.* 3d ed. Aurora, ON: Canada Law Book, 2006.
	Keith, Norman. *Workplace Health and Safety Crimes.* 2d ed. Markham, ON: LexisNexis, 2009.
	Keith, Norman & Adam Neave. *A Practical Guide to Occupational Health and Safety and Workers' Compensation Compliance in Alberta.* Aurora, ON: Canada Law Book, 2007.
	McDonald, Heather & Marguerite Mousseau. *Workers' Compensation in B.C.* Looseleaf. Markham, ON: LexisNexis, 2009.
	Robertson, Dilys. *ABCs of OH&S — Ontario.* Looseleaf. Toronto: Carswell, 1993.
	Robertson, Dilys. *Best Practices: Health & Safety.* Looseleaf. Toronto: Carswell, 2007.
	Rock, Nora & Fred Campbell. *Occupational Health and Safety in Ontario Health Care: A Risk and Compliance Manual.* Looseleaf. Markham, ON: Butterworths, 2002.
Journals	Health & Safety/Workers' Compensation Law Service (Lancaster House)
Encyclopedias	*Canadian Encyclopedic Digest*: Occupational Health and Safety (Ontario)
	Halsbury's Laws of Canada: Workplace Health and Safety*
	JurisClasseur Québec: Collection Droit du travail (Droit de la santé et de la sécurité du travail)
Case digests	*Canadian Abridgment* (Carswell): Labour and employment law
Websites	Canadian Centre for Occupational Health and Safety: www.ccohs.ca

JJ. PENSION LAW

Scope	Pension law is a fairly specialized subset of employment law focusing on federal and provincial pension legislation and case law interpreting that legislation. It is relevant in a number of areas of practice, particularly in family law (regarding valuation of matrimonial property), personal injury law, and employment law.
Subject headings	Pensions—Law and legislation—[jurisdiction] Pensions—Valuation—[jurisdiction]
Books	CCH Canadian. *Canadian Employment Benefits and Pension Guide Reports.* Looseleaf. Toronto: CCH Canadian, 1962.
Books	Kaplan, Ari N. *Pension Law.* Toronto: Irwin Law, 2006. Lloy, Douglas J. *CPP Disability Pension Guide.* Toronto: Butterworths, 2003. MacDonald, J. Bruce. *Carswell's Benefits Guide.* Looseleaf. Scarborough, ON: Carswell, 1999. McSweeney, Ian J. & David S. McFarlane. *Pension Benefits Law in Ontario.* Looseleaf. Scarborough, ON: Carswell, 1996. Mercer Human Resource Consulting. *The Mercer Pension Manual.* Looseleaf. Toronto: Carswell, 1988. Also available in a modified format as a CD-ROM called *Mercer Pension Manager.* Patterson, Jack & Catherine D. Aitken, ed. *Pension Division and Valuation: Family Lawyers' Guide.* 2d ed. Aurora, ON: Canada Law Book, 1995. Seller, Susan G. *Ontario Pension Law Handbook.* 2d ed. Aurora, ON: Canada Law Book, 2006.
Journals	*Compensation & Benefits Reporter* (Carswell) *Compensation and Benefits Review* (Carswell) *Estates, Trusts and Pensions Journal* (Canada Law Book)
Encyclopedias	*Canadian Encyclopedic Digest:* • Annuities • Pensions and Retirement Benefits *Halsbury's Laws of England:* • Pensions and Annuities*
Case digests	*Canadian Abridgment* (Carswell): Pensions LexisNexis Quicklaw: • Abrégé de jurisprudence—Régimes de retraite et pensions • Canada Pensions and Old Age Security Digest
Case law reporters	*Canadian Cases on Pensions and Benefits* (Carswell)

Databases and CD-ROMs	LexisNexis Quicklaw: • Pensions & Benefits Law Cases—Topical • Persons Law (Québec Civil Law) Cases—Topical
Websites	Canada Pension Plan: www.hrsdc.gc.ca/eng/isp/cpp/cpptoc.shtml

KK. PERSONAL PROPERTY SECURITY LAW

Scope	Personal property security law in Canada is a matter of provincial law that has been largely harmonized across most Canadian provinces. Case law interpreting provincial legislation is highly relevant.
Subject headings	Security (Law) — [jurisdiction] Personal property — [jurisdiction]
Books	Bennett, Frank. *Bennett on PPSA (Ontario)*. 3d ed. Markham, ON: LexisNexis Butterworths, 2006. Cuming, Ronald & Roderick J. Wood. *British Columbia Personal Property Security Act Handbook*. 4th ed. Toronto: Carswell, 1999. Cuming, Ronald *et al. Personal Property Security Law*. Toronto: Irwin Law, 2005. Cuming, Ronald & Roderick J. Wood. *Saskatchewan and Manitoba Personal Property Security Acts Handbook*. 4th ed. Toronto: Carswell, 1998. Duggan, Tony *et al. Secured Transactions in Personal Property*. 5th ed. Toronto: Emond Montgomery, 2009. Goldberg, Barry & Steven Golick. *Guide to Ontario Personal Property Security*. Looseleaf. Don Mills, ON: R. DeBoo, 1989. Hatzikiriakos, Kiriakoula. *Secured Transactions in Intellectual Property: Software as Collateral*. Markham, ON: LexisNexis Canada, 2006. Leppmann, Karl F. *Security Documents: An Annotated Guide*. Aurora, ON: Canada Law Book, 1999. McLaren, Richard H. *Secured Transactions in Personal Property in Canada*. Looseleaf. 2d ed. Toronto: Carswell, 1989. Also available on *InsolvencySource* on Westlaw Canada (by subscription) and by subscription online (Carswell eReference Library). Ziegel, Jacob S. & David L. Denomme. *The Ontario Personal Property Security Act: Commentary and Analysis*. Aurora, ON: Canada Law Book, 1994.
Journals	*Commercial Times* (CCH Canadian) *National Debtor/Creditor Review* (LexisNexis Canada)

Encyclopedias	*Canadian Encyclopedic Digest*: • Pledges • Secured Transactions in Personal Property (Ontario and Western) *Halsbury's Laws of England*: Personal Property and Secured Transactions *JurisClasseur Québec*: Collection Droit civil (Sûretés)
Case digests	*Canadian Abridgment* (Carswell): Personal property security
Case law reporters	*Personal Property Security Act Cases* (Carswell)

LL. PRIVACY LAW

Scope	Privacy law is increasingly relevant in modern society. In Canada, privacy is regulated by federal statutes such as the *Personal Information Protection and Electronic Documents Act*, S.C. 2000, c. 5 and the *Access to Information Act*, R.S.C. 1985, c. A-1, as well as parallel provincial statutes.
Subject headings	Freedom of information — Canada Privacy, Right of — Canada
Books	Charnetski, William A. *et al. The Personal Information Protection and Electronic Documents Act: A Comprehensive Guide.* Aurora, ON: Canada Law Book, 2001. Drapeau, Michel W. & Marc-Aurèle Racicot. *Federal Access to Information and Privacy Legislation.* Looseleaf. Toronto: Thomson Carswell, 2005. Edwards, Jennifer. *Human Resources Guide to Workplace Privacy.* Aurora, ON: Canada Law Book, 2003. Klein, Kris *et al. Privacy in Employment: Control of Personal Information in the Workplace.* 2d ed. Toronto: Carswell, 2009. Knight, Jamie. *Canada Personal Information and Electronic Documents Act.* Annual. Toronto: Thomson Carswell, 2004. McIssac, Barbara *et al. The Law of Privacy in Canada.* Looseleaf. Toronto: Thomson Carswell, 2000. Also available by subscription online (Carswell eReference Library). McNairn, Colin H. H. & Alexander K. Scott. *A Guide to the Personal Information Protection and Electronic Documents Act.* Markham, ON: LexisNexis Butterworths, 2000 [annual]. McNairn, Colin H.H. *et al. Privacy Law in Canada.* Toronto: Butterworths, 2001.

Books	Novakowski, Lorene & Karla Koles. *Personal Information Protection Act: British Columbia and Alberta: Quick Reference.* Toronto: Thomson Carswell, 2008. Platt, Priscilla *et al. Privacy Law in the Private Sector: An Annotation of the Legislation in Canada.* Looseleaf. Aurora, ON: Canada Law Book, 2002. Woodbury, Christopher D. & Colin H.H. McNairn. *Government Information: Access and Privacy.* Looseleaf. Scarborough, ON: Carswell, 1989.
Journals	*Canadian Privacy Law Review* (LexisNexis Canada) *The Klein & Kratchanov Report: The Canadian Source for Legal Developments in Privacy and Access* (Carswell)
Encyclopedias	*Canadian Encyclopedic Digest:* Privacy and Freedom of Information
Case digests	*Canadian Abridgment* (Carswell): Privacy and freedom of information
Databases and CD-ROMs	CanLII (www.canlii.org) has databases of decisions from the various federal and provincial privacy commissioners. PrivaWorks (www.privaworks.com) (Nymity)
Websites	Office of the Privacy Commissioner of Canada: www.privcom.gc.ca

MM. PROPERTY LAW (REAL AND PERSONAL)

Scope	Real property law is largely governed by provincial legislation too numerous to list here, although judicial interpretations of this legislation also impact real estate practice.
Subject headings	Vendors and purchasers—Canada Mortgages—Canada Real estate business—Law and legislation—Canada Condominiums—Law and legislation—[jurisdiction]
Books	Benson, Marjorie. *Understanding Property: A Guide to Canada's Property Law.* 2d ed. Toronto: Thomson Carswell, 2008. Bocska, Rosemary & Martin Rumack. *Legal Responsibilities of Real Estate Agents.* 2d ed. Markham, ON: LexisNexis Canada, 2009. Burke, Margaret R. *Ontario Real Estate Procedures.* 2d ed. Scarborough, ON: Carswell, 1994. Canada Law Book. *O'Brien's Encyclopedia of Forms: Division III, Conveyancing and Mortgages.* 11th ed. Aurora, ON: Canada Law Book, 1987. Also available on CD-ROM and by subscription on O'Brien's Internet.

Books

CCH Canadian. *Prairie Real Estate Law Guide*. Looseleaf. Toronto: CCH Canadian, 2004. Available in print and by subscription online.

Coburn, Frederick F. & Garth Manning. *Toxic Real Estate Manual*. Looseleaf. Aurora, ON: Canada Law Book, 1994.

DiCastri, Victor. *The Law of Vendor and Purchaser*. Looseleaf. 3d ed. Toronto: Carswell, 1988.

DiCastri, Victor. *Registration of Title to Land*. 3d ed. Looseleaf. Toronto: Carswell, 1988.

Donahue, Donald J. *et al. Real Estate Practice in Ontario*. 6th ed. Markham, ON: LexisNexis Butterworths, 2003.

Foster, William F. *Real Estate Agency Law in Canada*. 2d ed. Scarborough, ON: Carswell, 1994.

Gardiner, J. Robert. *The Condominium Act 1998: A Practical Guide*. Aurora, ON: Canada Law Book, 2001.

Gray, Wayne S. *Marriott and Dunn: Mortgage Remedies in Ontario*. Looseleaf. 5th ed. Toronto: Thomson Professional, 1991.

Kurtz, JoAnn *et al. Residential Real Estate Transactions*. 3d ed. Toronto: Emond Montgomery, 2009.

La Forest, Anne Warner. *Anger and Honsberger: Law of Real Property*. 3d ed. Aurora, ON: Canada Law Book, 2006.

Lamont, Donald H.L. *Lamont on Real Estate Conveyancing*. Looseleaf. 2d ed. Toronto: Thomson Carswell, 1991.

Law Society of Upper Canada. *Special Lectures 2002: Real Property Law*. Toronto: Irwin Law, 2003.

LexisNexis Canada. *Ontario Residential Real Estate Practice Manual*. Looseleaf. Toronto: Butterworths Canada, 1992.

Lipson, Barry. *The Art of the Real Estate Deal*. 2d ed. Toronto: Thomson Carswell, 2006.

Loeb, Audrey. *The Condominium Act: A User's Manual*. 3d ed. Toronto: Carswell, 2009.

Loeb, Audrey. *Condominium Law and Administration*. Looseleaf. 2d ed. Toronto: Carswell, 1989.

MacIntosh, C.W. *Nova Scotia Real Property Practice Manual*. Looseleaf. Markham, ON: LexisNexis, 1992.

Maguire, Robert & Rose H. McConnell. *British Columbia Real Estate Law Guide*. Looseleaf. Toronto: CCH Canadian, 1979. Available in print, on CD-ROM, and by subscription online.

McCallum, Margaret & Alan M. Sinclair. *Introduction to Real Property Law*. 5th ed. Toronto: LexisNexis Butterworths, 2005.

McConnell, Rose. *Document Registration Guide*, 5th ed. Toronto: CCH Canadian, 2002.

McDermott, Jim *et al. Canadian Commercial Real Estate Manual*. Looseleaf. Toronto: Carswell, 1986. Available in print, on CD-ROM, and by subscription online.

Books	McKenna, Bruce *et al. Ontario Real Estate Law Guide.* Loose-leaf. Toronto: CCH Canadian, 1975. Available in print, on CD-ROM, and by subscription online.

McKenna, Bruce. *Title Insurance: A Guide to Regulation, Coverage and Claims Process in Ontario.* Toronto: CCH Canadian, 1999.

Moore, Marguerite. *Title Searching and Conveyancing in Ontario.* 5th ed. Markham, ON: LexisNexis Butterworths, 2003.

Perell, Paul M. & Bruce H. Engell. *Remedies and the Sale of Land.* 2d ed. Toronto: Butterworths, 1998.

Petraglia, Philip & Lazar Sarna. *Annotated Real Estate Laws of Ontario.* Looseleaf. Markham, ON: LexisNexis Butter-worths, 2001.

Roach, Joseph E. *The Canadian Law of Mortgages of Land.* Toronto: Butterworths, 1993.

Sarna, Lazar & Asher Neudorfer. *The Law of Immovable Hypothecs in Québec.* Markham, ON: LexisNexis Butter-worths, 2006.

Smythe, Scott D. & E.M. Vogt. *McCarthy Tétrault Annotated British Columbia Strata Property Act.* Looseleaf. Aurora, ON: Canada Law Book, 2002.

Traub, Walter M. *Falconbridge on Mortgages.* Looseleaf. 5th ed. Aurora, ON: Canada Law Book, 2003.

Walma, Mark. *Advanced Residential Real Estate Transactions.* 2d ed. Toronto: Emond Montgomery, 2003.

Ziff, Bruce. *Principles of Property Law.* 4th ed. Toronto: Thomson Carswell, 2006.

Encyclopedias	*Canadian Encyclopedic Digest:*

- Absentees
- Bailment
- Boundaries and Surveys
- Condominiums (Ontario and Western)
- Drainage (Ontario and Western)
- Easements
- Expropriation
- Fraudulent Conveyances and Preferences
- Gifts
- Mortgages (Ontario and Western)
- Perpetuities and Accumulations
- Personal Property
- Planning and Zoning (Ontario and Western)
- Real Property (Ontario and Western)
- References and Inquiries (Ontario and Western)
- Sale of Land

Encyclopedias	*Halsbury's Laws of Canada*: • Absentees* • Boundaries and Surveys* • Real Property* • Condominiums and Cooperatives* • Expropriation* • Gifts • Mortgages* • Personal Property and Secured Transactions • Planning and Zoning • Waters and Drainage*
Case digests	*Canadian Abridgment* (Carswell): • Personal property • Real property caseAlert—Real Property (Canada Law Book) LexisNexis Quicklaw: Canada Real Property Law Digest
Case law reporters	*Land Compensation Reports* (Canada Law Book) *Real Property Reports* (Carswell)
Databases and CD-ROMs	LexisNexis Quicklaw: • Canada Property-Related Torts Quantums • Real Property Law Cases—Topical

NN. SECURITIES LAW

Scope	Securities law in Canada is highly regulated by provincial and federal securities and corporate legislation too numerous to list here.
Subject headings	Securities—Canada Stock exchanges—Law and legislation—Canada Investments—Law and legislation—Canada Mutual funds—Law and legislation—Canada
Books	Borden Ladner Gervais LLP. *Securities Law and Practice*. 3d ed. Looseleaf. Toronto: Carswell, 2003. Available by subscription on *SecuritiesSource* on Westlaw Canada. *Canadian Stock Exchanges Manual*. North York, ON: CCH Canadian, 1994. Dorval, Thierry. *Governance of Publicly Listed Corporations*. Markham, ON: LexisNexis Butterworths, 2005. Gillen, Mark R. *Securities Regulation in Canada*. 3d ed. Scarborough, ON: Carswell, 2007. Groia, Joseph & Pamela Hardie. *Securities Litigation and Enforcement*. Toronto: Thomson Carswell, 2007.

Books	Grottenthaler, Margaret E. & Philip J. Henderson. *The Law of Financial Derivatives in Canada.* Looseleaf. Toronto: Carswell, 1999.
	Hendrickson, Barbara. *Canadian Institutional Investment Rules.* Toronto: CCH Canadian, 2003.
	Hendrickson, Barbara. *Canadian Securities Law Reporter.* Toronto: CCH Canadian, 1996. Available in print, on CD-ROM, and by subscription online.
	Johnston, David L. & Kathleen Rockwell. *Canadian Securities Regulation.* 4th ed. Markham, ON: Butterworths, 2006.
	MacIntosh, Jeff & Christopher Nicholls. *Securities Law.* Toronto: Irwin Law, 2002.
	Marcone, Martin. *Eligible Financial Contracts: A Legal Analysis.* Markham, ON: LexisNexis Canada, 2009.
	Petraglia, Philip & Lazar Sarna. *Annotated Ontario Securities Act.* Looseleaf. Markham, ON: LexisNexis Canada, 2000.
	Petraglia, Philip & Lazar Sarna. *Corporate Securities Laws in Canada: with a Guide to U.S. Law.* Markham, ON: LexisNexis Butterworths, 2003.
	Puri, Poonam & Jeffrey Larsen. *Corporate Governance and Securities Regulation in the 21st Century.* Markham, ON: LexisNexis Butterworths, 2004.
	Puri, Poonam & Leslie McCallum. *Canadian Companies' Guide to the Sarbanes-Oxley Act.* Markham, ON: LexisNexis Butterworths, 2004.
	Sarna, Lazar (with the assistance of Noah Sarna). *Insider Trading: A Canadian Legal Manual.* Looseleaf. Rev. ed. Markham, ON: LexisNexis Butterworths, 2005.
	Stikeman Elliott. *Legal for Life: Institutional Investment Rules in Canada.* 6th ed. Scarborough, ON: Carswell, 1996.
	Toronto Stock Exchange Company Manual. Looseleaf. North York, ON: CCH Canadian, 1976. Available in print, on CD-ROM, and by subscription online.
Journals	*Canadian Securities Law Review* (Osler, Hoskin & Harcourt)
	Corporate Securities and Finance Law Report (LexisNexis Canada)
	Ontario Securities Commission Bulletin (Ontario Securities Commission)
Encyclopedias	*Canadian Encyclopedic Digest*: Securities and Stock Exchanges
	Halsbury's Laws of Canada: Securities Law*
	JurisClasseur Québec: Collection Droit des affaires (Valeurs mobilières)
Case digests	*Canadian Abridgment* (Carswell): Securities
Case law reporters	*Canadian Cases on the Law of Securities* (Carswell, 1993–1998)

Databases and CD-ROMs	CCH Online (Canadian Securities Law Reporter and other securities-related titles)
	DisclosureNet (www.disclosurenet.com)
	Securities Partner Plus [CD-ROM]. Scarborough, ON: Carswell. Updated regularly. Contains securities-related legislation, case law, and full-text commentary. Available in an expanded version as *SecuritiesSource* on Westlaw Canada (by subscription).
	Westlaw Business (business.westlaw.com)
Websites	SEDAR (Canadian stock exchange documents): www.sedar.com

OO. SPORTS AND ENTERTAINMENT LAW

Scope	Sports and entertainment law has developed in recent years into a fairly specialized practice area, focusing on contracting and licensing for entertainers and athletes. Entertainment and sports lawyers frequently deal with contract law, intellectual property law, and negotiations.
Subject headings	Motion pictures—Law and legislation—Canada
	Performing arts—Law and legislation—Canada
	Recreation—Law and legislation—Canada
	Sports—Law and legislation—Canada
	Television programs—Law and legislation—Canada
Books	Abe, Lisa. *Canadian Forms & Precedents: Information Technology & Entertainment.* Looseleaf. 2d ed. Markham, ON: LexisNexis, 2007. Available on CD-ROM and on LexisNexis Quicklaw.
	Barnes, John. *Sports and the Law in Canada.* 3d ed. Toronto: LexisNexis Canada, 1996.
	Bird, Stephen & John Zauhar. *Recreation and the Law.* 2d ed. Scarborough, ON: Carswell, 1997.
	Castel, Jacqueline. *Gaming Control Law in Ontario.* Looseleaf. Aurora, ON: Canada Law Book, 2001.
	Corbett, Rachel *et al. Legal Issues in Sport: Tools and Techniques for the Sport Manager.* Toronto: Emond Montgomery, 2008.
	Duarte, Tony. *Canadian Film & Television Business & Legal Practice.* Looseleaf. Aurora, ON: Canada Law Book, 2000.
	King, Jacqueline L. *Entertainment Law in Canada.* Looseleaf. Markham, ON: LexisNexis, 2000.
	Sanderson, Paul. *Musicians and the Law in Canada: A Guide to the Law, Contracts and Practice in the Canadian Music Business.* 3d rev. ed. Scarborough, ON: Carswell, 2000.

Encyclopedias	*Canadian Encyclopedic Digest*: Sports
	Halsbury's Laws of Canada: Athletics

PP. TAXATION LAW

Scope	Taxation law in Canada is governed primarily by the federal *Income Tax Act*, R.S.C. 1985 (5th Supp.), c. 1 and the *Excise Tax Act*, R.S.C. 1985, c. E-15, which are administered by Canada Customs and Revenue Agency (CCRA). The CCRA has extensive regulatory and administrative documentation on its website, including forms, information circulars, and interpretation bulletins. Provincial tax legislation is also relevant. There is a plethora of print and online legal resources on Canadian taxation law that are too numerous to list here, so the list of books below is only a partial list. Check the websites of the Canadian legal publishers for more information.
Subject headings	Excise tax—Law and legislation—Canada Goods and services tax—Law and legislation—Canada Income tax—Law and legislation—Canada
Books	Brown, Catherine & Cindy Radu. *Taxation and Estate Planning*. Looseleaf. Scarborough, ON: Carswell, 1996. Campbell, Colin. *Administration of Income Tax*. Toronto: Carswell, 2003 [annual]. *Canada Income Tax Law and Policy*. Looseleaf. Toronto: Thomson Carswell, 1990. CCH Canadian Limited. *Canadian Master Tax Guide*. Don Mills, ON: CCH Canadian, 1946 [annual updates]. Related income tax material available from CCH Canadian in print, on CD-ROM, and by subscription online (see link under CCH Tax Works). Chodikoff, David & James Horvath. *Advocacy & Taxation in Canada*. Toronto: Irwin Law, 2004. Cuperfain, Joel & Florence Marino. *Canadian Taxation of Life Insurance*. 4th ed. Toronto: Thomson Carswell, 2008. Davies Ward Phillips & Vineberg LLP. *Taxation of Corporate Reorganizations*. Toronto: Carswell, 2010. Drache, Arthur *et al. Charities Taxation, Policy and Practice*. Looseleaf. Toronto: Carswell, 2007. Duff, David & Harry Erlichman. *Tax Avoidance in Canada after Canada Trustco and Mathew*. Toronto: Irwin Law, 2007. Duff, David *et al. Canadian Income Tax Law*. 3d ed. Markham, ON: LexisNexis Butterworths, 2009.

Books	Erlichman, Harry, ed. *Tax Avoidance in Canada: The General Anti-Avoidance Rule in Canada.* Toronto: Irwin Law, 2002.
	Hanson, Suzanne. *Canada Tax Manual.* Looseleaf. Toronto: Carswell, 1990.
	Hogg, Peter H. *et al. Principles of Canadian Income Tax Law.* 6th ed. Toronto: Thomson Carswell, 2007.
	Horvath, James L. & David W. Chodikoff. *Taxation & Valuation of Technology: Theory, Practice, and the Law.* Toronto: Irwin Law, 2008
	Innes, William & Ralph Cuervo-Lorens. *Tax Evasion.* Looseleaf. Toronto: Carswell, 1995.
	Krishna, Vern. *Canada's Tax Treaties.* Looseleaf. Toronto: Butterworths, 1999.
	Krishna, Vern. *The Fundamentals of Income Tax Law.* Toronto: Carswell, 2009.
	Krishna, Vern. *Income Tax Law.* Concord, ON: Irwin Law, 1997.
	Li, Jinyan *et al. International Taxation in Canada: Principles and Practices.* Markham, ON: LexisNexis, 2006.
	McMechan, Robert & Gordon Bourgard. *Tax Court Practice.* Looseleaf. Toronto: Carswell, 1995.
	Pound, Richard. *Stikeman Annotated Income Tax Act.* Toronto: Carswell, 1949 [annual].
	PriceWaterhouseCoopers LLP. *Canadian Insurance Taxation.* 3d ed. Markham, ON: LexisNexis Butterworths, 2009.
	Schwartz, Alan. *GAAR Interpreted: The General Anti-Avoidance Rule.* Looseleaf. Toronto: Carswell, 2006.
	Sherman, David M. *Canadian Tax Research: A Practical Guide.* 4th ed. Toronto: Thomson Carswell, 2006.
	Sherman, David M. *The Practitioner's Goods and Services Tax Annotated.* Toronto: Carswell, 1991 [annual].
	Sherman, David M. *The Practitioner's Income Tax Act.* Toronto: Carswell, 1992 [annual].
	Sweeney, Terrance. *Annotated Ontario Retail Sales Tax Act.* Markham, ON: LexisNexis Butterworths, 2006.
	Tari, A. Christina. *Federal Income Tax Litigation in Canada.* Looseleaf. Markham, ON: LexisNexis Butterworths, 1997.
	Tobias, Norman C. *Taxation of Corporations, Partnerships and Trusts.* 3d ed. Toronto: Carswell, 2006.
Journals	*Canadian Current Tax* (LexisNexis Canada)
	Canadian Tax Journal (Canadian Tax Foundation)
	The Canadian Taxpayer (Carswell)
	GST & Commodity Tax (Carswell)
Encyclopedias	*Canadian Encyclopedic Digest:*
	• Customs and Excise
	• Income Tax

Encyclopedias	*Halsbury's Laws of Canada*: • Commodity Taxation* • Customs and Excise* • Income Tax (Corporate) • Income Tax (General) • Income Tax (International)*
Case digests	*Canadian Abridgment* (Carswell): Tax
Case law reporters	*Canada Tax Cases* (Carswell) *Dominion Tax Cases* (CCH Canadian)
Databases and CD-ROMs	CCH Online (extensive tax-related content) *GST Partner* [CD-ROM]. Toronto: Carswell. Updated regularly. Contains relevant legislation, case law, and commentary from Carswell's *GST Service*. *TaxPartner* [CD-ROM]. Toronto: Carswell. Updated regularly. Contains relevant legislation, case law, and commentary from Carswell-authored textbooks on tax law. TaxnetPRO (Thomson Carswell)
Websites	Canada Customs and Revenue Agency: www.ccra-adrc.gc.ca Canada Tax Foundation: www.ctf.ca

QQ. TORT LAW

Scope	Tort law is traditionally governed by case law, although provinces in Canada are increasingly introducing "no fault" insurance schemes governing injuries arising from motor vehicle accidents. Tort law can also be affected by provincial negligence legislation, such as British Columbia's *Negligence Act*, R.S.B.C. 1996, c. 333. Also included below are books dealing with fiduciary duties and products liability.
Subject headings	Negligence—Canada Products liability Torts—Canada
Books	Beaulac, Stéphane *et al.*, eds. *The Joy of Torts*. Markham, ON: LexisNexis Butterworths, 2003. Burns, Peter & Joost Blom. *Economic Interests in Canadian Tort Law*. Markham, ON: LexisNexis Canada, 2009. Cassels, Jamie & Craig Jones. *The Law of Large-Scale Claims: Product Liability, Mass Torts, and Complex Litigation in Canada*. Toronto: Irwin Law, 2005. Edgell, Dean F. *Product Liability in Canada*. Toronto: Butterworths, 2000.

Books	Ellis, Mark Vincent. *Fiduciary Duties in Canada*. Looseleaf. Toronto: Carswell, 1990. Also available by subscription online (Carswell eReference Library). Feldthusen, Bruce. *Economic Negligence: The Recovery of Pure Economic Loss*. 5th ed. Scarborough, ON: Thomson Carswell, 2008. Grace, Elizabeth & Susan Vella. *Civil Liability for Sexual Abuse and Violence in Canada*. Markham, ON: Butterworths, 2000. Fridman, Gerald. *Introduction to the Canadian Law of Torts*. Markham, ON: LexisNexis Butterworths, 2003. Fridman, Gerald. *The Law of Torts in Canada*. 2d ed. Toronto: Carswell, 2002. Kerr, Margaret, JoAnn Kurtz & Laurence M. Olivo. *Canadian Tort Law in a Nutshell*. 3d ed. Toronto: Carswell, 2009. Klar, Lewis. *Tort Law*. 4th ed. Toronto: Thomson Carswell, 2008. Klar, Lewis *et al*. *Remedies in Tort*. Looseleaf. Toronto: Carswell, 1987. Linden, Allen M. & Bruce Feldthusen. *Canadian Tort Law*. 8th ed. Markham, ON: LexisNexis Butterworths, 2006. Also available by subscription on LexisNexis Quicklaw. Osborne, Philip H. *The Law of Torts*. 3d ed. Toronto: Irwin Law, 2007. Pun, Gregory & Margaret Isabel Hall. *The Law of Nuisance in Canada*. Markham, ON: LexisNexis, 2010. Rotman, Leonard. *Fiduciary Law*. Toronto: Thomson Carswell, 2005. Theall, Lawrence G. *et al*. *Product Liability: Canadian Law and Practice*. Looseleaf. Aurora, ON: Canada Law Book, 2001. Waddams, Stephen. *Products Liability*. 4th ed. Toronto: Carswell, 2002.
Journals	*Canadian Class Action Review* (Irwin Law)
Encyclopedias	*Canadian Encyclopedic Digest*: • Malicious Prosecution and False Imprisonment • Negligence • Nuisance • Torts • Trespass *Halsbury's Laws of Canada*: • Negligence • Torts
Case digests	*Canadian Abridgment* (Carswell): Torts LexisNexis Quicklaw: Canada Tort Law Digest
Case law reporters	*Canadian Cases on the Law of Torts* (Carswell)

Databases and *CD-ROMs*	LexisNexis Quicklaw: • Quantum of Damages in Personal Injury Law Cases—Topical • Tort Law and Civil Liability Law Cases—Topical

RR. TRUSTS, WILLS, AND ESTATES LAW

Scope	Trusts and estates law are generally a combination of case law and (largely provincial) legislation, originally strongly influenced by English law.
Subject *headings*	Trusts and trustees—Canada Estate planning—Canada

Allen, William P.G. & John P. Allen. *Estate Planning Handbook.* 3d ed. Scarborough, ON: Carswell, 1999. Available on *Estates&TrustsSource* on Westlaw Canada (by subscription).

Armstrong, Anne. *Estate Administration: A Solicitor's Reference Manual.* Looseleaf. Toronto: Carswell, 1984.

Canada Law Book. *O'Brien's Encyclopedia of Forms: Division V, Wills and Trusts.* 11th ed. Aurora, ON: Canada Law Book, 1987. Also available on CD-ROM and by subscription on O'Brien's Internet.

CCH Canadian Limited. *Canadian Estate Administration Law Guide.* Looseleaf. North York, Ontario: CCH Canadian, 1995. Available in print, on CD-ROM, and by subscription online.

CCH Canadian Limited. *Executor's Handbook.* 2d ed. North York, ON: CCH Canadian, 2003.

Claxton, John B. *Studies on the Quebec Law of Trust.* Toronto: Thomson Carswell, 2005.

Crummey, Sheila M. *et al. Financial and Estate Planning for the Mature Client in Ontario.* Looseleaf. Markham, ON: LexisNexis Canada, 1997.

Doyle, Kelly R. *Asset Protection.* 2d ed. Markham, ON: LexisNexis Butterworths, 2009.

Easterbrook, Susan A. *Mediating Estate Disputes.* Aurora, ON: Canada Law Book, 2003.

Gibbs, Karen M. *et al. The Practical Guide to Ontario Estate Administration.* 5th ed. Scarborough, ON: Carswell, 2006.

Gillen, Mark & Faye Woodman, eds. *The Law of Trusts: A Contextual Approach.* Toronto: Emond Montgomery, 2000.

Gillese, Eileen & Martha Milczynski. *The Law of Trusts.* 2d ed. Toronto: Irwin Law, 2005.

Books

Greenan, Jennifer. *The Executor's Handbook*. 3d ed. Toronto: CCH Canadian, 2007.

Harvey, Cameron & Linda Vincent. *The Law of Dependants' Relief in Canada*. 2d ed. Toronto: Carswell, 2006.

Histrop, Lindsay Ann. *Estate Planning Precedents*. Looseleaf. Toronto: Thomson Carswell, 1995. Available on *Estates& TrustsSource* on Westlaw Canada (by subscription).

Howard, Judy & George Monticone. *Long-Term Care Facilities in Ontario: The Advocate's Manual*. Looseleaf. 2d ed. Toronto: Advocacy Centre for the Elderly, 2001.

Hull, Ian M. *Challenging the Validity of Wills*. Scarborough, ON: Carswell, 1996.

Hull, Ian M. *Power of Attorney Litigation*. Looseleaf. Toronto: CCH Canadian, 2000.

Hull, Rodney & Ian M. Hull. *Macdonell, Sheard and Hull on Probate Practice*. 4th ed. Scarborough, ON: Carswell, 1996.

Hunter, Fiona *et al*. *Financial and Estate Planning for the Mature Client in British Columbia*. Looseleaf. Markham, ON: Butterworths, 2000.

Jenkins, Jennifer J. & H. Mark Scott. *Compensation and Duties of Estate Trustees, Guardians and Attorneys*. Looseleaf. Aurora, ON: Canada Law Book, 2006.

Kessler, James & Fiona Hunter. *Drafting Trusts and Will Trusts in Canada*. 2d ed. Markham, ON: LexisNexis Canada, 2007.

MacGregor, Mary L. *Preparation of Wills and Powers of Attorney: First Interview to Final Report*. 3d ed. Aurora, ON: Canada Law Book, 2004.

MacKenzie, James. *Feeney's Canadian Law of Wills*. Looseleaf. 4th ed. Toronto: Butterworths, 2000.

McTeer, M.A. *Tough Choices: Living and Dying in the 21st Century*. Toronto: Irwin Law, 1999.

Rintoul, Margaret E. *Canadian Forms & Precedents: Wills and Estates*. Looseleaf. 2d ed. Markham, ON: LexisNexis, 2007. Available on CD-ROM and on LexisNexis Quicklaw.

Rintoul, Margaret E. *Ontario Estate Administration*. 5th ed. Markham, ON: LexisNexis Butterworths, 2005.

Schnurr, Brian A. *Estate Litigation*. Looseleaf. 2d ed. Toronto: Carswell, 1994. Available on *Estates&TrustsSource* on Westlaw Canada (by subscription).

Seller, Susan. *Ontario Pension Law Handbook*. 2d ed. Aurora, ON: Canada Law Book, 2006.

Scott Butler, Alison. *Tax Planned Will Precedents*. Looseleaf. 4th ed. Toronto: Carswell, 2006.

Sokol, Stan J. *Mistakes in Wills in Canada*. Scarborough, ON: Carswell, 1995.

Books	Solnik, Robyn & Mary-Alice Thompson. *Drafting Wills in Ontario: A Lawyer's Practical Guide*. Toronto: CCH Canadian, 2003.

Solnik, Robyn & Mary-Alice Thompson. *Drafting Wills in Ontario: A Lawyer's Practical Guide*. Toronto: CCH Canadian, 2003.

Spenceley, Robert. *Estate Administration in Ontario: A Practical Guide*. 2d ed. Toronto: CCH Canadian, 1999.

Sweatman, M. Jasmine. *Guide to Powers of Attorney*. Aurora, ON: Canada Law Book, 2002.

Thériault, Carmen, ed. *Widdifield on Executors and Trustees*. Looseleaf. 6th ed. Scarborough, ON: Carswell, 2002. Available on *Estates&TrustsSource* on Westlaw Canada (by subscription).

Waters, Donovan W.M. *et al. The Law of Trusts in Canada*. 3d ed. Toronto: Thomson Carswell, 2005. Available on *Estates&TrustsSource* on Westlaw Canada (by subscription).

Youdan, Timothy G. *Equity, Fiduciaries and Trusts*. Toronto: Carswell, 1989.

Journals

Annual Review of Estate Law (Carswell)
Estates, Trusts and Pension Journal (Canada Law Book)
Will Power (CCH Canadian)

Encyclopedias

Canadian Encyclopedic Digest:
- Burial and Cremation (Ontario and Western)
- Coroners and Medical Examiners
- Devolution of Estates (Ontario and Western)
- Executors and Administrators (Ontario and Western)
- Trusts
- Wills

Halsbury's Laws of Canada:
- Cemeteries and Internment
- Inquests, Coroners and Medical Examiners
- Trusts*
- Wills and Estates

JurisClasseur Québec: Collection Droit civil (Successions)

Case digests

Canadian Abridgment (Carswell):
- Religious institutions
- Trusts and estates

caseAlert — Wills, Estates & Trusts (Canada Law Book)

Case law reporters

Estates & Trusts Reports (Carswell)

Databases and CD-ROMs

Estates Partner (Ontario) [CD-ROM]. Updated regularly. Contains relevant legislation, case law, and Carswell-published textbooks on wills and estates. Available in an expanded version as *Estates&TrustsSource* on Westlaw Canada (by subscription).

SS. WORKERS' COMPENSATION LAW

Scope	Workers' compensation law is a specialized subset of employment and labour law that focuses on statutory regimes that determine the amount of money an injured worker is entitled to when injured on the job. It is generally governed by provincial legislation, such as *Ontario's Workplace Safety and Insurance Act*, 1997, S.O. 1997, c. 16, Sch. A, with disputes being heard before the relevant workers' compensation tribunal.
Subject headings	Workers' compensation—Law and legislation—[jurisdiction]
Books	Anstruther, Richard *et al. Employers' Guide to Ontario Workplace Safety & Insurance*. Looseleaf. Toronto: Carswell, 1999. Conlin, Ryan. *Employers' Guide to Ontario Workplace Safety and Insurance*. Toronto: Thomson Carswell, 1999. Dee, Garth *et al. Butterworths Workers' Compensation in Ontario Service*. Looseleaf. Toronto: LexisNexis Butterworths, 1993. Gilbert, Douglas G. & L.A. Liversidge. *Workers' Compensation in Ontario: A Guide to the Workplace Safety and Insurance Act*. 3d ed. Aurora, ON: Canada Law Book, 2001. Moher, Michael & Jane Adam. *Ontario Workplace Insurance: Claims Management and Return to Work*. Looseleaf. Scarborough, ON: Carswell, 1998. Robertson, Dilys. *CLV—Special Report—Accident Investigation in the Workplace*. Toronto: Thomson Carswell, 2004.
Journals	Health & Safety/Workers' Compensation Law Service (Lancaster House, E-Bulletin)
Encyclopedias	*Canadian Encyclopedic Digest*: Workers' Compensation (Ontario and Western) *JurisClasseur Québec*: Collection Droit du travail (Droit de la santé et de la sécurité du travail)
Case digests	*Canadian Abridgment* (Carswell): Labour and employment law
Databases and CD-ROMs	LexisNexis Quicklaw: • B.C. Workers' Compensation Appeal Tribunal Decisions • Ontario Workplace Safety and Insurance Appeals Tribunal Decisions

CHAPTER 9

SELECTING AND ACQUIRING LEGAL RESOURCES

A. INTRODUCTION

This book has focused on how to use legal resources. For some legal researchers, this will suffice since the focus of their work is hands-on legal research. Other lawyers or legal researchers, however, will need to choose or recommend for acquisition particular legal resources for a law library, be it as part of a small law firm or personal collection or as part of a larger organization. Very little has been written in the literature on how to acquire legal resources.[1] While it helps to have a good working knowledge of legal resources when deciding what to select or acquire, there are certain things that many lawyers or legal researchers may not be aware of on this topic, matters that often fall within the expertise of a law librarian. Therefore, this chapter is aimed at lawyers or other legal researchers who need to make decisions about selecting and acquiring legal resources. Information is provided on the following topics:

- deciding between print and electronic resources
- criteria for selecting material for a law library
- managing a small law firm law library

---

1 See, for example, Douglass MacEllven *et al.*, *Legal Research Handbook*, 5th ed. (Markham, ON: LexisNexis Butterworths, 2003) c. 16, "Law Firm Libraries," and the resources listed at the end of this chapter.

- negotiating licences for electronic resources

Additional resources are set out in Section G at the end of this chapter for those readers needing more detailed information on selecting and acquiring legal research resources.

B. DECIDING BETWEEN PRINT AND ELECTRONIC RESOURCES

Over the last decade or so, law libraries have faced the dilemma of deciding whether to acquire material in *print* versus material in *electronic format* (or both). In many cases, law libraries acquire both print and online resources, in part to cater to patrons who prefer one format over another and in part to experiment with the online version of a product. In some cases, material may only be available in one format and no decision between formats is required.

There are several advantages to acquiring material in print that are often regarded as disadvantages in an online environment:

- *Permanency*: Print materials can be stored or archived, thereby protecting the investment made in the books and ensuring long term accessibility. Online materials, however, tend to be more volatile, especially on the Internet, where addresses often change and sites get shut down.
- *Ownership*: Print materials are generally bought and owned by the purchaser, unlike many online materials which are merely licensed for access, thereby making the licensee subject to the pricing whims or viability of the publisher. If the user stops paying for licensing a CD-ROM, for example, the user usually loses access to the information, unlike print resources which would remain available on the shelf if the print subscription is cancelled.
- *Comfort level*: People generally prefer to read from books rather than computer screens; there is a comfort level in using print materials, whether it be in the ability to quickly flip through pages or read from page to page. In addition, most lawyers prefer the comfort of citing materials to specific pages in a book, something that is often more difficult in an online environment.
- *Wide availability*: For the foreseeable future, most law-related materials will continue to be available in print, especially books and other specialized monographs that are less likely to be available in electronic format.

Despite these advantages of print materials, there are also some fairly obvious disadvantages to law-related print materials that tend to be regarded as advantages in an online environment:

- *Storage and maintenance costs*: Print materials require space to be shelved; many law-related print publications, such as case reporters, grow larger every year. Looseleaf legal publications require staff to file the looseleaf pages on an ongoing basis. Online materials, on the other hand, tend to take up much less space, can be read from a laptop and accessed twenty-four hours per day.
- *Poor indexing*: Legal materials in print tend to be poorly indexed, due in part to the Canadian market for legal materials being so small, thereby giving less incentive for publishers to invest heavily in the cost of indexing print materials. Online materials, on the other hand, are searchable by keyword and often by sophisticated search strategies (by case name, by judge's name, and so on) making it easy to find relevant material in an online environment.
- *Publication delays*: There is typically a delay in publishing legal materials in print. Having current information in law is generally very important. This is a huge advantage of online legal materials where some databases are current to within twenty-four hours.
- *Bill back*: Lawyers generally are unable to bill back the cost of their overhead in maintaining a print law library but are able sometimes to bill back to the client the cost of online searches.[2] Thus, in theory, a law firm can run its research department and legal research by using online databases on a break-even basis where the cost of on-line searches is billed back to clients and there being little overhead investment in stocking and maintaining a print collection.

In deciding between print and online material, the following questions should be considered:

- Is there a strong preference for print resources among the primary users of the materials?
- Are there significant cost or content differentials between the print and online material?
- Does material need to be used primarily within the office?
- Is there storage room available for print material?
- Are there staff to maintain the shelving and looseleaf filing of print material? Conversely, is there adequate technical systems support if you emphasize material in electronic format?

---

2   See the discussion of this topic and a list of cases in which court costs have been awarded for legal research in Chapter 1, Section C.

- How computer literate are the primary users of the material?
- How receptive will your clients be to being billed for online searches?
- Are there public law libraries nearby that can be used?

There are no obvious answers regarding whether one should prefer print or online materials. The decision is often made on the following major criteria: the ability to store and maintain a print collection, the computer literacy of the primary users of the material, and the types and topics of material being acquired.

C. CRITERIA FOR SELECTION OF MATERIAL

Unfortunately, legal materials do not select themselves. From large academic law libraries to small law firm libraries, decisions must be made about what sort of materials to acquire, how much to spend, and who will maintain the collection once it is acquired.

Legal materials to be acquired can be broken down into the following broad categories:

- *Legislation*: Of most importance for the selection of legislation is federal legislation and legislation for the province in which the material is being acquired. Larger law libraries will also maintain legislation from other provinces. Consider using online sources for legislation (government websites, CanLII, LexisNexis Quicklaw, Canada Law Book, or Westlaw Canada, for example) unless print is strongly desired (if print materials are not being kept, you must consider how you will access older legislation in print—is there a nearby courthouse or law school law library that maintains a complete archive of historical legislation?). If print is chosen, consider your space needs for ever-expanding material. Regarding draft legislation in the form of bills, there is a move now towards relying upon free government websites or *CCH Legislative Pulse* for such information instead of subscribing to print versions of bills. Once again, this decision will often be made based on user preferences.
- *Case law*: Choices here for Canadian case law include national reporters (*Supreme Court Reports, Federal Court Reports, Dominion Law Reports*, and *National Reporter*), regional reporters (*Western Weekly Reports* or *Atlantic Provinces Reports*), and provincial reporters or topical reporters. Once again, consider obtaining electronic sources of case law (commercial legal databases or CanLII, for example) un-

less print is strongly desired. Chapter 8 identifies some of the major topical case law reporters.

- *Textbooks*: Textbooks are discussed in Chapter 2, Section A and are listed by topic in Chapter 8. Despite the increase in the availability of law-related e-books, most books are still being published in print only, and the decision to be made with books is often between preferring bound versus looseleaf publications. With looseleaf services comes the advantage of information being kept current. The disadvantage, of course, is the added cost of maintaining the subscription and of filing the updated supplemental pages (and the cost of replacing missing or stolen pages). Table 9.1 sets out the websites of some of the major Canadian legal publishers whose online bookstores can be searched for textbooks, usually by topic, author, title, or keyword. Alternatively, use the list of textbooks by topic in Chapter 8 to help decide which sort of materials may be required.

Table 9.1
Websites of Major Canadian Legal Publishers

Publisher	Web Address
Butterworths Canada	www.lexisnexis.ca
Canada Law Book	www.canadalawbook.ca
Carswell	www.carswell.com
CCH Canadian	www.cch.ca
Éditions Yvon Blais	www.editionsyvonblais.qc.ca
Emond Montgomery	www.emp.ca
Irwin Law	www.irwinlaw.com
Lancaster House	www.lancasterhouse.com
Maritime Law Book	www.mlb.nb.ca
Self-Counsel Press	www.self-counsel.com
SOQUIJ	www.soquij.qc.ca
Wilson & LaFleur	www.wilsonlafleur.com

- *Reference materials*: There are a wide variety of reference materials that lawyers or legal researchers should consider acquiring, including encyclopedias, legal dictionaries, legal directories, applicable Rules of Court, and forms and precedents materials. Chapter 2 discusses these materials in more detail and should be consulted. Reference materials are increasingly available in electronic format.

In general, when selecting any type of legal material, criteria to be applied should include:

- *Reputation of the author*: Is the author a lawyer or legal academic? Is the author known in her area of expertise? Has the author published before?
- *Reputation of the publisher*: The reputation of the publishers listed in Table 9.1 is strong for legal materials and these publishers can be relied upon to publish good quality material. When selecting law-related material from other publishers it is important to consider the reputation of that publisher for publishing reliable material.
- *Relevance of topic*: Only the largest law library will be able to acquire legal materials for all legal topics. Selection must often therefore be made based on user's needs and on what materials are essential for the lawyers or researchers using the collection.
- *Looseleaf versus bound*: As discussed above, decisions must often be made between looseleaf material and bound material. While looseleaf material has the advantage of being current, it costs time and money to continue the subscription and to ensure that the looseleaf filing is being properly done.
- *Standing orders*: Many publishers will encourage law libraries to subscribe to material that is published annually on a "standing order" basis. This means that material will automatically be shipped and invoiced when it is published. While this has its advantages, it can also result in less control to the law library. In addition, libraries on a budget may wish to consider a cost-saving measure by not ordering paper "supplements" to textbooks but to instead wait for a new "hardcover" edition to be issued.
- *Print versus online*: When assessing whether to acquire legal material in print or online (or both), it is important to evaluate whether one version provides the same or enhanced coverage compared to the other version and whether both versions are required in any event due to differing user needs and abilities.

There are a number of tools to help in the selection of materials. Publishers are more than happy to send out catalogues and brochures regarding their publications. The problem, if anything, is getting too much of this material. Another method is to simply check the websites of the Canadian legal publishers periodically or to check the publishers' advertisements that are found in a number of law-related publications. Some of the larger academic law libraries use "book-buying" agents (such as YBP Library Services) to create "approval plans" based on a profile of the individual library and the types of materials the library would like to acquire. Once set up, the agent will provide the library with customized "slips" of new titles for possible purchase by the library. For busy law firms, the easiest thing to do is hire a law librarian to make these sorts of decision for the firm.

D. MANAGING A SMALL LAW FIRM LAW LIBRARY

Legal researchers are often involved in the organization or running of a law firm's law library. For larger firms, a decision may be made to hire a part-time or full-time law librarian. As a rough rule of thumb, firms of thirty-five to forty-five lawyers can usually justify the need for a full-time librarian to manage their in-house law library. Larger firms will often have a team of librarians and other library technicians managing their collection. Smaller firms will often make do with a part-time librarian or will simply have some other person within the organization manage the library collection.

There are several things to consider about managing a small law firm law library:

- *Hiring a law librarian*: In Canada, a librarian is usually someone with a two-year Master's degree from a university library school program that is accredited by the American Library Association. The training would include a number of things, including how to catalogue and classify information, how to manage a library, how to provide reference and research services, and how to create and update web pages. In some cases, courses specifically on law librarianship are offered. To place an advertisement to hire a law librarian in Canada, there is the Jobs website at the Faculty of Information Studies[3] and the Jobline of the Foothills Library Association (emphasizing positions in Western Canada).[4] When advertising for a law librarian it is critical to be fairly specific in the technical skills that are expected (such as online searching, cataloguing, and Internet authoring).
- *Maintenance*: Regardless of who is hired to manage a law firm's library, there are a large number of things that the person must manage and maintain, including the selection and acquisition of material, cataloguing and labelling of material, shelving of material, weeding of material, and selective dissemination of information (informing

---

3   See www.ischool.utoronto.ca/alumni-careers/job-site.
4   See www.fla.org/jobline.php.

users about new material relevant to their research needs). The larger the law library, the greater the need to devote resources to the maintenance of the collection.

- *Research and reference support*: Another important aspect of managing a law firm law library is to set up procedures for providing research and reference support. Will the firm have a "stand-alone" research lawyer to conduct legal research or will the work instead fall to articling students or other (typically junior) lawyers in the firm? What will the relationship be between articling students and the library, and will there be training for the students? Will the library staff offer research training to lawyers in the firm? The answer to these sorts of questions will depend on the size and type of firm. Law librarians, unless they are also lawyers, should not be giving legal advice (and should be *seen* not to be giving legal advice). Despite this, it is possible to bill the services of a law librarian for some aspects of research and reference support.

- *Space planning and technology*: What amount of space will the library need (allowing for growth of any print resources in the collection)? Will the library house research computers with CD-ROM drives and Internet access? Will the library materials be catalogued in an online catalogue? If so, will the catalogue be available to each lawyer's desktop or only available on a library terminal? What sort of technical support will the library need?

- *Website and Intranet*: Increasingly, in-house law libraries play a key role in the firm's website and intranet as a means to disseminate information both externally and internally. Many organizations are now appreciating the value of institutionalizing their shared knowledge. This can be done in several ways regarding legal research matters: the firm—through a law librarian—can organize searchable or browsable databases of the firm's legal research memos, opinion letters, forms, and agreements. In addition, the firm can use an intranet to share information among lawyers within the firm, including information on clients, on practice management and on current awareness. When hiring a law librarian, it is therefore important to consider the Internet authoring skills of any applicants.

E. NEGOTIATING LICENCES FOR ELECTRONIC RESOURCES

As discussed above, a major disadvantage of electronic resources is the general lack of ownership of the materials being paid for. What one is paying for is *access* to the material, not ownership. Thus, once one stops paying for the CD-ROM or access to the database, there is generally no further access (for CD-ROMs, this happens where there is a built-in "time bomb" feature to disable the CD-ROM after the expiry of the licence period). Some care must therefore be taken when entering into licence agreements for CD-ROMs or online databases. The following points are usually the major issues that arise when entering into licence agreements to acquire law-related resources in electronic format:

- *Audience? Single user versus multiple users?* Most publishers quite naturally charge more where electronic resources are being accessed by multiple users. It is usually quite obvious when "single user" access is required, especially for sole practitioners or smaller law firms, and the cost of obtaining single user access is usually straightforward. What can often require negotiation and some explanation is where the electronic resource will regularly be used by more than one person via a computer network. Some vendors have policies to automatically calculate the number of licensed users based on the number of lawyers in the firm, even where not all lawyers in the firm will use the product. It therefore becomes necessary to evaluate how much the particular resource will be used and by how many people at the same time.
- *Controlling multi-user access*: For commercial online databases, passwords are often assigned to individual users, something that allows tracking of searches by individuals. In some settings, particularly academic law libraries, passwords to some law-related Internet subscription databases can be controlled by IP (Internet Protocol) address, thereby allowing any user within the organization to access the database. Regardless, care must be taken to prudently manage passwords to online databases, including access to the firm's intranet or other internal computer file folders that are related to legal research.
- *Hardware and software requirements*: In acquiring CD-ROMs, it is important to check any specific hardware or software requirements for the product. The move to electronic resources in legal research saves space and labour costs associated with print law-related materials but does involve fairly heavy investments in hardware technology. For larger firms, such matters will often be handled through technology departments that will assess the firm's technical needs. Fortunately, many legal publishers are moving away from CD-ROM technology to Internet platforms, lessening or eliminating the need for CD-ROM towers to network the CD-ROMs. For Internet subscriptions, it is important to check whether the product requires a newer or particular version of a Web browser interface.

- *Training and support*: It is important to check what level and sort of training the vendors will provide for use of their products. Do they provide training in your office or are you required to attend at their training centre? Is their training free? Do they provide useful handouts and training guides? With online databases made available through a Web browser, there is often a much smaller learning curve due to the more intuitive browser interfaces; Web browser interfaces also often include good online help or "how-to" information.
- *Scope of content*: Is the electronic resource being acquired full text? Does the online version contain the same or different information from the print equivalent, if any? What sort of search engine is used to find information? How easy is it to find information in the database?
- *Coverage*: What is the coverage of the electronic resources? How current is the resource? How often is it updated?
- *Costs*: How does the vendor bill for access to its electronic resources? Is it an hourly rate? If so, does it vary depending on what database you access? Is it based on the transaction and what information is downloaded? If so, is it easy to know in advance the cost of particular transactions? Does the vendor bill a monthly flat rate fee? If so, how is the flat rate fee calculated, how often is it adjusted, and on what basis is it adjusted?
- *Terms of licence*: What rights is the vendor/licensor granting regarding the downloading and storing of information? Is the vendor giving any representations or warranties regarding the information it is licensing? Is the licensee required to indemnify the vendor regarding any claims being made by a third party against the vendor regarding any alleged misuse by the licensee of the product?

By addressing these sorts of issues when negotiating acquisition of electronic resources, it is hoped that the researcher or law firm should be in a better position to negotiate terms that improve access to electronic resources.

F. CONCLUSIONS

The legal research and legal publishing fields are undergoing great change in recent times due to the impact of the Internet and other computer technology. While these changes have greatly improved the work lives of lawyers and legal researchers, they have added to the complexity of decisions that must be made regarding the acquisition of print and electronic legal resources. Change (and potential chaos) will likely continue to reign over the next few years as lawyers and legal researchers decide between print and electronic resources and how to rationalize material (if at all) during this period of change.

G. ADDITIONAL RESOURCES

Set out below are some additional resources on selecting and acquiring legal resources and managing a law library.

Ahlers, Glen-Peter. *The History of Law School Libraries in the United States: From Laboratory to Cyberspace.* Buffalo, NY: William S. Hein & Co., 2002.

Balleste, Roy *et al. Law Librarianship in the Twenty-First Century.* Lanham, MD: Scarecrow Press, 2007.

Bintliff, Barbara & Lee F. Peoples, eds. *Public Services in Law Libraries: Evolution and Innovation in the 21st Century.* Binghamton, NY: Haworth Information Press, 2008.

Chiorazzi, Michael & Gordon Russell, eds. *Law Library Collection Development in the Digital Age.* Binghamton, NY: Haworth Information Press, 2002.

Danner, Richard A. *Strategic Planning: A Law Library Management Tool for the 90's and Beyond.* 2d ed. Dobbs Ferry, NY: Glanville Publishers, 1997.

Denton, Vivienne & Neal Ferguson, "Libraries in Merged Law Firms: Challenges of Communication and Collaboration" (2003) 28 Can. L.L. 9.

Dragich, Martha J. & Peter C. Schanck, eds. *Law Library Staff Organization and Administration.* Littleton, CO: F.B. Rothman, 1990.

Fenner, Audrey, ed. *Selecting Materials for Library Collections.* Binghamton, NY: Haworth Information Press, 2004.

Fraser, Joan N., ed. *Law Libraries in Canada: Essays to Honour Diana M. Priestly.* Toronto, ON: Carswell, 1988.

Germain, Claire M. "Legal Information Management in a Global and Digital Age: Revolution and Tradition" (27 August 2007). Online: LLRX.com, www.llrx.com/features/legalinformationmanagement.htm.

Harris, Lesley Ellen. *Licensing Digital Content: A Practical Guide for Librarians*. Chicago: American Library Association, 2002.

Hazelton, Penny A. "How Much of Your Print Collection is Really on Westlaw or Lexis-Nexis?" (1999) 18 Legal Ref. Serv. Q. 3.

Howard, Paul E. & Renee Y. Rastorfer. "Do We Still Need Books—A Selected Annotated Bibliography" (2005) 97 Law Libr. J. 257.

How to Manage a Law School Library: Leading Librarians on Updating Resources, Managing Budgets, and Meeting Expectations. Boston, MA: Aspatore Books, 2008.

Licensing Digital Information: A Resource for Librarians. Online: Lib-License, www.library.yale.edu/~llicense. This website is the home page of the LibLicense listserv and contains useful information on licensing electronic resources, along with a detailed bibliography of additional materials.

MacEllven, Douglass T. *et al. Guide to Purchasing Law Reports*. Ottawa, ON: Canadian Law Information Council, 1985.

Managing the Law Library: Positioning for Change. New York, NY: Practising Law Institute, 1997.

Marke, Julius J. & Richard Sloane. *Legal Research and Law Library Management*. Looseleaf. Rev. ed. New York, NY: Law Journal Seminars-Press, 1990.

Matheson, Scott. "Access versus Ownership: A Changing Model of Intellectual Property" (2002) 21 Legal Ref. Serv. Q. 153.

Megantz, Robert C. *How to License Technology*. New York: Wiley, 1996.

Most, Marguerite. "Electronic Law Journals in the Academic Law Library—Law Reviews and Beyond" (2002) 21 Legal Ref. Serv. Q. 189.

Not a Box but a Window: Law Libraries and Legal Education in a Virtual World. Toronto: Faculty of Law, University of Toronto, 2001.

Pace, Andrew K. *The Ultimate Digital Library: Where the New Information Players Meet*. Chicago: American Library Association, 2003.

Panella, Deborah S. *Basics of Law Librarianship*. New York: Haworth Press, 1991.

Phillips, Kara. "Deal or No Deal—Licensing & Acquiring Digital Resources: License Negotiations Reprise" (15 January 2007). Online: LLRX.com, www.llrx.com/columns/deal3.htm.

Rae, Ann. "Preserving Canada's Law Collections: Is it Time for a National Strategy?" (2004) 29 Can. L.L. 16.

Ramsay, John T. *Ramsay on Technology Transfers and Licensing*. 2d ed. Markham, ON: Butterworths, 2002.

Reusch, Rita. "By the Book: Thoughts on the Future of Our Print Collections" (2008) 100 Law Libr. J. 555.

Robinson, Douglas. "Negotiating Licensing Agreements for Electronic Resources: A Selective Bibliography" Bibliography Series #7 (ISSN: 1203-2468). Online: www.collectionscanada.ca/6/7/s7-2604-e.html.

Runyon, Amanda M. "The Effect of Economics and Electronic Resources on the Traditional Law Library Print Collection" (2009) 101 Law Libr. J. 177.

Russell, Gordon. "Re-Engineering the Law Library Resources Today for Tomorrow's Users: A Response to 'How Much of Your Collection is Really on Westlaw or Lexis-Nexis?'" (2002) 21 Legal Ref. Serv. Q. 29.

Skalbeck, Roger & Iva Futrell. "Technology and Policy Issues With Acquiring Digital Collections" (12 February 2007). Online: LLRX. com, www.llrx.com/features/digitalcollections.htm.

Tjaden, Ted. "The Role of the Law Librarian in the Design, Maintenance and Promotion of Internet Sites" (1999) 18 Toronto Association of Law Libraries Newsletter 2.

Wu, Michelle M. "Why Print and Electronic Resources Are Essential to the Academic Law Library" (2005) 97 Law Libr. J. 233.

KNOWLEDGE MANAGEMENT FOR LAWYERS

This chapter discusses knowledge management and its importance to the practice of law along with its close relationship with legal research and writing. As a discipline, knowledge management is generally not discussed or taught in law school; instead, it is often only when the law student is in practice that the importance of knowledge management can be appreciated and put into use. And although technological advances in the practice of law over the last twenty years have both caused and supported the ascendancy of knowledge management in law firms, the reality is that lawyers have always practised forms of knowledge management, from the moment hundreds of years ago (or longer) that a lawyer first set aside a good sample agreement or figured out a better way of doing things. As will be seen in this chapter, knowledge management intersects with legal research and writing in a number of ways, with precedents and research memos being the two most obvious examples. In addition, although knowledge management in the legal industry is often associated with large law firms, even small firms and sole practitioners will benefit from adopting personal knowledge management principles to become more effective in their work.

A. WHAT IS KNOWLEDGE MANAGEMENT?

There are many definitions of knowledge management.[1] One reason for so many definitions is that knowledge management spans a number of disciplines (ranging from business management, to information science, to computer technology) and any number of industries and business. For our purpose, a basic definition is sufficient to introduce the topic:

> Knowledge management (KM) comprises a range of practices used in an organization to identify, create, represent, distribute and enable adoption of insights and experiences. Such insights and experiences comprise knowledge, either embodied in individuals or embedded in organizational processes or practice.[2]

From this definition we can observe a few key elements of the definition of knowledge management:

- Describing knowledge management as a "range of practices" reflects the broad nature of knowledge management and the fact that it can encompass a wide variety of activities related to information practices.
- A definition of "knowledge" as "insights and experiences" recognizes the two broad categories of knowledge: "tacit knowledge" (being the insights and experiences embodied in individuals) and "explicit knowledge" (being the insights and experiences embedded in organizational processes or practice, often found in documents or other "explicit" content).
- Knowledge management is not necessarily all about technology (the definition does not expressly mention technology). Although technology plays an important role in knowledge management "to identify, create, represent, distribute and enable adoption of insights and experiences," there is an important human element to this process.

Even though knowledge management has been practised in one form or another for hundreds of years,[3] modern law-related knowledge management makes its first major appearance in the Canadian legal

---

1   See, for example, the various definitions listed by Raymond Sims, "43 Knowledge Management Definitions—and Counting," Sims Learning Connections Blog, comment posted 16 March 2008, http://blog.simslearningconnections.com/?p=279.

2   Wikipedia contributors, "Knowledge Management," *Wikipedia, The Free Encyclopedia*, online: http://en.wikipedia.org/wiki/Knowledge_management.

3   An early KM technology was Agostino Ramelli'a bookwheel, invented over 400 years ago (in 1588). See the wonderful graphic of it in Figure 10.1, sourced from the Wikipedia entry for "Bookwheel."

literature just over one decade ago.[4] As such, within the legal community at least, knowledge management is still a relatively young industry with many firms trying different approaches, resulting in KM meaning different things to different firms.[5]

For our purpose, applying the foregoing elements of knowledge management to the legal industry results in a more specific definition applicable to lawyers: [6]

- The purpose of knowledge management in law firms[7] — aligned with the firm's specific operational and strategic goals — is to

---

In "Innovator, Fool, I Dream: Deploying Effective Knowledge Management Principles to Combat Information Overload in Law Firms" in *Knowledge Leadership Forum* (New York, 26 April 2007), I review the history of information overload, which dates back to the invention of the papyrus scroll (note: "Innovator, Fool, I Dream" is an anagram for "information overload"). As each generation faced an increase in the amount of information available, technological solutions — such as Ramelli's bookwheel as a solution for having too many books to read — were introduced to help cope with the information overload. As such, I see attempts by modern knowledge managers to organize legal knowledge content as part of an ongoing development: as technology causes (or allows to happen) an increase in legal information overload, so too does technology present likely solutions (along with the ever-present role of human beings as part of the process).

4   One of the earliest mentions of the phrase "knowledge management" in the Canadian legal literature appears to be from a 5 June 1998 article in *The Lawyers Weekly* by Joyce Hampton entitled "Lawyer Breaks Glass Ceiling in High-Tech Industry." In the United States, one of the earliest uses of the phrase "knowledge management" in the legal literature was from just over twenty years ago in the April 1989 newsletter of the American Association of Law Libraries: Robert L. Oakely, "Report on the Meeting of the Library of Congress Advisory Committee" (1988–89) 20 AALL Newsletter 258.

5   See the Additional Resources in Section J for a list of some of the leading resources on law firm knowledge management. The following two books are highly recommended: Matthew Parsons, *Effective Knowledge Management for Law Firms* (New York: Oxford University Press, 2004) and Gretta Rusanow, *Knowledge Management and the Smarter Lawyer* (New York: ALM, 2003).

6   My definition of legal knowledge management adapts a number of existing definitions, including, for example, a recent definition by Dave Snowden in "Defining KM," Cognitive Edge Blog, comment on 23 September 2009, online: www.cognitive-edge.com/blogs/dave/2009/09/defining_km.php. I also realize my definition — in an attempt to be fairly exhaustive — is likely far too lengthy for some.

7   My definition of legal knowledge management would also apply to corporate and government legal departments, entities that are increasingly applying knowledge management principles to organize and leverage the insights and experiences within their own departments and organizations. Government legal departments, such as the federal Department of Justice, for example, have more lawyers than the largest law firm in Canada, suggesting that their knowledge management needs are no less — and perhaps greater — than a typical law firm.

Figure 10.1
Agostino Ramelli's Bookwheel (1588)

An example of an early technology for providing quick access to information is Agostino Ramelli's bookwheel (1588).

» provide support for faster, more effective legal services to internal and external clients, thereby increasing profit margins for the firm at the same time as attracting and retaining clients;
» promote legal information literacy to make the work lives of lawyers and other firm members more productive, thereby indirectly nurturing employee retention and knowledge sharing;[8] and
» establish best practices and standards for legal services, thereby reducing the risk of errors and malpractice.

• This is achieved by
» helping create an environment that fosters information-sharing and that values lifelong education;
» capturing, organizing, updating, and making available explicit legal knowledge content (in the form of precedents, research, and best practices checklists); and
» supporting the training and mentoring of lawyers and staff to promote the transfer of tacit legal knowledge (using both human training and technology).

---

8   I realize that some may argue that this aspect of KM is slightly vague and that it is not the mandate of a KM department to worry about employee retention. Despite that concern, I truly believe that eliminating frustrations that lawyers experience when they cannot get the information they need when they need it goes a long way toward keeping them happy and improving employee retention.

In pragmatic terms, this definition of law-related knowledge management manifests itself in one or more of the following six knowledge-related activities undertaken by most law firms (or corporate or government legal departments):

• Document and records management
• Precedent development
• Legal research and intranet content delivery
• Professional development and training
• Litigation support and project management
• Practice management

A brief review of these six knowledge-related activities will show they are closely integrated and, in many cases, overlap or are mutually supported.

B. DOCUMENT AND RECORDS MANAGEMENT

The definition of legal knowledge management above includes the task of providing "support for faster, more effective legal services" to clients by "capturing, organizing, updating, and making available explicit legal knowledge content (in the form of precedents, research, and best practices checklists)." Document management and records management play an important role as part of this knowledge management task.

Although the paperless law firm remains a myth, legal professionals *are* increasingly working in a digital environment (word processors, e-mail, the Internet, and so on). As such, managing digital information (along with paper hard copies) is extremely important. A document management (DM) system is "a computer system (or set of computer programs) used to track and store electronic documents [or] images of paper documents."[9] Most DM systems have features that allow filing by specific location, that protect privacy settings on documents (when required), and that provide for authentication, traceability, and retrieval through browsing and searching.[10] Records management, on the other hand, is "the practice of maintaining the records of an organization from the time they are created up to their eventual disposal" and "may

---

9   Wikipedia contributors, "Document management system," *Wikipedia, The Free Encyclopedia*, online: http://en.wikipedia.org/wiki/Document_management_ system.
10   *Ibid.*

include classifying, storing, securing, and destruction (or in some cases, archival preservation) of records."[11] In a law firm, document management is often thought of as organizing documents for the lifecycle of a matter (i.e., while the matter is still open). Records management, on the other hand, is often thought of as a special form of managing documents at the end of that life cycle when the matter is closed and the documents are stored and retained for an appropriate period of time.

Although legal knowledge management can (obviously) be developed in a law firm or corporate legal department in the absence of a document management or records management system, for large, multi-office firms, these systems are an important foundation for housing the firm's explicit knowledge content (in the form of documents, e-mails, video, and the like). For a large law firm, it is almost unimaginable to operate without a document management system, something that helps organize documents by client or by matter and makes it easy to share information among firm members. For the knowledge manager, a document management system is an important source for harvesting knowledge content. Appropriate profiling or tagging of saved documents greatly increases the ease by which materials can be subsequently retrieved.

In many law firms, knowledge management staff are not necessarily responsible for records management despite the fact that (i) knowledge managers will know the legal and ethical issues that govern records retention, and (ii) at the time a file is closed, there is an excellent opportunity for knowledge managers to review the file for valuable content (in the form of research and sample documents with reuse value that might otherwise not have already been harvested).

Some of the major document management systems used in law firms in North America include Autonomy Interwoven,[12] OpenText (Hummingbird's Docs Open),[13] Worldox,[14] TimeMatters,[15] Microsoft SharePoint,[16] and Documentum[17] (with products such as CT Summation[18] or CaseMap[19] being used mainly in the context of organizing

---

11 Wikipedia contributors, "Records management," *Wikipedia, The Free Encyclopedia*, online: http://en.wikipedia.org/wiki/Records_management.

12 Autonomy Interwoven: www.interwoven.com.

13 OpenText: www.opentext.ca.

14 Worldox: www.worldox.com.

15 TimeMatters: www.lexisnexis.com/law-firms/practice-management/specialized-law/time-matters.aspx.

16 Microsoft SharePoint: http://sharepoint.microsoft.com.

17 Documentum: www.documentum.com.

18 CT Summation: www.ctsummation.com.

19 CaseMap: www.casesoft.com.

and searching documents on litigation matters). Some of the foregoing products also contain modules for records management; otherwise, firms will sometimes use their financial management system or develop their own home-grown solutions for tracking closed files.

Although document and records management can be expensive, it is simply a cost of doing business and a core or basic infrastructure for any large law firm; operating without document and records management would be inefficient and increase liability risks of a law firm breaching its statutory and ethical obligations to properly maintain documents.

Technology plays an important role in document and records management. However, due to the need to ensure the integrity of electronic documents and the privacy settings on documents, these systems require fairly significant investment in IT staffing and network and hardware infrastructure. In addition, until recently, most DM systems lacked effective search engines, causing frustration for users when they retrieve too many documents or not the anticipated ones. Fortunately, smart search engines are being developed[20] that improve both precision and recall and return results that are much more relevant. However, in addition to challenges of effective search, there is the challenge of effective e-mail management. The majority of documents in document management systems are increasingly e-mails. Although many e-mails are not important documents, some are, and most e-mails are integral to proper matter management (to ensure that all correspondence on a particular matter is properly stored).

C. PRECEDENT DEVELOPMENT

The documents in a DM with some of the highest "reuse" value can be precedents, which are the agreements and litigation documents drafted by lawyers on behalf of clients. Precedents—broadly defined—can include a variety of documents: model agreements or pleadings that, over time, have been developed and annotated to include the "ideal" or model document; sample precedent agreements or pleadings from past transactions or lawsuits; clause banks of boilerplate provisions or

---

20 Some of the smart enterprise search engines being used in law firms include Interwoven Universal Search (IUS) (www.interwoven.com), Recommind (www.recommind.com) and even Microsoft SharePoint (http://sharepoint.microsoft.com), the latter of which is discussed in more detail in the next section. For a recent article on the adoption of IUS by one Canadian law firm, see Gerry Blackwell, "The Knowledge Management Robot: Smart Search Tools Offer Easier and Faster Ways for Finding That Needle in a Haystack" *Canadian Lawyer* (June 2009) at 21.

important contractual provisions; checklists for typical transactions (e.g., for the purchase or sale of a business) or lawsuit procedures (e.g., a trial preparation checklist); transaction opinions; and deal closing documents (that many firms are now digitizing once the deal has been completed to make the full text searchable and easily accessible). Precedents, therefore, are an example of the core "explicit" knowledge or intellectual capital of a law firm (compared with the equally if not more important "tacit" knowledge of the law firm, being the knowledge or experience resident with the brains of firm members).

Even though there is typically no standard precedent perfect for every possible legal situation, many precedents can be reused and adapted for future transactions. The recycling of agreements as precedents has in fact been recognized (and implicitly endorsed) by the Supreme Court of Canada in the following comments of Mr. Justice Binnie:

> Recycling precedents is the life-blood of corporate law practice. A document prepared for Client A is part of the lawyer's work product and may go through numerous iterations in the service of other clients. The practice of law would be hopelessly inefficient and costly for clients if transactional documents had to be reinvented rather than customized.[21]

Precedents also help define a baseline standard of content to address the typical issues that might arise in connection with the issues for which the precedent was designed (for example, a model share purchase agreement may contain pages of sample representation and warranties clauses, not all of which might be needed or be relevant for a particular transaction in the future). However, it is easier to catalogue the most likely clauses in the model agreement as a "checklist" of issues for the drafter to consider and to later remove those that are not needed when the model document is applied to a particular transaction.

Although some lawyers are very effective at developing and maintaining their own personal sets of precedents, many are too busy to do so. Knowledge managers can therefore bring some discipline to the task of gathering, organizing, and maintaining precedents. This is achieved through a combination of people-powered resources and technology. The people-powered resources typically involve qualified lawyers (often given the title of "Professional Support Lawyer" or "Practice Support Lawyer," known by its acronym of PSL). PSLs usually have experience in the substantive areas of law related to the precedents in question and use their skills to evaluate the specific language and ap-

---

21 See *Strother v. 3464920 Canada Inc.*, 2007 SCC 24 at para. 111.

propriateness of particular precedents, in addition to—in most situations, time permitting—annotating the precedents with value-added commentary to alert the user to any particular issues to consider when using the particular precedent. Depending on the firm, PSLs may also write client bulletins and prepare "requests for proposals" (RFPs) for their department within the firm to bid on work from large corporate clients. And although technology plays an important role in helping to make precedents easily reusable, technology alone cannot (so far) replace the value in having some human-initiated review and organization process to make the precedents more easily browsable.

However, technology does play an important role in precedent development. For example, smart search engines will improve search recall by being able to have the system know to retrieve conceptually relevant documents that contain both the actual keywords used in the search ("confidentiality agreement") along with documents containing synonymous terms ("non-disclosure agreement"). Likewise, there are excellent document assembly software products that enable document assembly and clause banks to make document or precedent drafting both more efficient and less prone to errors.[22]

As mentioned above, most large law firms are also now digitizing their "deal closing books," often as a space-saving measure (since the hard copy of the closing books, once digitized, can more easily be returned to the client or sent to off-site storage).

Those knowledge management departments that integrate with their law library and legal research departments[23] can also supplement their internal precedents by providing access to commercially produced external precedents, many of which are available online by subscription.[24] The Practical Law Company[25] also has a subscription service providing access to fairly sophisticated corporate/commercial precedents developed by leading British and American deal lawyers.

---

22 Document assembly software includes such products as HotDocs, ContractExpress DealBuilder, Exari, KIIAC, Legal MacPac, and Microsystems.

23 Discussed more in Section D, below in this chapter.

24 As discussed in Chapter 12, Section G and elsewhere, the major commercial precedent services in Canada include *Canadian Forms and Precedents* and *Williston and Rolls Court Forms* (LexisNexis Butterworths, in print and online); *O'Brien's Encyclopedia of Forms and Precedents* (Canada Law Book, in print and online); and *Litigator* (court-filed litigation precedents, on Westlaw Canada). There are also numerous "print only" services available in Canada in addition to there being U.S. and U.K. forms and precedent services available on both LexisNexis Quicklaw and Westlaw Canada.

25 Practical Law Company UK: http://uk.practicallaw.com; Practical Law Company US: http://us.practicallaw.com.

Once again, just as most major law firms could not operate without a document management system, most major law firms will need to have some sort of process in place to access and develop corporate/commercial and litigation precedents. The degree of sophistication of any firm's precedents bank will depend in part on the nature of the firm's practice, the size of the firm, and the number of staff available to dedicate all or part of their time to precedent development. The investment cost in developing an internal precedent bank can be expensive but should provide returns on that investment in the form of being able to produce better agreements or court documents for clients more cost effectively. In addition, to the extent that firms need or want to address client demand for alternative fee arrangements, a necessary condition of being able to explore and offer alternative fee arrangements assumes access by the firm to a strong precedent bank in order to leverage such content more cost effectively.

One knowledge management activity that can often be impacted across all aspects of legal knowledge management is expertise location within the firm. In small organizations, people will know who the experts are on particular issues. However, as firms grow in size—especially when there are multiple offices—it becomes more difficult to know who does what well. Although online "contact information" systems such as InterAction[26] are commonly used by law firms, we are starting to see products that combine contact management with smart search to identify expertise within the organization based on activities an individual has done on particular transactions or documents and, for example, how much time the individual has billed on matters related to the area of expertise required (some of these smarter products include Recommind,[27] ContactNetworks,[28] and BranchIT[29]). Within the firm, locating experts is important when needing someone to draft particular documents or otherwise provide advice on a particular area of law (or provide training to firm members on that area of law).

D. LEGAL RESEARCH AND INTRANET CONTENT DELIVERY

An important part of legal knowledge management is legal research and its related elements, including research memos and opinion letters.

---

26   LexisNexis InterAction: www.interaction.com.
27   Recommind: www.recommind.com/solutions/enterprise_search.
28   ContactNetworks: www.contactnetworks.com/products/.
29   BranchIT: www.branchitcorp.com.

Many would typically think of traditional knowledge management as being the knowledge *inside* the firm (within the collective expertise of the lawyers and other firm members), whereas library and legal research is the knowledge *outside* the firm (within the decisions of judges or textbooks of leading academics, for example). Although this inside/outside distinction may be overly simplistic, there is some truth to it.

Despite how one characterizes the interdependency of knowledge management and legal research, it is clear that technology has radically transformed legal research and law libraries and lessened the inside/outside distinction, resulting in all sources of legal information being important, whether the information is physically within the firm or outside the firm. Technology has also transformed law librarianship—especially in the last decade—with the increasing digitization of both primary sources of law (legislation and case law) and secondary sources (treatises, journal articles, conference papers, encyclopedias, case digests, and reference tools).

Although in many law firms the knowledge management department and the law library may operate relatively independently, it makes sense for them to be formally integrated, given their interrelation, and to be seen as a "one-stop shop" for legal information, whether that information is sourced from internal sources (such as model agreements or best practices) or external sources (such as commentary from a book or cases from an online database).

In addition to technology providing greater access to sources of legal information, technology also allows the prospect of cost recovery for online legal research charges (on LexisNexis Canada or Westlaw Canada, for example), something which was generally not possible in a print-only environment (since the cost of library print subscriptions is generally regarded as office overhead, in the same way as rent and office supplies).[30] Technology has also enabled federated search, creating the ability to integrate and search on both internal content and external research databases (e.g., using such products as WestKM[31] and Lexis Search Advantage[32]).

In addition, law firm law libraries—on their own or in conjunction with knowledge management departments—are increasingly using Web 2.0 technologies such as RSS (really simple syndication) feeds to push relevant law-related information to members within the firm. As part of the role of pushing out information content, many knowledge management or library departments are given responsibility over their

---

30   As discussed in Chapter 1, Section C.
31   WestKM: http://west.thomson.com/products/services/westkm/default.aspx.
32   Lexis Search Advantage: http://law.lexisnexis.com/lexis-search-advantage.

organization's intranet portals. Intranets also play a unifying force in connecting organizations with multiple office locations, making communal resources easier to find. Products such as Microsoft SharePoint are currently in vogue in many law firms due to the capabilities of SharePoint to integrate content from different data sources within the law firm (the document management system, the firm's contact manager, the financial management system, and so on) and to provide improved search and browse capabilities.[33]

Other critical technologies for multi-office locations include IP-based phones and video conferencing.

E. PROFESSIONAL DEVELOPMENT AND TRAINING

To the extent that legal knowledge management is to "promote legal information literacy" and "establish best practices and standards for legal services," most knowledge management departments in law firms are involved (either formally or informally) in professional development and training. This training will often involve a combination of staff from the the library and the knowledge management, professional development, and IT departments, along with practising lawyers who are the experts within the firm. As mentioned earlier, the transfer of tacit knowledge—the information and experiences of a seasoned lawyer—can often be more valuable than the explicit knowledge contained in precedents and research memos. Unfortunately, until the Vulcan mind meld is perfected, one of the more effective ways of capturing tacit legal knowledge is through training and mentoring. However, technology is increasingly providing solutions to improve training of lawyers through the use of audio, video, and other online tools.

A positive side effect of in-house training—in addition to having lawyers develop their knowledge of substantive law and best practices in practicing law—is the atmosphere created in letting lawyers know that learning and sharing their knowledge is important.

In addition to in-house training, many lawyers will attend external continuing legal education (CLE) seminars, another excellent source of practical legal information and best practices. Most seminars provide

---

33   LawPort (www.svtechnology.com) is another popular intranet solution for law firms. For organizations with offices in Québec, IceFire (www.icefire.ca) is a software product that provides French/English translation on the fly for SharePoint menus and interfaces.

binders that are then kept in the firm's law library collection. Increasingly, CLE seminars are making their materials available online.[34] As discussed in Chapter 2, Section C, the *Canadian Legal Symposia Index* on LexisNexis Quicklaw is the best way to search for CLE papers (this database indexes CLE papers from 1986 to current). In the United States, the Practicing Law Institute[35] and West Legal EdCenter[36] are two major providers of online CLE for lawyers.

F. LITIGATION SUPPORT AND PROJECT MANAGEMENT

Litigation support is often a special subset of law firm knowledge management, focusing less on the litigation precedent and legal research aspect of litigation but instead dealing with case management, document review, and electronic discovery. Depending on the firm, the knowledge management department may or may not be directly involved in litigation support. For firms with large litigation departments, there may be embedded PSLs or a large contingent of litigation paralegals who will play an important role in managing what is, increasingly, a huge volume of electronic documents related to a particular lawsuit. One key aspect of litigation support—a topic not well taught in law school—is project management and the need for the litigation support team to have strong project management skills to help with early case assessment and managing appropriate levels of resources for particular lawsuits.

Most law firms will contract out the initial stages of the e-discovery process that (typically) involves the scanning of large volumes of the client's print and digital documents from the client's servers, and then will package that content for review using appropriate document review software.[37] There are a large number of software solutions dealing

---

34 In Ontario, for example, AccessCLE provides online access (for a fee) to a large number of CLE papers from Law Society of Upper Canada seminars. See online: http://ecom.lsuc.on.ca/home/accesscle.jsp. There are currently about 2,500 seminar papers available ranging across twelve different practice areas or topics.

35 Practising Law Insitute: www.pli.edu.

36 West Legal EdCenter: http://westlegaledcenter.com.

37 In Canada, for example, Platinum Legal Services (http://platinumlegalservices. com) and Commonwealth Legal Services (www.commonwealthlegal.com) are two firms that provide this type of service (as do many others). The trend towards e-discovery in Canada has also given rise to specialized, boutique law firms such as Wortzman Nickle (www.wortzmannickle.com), a law firm whose work focuses on e-discovery.

with document review and case management, including CaseMap,[38] CT Summation,[39] and Recommind's Axcelerate eDiscovery Software.[40] One challenge North American law firm knowledge managers are dealing with is the availability and suitability of outsourcing some or all of this document review work (and potentially other KM-related work) to India and other countries where the hourly wages of lawyers are much lower (this outsourcing is often called "Legal Process Outsourcing" (LPO)).[41]

G. PRACTICE MANAGEMENT

Many legal knowledge managers play some role in practice management for their firm or organization. Like knowledge management, however, "practice management" may mean different things to different people. In the context of legal knowledge work, practice management will often involve establishing professional standards or best practices that cover one or more of the following activities:

- establishing and maintaining document standards, such as creating standard word processing templates for the "look and feel" and formatting of the firm's documentation, or establishing criteria that governs how the firm provides reasoned opinions to clients or transaction opinions to other parties;
- helping the firm manage its conflicts of interest procedures and the establishment of ethical walls; and
- supporting competitive intelligence on competitor law firms.

Knowledge managers' support of practice management within the law firm will often involve leveraging a variety of technologies, including the document management system, the financial management system, and various legal research databases (for competitive intelligence, for example).

For the knowledge manager, any work in support of practice management provides the opportunity to work more closely with the firm's top management, something which can help raise the profile of the knowledge management work being done. It is always important for

---

38   CaseMap: www.casesoft.com.
39   CT Summation: www.ctsummation.com/.
40   Recommind Axcelerate eDiscovery Software: www.recommind.com/solutions/ediscovery_compliance.
41   See, for example, Gavin Birer, "The Winds of Change: Law Firms & LPO," SLAW Blog, comment posted on 13 June 2009, online: www.slaw.ca/2009/06/13/the-winds-of-change-law-firms-lpo.

anyone doing legal knowledge management to remember that it is not about implementing processes or projects for the sake of something to do—it is about clients and trying to ensure that any knowledge management initiatives are implemented with the bottom line—to increase revenues, decrease expenses, and promote lawyer and employee retention, all with the goal of improving client service, important things that are constantly in the minds of upper management. In the words of Matthew Parsons: "The point of a knowledge-based strategy is not to save the world; it's to make money."[42]

Closely related to practice management are initiatives by the firm to attract and maintain clients through a variety of methods. For the knowledge manager, these methods can involve a wide range of activities, and will often involve working closely with the firm's management and the marketing and finance departments:

- *Business intelligence*: Many firms track news stories on clients and on industry trends in an attempt to better know the client and anticipate the client's business and legal needs.
- *Extranets*: In response to client demand or the desire to work more efficiently with clients, law firms establish and maintain shared online (and secure) workplaces for clients in the forms of extranets or wikis to allow clients to remotely review and monitor work being done on their behalf.
- *Bulletins*: Most law firms regularly publish bulletins or newsletters on legal topics of interest to their client and then distribute these to important clients and otherwise make them available on their websites.[43]

---

42 Parsons, above note 5 at 21. Determining the return on investment (ROI) on knowledge management projects can be a challenge, due in part to the sometimes intangible nature of knowledge management initiatives and to the difficulty in effectively measuring input and outputs. See, for example, Kingsley Martin, "'Show Me the Money'—Measuring the Return on Knowledge Management" (15 October 2002), online: LLRX.com, www.llrx.com/features/kmroi.htm; John I. Alber, "Rethinking ROI: Managing Risk and Rewards in KM Initiatives" (23 February 2004), LLRX.com, online: www.llrx.com/features/rethinkingroi. htm; Mary Abraham, "Measuring Knowledge Management ROI," Above and Beyond KM Blog, comment posted on 20 May 2008, online: http://aboveandbeyondkm.blogspot.com/2008/05/measuring-knowledge-management-roi.html.

43 I have created a Custom Google Search that searches the websites of major Canadian law firms, Canadian law-related blogs, and Canadian law journal websites that can be used to find bulletins on particular legal topics (by searching on the applicable keywords). See: http://tinyurl.com/canadianlawfirms. In addition, Lexology (www.lexology.com), Linex Legal (www.linexlegal.com), and lawday (www.lawday.ca) are Web services that compile law firm bulletins.

An increasingly important issue for law firms and their clients is the likely trend towards alternative fee billing that provides the client ways of paying for legal services that are not necessarily based solely on the hourly rate of the lawyer.[44] For alternative fee billing to work, firms will need to be able to leverage its intellectual capital more effectively, and here is where legal knowledge management plays an important role. A firm that can provide its services faster while still maintaining high standards for quality will be in a better position to move away from traditional hourly billing and consider value billing or flat-fee arrangements, where appropriate. Technology can play an important role in helping the firm predict appropriate billing amounts for particular transactions by analyzing data of past transactions and the amount of time and work done.[45] There are a number of products that can help with fee estimation, profitability analysis, and task-based billing.[46]

H. PERSONAL KNOWLEDGE MANAGEMENT FOR LAWYERS

The foregoing discussion focuses on knowledge management at the firm-wide level and assumes some level of infrastructure and staffing to implement knowledge management initiatives. However, not all firms or organizations will have the size or infrastructure to support such initiatives. As such—and even for large firms with some sort of infrastructure for knowledge management—there is something to be said for personal knowledge management where the individual lawyer takes responsibility for his own efforts to work smarter. Personal knowledge management for lawyers will often involve one or more of the following activities:

- *Current awareness*: It is important for lawyers to stay current with legal trends and recent changes in substantive law relevant to their practice. Staying current can be achieved through any number of

---

44 See, for example, Mark A. Robertson & James A. Calloway, *Winning Alternatives to the Billable Hour*, 3d ed. (Chicago, IL: American Bar Association, 2008). See also: The Alternative Fee Lawyer Blog (http://thealternativefeelawyer.blogspot.com).

45 See, for example, Mary Abraham, "Alternative Billing Alternatives (ILTA09)," Above and Beyond KM blog, comment posted on 30 September 2009, online: http://aboveandbeyondkm.com/2009/09/alternative-billing-alternatives-ilta09. html and Mary Abraham, "Using Technology to Manage Costs," Above and Beyond KM blog, comment posted on 1 October 2009, online: http://aboveand-beyondkm.com/2009/10/using-technology-to-manage-costs.html.

46 See, for example, Redwood Analytics, Satori, Elite 3e, and viEval.

commercially available products and through subscribing to RSS feeds to law-related blogs and websites (some of these blogs and websites are listed in Section J, below in this chapter).

- *Continuing legal education*: Closely related to current awareness is the need for lifelong learning for lawyers. Increasingly, continuing legal education (CLE) is being made mandatory by individual provincial law societies.[47] There is usually a valuable transfer of knowledge made possible by attending CLE seminars (or, increasingly, webinars). Most sessions are taught by experts in their field and are practitioner-focused (as opposed to being too theoretical).
- *Precedent and research binders*: It is relatively simple for the individual lawyer to set aside copies of good examples of agreements, clauses, or research. The old-fashioned method of keeping such material in a tabbed binder is actually quite simple and produces an easy-to-organize and easy-to-access body of knowledge content. Taking the process one step further, it is relatively easy to digitize this material and organize it on your computer with any value-added annotations you want to make on the digital copies.
- *Information literacy*: Lawyers process a large volume of information. By training, they are taught to be logical and question everything. As such, most lawyers are good at evaluating information. However, since law-related information is increasingly being consumed online, there may be a need for some lawyers to improve their digital information literacy (discussed in more detail in Chapter 1, Section A). This literacy includes needing to know how reliable and current the information is and the best online sources (both fee and free) for a particular matter. Information literacy today also requires lawyers to be technologically savvy to be able to access the increasingly large volume of online law-related information.

One advantage of personal knowledge management is that it usually requires less effort and resources than large firm-wide projects. In addition, lawyers sometimes may be more motivated to develop their own knowledge content rather than to contribute to the common good. Ideally—where personal knowledge management is practised in a large law firm—materials developed by individual lawyers will be stored on network drives with lawyers making available their personally developed content to others within the firm, when appropriate.

---

47 Natalie Fraser, "Technological Innovation Makes Mandatory CLE a Realistic Goal" *The Lawyers Weekly* (8 February 2008).

I. CONCLUSIONS

Expect to see and hear more about legal knowledge management in the coming years due to the increasing pressures on lawyers to work more effectively and cost efficiently. For lawyers in large law firms, there will ordinarily be some level of knowledge management infrastructure that will involve one or more of the following activities: document and records management, precedent development, legal research and intranet content delivery, professional development and training, litigation support and project management, and practice management.

Each of these aspects of knowledge management can involve different skill sets and technologies, in addition to the need to work with various departments within the organization. For some of these tasks, technology plays a huge role, whether in document management, smart search, or online training, to name but a few examples. Just as the definition of legal knowledge management may change and grow over time, expect to see technology change and grow to address new and better ways of helping lawyers capture and organize both their explicit and tacit knowledge content.

For lawyers in smaller firms or sole practice, knowledge management can and should be implemented on a personal level. This will usually involve a mix of staying current and engaging in continuing legal education, collecting your own knowledge content in the form of precedents and research, and developing your information literacy, especially with new technologies that will assist with research and precedent development.

J. ADDITIONAL RESOURCES ON KNOWLEDGE MANAGEMENT

Set out below are some additional resources on knowledge management, with a focus on knowledge management in law firms.

1) Selected Books on Knowledge Management for Lawyers

Battersby, Karen. *Know How in the Legal Profession*. Edited by Caroline Poynton. London: Ark Group, 2006.

Kennedy, Dennis & Tom Mighell. *The Lawyer's Guide to Collaboration Tools and Technologies: Smart Ways to Work Together*. Chicago, IL: American Bar Association Law Practice Management Section, 2008.

Parsons, Matthew. *Effective Knowledge Management for Law Firms*. New York: Oxford University Press, 2004.

Rusanow, Gretta. *Knowledge Management and the Smarter Lawyer*. New York: ALM, 2003.

Susskind, Richard. *The End of Lawyers? Rethinking the Nature of Legal Services*. Oxford: Oxford University Press, 2008.

Susskind, Richard. *Transforming the Law*. Oxford: Oxford University Press, 2003.

2) Selected Journals and Articles

Ash, Jerry, ed. *InsideKnowledge* (magazine). Ark Publishing. Online: www.ikmagazine.com.

Blackwell, Gerry. "Sharing Knowledge Is Power" *Canadian Lawyer* (February 2009) at 21.

Bontis, Nick. "The Rising Star of the Chief Knowledge Officer" (Mar. 2002) 66 Ivey Business Journal 20.

Crysler, Susan. "Engagement with Knowledge: Law Firms and KM" (Spring 2003) 28 Can. L. L. 15.

Gottschalk, Petter. "Knowledge Management in the Professions: Lessons Learned from Norwegian Law Firms" (1999) 3(3) Journal of Knowledge Management 203.

Gottschalk, Petter. "Predictors of Inter-Organizational Knowledge Management: Lessons Learned from Law Firms in Norway" (2001) 8(3) Knowledge and Process Management 186.

Hunter, Laurie. *et al.* "Knowledge Management Practice in Scottish Law Firms" (2002) 12(2) Human Resource Management Journal 4.

Jabbari, David *et al.*, eds. *KMLegal* (magazine). Ark Publishing. Online: www.kmlegalmag.com.

Kay, Stuart. "Benchmarking Knowledge Management in U.S. and UK Law Firms" (15 August 2002). Online: LLRX.com, www.llrx.com/features/benchmarkingkm.htm.

Khandelwal, Vijak K. & Petter Gottschalk. "Information Technology Support for Interorganizational Knowledge Transfer: An Empirical Study of Law Firms in Norway and Australia" (2003) 16(1) Information Resources Management Journal 14.

Rusanow, Gretta. "Culturing Lawyers in Knowledge Management (1999) 1(1) Knowledge Management Asia-Pacific 1.

Saunders, Chad. "Knowledge Sharing in Legal Practice" in David Schwartz, ed., *Encyclopedia of Knowledge Management*. Hershey, PA: Idea Group Reference, 2006 at 515.

Terrett, Andrew. "Knowledge Management and the Law Firm" (1998) 2(1) Journal of Knowledge Management 67.

Tjaden, Ted. "Managing Legal Knowledge: KM Demystified." (February 2008) CCH Law Student eMonthly. Online: www.cch.ca/news-letters/LawStudent/February2008/article2.htm.

Tjaden, Ted. "The Role of Law Firm Culture in Knowledge Management." Posted on slaw.ca (29 June 2007), www.slaw.ca/2007/06/29/the-role-of-law-firm-culture-in-knowledge-management/.

Weiss, Leigh. "Collection and Connection: The Anatomy of Knowledge Sharing in Professional Service Firms" (1999) 17(4) Organization Development Journal 61.

3) KM Blogs, Listservs, and Websites

The best list of Canadian law-related blogs is available at Lawblogs (www.lawblogs.ca), a site that documents well over 100 Canadian law-related blogs, including blogs that focus on substantive areas of law (ranging from copyright to wills and estates) and those that focus on the practice of law or on legal research and technology.

Another good general site is the American Bar Association Journal Blawg Directory, available at www.abajournal.com/blawgs.

For a general Canadian blog covering legal research, technology, and general legal issues, I can highly recommend the award-winning SLAW blog at www.slaw.ca, which benefits from a large number of contributors (including me) with various backgrounds in law and law-related technology and research.

Set out below are some of the law-related blogs I most closely monitor:

a)   Legal Research Blogs
- *BeSpacific*: www.bespacific.com
- *Connie Crosby*: http://conniecrosby.blogspot.com
- *inter alia*: http://inter-alia.net
- *Library Boy*: http://micheladrien.blogspot.com
- *Shaunna Mireau on Canadian Legal Research*: http://mireau.blogspot.com
- *Strategic Librarian*: http://strategiclibrarian.com

- *SLAW*: www.slaw.ca

b)   Legal Writing Blogs
- *AdamsConsulting*: www.adamsdrafting.com/system
- *Legal Writing Prof Blog*: http://lawprofessors.typepad.com/legal-writing

c)   Law-Related Knowledge Management Blogs
- *Above and Beyond KM*: http://aboveandbeyondkm.com
- *Caselines*: http://caselines.blogspot.com
- *Dennis Kennedy*: www.denniskennedy.com
- *Knowledgeline*: http://kmpipeline.blogspot.com
- *Lawsites*: www.legaline.com/lawsites.html
- *LawyerKM*: http://lawyerkm.com
- *Strategic Legal Technology*: www.prismlegal.com/wordpress
- *Wired GC*: www.wiredgc.com

d)   Practice of Law / Law Firm Management Blogs
- *Adam Smith, Esq.*: www.bmacewen.com/blog
- *ALM Legal Blog Watch*: http://legalblogwatch.typepad.com
- *AvoidAClaim.com*: http://avoidaclaim.com
- *Law 21*: www.law21.ca
- *Thoughtful Legal Management*: www.thoughtfullaw.com

e)   Current Awareness for Lawyers
The following resources are good for staying current:

- *Custom Google Search of Canadian Law Firms*: http://tinyurl.com/canadianlawfirms
- *Lexology*: www.lexology.com
- *Linex Legal*: www.linexlegal.com
- *Fee Fie Foe Firm*: www.feefiefoefirm.com

LEGAL RESEARCH AND WRITING MALPRACTICE

A. INTRODUCTION

The concept of legal research malpractice and the extent to which a lawyer has adequately carried out legal research on behalf of a client is not widely discussed in Canada, although there have been several cases where the topic has been raised. The issue, however, has been more widely litigated in the United States, and there is every reason to believe that Canadian courts will readily apply principles of legal research malpractice in appropriate cases where a lawyer has failed to conduct legal research or has done so incompetently. What is less certain is the extent to which Canadian courts will impose a duty on lawyers to conduct *online* legal research in appropriate cases. Given the increase of material online, and given the depth, accuracy, and speed of commercial online law-related databases, it is likely that courts will regard online legal research skills as a standard by which all lawyers and legal researchers should be judged.

In Chapter 1, Section A, brief mention was made of the importance of legal research as a skill that every competent lawyer should possess. The very essence of lawyering assumes that the lawyer, as a legal specialist, either knows the law or can identify and find the relevant law in order to provide a competent legal opinion to the client. In recent years, continuing legal education or life-long learning for lawyers has been an important issue for Canadian provincial law societies and the liability insurers for Canadian lawyers. While there are relatively few cases dealing specifically with legal research malpractice, it is reasonable to assume that the improvement by all lawyers of legal research skills and the other competencies identified by the Law Society of Upper Canada can only reduce the incidences of malpractice claims against lawyers. This chapter looks at Canadian and American cases dealing with legal research malpractice and the consequences of sloppy drafting of court documents, and then attempts to provide some basic tips that lawyers can apply to reduce the risk of being liable for legal research and writing malpractice.

B. CANADIAN CASES ON LEGAL RESEARCH MALPRACTICE

As a general rule, lawyers are required to bring reasonable care, skill, and knowledge to the performance of the professional services they have undertaken to perform.[1] Rule 2 of Chapter II (Competence and Quality of Service) of the Canadian Bar Association *Code of Professional Conduct*, for example, admonishes the lawyer to "serve the client in a conscientious, diligent and efficient manner so as to provide a quality of service at least equal to that which lawyers would expect of a competent lawyer in a like situation."[2]

From this general standard of care, Canadian courts have discussed a specific standard of care required for conducting legal research. In *Central & Eastern Trust Co. v. Rafuse*, for example, at issue was whether the lawyers were negligent in failing to ensure that their clients' mortgage security constituted a valid charge in a situation where the mortgage was later held to be void under Nova Scotia corporate legislation. In holding that the liability of lawyers could arise in both tort and contract for negligently performing services for which they were retained, the Court went further to hold that the lawyers in that particular case were negligent for failing to have ascertained the existence of the relevant corporate legislation that would have affected the enforceability of the mortgage. In so holding, the Supreme Court of Canada applied both American and British law in suggesting that a lawyer, to avoid being negligent, may have a duty to adequately research the law in order to properly advise a client:

1   See *Central & Eastern Trust Co. v. Rafuse*, [1986] 2 S.C.R. 147 at 208.
2   Canadian Bar Association, *Code of Professional Conduct* (Ottawa: Canadian Bar Association, 2009) at 5, online: www.cba.org/CBA/activities/pdf/codeofconduct.pdf.

The requirement of professional competence that was particularly involved in this case was reasonable knowledge of the applicable or relevant law. A solicitor is not required to know all the law applicable to the performance of a particular legal service, in the sense that he must carry it around with him as part of his "working knowledge," without the need of further research, but he must have a sufficient knowledge of the fundamental issues or principles of law applicable to the particular work he has undertaken to enable him to perceive the need to ascertain the law on relevant points. The duty in respect of knowledge is stated in 7 Am. Jur. 2d, "Attorneys at Law" ¶200, in a passage that was quoted by Jones J.A. in the Appeal Division, as follows [(at pp. 269–70): pp. 269, 147 D.L.R.]: "An attorney is expected to possess knowledge of those plain and elementary principles of law which are commonly known by well-informed attorneys, and to discover those additional rules of law which, although not commonly known, may readily be found by standard research techniques." See *Charlesworth and Percy on Negligence* (7th ed., 1983), pp. 577–78 to similar effect, where it is said: "Although a solicitor is not bound to know the contents of every statute of the realm, there are some statutes, about which it is his duty to know. The test for deciding what he ought to know is to apply the standard of knowledge of a reasonably competent solicitor." The duty or requirement of professional competence in respect of knowledge is put by Jackson and Powell, *Professional Negligence* (1982), at pp. 145–46 as follows: "Although a solicitor is not 'bound to know all the law,' he ought generally to know where and how to find out the law in so far as it affects matters within his field of practice. However, before the solicitor is held liable for failing to look a point up, circumstances must be shown which would have alerted the reasonably prudent solicitor to the point which ought to be researched." [3]

Similar judicial sentiment was expressed in *World Wide Treasure Adventures Inc. v. Trivia Games Inc.*, in which the court applied the *Rafuse* decision in holding the negligent lawyer liable for his client's costs in a botched application for an interim injunction. The court ruled in essence that if the lawyer had properly conducted legal research, he would have uncovered the burden of proof facing his client and would not have proceeded (or presumably would have more carefully advised the client of the risks of failing if the injunction application proceeded):

---

3   Above note 1 at 208–9.

In my opinion the conduct of the Plaintiff's solicitors in this case fell far short of the reasonable care, skill and knowledge which the Plaintiff was entitled to expect. The *American Cyanamid* principles ought by now to be part of the working knowledge of a competent counsel in this jurisdiction. *If they are not, then any counsel contemplating an injunction application ought to be able to perceive the need to research the law before preparing the material to be filed. It may be that the Aetna Financial case is not as well known, however a moderate amount of research would quickly have brought it to light, and that research should have been undertaken as part of the preparation for a bid for what are known to competent counsel to be extraordinary remedies not lightly granted by the Court.* It is for these reasons, and in accordance with the principles I have read from the *Rafuse* case that I conclude that the Plaintiff's solicitors were negligent in the performance of their duty to him.[4]

Likewise, in *285614 Alberta Ltd v. Burnet Duckworth & Palmer*, the law firm was held liable to the client for the firm's professional negligence in structuring a shareholder's loan to allow the clients to purchase a home by securing the loan with a demand promissory note, something that later resulted in the client being subject to adverse income tax consequences. In holding the law firm liable, the court concluded that the lawyer responsible had failed to adequately research the issue regarding the income tax effect of the demand promissory note:

> In my view, Spackman did breach the standard of care of a reasonably competent lawyer both in failing to adequately consider or research the requirements of the legislation, and in failing to advise Mrs. Maplesden of the potential for tax consequences.[5]

In *Renner v. O'Connell*,[6] the client was "taxing" his lawyer's account as being excessive. The account was reduced, in part, because the lawyer did not provide exhaustive research for the legal opinion required by the retainer where the lawyer failed to make use of online legal databases.

Although no negligence *per se* was involved in *Gibb v. Jiwan*,[7] the court spent a fair bit of time chastising counsel and suggesting that there would be negative costs implications for their failure to properly

---

4   (1987), 16 B.C.L.R. (2d) 135 at 141–42 (S.C.) [emphasis added].

5   [1993] 4 W.W.R. 374 at 384 (Q.B.). For a case to the contrary in which the lawyer was not held to be negligent because he had adequately researched the quantum of the client's potential damages (despite a jury subsequently awarding a higher amount), see *Maillet v. Haliburton & Comeau* (1983), 55 N.S.R. (2d) 311 (S.C.T.D.).

6   (1989), 97 N.B.R. (2d) 200 (Q.B.).

7   [1996] O.J. No. 1370 (Gen. Div.)

conduct research and uncover relatively straightforward commentary and case law on a point of law involving priority interests in land involving a prior unregistered interest:

> Counsel cannot fulfil their duties to the client or the court unless they conduct reasonable research on points of law which are known in advance to be contentious. The court must rely on counsel to conduct reasonably complete research on points of law they raise. That is part of counsel's professional duty. It is desirable that counsel look up difficult or important points on Quicklaw but I can appreciate that this may not be economical in many cases. However, in my view it is not acceptable for any counsel or articling student to come to court intending to argue a contentious point of law without first researching the point at least to the extent of looking up the issue in basic reference books.
>
> In a case like this where counsel know there is a contest as to which cases may be authoritative, I think they also have a duty to cite up cases they rely on to determine whether they are still good law. (I recall that citing up a case was one of the first things I learned in law school and its importance in litigation was emphasized repeatedly during articles.)
>
> The judicial system cannot function effectively unless counsel fulfil this duty because judges cannot possibly know the law on all issues which come before them. Counsel must bear in mind that most justices in the General Division are generalists and hear cases of all kinds.[8]

The judge in *Gibb v. Jiwan* pointed out how easy it was for him to find the relevant case law by looking in the index to Carswell's *Canadian Abridgment* and *Canadian Encyclopedic Digest* and by checking out textbooks on debtor/creditor law and real property law.

In *Nichols v. Warner, Scarborough, Herman & Harvey,*[9] an allegation was made that the law firm was negligent in allowing the plaintiff to settle a motorcycle accident claim without first having researched the need to include the telephone company as a possible defendant for its alleged negligence in the placement of the telephone pole that the plaintiff struck in the accident (near an intersection). In ruling that the law firm was not negligent for not carrying out research on this issue, the court noted that the lawyers involved made a conscious decision, based

---

8   *Ibid.* at paras. 34–36.
9   2007 BCSC 1383, aff'd 2009 BCCA 277, leave to appeal to SCC refused, [2009] S.C.C.A. No. 355.

on their experience in this area, that research was not required and that there was no advantage in joining the telephone company to the action:

> The plaintiff has not established, in my view, that the circumstances were such that the reasonably competent solicitor at the time would have been alerted that further research ought to have been conducted or . . . that such research was required. The [action] was an area in which [the plaintiff's lawyers] carried out the majority of their practice. They were alive to the issue. They concluded that research was not required. The plaintiff has not established that this was a conclusion that a reasonably competent solicitor would not have reached in those circumstances.[10]

C. AMERICAN CASES ON LEGAL RESEARCH MALPRACTICE

American cases dealing with legal research malpractice raise similar issues as the foregoing Canadian cases despite the fact that none of these American cases appear to have been considered or applied by any Canadian court. American courts have regularly held that a lawyer is under a duty to her client to conduct adequate legal research in order to fully advise the client of the client's rights or risk being held liable in damages for research malpractice.[11]

---

10   *Ibid.* at para. 132 (S.C.).
11   *Lawhorn v. Allen*, 519 F.3d 1272 (11th Cir. 2008) [criminal defence lawyer negligent in failing to conduct adequate legal research in support of decision to waive closing argument]; *Kempf v. Magida*, 37 A.D.3d 763, 832 N.Y.S.2d 47 (2007) [allegation that the lawyer was negligent for failing to become familiar with forfeiture law]; *TCW/Camil Holding L.L.C. v. Fox Horan & Camerini L.L.P.*, 330 B.R. 117 (D. Del. 2005) [law firm failed to adequately research and investigate plaintiff's obligation under merger agreement; *Janik v. Rudy, Exelrod & Zieff*, 2004 WL 1386171 (Cal. App. 2004) [labour law class action law suit, failure to uncover alternative theory of recovery]; *Village Nurseries v. Greenbaum*, 101 Cal. App. 4th 26 (2002) [bankruptcy liens, lawyer liable, failed to establish that his advice was based on informed judgment at the time he advised his client]; *Frank v. Pepe*, 717 N.Y.S.2d 873 (2000) [divorce action]; *Lieber v. ITT Hartford Ins. Center, Inc.*, 15 P.3d 1030 (Utah 2000) [insurance company brief inaccurate]; *Shopsin v. Siben & Siben*, 702 N.Y.S.2d 610 (App. Div. 2000) [real estate transaction]; *Sun Valley Potatoes, Inc. v. Rosholt, Robertson & Tucker*, 981 P.2d 236 (Idaho 1999) [conduct of counsel at trial]; *McCoy v. Tepper*, 690 N.Y.S.2d 678 (App. Div. 1999) [limitation period]; *Schutts v. Bentley Nevada Corp.*, 966 F. Supp. 1549 (D. Nev. 1997) [lawyer's liability for costs for filing weak employment law/discrimination claim]; *Fiorentino v. Rapoport*, 693 A.2d 208 (Pa. Super. Ct. 1997) [corpor-

In the oft-cited *Smith v. Lewis*, for example, the defendant lawyer was held liable in negligence to his client for failing to research and properly advise his client regarding the likelihood of the client's pension being "community property":

> In any event, as indicated above, had defendant conducted minimal research into either hornbook or case law, he would have discovered with modest effort that General Smith's state retirement benefits were likely to be treated as community property and that his federal benefits at least arguably belonged to the community as well . . . . Even as to doubtful matters, an attorney is expected to perform sufficient research to enable him to make an informed and intelligent judgment on behalf of his client.[12]

---

ate matter]; *Massey v. Prince George's County*, 918 F. Supp. 905 (D. Md. 1996) [dog bite case law, under ethical rule requiring attorney to provide competent representation, attorney must have ability to research law, court specifically comments on the ease of "natural language" searches on Westlaw]; *Hart v. Carro, Spanbock, Kaster & Cuiffo*, 620 N.Y.S.2d 847 (App. Div. 1995) [negligence relating to stock purchase transaction]; *Finkelstein v. Collier*, 636 So. 2d 1053 (La. App. 5th Cir. 1994) [negligence in missing limitation period in tort claim]; *Harline v. Barker*, 854 P.2d 595 (Utah Ct. App. 1993) [negligence relating to lack of knowledge of bankruptcy court procedure]; *Niziolek v. Chicago Transit Authority*, 620 N.E.2d 1097 (Ill. App. Ct. 1993) [limitation period]; *Collas v. Garnick*, 624 A.2d 117 (Pa. Super. Ct. 1993) [settlement of lawsuit]; *Youngworth v. Stark*, 283 Cal. Rptr. 668 (Ct. App. 1991) [civil procedure, "local rules"]; *Goebel v. Lauderdale*, 214 Cal. App. 3d 1502 (1989) ["total failure to perform even the most perfunctory research" in negligently advising client to divert money in a bankruptcy proceeding in violation of bankruptcy code]; *Blake v. National Casualty Co.*, 607 F. Supp. 189 (C.D. Cal. 1984) [lawyer sanctioned for failing to conduct reasonable research — noting up cases, using an annotated code, or doing a computer search would have uncovered controlling precedents]; *Copeland Lumber Yards, Inc. v. Kincaid*, 684 P.2d 13 (Or. Ct. App. 1984) [limitation period]; *Horne v. Peckham*, 158 Cal. Rptr. 714 (Ct. App. 1979) [negligence in drafting trust agreement without due regard to tax implications]; *Smith v. Lewis*, 530 P.2d 589 (Cal. 1975) [family law, division of property]. See also *American Jurisprudence* at §204:

> An attorney is expected to possess knowledge of those plain and elementary principles of law which are commonly known by well-informed attorneys, and to discover those additional rules of law which, although not commonly known, may readily be found by standard research techniques. In addition, while a legal malpractice action is unlikely to succeed where an attorney erred because an issue of law was unsettled or debatable, an attorney may be liable for a failure to conduct adequate legal research. A law firm will be liable for failure to comply with requirements of a statute, even though the firm claims that compliance would be costly and that the client was preoccupied with costs [footnotes omitted].

12   530 P.2d 589 at 596 (Cal. 1975).

Likewise, in *Horne v. Peckham*,[13] the lawyer was found liable for his negligence in drafting a trust agreement that had negative tax consequences for the client, consequences that would have been obvious if the lawyer had conducted basic legal research. In holding the lawyer liable, the court pointed out the lawyer's duty to either research the law or at least make the client aware of the uncertainty with the law by stating that "an attorney has a duty to avoid involving his client in murky areas of the law if research reveals alternative courses of conduct."[14]

In addition to the risk of being liable in damages to the client, there is the almost worst sanction of public embarrassment. In *Bradshaw v. Unity Marine Corp.*,[15] note the court's sarcasm regarding counsel's inability to properly cite precedents in support of their written arguments in their briefs regarding a claim under maritime law for damages for personal injury to a seaman sustained while working aboard a ship at dock:

> Defendant begins the descent into Alice's Wonderland by submitting a Motion that relies upon only one legal authority. The Motion cites a Fifth Circuit case which stands for the whopping proposition that a federal court sitting in Texas applies the Texas statutes of limitations to certain state and federal law claims . . . . That is all well and good — the Court is quite fond of the *Erie* doctrine; indeed there is talk of little else around both the Canal and this Court's water cooler. Defendant, however, does not even cite to *Erie*, but to a mere successor case, and further fails to even begin to analyze why the Court should approach the shores of *Erie*. Finally, Defendant does not even provide a cite to its desired Texas limitation statute. A more bumbling approach is difficult to conceive — but wait folks, There's More!
>
> Plaintiff responds to this deft, yet minimalist analytical wizardry with an equally gossamer wisp of an argument, although Plaintiff does at least cite the federal limitations provision applicable to maritime tort claims . . . . Naturally, Plaintiff also neglects to provide any analysis whatsoever of why his claim versus Defendant Phillips is a maritime action. Instead, Plaintiff "cites" to a single case from the Fourth Circuit. Plaintiff's citation, however, points to a nonexistent Volume "1886" of the Federal Reporter Third Edition and neglects to provide a pinpoint citation for what, after being located, turned out to be a forty-page decision . . . . The Court cannot even begin to comprehend why this case was selected for reference. It is almost as if Plaintiff's counsel

---

13   158 Cal. Rptr. 714 (Ct. App. 1979).
14   *Ibid.* at 720.
15   147 F. Supp. 2d 668 at 670 (S.D. Tex. 2001).

chose the opinion by throwing long range darts at the Federal Reporter (remarkably enough hitting a nonexistent volume!). And though the Court often gives great heed to dicta from courts as far flung as those of Manitoba, it finds this case unpersuasive.[16]

To the contrary, in the United States, courts have dismissed legal research malpractice claims against lawyers where the law in question was unsettled and the lawyer at least made good faith efforts to determine the law and made a mistake of law or error in judgment on a point on which reasonable lawyers might differ, or the lawyer, although subsequently wrong in his opinion, at least made the client aware at the time of the risk of the law being reversed or changed in the future.[17]

D. CONSEQUENCES OF CARELESS DRAFTING

The consequences of inadequate research can be devastating to both the client and ultimately the lawyer in the form of embarrassment and

---

16   *Ibid.* at 670–71 (citations omitted). See also *Roeder v. Islamic Republic of Iran*, 195 F. Supp. 2d 140 at 184 (D.D.C. 2002) where counsel was criticized for meritless arguments, repeatedly failing to substantiate their arguments by reference to any supporting authority, and repeatedly failing to bring to the court's attention the existence of controlling authority that conflicted with those arguments: "An attorney can not carry out the practice of law like an ostrich with her head in the sand, ignoring her duty to research and acknowledge adverse precedent and law. Attorneys are not free to assert any and all legal arguments they wish on behalf of their clients, without regard to existing precedent."

17   *Bergstrom v. Noah*, 974 P.2d 531 (Kan. 1999) [alleged error regarding trial strategy]; *Villavicencio v. State*, 719 So. 2d 322 (Fla. Dist. Ct. App. 1998) [defence counsel's alleged lack of knowledge of criminal procedure]; *Wood v. McGrath, North, Mullin & Kratz, P.C.*, 589 N.W.2d 103 (Neb. 1999) [family law settlement agreement, lawyer allegedly failed to advise client of uncertainties]; *Collins v. Miller & Miller, Ltd.*, 943 P.2d 747 (Ariz. Ct. App. 1996) [limitations period]; *U.S. v. Vastola*, 25 F.3d 164 (3d Cir. 1994) [prosecutor conducted adequate legal research regarding sealing of wiretap evidence]; *Bush v. O'Connor*, 791 P.2d 915 (Wash. Ct. App. 1990) [civil procedure, limitation period]; *Meir v. Kirk, Pinkerton, McClelland, Savary & Carr, P.A.*, 561 So. 2d 399 (Fla. Dist. Ct. App. 1990) [limitation period]; *Molever v. Roush*, 152 Ariz. 367, 732 P.2d 1105 (Ct. App. 1986) [defamation action]; *Sharpe v. Superior Court, Sacramento County*, 192 Cal. Rptr. 16 (Ct. App. 1983) [family law, pension rights]; *Wright v. Williams*, 121 Cal. Rptr. 194 (Ct. App. 1975) [maritime law, documents of title]; *Young v. Bridwell*, 437 P.2d 686 (Utah 1968) [failing to file an appeal]; *Martin v. Burns*, 429 P.2d 660 (Ariz. 1967) [civil procedure]. See also David D. Dodge, "Lawyer Not Liable for Negligence Regarding Unsettled Issues of Law" (2000) 36 Ariz. Att'y 20 and cases cited therein.

potential professional liability. Equally embarrassing are those situations where courts have sanctioned lawyers for their careless drafting of court documents, such as motions, pleadings, and facta (or briefs). There are a number of Canadian and American decisions in which courts have denied costs to lawyers (and their clients) as a form of punishment for sloppy legal writing that has caused confusion or extra work for the court or the other party; some American decisions go further and sanction or penalize the individual lawyer.

A recent Canadian example that received national newspaper coverage[18] was the "missing comma" case in Telecom Decision CRTC 2007-75 involving the interpretation of a Support Structure Agreement between Bell Aliant and Rogers Communications Inc.[19] In the original decision a year prior, Bell Aliant was successful in arguing that a misplaced comma in an English version of their contract with Rogers allowed them to terminate the contract early. However, on appeal, Rogers was successful in arguing that the commas in the French version of the contract were in their proper position and that it was clear, based on the French version, that Bell Aliant could not terminate early. Although this case did not (appear to) involve professional liability issues, the ambiguity in drafting did result in extended litigation and expense.

Another recent Canadian decision involving negligent drafting was *V.C.P. Homes Inc. v Fast.*[20] In that dispute, at issue was whether a lawyer negligently drafted clauses in a joint venture agreement regarding which party was responsible for financing the construction project under consideration. The court noted that "the issue to be decided is not whether in a general way the agreement was negligently drafted" but that to succeed "the plaintiffs must point to the presence or absence of particular provisions which demonstrate a breach of the standard of care and which caused a loss to the plaintiffs."[21]

In noting an ambiguity in the agreement on this issue, the court ruled that "the plaintiff sufficiently demonstrated that a reasonably prudent solicitor would not have left the clause on borrowing so open to misinterpretation."

---

18   See Barbara Shecter, "Rogers Wins 'Comma' Contract Dispute" *National Post* (21 August 2007) FP2; Kenneth A. Adams, "Behind the Scenes of the Comma Dispute" *The Globe & Mail* (28 August 2007).

19   Telecom Decision CRTC 2007-75, Rogers Communications Inc. — Application to review and vary Telecom Decision 2006-45 regarding the termination and assignment of a support structure agreement (20 August 2007), online: www.crtc. gc.ca/eng/archive/2007/dt2007-75.htm.

20   2002 BCSC 446.

21   *Ibid.* para. 40.

Careless drafting can also apply to court-filed pleadings. In *Toll v. Marjanovic*, for example, even though the defendant's lawyer was ultimately successful on a summary judgment motion to dismiss the plaintiff's application for specific performance, the court denied the defendant costs on this motion due to the sloppy nature of the motion materials prepared by the defendant's lawyer:

> The fact that there was confusion generated by the drafting of the notice of motion, which came close to requiring an adjournment of the motion after the better part of the argument had taken place, inevitably means that there was a waste of some time and effort resulting in avoidable costs being incurred. The defendant must bear the consequences of that result.[22]

In *AMJ Campbell Inc. v. Kord Products Inc.*,[23] even though there was no suggestion of sloppy drafting, the court had to resolve a dispute over the drafting of a letter of intent. In what is known as the "million dollar comma case," at issue was the insertion of a comma in the definition of "Average Selling Price," which resulted in a difference to the parties of one million dollars, depending on whether or not the comma was placed after the word "freight" in the definition. In denying rectification of the agreement, the court was satisfied that the vendor—the party now complaining about the insertion of the comma—was aware of the insertion, which was in fact inserted by its counsel in an earlier draft of the document.

In the United States, there have been a number of recent decisions in which the court has drawn attention to sloppy drafting.

In *Precision Specialty Metals, Inc. v. U.S.*, for example, the United States Court of Appeal upheld sanctions on a Department of Justice lawyer for "misquoting and failing to quote fully from two judicial opinions in a motion for reconsideration she signed and filed."[24] In that

---

22   [2001] O.J. No. 1529 at para. 5 (S.C.J.). For similar results, see *National Bank of Canada v. Pelletier et al.* (1980), 34 N.B.R. (2d) 614 (Q.B.); *Humby Enterprises Ltd. v. A.L. Stuckless & Sons Ltd.* (2003), 225 Nfld. & P.E.I.R. 268 (C.A.); *Bouteiller v. Bouteiller* (1997), 116 Man. R. (2d) 153 (Q.B.); and *Royal Bank v. Robb* (1977), 19 N.S.R. (2d) 368 (C.A.).

23   (2003), 63 O.R. (3d) 375 (S.C.J.).

24   315 F.3d 1346 at 1347 (Fed. Cir. 2003) [*Precision Specialty Metals*]. For additional cases where counsel were sanctioned or criticized for mis-citations, see *Espitia v. Fouche*, 314 Wis. 2d 507, 758 N.W.2d 224 (Ct. App. 2008) [counsel fined $100 for providing faulty citation to a decision]; *Walder v. State*, 85 S.W.3d 824 (Tex. App.—Waco 2002) [court-appointed counsel required to file an amended brief for, among other things, inadequate citation to relevant authority]; *Abbs v. Principi*, 237 F.3d 1342 (Fed. Cir. 2001); and *Porter v. Farmers Sup-*

case, the lower court—the Court of International Trade—had denied the lawyer's motion for reconsideration when she failed to file materials "forthwith" as demanded by the court (she filed them some twelve days later). In a motion for reconsideration, the lawyer signed and filed a brief setting out arguments on the definition of "forthwith." In support of her arguments, she allegedly intentionally omitted parts of the *Black's Law Dictionary* definition of "forthwith" and "cropped" parts of quotes from judicial decisions that were unfavourable to her argument and changed the meanings of the quotes. She also failed to cite a leading U.S. Supreme Court decision that defined the term as usually meaning within twenty-four hours:

> The effect of Walser's editing of this material and ignoring the Supreme Court decision that dealt with the issue—a decision that seriously weakened her argument—was to give the Court of International Trade a misleading impression of the state of the law on the point. She eliminated material that indicated that her delay in filing the motion for reconsideration had not met the court's requirement that she file "forthwith," and presented the remaining material in a way that overstated the basis for her claim that a "forthwith" filing requirement meant she could take whatever time would be reasonable in the circumstances. This distortion of the law was inconsistent with and violated the standards of Rule 11.
>
> By signing the motion for reconsideration, Walser certified that the "claims, defenses, and other legal contentions therein are warranted by existing law." Inherent in that representation was that she stated therein the "existing law" accurately and correctly. She did not do so, however, because her omissions from and excisions of judicial authority mischaracterized what those courts had stated. The effect of her doctored quotations was to make it appear that the weight of judicial authority was that "forthwith" means "a time reasonable under the circumstances." This was quite different from the Supreme Court's statement in *Dickerman* that "[i]n matters of pleading and practice," forthwith "is usually construed, and sometimes defined by rule of court, as within twenty-four hours." By suppressing any reference to *Dickerman*, which both the Second Circuit in *McAllister* and Justice Thomas in his dissent in *Henderson* cited and which the

---

ply Service, 790 F.2d 882 (Fed. Cir. 1986). For additional cases where counsel were sanctioned for misstating the law, see: *Teamsters Local No. 579 v. B & M Transit., Inc.*, 882 F.2d 274 at 280 (7th Cir. 1989); *Borowski v. DePuy, Inc.*, 850 F.2d 297 at 304–5 (7th Cir. 1988); and *Jewelpak Corp. v. United States*, 297 F.3d 1326 (Fed. Cir. 2002).

Second Circuit quoted, Walser gave a false and misleading impression of "existing law" on the meaning of "forthwith."[25]

In *B.A.M. Development, L.L.C. v. Salt Lake County*, the dissenting judge drew attention in a footnote to the decision of the inappropriate drafting style of the brief filed by the appellant's lawyer, a brief that used unnecessary bolding, underlining, and use of "all caps" and exclamation points:

> To the extent BAM has successfully persuaded me of the fundamental soundness of its position, that success should not be attributed, in any degree, to its counsel's unrestrained and unnecessary use of the bold, underline, and "all caps" functions of word processing or his repeated use of exclamation marks to emphasize points in his briefs. Nor are the briefs he filed in this case unique. Rather, BAM's counsel has regularly employed these devices in prior appeals to this court. While I appreciate a zealous advocate as much as anyone, such techniques, which really amount to a written form of shouting, are simply inappropriate in an appellate brief. It is counterproductive for counsel to litter his brief with burdensome material such as "WRONG! WRONG ANALYSIS! WRONG RESULT! WRONG! WRONG! WRONG!"[26]

Likewise, in *Devore v. City of Philadelphia*, the court took exception to the poorly drafted pleadings of the plaintiff's counsel, even though the plaintiff was ultimately successful in his jury trial alleging employment discrimination against the City. In addition to a substantial jury verdict, the plaintiff was awarded his costs, but the City objected to the fees submitted by the plaintiff's lawyer, a Mr. Puricelli, as being excessive, especially in light of his poor paperwork. The court agreed and significantly reduced the amount of fees Mr. Puricelli was entitled to:

> Mr. Puricelli's written work is careless, to the point of disrespectful. The Defendants have described it as "vague, ambiguous, unintelligible, verbose and repetitive." See Response, at 2. We agree. Although the Defendants have taken issue with some of the typographical errors present in Mr. Puricelli's filings, the problems with his pleadings have gone beyond typos.
>
> . . .
>
> As previously mentioned, Mr. Puricelli's filings are replete with typographical errors and we would be remiss if we did not point out

---

25 *Precision Specialty Metals, ibid.* at 1355–56.
26 87 P.3d 710 at 734 (Utah App. 2004).

some of our favorites. Throughout the litigation, Mr. Puricelli identified the court as "THE UNITED STATES DISTRICT COURT FOR
THE EASTER [sic] DISTRICT OF PENNSYLVANIA." Considering the
religious persuasion of the presiding officer, the "Passover" District
would have been more appropriate. However, we took no personal
offense at the reference. In response to the attorneys' fees petition,
the Defendants note that the typographical errors in Mr. Puricelli's
written work are epidemic. In response to this attack, Mr. Puricelli
writes the following:

> As for there being typos, yes there have been typos, but these
> errors have not detracted from the arguments or results, and
> the rule in this case was a victory for Mr. Devore. Further,
> had the Defendants not tired [sic] to paper Plaintiff's counsel
> to death, some type [sic] would not have occurred. Further-
> more, there have been omissions by the Defendants, thus
> they should not case [sic] stones.

If these mistakes were purposeful, they would be brilliant. However, based on the history of the case and Mr. Puricelli's filings, we
know otherwise. Finally, in the most recent letter to the court, asking
that we vacate the settlement agreement, Mr. Puricelli identifies the
undersigned as "Honorable Jacon [sic] Hart." I appreciate the eleva-
tion to what sounds like a character in the Lord of the Rings, but alas,
I am but a judge.[27]

The decision of *In re Wilkins* also involved the wording of a brief but
involved the disrespectful and sarcastic language in an appeal brief the
lawyer had filed seeking an appeal:

The Court of Appeals' published Opinion in this case is quite disturb-
ing. It is replete with misstatements of material facts, it misapplies
controlling case law, and it does not even bother to discuss relevant
cases that are directly on point. Clearly, such a decision should be
reviewed by this Court. Not only does it work an injustice on appellant Michigan Mutual Insurance Company, it establishes dangerous
precedent in several areas of the law. This will undoubtedly create
additional problems in future cases.[2]

FN2: Indeed, the Opinion is so factually and legally inaccurate that
one is left to wonder whether the Court of Appeals was determined to
find for Appellee Sports, Inc., and then said whatever was necessary

---

27   2004 WL 414085 (E.D. Pa. Feb 20, 2004) (No. Civ. A. 00-3598).

to reach that conclusion (regardless of whether the facts or the law supported its decision).[28]

In a 3:2 split decision, the Supreme Court of Indiana ordered a thirty-day suspension for the lawyer's use of such disrespectful language, although the dissenting judges held that the language in the footnote was speech protected by the First Amendment, even if it was "heavy-handed."[29]

There are, however, a number of "sanctions" cases where lawyers were *not* sanctioned for failing to uncover relevant precedents (i.e., for inadequate research).[30] In these cases, the lawyer's "offence" was not sanctionable as being an attempt to mislead the court, but in the right circumstances, might amount to a malpractice claim by the client if the lawyer's failure to adequately research resulted in a loss to the client.

The lesson from these examples is obvious: litigators must be careful to accurately state the law, avoid unnecessary sarcasm or hyperbole, and not be misleading.

E. TIPS TO AVOID LEGAL RESEARCH AND WRITING MALPRACTICE

Based on the foregoing Canadian and American case law, and based on the general standards that courts apply in determining whether a lawyer was negligent in a particular transaction, there are a number of things that lawyers can do to reduce the risk of legal research malpractice. Before discussing these tips, it is useful to consider the factors that courts would take into account in determining whether a lawyer will be found liable for legal research malpractice. These factors include:

- the complexity of the legal issues and whether the law is unsettled in that particular area;
- the urgency of the matter;
- the steps actually taken by the lawyer using either print or online resources to ascertain the law for the particular issue; and
- the relationship with the client and whether the lawyer discussed with the client the advisability of further research being done and

---

28   777 N.E.2d 714 at 715–16 (Ind. 2002).
29   *Ibid.* at 719 *et seq.*
30   See *United States v. Stringfellow*, 911 F.2d 225 at 227 (9th Cir.1990); *Thompson v. Duke*, 940 F.2d 192 at 197–98 (7th Cir.1991); and *Golden Eagle Distrib. Corp. v. Burroughs Corp.*, 801 F.2d 1531 at 1541–42 (9th Cir.1986).

the risk and consequences the client would face where the law is unsettled for a particular issue.

To minimize careless drafting errors, lawyers should regularly consult "forms and precedents" materials for sample pleadings and agreements and actively edit these sample documents to conform to a client's specific needs. Legal writing is discussed in detail in Chapter 12.

What is less clear in the American (and Canadian) case law is the extent to which a lawyer is obliged to conduct *online* legal research or risk being held negligent for not uncovering relevant law.[31] Given the increasing use of computers and the availability of flat-rate fees for many of the online commercial databases, the time has likely come where a Canadian court, in the right circumstances, could easily conclude that failure to research a point of law online will result in professional negligence.

Ultimately, the focus should be on conducting good quality legal research that uses the most appropriate sources of information, whether print or online, depending on the circumstances, the issues being researched, the instructions from the client, and the importance of the matter. In certain situations, it may be that resorting to print-based textbooks would be a prudent source of information, whereas in other situations there may be no choice but to conduct full-text keyword searches in online databases to locate otherwise hard to find information:

> Whether a lawyer should resort to Westlaw or Lexis to find the latest case or utilize other electronic media resources or go to a law library depends on the circumstances. The fact that technology provides greater efficiencies and may afford lawyers a competitive advantage does not mean that it is unethical not to use technology. In the end it is the quality of the legal work and not the speed at which it is done that matters. Given today's technologies and the inventions that will serve lawyers in the future, the practice of law still requires the exer-

---

31   See Ola Najar, "Computerized Research in the Legal Arena: Developing a Standard of Research Sufficiency in Legal Malpractice and Rule 11 Actions" (1993) 39 Wayne L. Rev. 1683; Simon Chester, "Electronic Malpractice: Does Competence Require Computer Research?" (1991) 17:8 L. Prac. Mgmt 23; Teresa N. Pritchard, "Attorneys in the Electronic Information Age: Is there a Duty to Make the Transition?" (1988) 62 Fla. B.J. 17. See also Ronald E. Mallen & Jeffrey M. Smith, *Legal Malpractice*, 5th ed. (St. Paul, MN: West Group, 2000) at §19:6 where the authors suggest "There is no doubt, however, that the issue of electronic research and the Internet will be injected into legal malpractice litigation, concerning whether expert witnesses should be allowed to offer such testimony. Then, the question will be for the courts about the technology skills required of the modern lawyer."

cise of judgment by the legally trained mind. Although access to law may become automated, the practice of law will not.[32]

Considering the factors discussed above that courts would likely apply to judge whether a particular lawyer was liable for legal research malpractice, it is prudent for lawyers and legal researchers to develop standard practices or checklists that will help remind them of the multiple steps involved in legal research. The legal research checklist set below provides a reminder of some of the fundamental research techniques that should be used. Equally important, of course, is ensuring that one has a correct and complete understanding of the facts that drive the legal research question and that the researcher (or lawyer to whom the researcher reports) has fully informed the client whether the law being researched is settled or unsettled.

Legal Research Checklist
1. **Facts**: Do you have all of the relevant facts?
    Assumptions: What assumptions are being made?
    The facts and assumptions on which the legal research opinion is based should be set out in the legal research memorandum or in the report for the client. Where the client has documents, these should obviously be reviewed to confirm what the client has been saying and to check for things such as "choice of law" provisions (assuming it is a contractual dispute).

2. **Preliminary questions and issues**:
    *   Is there federal, provincial, or municipal legislation that governs this problem?
    *   Is there a limitation period problem? If so, consult the applicable federal or provincial limitation period legislation. If the calculation of time is involved, consult the applicable federal or provincial *Interpretation Act*.
    *   How urgently is the answer needed?
    *   How much time and money can be spent on research for this problem?
    *   Has anyone else within the organization looked at this problem?
    *   Is there someone you can speak to about this sort of research problem for guidance or ideas?

3. **Secondary research (start broad)**:
    *   *Treatises*: check books for explanations and overviews

---

32 Mark Tuft, "Not Using New Technology: Ethical and Liability Risks? A Lawyer's Judgment Will Never Be Automated" (2003) 20 GP Solo 21 at 28.

- *Journals*: Check journal literature for explanations and overviews.
- *CLE Seminar papers*: Check for papers presented at conferences.
- *Encyclopedias of law*: Consult Canadian, U.K, or U.S. legal encyclopedias
- *Reference material*: Consult dictionaries, directories, and other reference materials.
- *Case law digests*: Consult standard case law digests (*Canadian Abridgment* in print or on Westlaw Canada or Quicklaw's Canada Digest database) to ensure obvious case law is not being overlooked.
- *Internet searches*: Are their websites relevant to your area of research? Have you conducted a Web search on Google or other search engine?
- *Other jurisdictions*: Have you searched for journals, textbooks, law reform commission reports, cases, or legislation from other jurisdictions, including the U.K, the United States, Australia, or New Zealand?

4. **Primary research (focus and update)**:
   - Read and note up relevant case law.
   - Read and note up relevant statutes and regulations.
   - Keep a good dated log of the sources searched, including the syntax of online searches and the databases searched.

5. **Repeat steps 1 to 4, as needed**.
   It is time to stop the research when you start to repeatedly see references to the same cases or the same materials.

F. CONCLUSIONS

By following the basic legal research skills described in this book, it is hoped that lawyers and legal researchers can avoid or at least minimize the risk of being found liable for legal research malpractice. A common factor of many cases of any sort of professional negligence is likely a combination of inattention to detail, working too quickly, or making incorrect assumptions. By conducting legal research methodically and in a consistent manner that forces you to follow steps like those set out in the checklist, you should be able to avoid any possible claims at the same time as improving the effectiveness and results of your legal research.

G. RESOURCES ON LEGAL RESEARCH MALPRACTICE

Bast, Carol M. & Susan W. Harrell. "Ethical Obligations: Performing Adequate Legal Research and Legal Writing" (2004) 29 Nova L. Rev. 49.

Bigelow, Robert. "Be Careful How You Use Computerized Search Services" (2003) 5 The Journal of Law Office Economics and Management 17.

Butler, Marguerite L. "Rule 11 Sanctions and a Lawyer's Failure to Conduct Competent Legal Research" (2000) The Professional Lawyer 2.

Chester, Simon. "Electronic Malpractice: Does Competence Require Computer Research?" (1991) 17:8 L. Prac. Mgmt. 23.

Daiker, Duane. "Computer-Related Legal Malpractice: An Overview of the Practitioner's Potential Liability" (1995) 69 Fla. B.J. 12.

Davis, Susan E. "Duty to Surf: Do Lawyers Have a Responsibility to Surf the Web for Every Case?" (1998) 18 California Lawyer 63.

Dodge, David D. "Lawyer Not Liable for Negligence Regarding Unsettled Issues of Law" (2000) 36 Ariz. Att'y 20.

Gertner, Eric. "Case Comment: *World Wide Treasure Adventures Inc. v. Trivia Games Inc.*" (December 1987) 2 Leg. Res. Update 10.

Hamner, Claire. "Computer Assisted Legal Research and Legal Malpractice: Is the Future Here?" (1997) 16 Trial Advocate Quarterly 4.

Howe, Robert J. "The Impact of the Internet on the Practice of Law: Death Spiral or Never-Ending Work?"(2003) 18. 8 Va. J.L. & Tech 5.

Karpman, Diane. "Not Using New Technology: Ethical and Liability Risks? Keep up or Face Peril" (2003) 20 GP Solo 20.

MacLachlan, Lawrence Duncan. "Gandy Dancers on the Web: How the Internet has Raised the Bar on Lawyers' Professional Responsibility to Research and Know the Law" (2000) Geo. J. Legal Ethics 607.

Macmillan, John. "The Information Age, Lawyers and Negligence" (1992) 66 Law Institute Journal 138.

Margolis, Ellie. "Surfin' Safari—Why Competent Lawyers Should Research on the Web" (2007) 10 Yale J. L. & Tech. 82.

McCormack, Nancy & Michael Silverstein. "Is Taxonomy Dead? Some Observations on Teaching and Learning How To Do Legal Research in Canada at the Start of the 21st Century" (2007) Can. Legal Educ. Ann. Rev. 145.

Najar, Ola. "Computerized Research in the Legal Arena: Developing a Standard of Research Sufficiency in Legal Malpractice and Rule 11 Actions" (1993) 39 Wayne L. Rev. 1683.

Nayyer, Kim. "The Information Literate Legal Researcher" (2008) 33 Can. L. Libr. Rev. 450.

Newman, Mark J. "Attorney Research Malpractice" (1991) 590 PLI/Comm 11.

North, Ronwyn. "Can You Learn to Think More Carefully" (1995) 33 Law Society Journal 31.

O'Connell, Laura. "Legal Malpractice: Does the Lawyer Have a Duty to Use Computerized Research?" (1984) 35 Federation of Insurance Counsel Quarterly 77.

Pritchard, Teresa N. "Attorneys in the Electronic Information Age: Is There a Duty to Make the Transition" (1988) 62 Fla. B.J. 17.

Richards, J. Kent. "Lawyer Malpractice: The Duty to Perform Legal Research" (1982) 32 Federation of Insurance Counsel Quarterly 199.

Sloane, Richard. "When Ineptness Becomes Frivolous Conduct" (1996) 215 N.Y.L.J. 5.

Sullivan, J. Thomas. "The Perils of Online Legal Research: A Caveat for Diligent Counsel." (2005) 29 Am. J. Trial Advoc. 81.

Tuft, Mark. "Not Using New Technology: Ethical and Liability Risks? A Lawyer's Judgment Will Never Be Automated" (2003) 20 GP Solo 21.

Whiteman, Michael. "The Impact of the Internet and Other Electronic Sources on an Attorney's Duty of Competence under the Rules of Professional Conduct" (2000) Alb. L.J. Sci. & Tech. 89.

Whiteway, Ken. "Research Malpractice" (1990) 15 Can L. Libraries 51.

CHAPTER 12

LEGAL WRITING

A. INTRODUCTION

There is a large number of books already published on legal writing, as witnessed by the lengthy list of legal writing resources listed in Section I at the end of this chapter. Rather than trying to duplicate the effort of other authors on this topic, an attempt is made in this chapter to highlight some of the main points to be made about effective legal writing. To start, there is a discussion of effective legal writing principles. This is followed by a discussion of specific types of legal writing, including case comments, research memos, factums, drafting agreements, and court documents. Readers wanting more details on legal writing can consult the many resources listed in Section I.

B. WHY LAWYERS WRITE LIKE LAWYERS

It is, of course, an indispensable part of a scrivener's business to verify the accuracy of his copy, word by word. Where there are two or more scriveners in an office, they assist each other in this examination, one reading from the copy, the other holding the original. It is a very dull, wearisome, and lethargic affair. I can readily imagine that, to some sanguine temperaments, it would be altogether intolerable.

—Herman Melville, *Bartleby, the Scrivener*

What does it mean to say that lawyers write "like lawyers"? Unfortunately, the impression that some non-lawyers have is that lawyers tend to use too much gobbledygook (or "legalese") when they write and speak. There are several reasons why this has been so. Perhaps the main reason is that lawyers have traditionally been quite conservative, relying upon "tried and true" past precedents.[1] This can sometimes be a good thing since it ensures consistency and safe practice. The problem, however, is that many older precedents used archaic language, Latin phrases, notoriously bad legalese ("the Defendant struck the *said* car"), and redundant expressions or "freight trains" (for example, "null and void"—using void alone is sufficient).[2] Since scriveners were often paid by the number of words they transcribed, there was little incentive for brevity and every motivation to be as wordy as possible, as would have been the case with Melville's Bartleby.

Combined with these factors is the very essence of lawyering—trying to anticipate every possible scenario or risk by "crossing every 't' and dotting every 'i'" when drafting legal documents. This is not always a bad thing but can sometimes be unnecessary, especially when it is being done unconsciously when lawyers are blindly copying past precedents.

Another reason why lawyers write like lawyers is the monopolistic nature of the legal profession and its perceived elite nature. Lawyers were seen to belong to an exclusive, upper-class "club" that did not include the "unlearned" among its members. The very use of legal language—especially when it is capitalized and uses Latin phrases—sounds impressive and was likely used by some lawyers to intimidate people.

In defence of "writing like a lawyer," lawyers do need to use precise language since some legal problems are complex, involve important issues, and must therefore be described in precise terms. In addition, some Latin phrases, such as *res ipsa loquitur* (the "thing" or negligence speaks for itself), have meaning for lawyers and judges and are understood by them without the need for additional explanation.

Fortunately, there has been a movement in North America and elsewhere towards the use of plain English in legal writing, a topic briefly discussed in the next section.

---

1   Timothy Perrin, *Better Writing for Lawyers* (Toronto: Law Society of Upper Canada, 1990) at 3–4.
2   "Freight trains" is a phrase used by Perrin, *ibid.* at 136.

C. THE PLAIN ENGLISH MOVEMENT

In the last thirty years or so there has been a gradual development of the use of plain English in legal writing. Part of this development is likely due to a rise in consumer rights and consumer awareness combined with an increase in the number of lawyers graduating from law schools, lawyers who are no longer coming from an "elite" part of society. These factors from both within and outside the legal profession have resulted in a growing awareness by lawyers of the advantages of using plain English in legal drafting.

The plain English movement in law, however, is not a defined group or organization but instead represents the notion that legal documents should be written using plain words that can be understood by average people. Plain English does *not* mean childish language or simplistic English; instead, it suggests that lawyers should more carefully choose the words they use to be precise and unambiguous (assuming this is desired) yet simple and easily understood (once again, assuming this is desired).

The legal writing literature is full of horrific examples of "legalese" that tend to fall into the following categories:[3]

Table 12.1
Examples of Legalese

Archaic/Bad English	Comments
Aforesaid, henceforth, hereafter, hereby, herein, hereinafter, heretofore, herewith, theretofore	These "chestnuts" are usually redundant or a signal that the sentence should be reworked.
Freight Trains	**Comments**
Have and hold, save and except, keep and maintain, each and every, fit and proper, "situate, lying, and being in"	These "paired" expressions are unnecessary and can usually be reduced to a single term.
Legalese	**Comments**
The undersigned Witnesseth Wherefore the Plaintiff prays that . . . Know All Men By These Presents Said contract	Terms like these are holdovers from days past and should be dropped in favour of plain English equivalents.

---

3   These examples are culled from the various legal writing resources listed in Section I, resources that should be consulted for more detail on effective legal writing.

Clients are often openly grateful when you use language they can easily understand. It is well worth the effort, therefore, to consciously think about your audience and the language you use as you prepare law-related documents.

D. CASE COMMENTS

One of the first legal writing tasks assigned to first-year law students is to write a case comment, often with little or no explanation of what a case comment is or how one goes about writing a case comment. This section will seek to explain such matters.[4]

What is a case comment? Simply put, case comments are short essays that usually analyze a single, recent decision of general interest to practising lawyers or the academic legal community. Case comments abound in a wide variety of formats and styles and are not necessarily entitled "case comments." It is quite easy to find case comments by using legal periodical indexes such as the online version of the *Index to Canadian Legal Literature* (discussed in detail in Chapter 2, Section B). One need merely type in the case name (i.e., the style of cause or the names of the parties) in the *Index* and this will generally identify or list any articles giving significant treatment to that case. Figure 12.1 sets out an example from Westlaw Canada (from the *Index to Canadian Legal Literature*) where a search was conducted on "semelhago /5 paramadevan," which resulted in ten articles regarding that decision.

There are usually no strict requirements or rules for writing a case comment unless one is submitting it for publication in a journal that has its own specific requirements (regarding formatting and footnoting, for example). A typical case comment has the following characteristics:

- *Facts*: There is usually a very brief recitation of the relevant facts to remind the reader about what lead to the dispute. If the facts are not highly relevant to the analysis to be made, this section of the case comment should be kept very brief.
- *Ruling/history*: A case comment also usually provides a brief overview of the history of the case, along with the ruling of the court. This can also usually be kept very brief.

---

4   This material on case comments is based on materials prepared by Shikha Sharma, former Reference Librarian, Bora Laskin Law Library, Faculty of Law, University of Toronto, and training sessions developed by her and the author.

Figure 12.1

Search Results from the *Index to Canadian Legal Literature* on Westlaw Canada

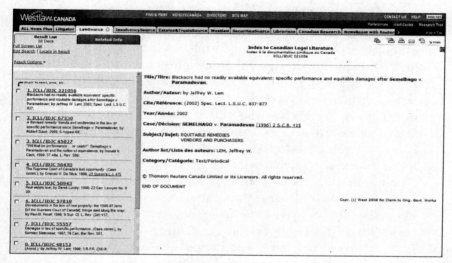

- *Point of law*: It is also fairly standard for a case comment to summarize the relevant point of law for which the case stands and to place this point of law in a larger context, where appropriate.
- *Analysis/argument*: The most important part of a case comment, and the part least susceptible to standardization, is the analysis or argument that the writer brings to the case comment. Possible approaches include but are not limited to the following ideas:
  - » Faulty reasoning or conclusions—the case comment may take the approach, supported by arguments and examples, that the court has applied faulty reasoning or reached the wrong conclusion.
  - » Ground-breaking—alternatively, the case comment may be supportive of the decision in showing how it is a ground-breaking ruling.
  - » Policy issues—another approach is to analyze the decision from a policy point of view. What will the effect of the decision be on Canadian society? Does the decision have implications beyond the needs or rights of the parties to the lawsuit?
  - » Grounds for appeal—if the decision is a trial or provincial Court of Appeal decision, another approach is to write the case comment from the arguments that the losing party would make if the decision were being further appealed.

To prepare for writing a case comment, there are a number of steps that can be taken:

1) *Carefully read the decision*: It is trite advice, of course, for the case commentator to carefully read the decision being commented upon, but this is a critical first step and must often be repeated to carefully analyze the decision, and to follow up and read cases and other academic commentary (if any) cited by the court in its decision.

2) *Note up the decision*: It is usually prudent to note up the decision being commented upon to see if other courts have yet cited the decision. If there is any judicial treatment, these subsequent decisions should ordinarily be reviewed to see if any of them have given any unique or significant analysis of the case being commented upon.

3) *Search for journal articles*: Unless the case being commented upon is a newly released decision, it can be useful to check legal periodical indexes to see if any other writers have commented on the case in question. Even if the case is new, or if there are no other case comments in the case in question, it may be fruitful to search for articles that deal with the same subject matter to see how other authors have dealt with the subject matter.

4) *Look to other jurisdictions*: Another possible approach is to see how courts or academics from other jurisdictions have treated or commented upon the subject matter of the case. To find such viewpoints, use journal indexes, textbooks, or encyclopedias for these foreign jurisdictions, resources that are discussed in more detail in Chapter 2.

E. RESEARCH MEMOS

Another common form of legal writing used by lawyers is the ubiquitous legal research memo (law students, as part of an assignment, are often asked to prepare a memo setting out their opinion or conclusions of law given a particular set of hypothetical facts). More so than case comments, legal research memos have no set format other than the standard opening identifying to whom the memo is being sent, by whom, the date of the memo, and the subject matter of the memo (see the Appendix for a sample legal research memo).

What separates good legal research memos from bad ones are a few basic features:

* *Purpose*: It should be obvious to the reader of the memo why the memo has been prepared. This can be most simply achieved by setting out the purpose of the memo near the beginning (e.g., "You have asked me to research whether an RSP is exigible by a creditor of the holder of the RSP.").

- *Structure*: Good memos have a natural flow or structure. If helpful, "bolded" headings and sub-headings should be used to divide the memo into its constituent parts (e.g., facts, law, academic commentary, analysis, and conclusions).
- *Clarity in writing*: The purpose of a research memo is to impart information clearly and directly with the goal of helping the reader make a decision. Anything in the memo that distracts from this purpose should be eliminated.
- *Footnoting*: There is no strict rule or requirement regarding the footnoting of case and legislative citations in legal research memos. Many people tend to simply cite their material in the text of the memo, without resorting to footnotes. Others, however, find that the use of footnotes is cleaner or neater and can actually act more like a checklist of cases cited, making it easier for office staff to later retrieve those cases, if needed, for a book of authorities if the matter proceeds to a court hearing.
- *Statement of research limitations*: As a general rule, to the extent the legal research memo is a document internal only to the law firm, it is ordinarily important for the writer to explore both sides of any issue being researched and to point out both strengths and weaknesses, along with any limitations on the research being done (i.e., a lack of time) or areas for further research if the matter proceeds further.

Many law firms will archive legal research memos by storing copies of them in separate folders or online databases. This allows the firm to later retrieve the memo if a similar issue on a different file arises.

F. FACTUMS

Factums—or *facta* for the Latin perfectionists—are written arguments or briefs filed in court to advocate a client's legal position before the court. There are technical requirements prescribed by the rules of court for most jurisdictions regarding the length, content, and format of factums. In law school, law students are usually required to participate in a moot court hearing—a mock appeal-level hearing—and as part of this process are required to prepare and file factums. Moot court factum requirements are often prescribed specifically by the law school but often mirror "real life" factums.

Much has already been written about in the legal literature regarding factum preparation (see the resources listed in Section I, below in this chapter), so what follows in this section is nothing more than a simple overview of tips for drafting effective court factums. Readers needing more details should consult the resources at the end of this chapter and any specific court rule requirements of the applicable jurisdiction.

The following pointers apply to most factums, regardless of jurisdiction or level of court; ultimately, one must always check specific requirements before preparing and filing a factum:

- **What is a factum?** A factum is a concise statement, without argument, of the facts and law a party relies upon in an argument before the court.[5] The style of factums in Canada is regarded as a hybrid of the British and American legal practice. The British practice tends to emphasize oral advocacy over written advocacy, such that barristers in England ordinarily only use written "skeletal arguments" on appeal matters, which tend to be only general outlines of their position, requiring instead that they rely upon their oral advocacy. The American practice, however, is to emphasize written argument, since on many applications, counsel may not even be called upon to make submissions or may be under strict time limitations for oral argument. The court will instead rely upon written material (sometimes called a "Brandeis brief") filed in advance of the hearing to make their ruling. In Canada, factums are not usually as detailed as the American approach and are often meant as an outline of counsel's position on the facts and the law. Remaining concise is still very important in Canada, no matter how complicated the issues may be.
- **Structure**: Typical factum requirements suggest an outline or structure that divides the written argument into the following parts:
  - » *Introduction*: Often entitled "Part 1—Nature of the Motion," this part of the factum briefly introduces the party to the lawsuit and the type of relief that is being sought.
  - » *Facts*: Often entitled "Part 2—The Facts," this part of the factum sets out a concise statement of the *relevant* facts. This part does not include extraneous information. Consider using charts or tables if you are compiling a chronology of events. All facts must be supported by affidavit evidence or material forming part of the court record.
  - » *Issues and the Law*: Often entitled "Part 3—Issues and the Law," this part of the factum sets out the issues and legal argument. Stating the issues as statements rather than questions is often more forceful (e.g., "The trial judge erred in her charge to the jury on the issue of reasonable doubt."). The legal argument is often more effective if divided into sections with separate headings. Be

---

5   See, for example, Rule 20.03 of the Ontario *Rules of Civil Procedure*, R.R.O. 1990, Reg. 194.

forceful in your arguments and support all legal propositions with pinpoint citations to relevant case law, preferably from the same or higher jurisdictions.

» *Order sought*: Often entitled "Part 4—Order Sought," this part of the factum sets out the terms of the order the court is being asked to grant.

- **Practice tips**: Effective counsel keep their own library of factums to redeploy and adapt for future hearings, especially for commonly encountered applications such as leave to appeal hearings or applications for security for costs. In addition, although factums are often only required for contentious hearings, it is sometimes effective to prepare factums even where they are not specifically required. This helps to focus your arguments, and if the judge has read the court file before the hearing, this will help focus the judge's mind on your arguments. In the future, expect to see requirements in most jurisdictions for counsel to also file an electronic version of the factum, along with electronic versions of cases being relied upon.

- **Precedents**: The Litigator database on Westlaw Canada is unique in the access provided to court-filed factums (in HTML and the original PDF) from the various leadings cases reported in Carswell print reporters and selected newer cases as well.

G. DRAFTING AGREEMENTS AND COURT DOCUMENTS

Agreements and pleadings are the final major category of legal writing to be discussed in this book. Agreements fall within the realm of traditional solicitor's work—drafting contracts, wills, and corporate documents. Pleadings fall within the realm of traditional barrister's work—drafting court documents, such as pleadings and affidavits, on behalf of a client. Resources on drafting agreements and pleadings are listed in Section I, below in this chapter.

1) Agreements

Lawyers very rarely draft agreements from scratch. We are heavily dependent on forms and precedents available from various commercial publications and on precedents compiled by individual lawyers and law firms and kept internally by the firm. Precedents can be particularly useful for "boilerplate" provisions, which are those standard provisions found at the end of agreements. Boilerplate provisions often include such topics as governing law, resolution of disputes by arbitration, provisions for modifying the agreement, "entire agreement" provisions, warranty provisions, provisions for Acts of God ("force majeure" clauses), time being of the essence, and restrictions on assignment of the agreement. Although boilerplate provisions are not ordinarily required by law, prudence warrants their inclusion in most agreements since these provisions usually anticipate what might otherwise be unforeseen events. As with reliance on any precedent, care must be taken not to slavishly copy the language from the precedent without first adapting it, where necessary, to suit the needs of the client entering into the agreement. There are two major "forms and precedents" sets in Canada—one offered by LexisNexis Canada (*Canadian Forms and Precedents*) and the other offered by Canada Law Book (*O'Brien's Encyclopedia of Forms*).

There are currently a number of titles or topics in the LexisNexis Canada *Canadian Forms & Precedents* series (red and blue binders in print, also available on CD-ROM and by subscription on LexisNexis Quicklaw):

- *Banking & Finance*
- *British Columbia Court Forms*
- *Commercial Tenancies*
- *Corporations*
- *Debtor/Creditor*[6]
- *Employment*
- *Information, Technology & Entertainment*
- *Land Development*
- *Licensing*
- *Sale & Operation of a Business*
- *Sale, Distribution & Transportation of Goods*
- *Wills & Estates*

Canada Law Book has a large, multi-volume series called *O'Brien's Encyclopedia of Forms* (burgundy binders in print, also available online by subscription). The set is currently divided into ten "divisions" or topics, with the forms and precedents being written and commented on by leading practitioners within each field (CD-ROMs are included):

- Division I: Commercial and General

---

6   Coverage in Debtor/Creditor includes bankruptcy, receiverships, restructuring, construction liens, levying execution, commercial landlords' remedies, repair and storage liens, personal property security, bulk sales, oppressive conduct, and fraudulent preferences and conveyances.

- Division II: Corporations
- Division III: Conveyancing and Mortgages
- Division IV: Leases
- Division V: Wills and Trusts
- Division VI: Ontario—Family Law
- Division VII: Labour Relations and Employment
- Division VIII: Ontario—Court Forms
- Division IX: Municipal Corporations
- Division X: Computers and Information Technology

There is a separate "Master Subject Index" volume that provides more detailed access points to help you decide which division or volume to access. There is an online subscription version of this product called O'Briens Internet (www.obriensforms.com) that allows subscribers to fill out forms and precedents via a Web browser and then save them into their desired word processing format.

In addition, the following individual titles provide excellent guidance on drafting commercial documents for the various topics represented by their titles:[7]

- Abe, Lisa K. *Internet and E-Commerce Agreements: Drafting and Negotiating Tips.* 2d ed. Toronto: LexisNexis Butterworths, 2004 (includes CD-ROM).
- Aird & Berlis LLP. *Shareholders Agreements: An Annotated Guide.* 2d ed. Aurora, ON: Canada Law Book, 2009 (includes CD-ROM).
- Beaudin, Patrice & Anne-Marie Laberge. *Recueil des conventions commerciales.* Looseleaf. Montreal: LexisNexis, 2008.
- Earle, Wendy J. *Drafting Arbitration and ADR Clauses for Commercial Contracts: A Solicitor's Manual.* Looseleaf. Toronto: Carswell, 2001.
- Elderkin, Cynthia L. & Julia S. Shin Doi. 2d ed. *Behind and Beyond Boilerplate: Drafting Commercial Agreements.* Scarborough, ON: Carswell, 2005.
- Ewasiuk, Ricky W. *Drafting Shareholders' Agreements: A Guide.* Scarborough, ON: Carswell, 1998.
- Kessler, James & Fiona Hunter. *Drafting Trusts and Will Trusts in Canada.* 2d ed. Markham, ON: LexisNexis Canada, 2007 (includes CD-ROM).
- Klotz, James M. *International Sales Agreements: An Annotated Drafting and Negotiation Guide.* Aurora, ON: Canada Law Book 1997 (includes CD-ROM).

---

7   See also Chapter 8 where resources are organized by topic, including those resources that contain precedents.

- Thibault, Gilles (with the assistance of Denise Trottier). *Carswell's Form and Precedent Collection: Corporate Precedents*. Looseleaf. Scarborough, ON: Thomson Carswell, 2007.
- Watt, David. *Carswell's Form and Precedent Collection: Criminal Precedents*. Looseleaf. 2d ed. Toronto: Carswell, 2007.

2) Pleadings

Pleadings, which are court documents filed on behalf of a client, present a wonderful opportunity for litigation lawyers to be effective legal drafters. Unfortunately, this opportunity is sometimes missed (often due to time constraints) when lawyers fail to appreciate the two main (related) purposes of pleadings: (i) to tell the judge a compelling and easy-to-understand story, and (ii) to resolutely advocate the client's position and win the argument. This opportunity is most often missed when lawyers blindly copy precedents without adapting them to the client's individual situation or when lawyers fail to write vigorously and concisely (i.e., they sometimes ramble on incessantly).

The move to plain English in court documents is welcomed by judges, where documents are organized with headings, are written with short sentences, and do not ramble on. Smart lawyers use the active voice in favour of the passive voice to make their pleadings easier to read and more forceful. Fortunately, there are a number of useful resources to help litigators with drafting:

- Bullen, Edward & Stephen Martin Leake. *Bullen & Leake & Jacob's Precedents of Pleadings*. 16th ed. London: Sweet & Maxwell, 2008.
- Ewaschuk, Eugene G. *Criminal Pleadings & Practice in Canada*. Looseleaf. 2d ed. Aurora, ON: Canada Law Book, 1987. Available on CD-ROM and by subscription online.
- *How Do You Plead? Breaking the Bonds of Boilerplate*. Toronto: Department of Continuing Legal Education, Law Society of Upper Canada, 1994.
- Cromwell, Thomas. *Effective Written Advocacy*. Aurora, ON: Canada Law Book, 2008.
- Van Kessel, Robert J. *Dispositions Without Trial*. 2d ed. Markham, ON: LexisNexis Canada, 2007.
- *Williston and Rolls Court Forms*. Looseleaf. 2d ed. Markham, ON: Butterworths, 1986. Also available on CD-ROM and by subscription on LexisNexis Quicklaw.

H. CONCLUSIONS

Most legal researchers must apply their research in the form of a written memo or opinion letter to the client. Most legal writing is not mandated to follow particular forms, perhaps with the exceptions of court factums, court forms, and other forms of documents or contracts which are regulated by legislation. It is hoped that this chapter has provided a good overview of legal writing issues and that the bibliography that follows can provide readers with additional resources that can answer more detailed questions about legal writing.

I. BIBLIOGRAPHY OF LEGAL WRITING MATERIAL

This section lists some of the more recent publications that discuss legal writing, essays and research papers, factums and court briefs, and agreements. Many of these materials are held by academic law libraries or are available directly from the respective publishers.

1) Legal Writing

Asprey, Michele M. *Plain Language for Lawyers*. 4th ed. Annandale, NSW: Federation Press, 2010.

Bahrych, Lynn & Marjorie Dick Rombauer. *Legal Writing in a Nutshell*. 4th ed. St. Paul, MN: Thomson/West, 2009.

Block, Gertrude. *Effective Legal Writing for Law Students and Lawyers*. 5th ed. New York: Foundation Press, 1999.

Bouchoux, Deborah E. *Aspen Handbook for Legal Writers: A Practical Reference*. 2d ed. New York: Aspen, 2009.

Bronsteen, John. *Writing a Legal Memo*. St. Paul, MN: Thomson/West, 2006.

Brostoff, Teresa & Ann Sinsheimer. *Legal English: An Introduction to the Legal Language and Culture of the United States*. 2d ed. Dobbs Ferry, NY: Oceana, 2003.

Butt, Peter & Richard Castle. *Modern Legal Drafting: A Guide to Using Clearer Language*. 2d. Cambridge: Cambridge University Press, 2006.

Calleros, Charles R. *Legal Method and Writing*. 5th ed. New York: Aspen Law and Business, 2006.

Campbell, Enid, Richard Fox, & Melissa De Zwart. *Students' Guide to Legal Writing and Law Exams*. 3d ed. Annandale, NSW: Federation Press, 2010.

Charrow, Veda *et al*. *Clear and Effective Legal Writing*. 4th ed. Austin, TX: Aspen, 2007.

Clary, Bradley G. & Pamela Lysaght. *Successful Legal Analysis and Writing: The Fundamentals*. 2d ed. St. Paul, MN: Thomson/West, 2006.

Dave, Sandeep. *Plain Language in Law* (8 November 2002). Online: LLRX.com, www.llrx.com/features/plainlanguage.htm.

Dernbach, John et al. *A Practical Guide to Legal Writing and Legal Method*. 3d. ed. New York: Aspen, 2007.

Dick, Robert C. *Legal Drafting in Plain Language*. 3d ed. Scarborough, ON: Carswell, 1995.

Edwards, Linda. *Legal Writing: Process, Analysis & Organization*. 5th ed. New York: Aspen, 2010.

Fitzgerald, Maureen F. *Legal Problem Solving: Reasoning, Research and Writing*. 4th ed. Markham, ON: LexisNexis Canada, 2007.

Garner, Bryan A. *Elements of Legal Style*. 2d ed. New York: Oxford University Press, 2002.

Garner, Bryan A. *The Redbook: A Manual on Legal Style*. 2d ed. St. Paul, MN: Thomson/West, 2006.

Gender-Free Legal Writing: Managing the Personal Pronouns. Vancouver, BC: British Columbia Law Institute, 1998.

Goldstein, Tom & Jethro K. Lieberman. *The Lawyer's Guide to Writing Well*. 2d ed. Berkeley, CA: University of California Press, 2003.

Gordon, Suzanne. *The Law Workbook: Developing Skills for Legal Research and Writing*. Toronto: Emond Montgomery Publications, 2001.

Haggard, Thomas R. *The Lawyer's Book of Rules for Effective Legal Writing*.Littleton, CO: F.B. Rothman, 1997.

Haggard, Thomas R. & George W. Kuney. *Legal Drafting in a Nutshell*. 3d ed. St. Paul, MN: Thomson/West, 2007.

Haggard, Thomas R. & Elizabeth Scott Moïse. *The Scrivener: A Primer on Legal Writing*. 3d ed. Columbia, SC: South Carolina Bar, 2009.

LeClercq, Terri. *Guide to Legal Writing Style*. 4th ed. New York: Aspen, 2007.

Mowat, Christine. *A Plain Language Handbook for Legal Writers*. Scarborough, ON: Carswell, 1999.

Neumann, Richard K. *Legal Reasoning and Legal Writing: Structure, Strategy and Style*. 6th ed. New York: Aspen, 2009.

Oates, Laurel Currie & Anne Enquist. *The Legal Writing Handbook: Analysis, Research and Writing*. 4th ed. New York: Aspen, 2006.

Perrin, Timothy. *Better Writing for Lawyers*. Toronto: Law Society of Upper Canada, 1990.

Ray, Mary Barnard & Barbara J. Cox. *Beyond the Basics: A Text for Advanced Legal Writing*. 2d ed. St. Paul, MN: Thomson/West, 2003.

Ray, Mary Bernard & Jill J. Ramsfield. *Legal Writing: Getting It Right and Getting It Written*. 4th ed. St. Paul, MN: Thomson/West, 2005.

Rossini, Christine. *English as a Legal Language*. 2d ed. London: Kluwer Law International, 1998.

Schiess, Wayne. *Writing for the Legal Audience*. Durham, NC: Carolina Academic Press, 2003.

Shapo, Helene S. *et al. Writing and Analysis in the Law*. 5th ed. New York: Foundation Press, 2008.

Smith, Michael R. *Advanced Legal Writing: Theories and Strategies in Persuasive Writing*. 2d ed. Austin, TX: Aspen, 2008.

Stephens, Cheryl M. *Plain Language Legal Writing*. Vancouver, BC: Plain Language Wizardry Books, 2008. Preview available for on-line download at http://plainlanguage.com.

Tiersma, Peter Meijes. *Legal Language*. Chicago: University of Chicago Press, 2000.

Volokh, Eugene. *Academic Legal Writing: Law Review Articles, Student Notes, and Seminar Papers and Getting on Law Review*. 3d ed. New York: Foundation Press, 2007.

Wojcik, Mark E. *Introduction to Legal English: An Introduction to Legal Terminology, Reasoning, and Writing in Plain English*. 3d ed. Washington, DC: International Law Institute, 2009.

Wydick, Richard C. *Plain English for Lawyers*. 5th ed. Durham, NC: Carolina Academic Press, 2005.

2) Essays/Research Papers

Booth, Wayne C. *et al*. *The Craft of Research*. 3d ed. Chicago: University of Chicago Press, 2008.

Chicago Manual of Style. 15th ed. Chicago: University of Chicago Press, 2003.

Clark, Jessica L. & Kristen E. Murray. *Scholarly Writing: Ideas, Examples, and Execution*. Durham, NC: Carolina Academic Press, 2010.

Fajans, Elizabeth & Mary R. Falk. *Scholarly Writing for Law Students: Seminar Papers, Law Review Notes, and Law Review Competition Papers*. 3d ed. St. Paul, MN: Thomson/West, 2005.

Foster, Steve. *How to Write Better Law Essays: Tools and Techniques for Success in Exams and Assignments*. 2d ed. New York: Pearson Education, 2009.

Turabian, Kate. *A Manual for Writers of Term Papers, Theses and Dissertations*. 7th ed. Chicago: University of Chicago Press, 2007.

Volokh, Eugene. *Academic Legal Writing: Law Review Articles, Student Notes, and Seminar Papers*. 3d ed. New York: Foundation Press, 2007.

3) Factums/Moot Court Briefs

Beazley, Mary Beth. *A Practical Guide to Appellate Advocacy*. 2d ed. New York: Aspen, 2006.

Berry, Carole C. *Effective Appellate Advocacy: Brief Writing and Oral Argument*. 4th ed. St. Paul, MN: Thomson/West, 2009.

Bucholtz, Barbara K. *The Little Black Book: A Do-It-Yourself Guide for Law School Competitions*. Durham, NC: Carolina Academic Press, 2002.

Bullen, Edward & Stephen Martin Leake. *Bullen & Leake & Jacob's Precedents of Pleadings*. 16th ed. London: Sweet & Maxwell, 2008.

Ciampi, Maria L. & William H. Manz. *The Question Presented: Model Appellate Briefs*. Cincinnati, OH: Anderson, 2000.

Cromwell, Thomas. *Effective Written Advocacy*. Aurora, ON: Canada Law Book, 2008.

Crowne-Mohammed, Emir Aly & Mohamed R. Hashim, *The Essential Guide to Mooting: A Handbook for Law Students*. Toronto: Irwin Law, 2010.

Fontham, Michael *et al. Persuasive Written and Oral Advocacy in Trial and Appellate Courts*. 2d ed. New York: Aspen, 2007.

Garner, Bryan A. *The Winning Brief: 100 Tips for Persuasive Briefing in Trial and Appellate Courts*. 2d ed. New York: Oxford University Press, 2004.

Glaser, Cathy *et al. Lawyer's Craft: An Introduction to Legal Analysis, Writing, Research and Advocacy*. Cincinnati, OH: Anderson, 2004.

How Do You Plead? Breaking the Bonds of Boilerplate. Toronto: Department of Continuing Legal Education, Law Society of Upper Canada, 1994.

Morton, James & Michael E. Freeman. *Written Advocacy*. Toronto: Butterworths, 2000.

Perell, Paul M. *Written Advocacy*. Toronto: Law Society of Upper Canada, 1994.

Scalia, Antonin & Bryan A. Garner. *Making Your Case: The Art of Persuading Judges*. St. Paul, MN: Thomson/West, 2008.

Sopinka, John & Mark A. Gelowitz. *The Conduct of an Appeal*. 2d ed. Toronto: Butterworths, 2000.

van Kessel, Robert J. *Dispositions Without Trial*. 2d ed. Markham, ON: LexisNexis Canada, 2007.

Williston and Rolls Court Forms. Looseleaf. 2d ed. Markham, ON: Butterworths, 1986. Also available on CD-ROM and by subscription on LexisNexis Quicklaw.

4) Legal Agreements

Abe, Lisa K. *Internet and E-commerce Agreements: Drafting and Negotiating Tips*. 2d ed. Toronto: LexisNexis Butterworths, 2004 (includes CD-ROM).

Adams, Kenneth. *A Manual of Style for Contract Drafting*. 2d ed. Chicago, IL: American Bar Association, 2008.

Beaudin, Patrice & Anne-Marie Laberge. *Recueil des conventions commerciales*. Looseleaf. Markham, ON: LexisNexis, 2008.

Beaudoin, Louis. *Expressions juridiques en un clin d'oeil*. 3d ed. Cowansville, QC: Éditions Y. Blais, 2005.

Canadian Forms & Precedents (LexisNexis Canada) — various topics (see Section G, above in this chapter, for more details). Available in looseleaf, on CD-ROM, and by subscription on LexisNexis Quicklaw.

Child, Barbara. *Drafting Legal Documents: Principles and Practices*. 2d ed. St. Paul, MN: West, 1992.

Earle, Wendy J. *Drafting Arbitration and ADR Clauses for Commercial Contracts: A Solicitor's Manual*. Looseleaf. 2d ed. Toronto: Carswell, 2001.

Elderkin, Cynthia L. & Julia S. Shin Doi. *Behind and Beyond Boilerplate: Drafting Commercial Agreements*. 2d ed. Toronto: Thomson Carswell, 2005.

Encyclopaedia of Forms and Precedents other than Court Forms. 4th ed. London: LexisNexis United Kingdom, 1964.

Ewasiuk, Ricky W. *Drafting Shareholders' Agreements: A Guide*. Scarborough, ON: Carswell, 1998.

Fox, William F. *International Commercial Agreements: A Primer on Drafting, Negotiating, and Resolving Disputes*. 4th rev. ed. Austin, TX: Wolters Kluwer Law & Business, 2009.

Kessler, James & Fiona Hunter. *Drafting Trusts and Will Trusts in Canada*. 2d ed. Markham, ON: LexisNexis Butterworths, 2007 (includes CD-ROM).

Klotz, James M. *International Sales Agreements: An Annotated Drafting and Negotiation Guide*. Aurora, ON: Canada Law Book, 1997 (includes CD-ROM).

O'Brien's Encyclopedia of Forms. Looseleaf. 11th ed. Aurora, ON: Canada Law Book, 1987. Various topics (see Section G, above in this chapter, for more details). Available in looseleaf, on CD-ROM and by subscription on O'Brien's Internet.

Stark, Tina. *Drafting Contracts: How and Why Lawyers Do What They Do*. New York: Aspen, 2007.

Stark, Tina. *Negotiating and Drafting Contract Boilerplate*. New York: ALM Publications, 2003.

5) Legal Writing Blogs

- AdamsConsulting: www.adamsdrafting.com/system
- Legal Writing Prof Blog: http://lawprofessors.typepad.com/legalwriting

PUTTING IT ALL TOGETHER—A SAMPLE RESEARCH PROBLEM AND MEMORANDUM OF LAW

A. INTRODUCTION

This chapter sets out a hypothetical legal problem and then seeks to answer it using the Legal Research Checklist in Chapter 11, Section E, and the other resources and techniques described in this book. This research culminates in a sample law office memo set out in Section D, below in this appendix.

B. HYPOTHETICAL PROBLEM[1]

You work as a student at the law firm of Berger and Khan in Toronto. A client of the firm is purchasing the ESL 123 Learning Centre chain of private schools (the "new business"). The new business has developed a good reputation for teaching English as a Second Language due to the innovative teaching programs and materials developed by its founder, Monica Lee. As part of the purchase, the client wishes to restrict Monica

---

1   The law firm, company, and facts are fictitious. Although I have made an effort to be thorough and accurate in answering this hypothetical problem, readers of this book should not rely on this research and sample memo for any particular issue on similar facts since the law can change and the research and sample memo may not apply to particular fact situations. Readers needing legal advice should consult their own lawyer.

Lee, the vendor, from competing with the new business after the sale has been completed. The partner acting on behalf of the client has asked you to research the enforceability of non-compete clauses in takeovers and the likely maximum length of time and geographic distance a court would enforce against Monica Lee to prevent her or a new company she controlled from competing with the business being purchased.

C. ANALYSIS AND APPROACH

Since legal research remains an art rather than a science, there is never only one correct way to answer a problem. Instead, so long as one takes a methodical and thorough approach using the major secondary and primary legal resources, there is usually some assurance of finding relevant legal information.

1) Step 1: Facts

Do you have all of the relevant facts? What assumptions are being made? This is the first step of the Legal Research Checklist and also corresponds to the first step of the "FILAC" legal research process discussed in more detail in Chapter 1, Section B.

Arguably, the legal researcher can take the position that he need only research the problem as presented, without having to worry about other possibly relevant facts. This can be dangerous, however, since a change in facts can change the issues which need to be researched. In many cases, the lawyer representing the client is also the same person who conducts the legal research, so there is less chance of miscommunication or a misunderstanding of relevant facts. Where the researcher is not the lawyer dealing directly with the client, however, it is important for the researcher to anticipate questions that may be relevant to the legal issues and to communicate any concerns to the lawyer responsible for the client's file. In the hypothetical scenario above, the legal researcher might consider some of the following questions before beginning the research; alternatively, some of these questions might only arise after the research has begun. It would ordinarily be prudent for the legal researcher to raise these questions or issues with the lawyer (or the client, if appropriate) as the research progresses:

- In what jurisdictions and specifically where do the ESL 123 Learning Centres operate? The answer to this question will impact how broadly the geographic scope of the non-competition clause could be.

- What is the purchase price for the new business? What comprises the goodwill and how much of the purchase price is being allocated towards goodwill? Will Monica Lee continue on as a consultant after the purchase? What is the exact nature of the business and the scope of its contracts, students, copyright, technology, or trade secrets? These questions might not be obvious to the student when starting the research but the issue could affect the duration of the non-competition clause.

- Is Monica Lee represented by her own lawyer? Are there any family members involved in the business against whom non-compete clauses should also be sought? One can likely safely assume that the vendor will have her own counsel (thereby eliminating the need for the vendor to receive independent legal advice), but it is worth determining whether there are other relatives or key employees in the business against whom restrictive covenants should be sought.

2) Step 2: Preliminary Questions and Issues

Once you have considered the facts, it is then important to ask yourself some preliminary questions to help identify the relevant issues. This corresponds to the second step of the FILAC legal research process discussed in more detail in Chapter 1, Section B.

The first two preliminary questions in this step of the Legal Research Checklist are basic questions that should be asked at the start of any legal research problem, even if the research has not formally begun and even if these questions end up being irrelevant:

a) Is there federal, provincial, or municipal legislation that governs this problem?

At this stage, many researchers may not know the answer to this question from first-hand knowledge. If so, it is worth keeping this question in mind as the research progresses. Since, as it turns out, the enforceability of restrictive covenants is governed largely by the common law (i.e., judicial decisions), the question of what legislation governs is not so applicable in this research problem. However, there would likely be legislation impacting the transaction, and the lawyer advising your client would want to check for any applicable legislation governing private schools, for example, and whether the new business is governed by such legislation.[2] In addition, if the purchase is taking place in Ontario

---

2   Depending on the particular programs offered by the ESL 123 Learning Centres, the *Private Career Colleges Act, 2005*, S.O. 2005, c. 28, Sch. L, for example,

and is a purchase of all of the assets of the ESL 123 Learning Centres, the *Bulk Sales Act*[3] might also apply.

The point to make for now is that many, if not most, legal problems are affected by legislation, and it is therefore important to always consider what legislation might apply to the problem. In reality, there is a good chance the instructing lawyer or client may already be familiar with any relevant statutes or regulations governing the operations of the new business or the issues at hand. It would therefore be worth asking the instructing lawyer or the client about this, if only to save time and avoid unnecessary work or research.

b) Is there a limitation period problem?

Once again, the answer to this question may not be immediately obvious, but you should consider potential limitation period issues for every legal research problem. If the client is facing a deadline by which to sue and you or your firm miss the filing deadline pending your research and investigation into the client's more substantive rights, your work on the substantive issues would be wasted and you or your firm would risk being liable for professional negligence in failing to identify the client's limitation period problem.

Since this hypothetical problem anticipates a successful takeover (instead of a dispute), no limitation problem exists *per se*. Assuming this transaction takes place entirely within Ontario (or assuming the parties choose in their contract to have the laws of Ontario apply to the transaction), the client may not be aware of new limitations legislation in Ontario. Section 4 of Ontario's *Limitations Act, 2002*,[4] for example, sets out a basic limitation period of two years that would likely apply if the vendor were to sue for breach of contract or if your client determined that the vendor was carrying on business in violation of the restrictive covenant and wished to sue the vendor:

> 4. Unless this Act provides otherwise, a proceeding shall not be commenced in respect of a claim after the second anniversary of the day on which the claim was discovered.

---

might be relevant and govern their operations. The lawyer acting on behalf of your firm's client would therefore need to work with your client on ensuring all statutory and regulatory requirements for operating the new business have been complied with.

3   R.S.O. 1990, c. B.14. Ontario is the sole remaining jurisdiction in Canada with bulk sales legislation and it is reasonable to assume that its Act will be repealed in the near future.

4   *Limitations Act, 2002*, S.O. 2002, c. 24, Sch. B.

Section 5 of this new Act also codifies the discoverability principle (i.e., that the claim is discovered only when the person knew about it or ought to have known about it). To ensure more certainty, parties in a commercial transaction will often agree to vary or exclude any limitation periods by which either party may sue the other.[5] As such, even though this hypothetical problem does not raise limitation issues, it is worth raising the issue, if only as a trigger to consider whether to vary or exclude limitation periods as part of the purchase contract. Unless the limitation period is an issue, it is not always mentioned in a legal research memo on the more substantive issues.

The other points mentioned in this section of the Legal Research Checklist have you consider how urgently the research is needed, how much time and money can be spent, and whether this research has already been done on another file in the law firm or whether there is someone with expertise on the subject that you can speak to, all important things to consider before beginning the substantive research.

At this stage, you would try to identify the issues that need to be researched. For this problem, the issues are relatively straightforward; with what is known at present, it might be reasonable to frame the issues as follows, keeping in mind the possible need to redefine them as the research progresses:

- What is the likely maximum length of time and geographic distance a court would enforce against a vendor of a chain of English language instruction schools to restrict the vendor from competing with the purchaser after the sale is completed?
- What factors does a judge consider in determining whether restrictive covenants are enforceable?

For the first-time researcher not familiar with this area of law, it may take some time to uncover the various terminology used to describe clauses that attempt to restrict another person from competing. The instructing lawyer referred to "non-compete" clauses, so that is one term to use: Another term you would likely come across is "restrictive covenants" (but realize that the term "restrictive covenants" is also used in real estate law to describe a charge on title). Even if you did not know the possible terminology, you would have also eventually come across "restraint of trade" or "covenant not to compete" as possibly relevant terminology.

---

5   Section 22(5) of the *Limitations Act, 2002, ibid.,* for example, allows parties to a "business agreement" to vary or exclude limitation periods.

3) Step 3: Secondary Research (Start Broad)

By systematically reviewing standard secondary legal resources, you increase the chance of finding commentary that can lead to relevant cases and legislation. This stage of the research roughly corresponds to the third step in the FILAC approach. What follows next is a partial listing of some of the background resources used for this hypothetical research problem, using the categories in the Legal Research Checklist.

a) Treatises

Generally speaking, law-related books are an excellent starting point for any research. You should assume that for any legal issue, someone, somewhere, has written a book or chapter on the topic.

For this topic, some researchers might initially have trouble finding relevant books since the topic of non-competition clauses may be too narrow to warrant a book just on that topic.[6] If you were instead able to identify the issue as falling more generally under contract law, it would be easy to check the indexes of the major Canadian contract treatises to find relevant commentary. Alternatively, searching on Swan's *Canadian Contract Law*, 2d ed., on LexisNexis Quicklaw on the truncated search term <non-compet!>, resulted in eighteen hits, one of which is "9.5.1.—Non-competition Clauses between Buyers and Sellers" (falling under Chapter 9, being "The Control of Contract Power"). Another approach was to search the AMICUS catalogue of Library and Archives Canada[7] on a title keyword search on <non-competition>. This resulted in a number of hits, including reference to a Carswell book from 1995. Clicking on the full record for that title revealed that one of the Library of Congress Subject Headings it was catalogued under was "Covenants not to compete—Canada." Clicking on this link lists out all of the books catalogued on that title (you could then search on only "Coven-

---

6   Even I initially missed (and forgot that at one time I knew about) the following books mentioned in a footnote in Waddam's treatise on contract law: John D. Heydon, *The Restraint of Trade Doctrine* (London: Butterworths, 1971) and Michael J. Trebilcock, *The Common Law of Restraint of Trade* (Toronto: Carswell, 1986). The latter text, although somewhat dated, provides an excellent overview of the history of the common law and also has a chapter specifically devoted to the issue of the enforceability of non-competition clauses in the sale of a business that will be mentioned in the research memo later in this appendix. The point here is to realize the iterative nature of research—even if you miss a resource the first time around, if you are thorough you will often find subsequent references to relevant material, as happened here.

7   The AMICUS catalogue (http//amicus.collectionscanada.ca/aaweb/aalogine.htm) of Library and Archives Canada, in theory, catalogues every book published in Canada. As such, it is an excellent tool to "scope out" possible titles.

ants not to compete" in the Subject field to get a listing of all books on that topic, regardless of jurisdiction).

The relevant passages from the foregoing textbooks were relatively easy to find (using the index or tables of contents in each book or searching by keyword for those books that were available online). If these access points were not obvious enough, another good access point is the Table of Cases to look up known, relevant cases to see if they were discussed in the book. Even if you did not have a known case at hand when starting this stage of the research, you would soon come across references to cases such as *J.G. Collins Insurance Agencies v. Elsley*, [1978] 2 S.C.R. 916, as being a relevant Supreme Court of Canada decision. Looking up this decision in the Table of Cases of the contract law books, for example, leads you to the relevant commentary on this issue, including references to other cases. All of these textbooks provide an excellent overview of the Canadian law and leading cases (and most books also identified relevant case law from England, which has influenced the law in Canada on this issue). From an initial review of some of this material, you start to notice that courts treat non-compete clauses in the sale of a business more liberally than non-compete clauses in an employment context. Reference will be made to some of this material in the sample research memo in Section D, below in this appendix.

Even if you struggled to find relevant books, if you proceeded through the Legal Research Checklist, there is a good chance you would have found other relevant secondary sources, discussed below, that would have alerted you to consider checking a contract law treatise.

b) Journals

Law journals are another excellent source of commentary and will typically discuss relevant case law and legislation, often from a critical or analytical point of view.

A search for article citations in the *Index to Canadian Legal Literature* (the *Index*)[8] on Westlaw Canada revealed a number of relevant hits. The following Boolean operator search commands were used to start, using the exclamation mark to truncate the term: <non-compet!>.This resulted in forty hits, perhaps a large result, but the following items were identified as being potentially relevant from this list:

- Lelia Constantini, Alex Colangelo, & Stuart Carruthers, "Supreme Court Says Ambiguous Non-Competition Clauses not Enforceable: *Shafron v. KRG* and Best Practices in Drafting Restrictive Covenants" (2009) 2 Can. Ins. Reg. Rep. 21.

---

8   The *Index to Canadian Legal Literature* is also available on LexisNexis Quicklaw.

- Jeremy Herbert, "New Tax Laws Put the Squeeze on Non-Competition Payments" (2008) 27 Lawyers Wkly. No. 42 7.
- Jim Hassell & Rebecca Reasner, "Drafting Enforceable Non-Compete Restrictions: 'Shooting for the Moon Will Not Land You in the Stars'" (2007) 16 Can. Corp. Counsel 113.
- Joel Nitikman, "The Nature of a Non-competition Payment" (2005) 63 Advocate (Van.) 49.

In checking the full record of some of these hits, you realize that the *Index* is using "Covenants not to compete" as an official subject heading for this topic. Rerunning your search in the index on that subject heading produces sixty-six hits, which included a few hits not found in the original search, including:

- Sunil Kapur & Brian G. Wasyliw, "*KRG Insurance Brokers (Western) Inc. v. Shafron*: Supreme Court of Canada Rules on Restrictive Covenants and Notional Severance" (2009) 18 Can. Corp. Counsel 49
- Malcolm J. MacKillop, "Enforcement of Restrictive Covenants" (2007) Spec. Lect. L.S.U.C. 297

One thing to notice from the sixty-six hits was mention in several article titles of the tax consequences of non-competition clauses. Although this would ordinarily be of more concern to the vendor, it is important to understand the tax consequences since these might affect the negotiations over the amount of the purchase price to be allocated to goodwill or how to structure the transaction to minimize any adverse tax implications of the purchase.[9]

Although journal indexes are usually the better starting place to look for journal articles, it is often a good idea to complement your journal index searching with searches of full-text journal databases on HeinOnline, LexisNexis Canada, and Westlaw Canada. Searching on HeinOnline has an additional advantage since most of the Canadian law journals on that database predate the *Index to Canadian Legal Literature*, meaning that you can find (older) articles on HeinOnline that you would not find using the *Index* (although for this research problem, older, historical material is going to be less useful).

---

9   The memo that follows raises the issue of tax implications but excludes any detailed analysis from the scope of the memo (i.e., the lawyer did not ask about tax implications so it might be reasonable to assume that the lawyer is familiar with those issues; however, it doesn't hurt to mention the issue in case the lawyer was not aware of that aspect).

c) CLE/Seminar Papers

Papers presented by lawyers at continuing legal education conferences or symposia can be a useful source of research, typically providing a practical—as opposed to academic—point of view. A search on the *Canadian Law Symposia Index* on LexisNexis Quicklaw on <non-compet!> had thirty-five hits, many of which looked possibly relevant, including the following four papers, all of which appear to be very practitioner oriented:

- Mark C. Hogan, "Drafting Non-Solicitation/Non-Competition Covenants" in *The Six-Minute Business Lawyer* (Toronto: Law Society of Upper Canada, 2008).
- Peter H. Griffin, "Non-Competition Covenants" in *The Six-Minute Business Lawyer* (Toronto: Law Society of Upper Canada, 2005).
- Jonathan Levin, "Confidentiality and Non-Competition Clauses and Agreements: What's Effective? What's Enforceable?" in *Negotiating and Drafting Key Business Agreements* (Toronto: Canadian Institute, 2003).
- Philip R. Rosenblatt & Tracy R. Schubert, "Confidentiality and Non-Compete Agreements in Mergers and Acquisitions" in *Negotiating and Drafting Major Business Agreements* (Toronto: Insight Information, 2002).

d) Encyclopedias

Law-related encyclopedias are also an excellent way to get an overview of an area of law and to identify leading cases and relevant legislation. In Canada, there is the *Canadian Encyclopedic Digest* (CED) (Carswell) and *Halsbury's Laws of Canada* (LexisNexis Canada), both discussed in more detail in Chapter 2, Section D.[10]

A search on the CED on <non-compet!> had ninety hits, perhaps too many to bother reviewing (although the relevant results from the "Contracts" title appear early in the results). Narrowing the search to <non-compet! and (sale or purchase or acquir!) /5 business> had nineteen results, which were much more focused. From these results, it was fairly easy to determine that the most relevant section of the CED was under the "Contracts" title within the section on substantive illegality in contract law dealing with contracts in restraint of trade:

---

10 There is also, of course, *JurisClasseur Québec* for civil law, but this hypothetical problem assumes there are no operations within Québec and therefore no need to consult civil law resources.

Contracts

VII Substantive Illegality in Contract Law
    5   Contracts in Restraint of Trade
        (b) Agreements of Employment, Sale and Partnership
            (i)   General
            (ii) Legitimate Interest Requiring Protection
            (iii) Restrictions Respecting Customers
            (iv) Restrictions Respecting Businesses and Employee Capacities
            (v) Geographic and Temporal Restrictions
            (vi) Deprivation of Benefits

These sections contained a lot of relevant commentary and identified a number of cases in the footnotes, cases that will be consulted in Step 4 below. If you only had access to a print version of the CED in a law library, you would find it fairly easy to use, starting with looking up "Contracts" in the Index and looking for entries dealing with illegality and restraint of trade.

For *Halsbury's Laws of Canada*, you can search the online version or use the print Index. Using the Index to the print version was straight-forward, with there being an entry under "N" for "Non-Competition Clauses, between buyer and seller, HCO-152" (note: the content from the encyclopedia mirrors the text of Swan's *Canadian Contract Law* quite closely, presumably since Swan is also the editor of this volume of the encyclopedia).

e) Reference Tools

For this hypothetical problem, it may be unnecessary to consult reference tools such as legal dictionaries, words and phrases services, or legal directories, given that there seems to be sufficient background material from other resources already identified. If during the course of research you came across the various phrases used to describe non-competition clauses, you could look up these phrases using Carswell's print *Words and Phrases* or use its online version or the Canadian Legal Words and Phrases service on LexisNexis Quicklaw. Westlaw Canada's *Words and Phrases* service, for example, defined a "covenant in restraint of trade" by referring to how that phrase was interpreted in two Supreme Court of Canada decisions, both of which appear to be relevant to the issue being researched. As such, using words and phrases services is another technique that can be used to identify possibly relevant case law.

f)   Case Law Digests

Because the enforceability of non-compete clauses is determined by case law, a key part of this research will be checking the standard case law digests to help identify possibly relevant cases.

One easy way to access cases on the *Canadian Abridgment* online is to link to the relevant category from the link provided in the CED. The CED commentary discussed above in Section C.3.d provided links to the following two case digest topics:

- CON.VI.3 Contracts—Illegal contracts (substantive validity)—Contrary to public policy, and
- CML.VI.4 Commercial law—Trade and commerce—Restraint of trade.

Of these two categories, the second seemed to have more relevant cases. Burrowing down within the topic of Commercial law—Trade and Commerce—Restraint of trade, one gets to twenty-three case digests dealing with restrictive covenants in the context of a sale of a business under the following classification:

- Commercial law: VI.4.b.iv.B.1—Trade and commerce—Restraint of trade—Restrictive covenants—Particular situations—Sale of business—General principles

For the print version of the *Canadian Abridgment*, it is simple enough to check the General Index, where there were multiple access points. Under "R" for "Restraint of Trade," for example, there were entries under "Particular situations—Non-competition clauses—Sale of business" referring the reader to specific digest numbers in the "Commercial" volume. There were also relevant entries under "C" for "Contracts" in the General Index. Alternatively, like the situation with the CED, if you had a known case at hand, you could look up the case (in print or online) to see where it fell within the Abridgment classification scheme. If for example, you had earlier found a reference to *Yellowhead Petroleum Products Ltd. v. United Farmers of Alberta Co-operative Ltd.* (2004), 362 A.R. 171 (Q.B.) as possibly being a relevant case, you could find other "like" cases by looking up this decision in the *Canadian Abridgment* to see how it was classified and where it fell within the *Canadian Abridgment* classification scheme (which for that decision was "Commercial law (VI.4.b.ii): Trade and commerce—Restraint of trade—Restrictive covenants—Whether covenant reasonable"). You could then browse any applicable *Abridgment* categories for additional relevant cases.

The Canada Contracts Digest on LexisNexis Quicklaw indexes cases on this topic under the following tree structure of categories:

Canada Contracts Digest
  Validity
  Public Policy
  – Agreements in restraint of trade CTR780
  – Restrictive covenants CTR 785

The cases found using the *Canadian Abridgment* and the Canada Contracts Digest and those mentioned in the various other secondary resources will be reviewed and noted up in Step 4 below, and the relevant cases will be discussed in detail in the research memo.

g) Internet Search

Google should never be your sole source for conducting legal research. However, searching on the Internet is worthwhile to supplement the results you have uncovered using the resources above. For this hypothetical problem, searching for the words <non-compete sale business> in my custom Google search engine of the websites of Canadian law firms and law-related blogs (http://tinyurl.com/canadianlawfirms) produced some useful results identifying leading cases and dealing with strategies to consider for buying or selling a business. Because it is now so easy to do, never rule out doing a quick Internet search on your topic to supplement your other research of secondary resources. You might be surprised by what you find.

h) Resources from Other Jurisdictions

The final part of this section of the Legal Research Checklist exhorts the researcher to consider the need to research the law in other jurisdictions. This is important especially where you are not finding a lot of relevant Canadian federal or provincial material. The quickest way to get an overview of the law in a different jurisdiction is to check for textbooks, journal articles, or legal encyclopedia entries for the jurisdiction in question. In this particular hypothetical situation, since there appears to be no lack of material on point, and since some of the Canadian textbooks already identified British cases, it is likely unnecessary to do a separate check for British, American, or Australian resources.

Having said that, however, you should try to develop instincts for when to look at the law in other jurisdictions. British law, for example, is often worth checking on issues of common law where one wishes to get a "classic" view of the law. Whenever researching the law outside of Canada, however, it is always necessary to be wary of possible differences between the law and policies in the foreign jurisdiction and in Canada.

For this hypothetical problem, out of curiosity, I checked *Halsbury's Laws of England* on LexisNexis Quicklaw, where there was relevant commentary under the topic "Competition—Trade and Freedom to Trade—Restraint of Trade." On a quick glance, the position in England appears to be similar to the Canadian position. Likewise, the American *Corpus Juris Secundum* encyclopedia on Westlaw Canada identified relevant commentary under "Contracts, IX. Illegality, C. Agreements Contrary to Public Policy, 5. Agreements in Restraint of Trade, a. In General" that also appeared to be consistent with the Canadian position:

> § 252 CJS: Where the covenant in restraint of trade is an incident of a business transaction, such as the sale of a business or the dissolution of a partnership, the courts are more liberal in their determination of what is a reasonable restraint than where the covenant is an incident of an employment contract.

At this stage of the research, you will have likely uncovered some relevant commentary. What is not clear from the foregoing description, however, is the fact that you often uncover more material once you start reading what you have uncovered on your first "go around" and that once you start checking various references, you will end up with additional commentary you might have missed the first time around. Hence, the importance to treat the research process as iterative or circular and the need to be both flexible and tenacious to pick up on cross-references to other material as you go through the material you have uncovered.

4) Step 4: Primary Research (Focus and Update)

Once the foregoing secondary or background resources have been reviewed, the researcher is then obliged to consult any relevant legislation or case law identified within the secondary literature and also to search for any additional legislation or case law that may have been overlooked or not yet identified in the secondary literature. It is also necessary to note up any relevant legislation or case law, a step that can sometimes identify other relevant, more recent information.

a) Legislation
Legislative research for this hypothetical problem was already briefly mentioned in Section C(2), above in this appendix, when asking one of the preliminary questions—is there federal, provincial, or municipal legislation governing this problem? Because the reasonableness of non-compete clauses in the sale of a business is determined by the courts, there is not any relevant legislation on the specific topic of the reasonableness of a covenant not to compete in this particular hypothetical problem.

b) Case Law

At this stage of the research, it is critical for the researcher to carefully read the cases uncovered so far and to consider searching for additional or more recent cases not yet identified in the secondary resources.

In addition to the searches mentioned in Step 3 using the *Canadian Abridgment* and other resources, a number of Boolean searches were also conducted in the full-text case law databases on LexisNexis Quicklaw and Westlaw Canada, using a variety of terms to identify cases involving the enforceability of non-compete clauses. The full-text searches that were done resulted in similar cases as those that were found above using the classification scheme in the *Canadian Abridgment*.

It is then important to note up relevant cases to ensure those cases were not reversed on appeal and to see how they have been cited by subsequent judges. Noting up cases can also help you identify other cases, since later cases that have considered the case being noted up are usually relevant either on the facts or the law or both.

Where time and money permit, and depending on the importance of the issue or how certain the law appears to be, the careful legal researcher will also note up all cases using the online citators from more than one service, whether it be the free noter-upper on CanLII or the subscription-based services on BestCase, LexisNexis Quicklaw, or Westlaw Canada, since differences in scope, coverage, and treatment do arise among the various noter-uppers.[11]

5) Step 5: Repeat Steps 1 to 4 (as Needed)

It is time to stop the research when you start to see references to the same cases or materials repeatedly.

Repeating Steps 1 to 4 of the Legal Research Checklist is not always done in real life, either due to a shortage of time or money, or because the issues and law are not that difficult and sufficient resources were found. In a real-life situation, unless the client has a lot of money to spend, it is unlikely that you would be able to necessarily exhaust all of the resources and follow all of the steps listed above due to the costs involved. At a minimum, starting with textbooks and perhaps the *Canadian Encyclopedic Digest* alone may be a sufficient starting point for researchers on a budget, followed up by checking a few of the leading cases. Regardless, it is somewhat comforting that many of the second-

---

11   See, for example, Greg Wurzer, Aleksandra Zivanovic, & Rhonda O'Neill, "Canadian Electronic Citators: An Evaluation of their Accuracy and Efficiency" (2004) 29 Canadian Law Libraries Review 68.

ary resources explored here referred to the same or similar cases and issues, something that helps confirm the analysis to be given in the legal research memo, a sample of which follows in Section D below.

D. SAMPLE RESEARCH MEMO

Based on the foregoing research, the following legal research memo was drafted. Following this memo are comments on specific sections of the memo.[12] The persons named in the sample memo are fictitious and any resemblance to real persons or situations is purely coincidental. In addition, although the memo is believed to be accurate as of the date indicated in it, readers of this book should not rely on the memo as legal advice but should instead consult their own lawyers if they have questions regarding the appropriateness or enforceability of a non-compete clause in connection with the sale of a business.

---

12   Footnotes in the memo that follow assume that the memo is separate from both this appendix and the footnotes in the appendix up to this point.

MEMORANDUM

To: Pat Partner
From: Robin Researcher
Date: 1 February 2010

Subject: File 96,344—Non-compete Clauses in the Purchase of a Business

---

You asked me to research the enforceability of a covenant made by a vendor of a business to not compete with the business after the sale has completed, and the likely maximum duration and geographic limitation of restrictions a court would enforce against the vendor. We act for the proposed purchaser of the ESL 123 Learning Centre chain of English language instruction schools. As part of the purchase, our client wishes to restrict Monica Lee, the owner of ESL 123, from competing with the business once our client has purchased it.

Conclusions

1. A covenant by Monica Lee for her or any entity under her control to not compete with the new business will be enforceable where she has been paid for the goodwill in the business and the time and geographic scope of any limitation on her competing with the business are reasonable to protect our client's investment.

2. Because each sales transaction will have unique aspects, there is no "chart" that can be consulted to determine what time or geographic restriction will be reasonable in any given situation. However, based on what you have told me, and based on past court decisions involving the sales of similar businesses, an agreement to not compete for anywhere from three to five years within the cities where the schools operate would most likely be upheld as being reasonable. If the client can show the need for a longer period of time or wider geographic scope to protect his investment, it might be possible to seek longer and wider restrictions.

3. Despite the deference by courts to the wishes of parties of equal bargaining power to agree to a non-competition clause in the context of a sale of a business, there is a risk in seeking an overly lengthy time restriction or broad geographic scope since some courts have questioned their power to either "blue pencil edit" or notionally sever any offending term of the restrictive covenant, resulting in

some situations where the clause is instead held unenforceable (as opposed to being "read down" to reasonable terms).

4.   However, there are a number of drafting considerations identified in the literature you should consider to help minimize such risk and to ensure the enforceability of the non-compete clause. These considerations are discussed in the Analysis section of this memo.

Facts and Assumptions

My research assumes the following facts:

1.   The vendor, Monica Lee, is selling the ESL 123 Learning Centre chain of English language schools to our client. As you mentioned, Lee is the "heart and soul" of the business and has developed innovative training materials and techniques to improve the ease by which students can learn. These materials, including various trademarks and copyrighted teaching materials, will be assigned to the client as part of his purchase.

2.   The ESL 123 Learning Centres operate in 7 cities throughout southern Ontario.

3.   The vendor is represented by her own counsel.

4.   Our client is concerned to not have Monica Lee go into competition with the business after he has acquired it.

I confirm that you are handling any tax issues arising out of our client's acquisition as well as investigating any regulatory requirements our client may face in operating the business.

Analysis

1)   Restraints of Trade at Common Law

The traditional view is that any attempt to restrain a person from carrying on his or her trade is contrary to public policy and *prima facie* void. In reviewing the history of the common law of restraint of trade from the Elizabethan era to modern times, Professor Trebilcock comments on why such restraints were disfavoured:

> Protection of the right to work was considered to be in the public interest, not only because the maintenance of a fair and just economic order was in the public interest, but also because it was understood as preventing the collective labouring potential of the society from being reduced and wasted.[1]

---

1   Michael J. Trebilcock, *The Common Law of Restraint of Trade* (Toronto: Carswell, 1986). at 1–2.

However, an absolute ban on restraints of trade was too harsh in some circumstances. As such, the early common law eventually developed to the point where restraints of trade, while *prima facie* void, could be enforced, if the restraint was reasonable. This more modern view was first articulated just over 100 years ago in England in *Nordenfelt v. Maxim Nordenfelt Guns and Ammunition Co. Ltd.*[2] That case involved an inventor of quick-firing guns who sold his patents and business and agreed, on a worldwide basis, to not carry on the business of the manufacture of guns and ammunition for twenty-five years or otherwise compete against the purchaser "in any way." In upholding the restrictive covenant (except for the latter part on not competing "in any way," which was too broad), the court held that, under the circumstances, the restrictive covenant was reasonable. In so doing, it looked to whether the restraint was reasonable in reference to both the interests of the parties and the interests of the public:

> [R]estraints of trade and interference with individual liberty of action may be justified by the special circumstances of a particular case. It is a sufficient justification, and indeed it is the only justification, if the restriction is reasonable—reasonable, that is, in reference to the interests of the parties concerned and reasonable in reference to the interests of the public, so framed and so guarded as to afford adequate protection to the party in whose favour it is imposed, while at the same time it is in no way injurious to the public.[3]

In that decision, the House of Lords commented on the fact that restrictive covenants given by the seller of a business are different than those imposed upon an employee and should be treated more liberally since there is more freedom of contract between the vendor and purchaser of a business:

> To a certain extent, different considerations must apply in cases of apprenticeship and cases of that sort, on the one hand, and cases of the sale of a business or dissolution of partnership on the other. A man is bound an apprentice because he wishes to learn a trade and to practise it. A man may sell because he is getting too old for the strain and worry of business, or because he wishes for some other reason to retire from business altogether. Then there is obviously more freedom of contract between buyer and seller than between master and servant or between an employer and a person seeking employment.[4]

---

2   [1894] A.C. 535 (H.L.).
3   *Ibid.* at 565.
4   *Ibid.* at 566.

2)   Restrictive Covenants in the Sale of a Business

In Canada, numerous commentators have noted that courts have consistently viewed restrictive covenants in the context of the sale of a business more liberally than those in employment contracts. For example, in *Canadian Contract Law*,[5] Swan comments on the fact that where vendors are being fairly compensated for the sale of their business, giving up the right to compete will ordinarily not be unfair:

> When the goodwill has been purchased for a significant amount and the bargain is fair — as with legally advised parties it is almost certain to be — the seller who argues that the restriction on its right to compete with the purchaser [is unenforceable] cannot expect to find a sympathetic court.[6]

Likewise, in *Canadian Contractual Interpretation Law*,[7] Hall notes that the courts' concern over restricting employees from working in an employment situation is due to a concern over inequality of bargaining power between employer and employee, a concern not usually present in a commercial transaction where the parties usually have some sophistication and are represented by counsel:

> The balancing of competing interests generally plays out differently in the case of a contract for the sale of a business (in which a party sells a business and agrees not to compete with the business for a period of time) and in the case of an employment contract (in which an employee agrees not to undertake certain lines of business in competition with his or her employer for a period of time after leaving the employer). In the employment context, courts are less apt to enforce a restrictive covenant because of concerns about inequality of bargaining power, a policy concern affecting the interpretation of employment contracts generally, whereas there can be very good reasons having no taint of oppression for a contract for the sale of a business to contain a restrictive covenant.[8]

---

5   Angela Swan (with the assistance of Jakub Adamski), *Canadian Contract Law*, 2d ed. (Markham, ON: LexisNexis Butterworths, 2009). See also Stephen M. Waddams, *The Law of Contracts*, 5th ed. (Aurora, ON: Canada Law Book, 2005) at paras. 564–66 and Gerald H.L. Fridman, *The Law of Contract in Canada*, 5th ed. (Toronto: Carswell, 2006) at 390–93.

6   *Swan, ibid.* at §9.263

7   Geoff R. Hall, *Canadian Contractual Interpretation Law* (Markham, ON: LexisNexis, 2007).

8   *Ibid.* at 277.

In addition, in *The Law of Contracts*,[9] McCamus notes the mutual benefits of a non-competition clause to each the seller and buyer:

> [B]oth the seller and the purchaser of the business have a legitimate interest in the enforceability of the restraint for it is only if the restraint can be enforced that the seller can effectively transfer the goodwill of the business. It is in the interest of the buyer to acquire the goodwill and in the interest of the seller to receive consideration for its transfer.[10]

A series of Supreme Court of Canada decisions documents the Court's more liberal attitude towards enforcing non-competition agreements given in the context of the sale of a business:

- In *Hecke c. Cie de gestion Maskoutaine*,[11] at issue was a non-competition clause to not "carry on, whether directly or indirectly, the business of manufacturing sash and doors, general woodwork" for a period of ten years given by a manufacturer of doors when he sold his business to the plaintiff. In upholding the reasoning of the trial judge in ruling that the clause was not unreasonable, the Supreme Court of Canada agreed that "it is well settled that a restrictive covenant of the type in issue here, contained in a contract of sale, is valid if it does not go beyond what is reasonably necessary for the protection of the purchaser."[12]
- A few years later, the Supreme Court of Canada issued its ruling in *J.G. Collins Insurance Agencies v. Elsley*,[13] regarded by many as the leading case in this area. Although in that case there was a restrictive covenant preventing the seller of an insurance agency from competing for ten years, at issue was a separate employment agreement governing the vendor's post-sale employment in which the vendor agreed to work for the new business and not compete for a period of five years after he left employment, with the parties agreeing to liquidated damages if that covenant were broken. As such, this decision involved interpretation of a restrictive covenant in the employment context. When the seller resigned from the business he had sold, and started a new general insurance agency, he was found to have been in breach of that employment covenant—which was held to be reasonable—and an injunction was granted and damages

---

9   John D. McCamus, *The Law of Contracts* (Toronto: Irwin Law, 2005).
10   *Ibid.* at 449.
11   [1972] S.C.R. 22.
12   *Ibid.* at 24.
13   [1978] 2 S.C.R. 916 [*Elsley*].

awarded based on the stipulated amount. In so ruling, the Supreme Court of Canada applied the "reasonableness test" as to whether the restrictive covenant was reasonable between the parties and with reference to the public interest:

> A covenant in restraint of trade is enforceable only if it is reasonable between the parties and with reference to the public interest. As in many of the cases which come before the courts, competing demands must be weighed. There is an important public interest in discouraging restraints on trade, and maintaining free and open competition unencumbered by the fetters of restrictive covenants. On the other hand, the courts have been disinclined to restrict the right to contract, particularly when that right has been exercised by knowledgeable persons of equal bargaining power. In assessing the opposing interests the word one finds repeated throughout the cases is the word "reasonable." The test of reasonableness can be applied, however, only in the peculiar circumstances of the particular case. Circumstances are of infinite variety. Other cases may help in enunciating broad general principles but are otherwise of little assistance.[14]

The court noted the benefit to the vendor in agreeing to not compete and that the sale of a business context usually does not raise concerns about inequality of bargaining power as can be present in an employer/employee situation:

> The distinction made in the cases between a restrictive covenant contained in an agreement for the sale of a business and one contained in a contract of employment is well-conceived and responsive to practical considerations. A person seeking to sell his business might find himself with an unsaleable commodity if denied the right to assure the purchaser that he, the vendor, would not later enter into competition. Difficulty lies in definition of the time during which, and the area within which, the non-competitive covenant is to operate, but if these are reasonable, the courts will normally give effect to the covenant.
>
> A different situation, at least in theory, obtains in the negotiation of a contract of employment where an imbalance of bargaining power may lead to oppression and a denial of the right of the employee to exploit, following termination of employment, in the public interest and in his own interest, knowledge and skills obtained during employment. Again, a distinction is made. Al-

---

14 *Ibid.* at 923.

though blanket restraints on freedom to compete are generally held unenforceable, the courts have recognized and afforded reasonable protection to trade secrets, confidential information, and trade connections of the employer.[15]

- Two years later in *Doerner v. Bliss & Laughlin Industries Ltd.*,[16] the Supreme Court of Canada upheld a five-year agreement to not compete North American–wide by the vendor of a business that manufactured chair bases and controls (for adjusting chair heights). In noting the different treatment given to non-competition clauses in the context of the sale of a business, the Court confirmed the reasonableness of the clause:

> In my view, the covenant was clearly reasonable considering the interests of the parties. The purchaser, having paid for the goodwill, was entitled to the five-year protection. The business had been conducted by the [vendors] personally. They knew all the customers and enjoyed a virtual monopoly in the field in Canada. In the eyes of the public they were the business. It was this fact which made their continuation in the business so desirable, and their competition with the business so dangerous. The falloff in the business done by the company after the [vendors] commenced a competitive operation in 1974 bears testimony to this proposition. While, as Dickson J. has said in *Elsley*, each case must be decided on the basis of its own peculiar facts, a review of the various cases on this subject . . . would indicate that the restrictions imposed in the case at Bar fall within the range of others which have been found acceptable.[17]

- Most recently, the Supreme Court of Canada in *Shafron v. KRG Insurance Brokers (Western) Inc.*[18] confirmed its adoption of the reasoning in *Nordenfelt v. Maxim Nordenfelt Guns and Ammunition Co. Ltd.* that restrictive covenants in the context of the sale of a business are different and should be treated more leniently:

> It is important at this juncture to differentiate between a contract for the sale of a business and an employment contract.
>
> . . .
>
> The sale of a business often involves a payment to the vendor for goodwill. In consideration of the goodwill payment, the cus-

---

15 *Ibid.* at 924.
16 [1980] 2 S.C.R 865.
17 *Ibid.* at 874.
18 2009 SCC 6.

tom of the business being sold is intended to remain and reside with the purchaser . . .

And as stated by Dickson J. (as he then was) in *Elsley v. J. G. Collins Insurance Agencies Ltd.*, [1978] 2 S.C.R. 916, at p. 924:

> A person seeking to sell his business might find himself with an unsaleable commodity if denied the right to assure the purchaser that he, the vendor, would not later enter into competition.[19]

The *Shafron* decision will be reviewed in more detail below on the issue of whether a court may sever all or part of an unreasonable non-competition clause.

3) Onus of Proving Reasonableness of Non-competition Clause

Although in some cases the court does not specifically address the onus of proving the reasonableness of a non-competition clause, in *Elsley* the Supreme Court of Canada stated that the onus is on the party seeking to enforce a covenant in restraint of trade to establish that it is reasonable in the interests of the parties and the onus for establishing that it is not reasonable in the public interest is on the party opposing enforcement.[20] However, in many of the cases, the focus is on the reasonableness of the clause in relation to the parties, with there being much less of an analysis of the impact on the public interest. In many situations where there is a competitive industry—such as with insurance and travel agencies and likely, one could argue, with English language instruction schools—a vendor would be hard-pressed to establish a negative impact on the public interest. Certainly, this was the attitude of the Supreme Court of Canada in *Elsley* regarding the non-impact of the transaction in that case on competition within the insurance industry:

> There were twenty to twenty-two general agents in Niagara Falls according to the evidence as of the date of trial, employing eighty to ninety employees. There was nothing to suggest that the people of Niagara Falls would suffer through the loss, for a limited period, of the services of Elsley in the general insurance business.[21]

To give you a sense of the approach of other Canadian courts, set out below from oldest to most recent is a brief summary of some of the

---

19   *Ibid.* at paras. 18 and 21.
20   *Elsley*, above note 13 at 928.
21   *Ibid.* at 929.

more important cases involving the enforceability of non-competition clauses in the context of the sale of a business:

- *Cope v. Harasimo*:[22] A covenant by a vendor—unlimited in time—to not compete within a twenty-five-mile radius of the beauty shop she sold to the plaintiff was upheld as being reasonable in time and geographic scope.
- *Tank Lining Corp. v. Dunlop Industrial Ltd.*:[23] The court upheld a two-year covenant to not compete anywhere in Canada regarding the sale of a business for lining the inside of railway tanker cars.
- *Gelco Express Ltd. v. Roberts*:[24] The B.C. Court of Appeal upheld an injunction restraining the vendor of a courier company who sold his business for $200,000 from engaging in the courier business for a period of five years in Victoria, Nanaimo, and within 100 miles of Vancouver. The court noted that the agreement had a clause indicating that a breach of the covenant would result in irreparable harm and that the purchaser had a legitimate business interest to protect.
- *Blair v. Reynaud*:[25] In this case, the court enforced a five-year covenant to not compete within a fifty-mile radius against the vendor of a bulk food business who sold his interest in the business to his father-in-law for $25,000 cash.
- *Woodward v. Telco Inc.*:[26] Although this case involved a restrictive covenant in an employment context, the court upheld the covenant where the employee, a senior member of management, agreed to a special retirement package in return for not competing with the company upon retirement. The court was satisfied that there was no inequality of bargaining power and that the agreement was otherwise reasonable.
- *Capital Safe & Lock Service Ltd. v. Sleeves*:[27] The court upheld a ten-year restrictive covenant given by a vendor of a locksmith business who agreed to not compete within 100 miles of Fredericton. The court deferred to the parties' agreement as evidence of reasonableness of the transaction:

> In a sale of business context, deference for the views and wishes of the parties, as expressed in their contractual arrangements, should

---

22 (1964), 48 D.L.R. (2d) 744 (B.C.C.A.).
23 (1982), 40 O.R. (2d) 219 (C.A.).
24 1985 CarswellBC 1729 (C.A.).
25 (1992), 41 C.P.R. (3d) 169 (Ont. Ct. Gen. Div.).
26 (1998), 80 C.P.R. (3d) 319 (Ont. C.A.), leave to appeal to the S.C.C. refused, 1999 CarswellOnt 5723 (S.C.C.).
27 2000 NBCA 1.

weigh heavily in the balance when courts pass judgment on the vendor's post-sale contention that his or her restrictive covenant is unreasonable.[28]

- *Burns v. Shoppers Drug Mart (London) Ltd.:*[29] The court upheld a ten-year covenant to not compete within ten miles of Brockville given by the vendor of a pharmacy business: "[The vendor] had the benefit of legal advice and accounting advice and discussed the non-competition clause with his legal counsel and his accountants."[30]
- *Brouwer Claims Canada & Co. v. Doge:*[31] In this case, there was a non-competition agreement of twelve months and a fifty-mile radius entered into by the defendant when he sold his insurance business to the plaintiff and became an employee of the plaintiff in Vancouver. On leaving that employment and opening up his own insurance business in Abbotsford outside the fifty-mile radius, he was still found to be in breach of the non-competition agreement because, although contracts were entered into in the Abbotsford office outside of the restricted zone, he was dealing with clients within that restricted zone.
- *Industrial Rush Supply & Service Ltd. v. Farina:*[32] In this case, the court enforced an injunction restricting the vendor of a business that distributed ball bearings, power transmission, hydraulics, and pneumatics from competing with the business. In this case, the vendor had also entered into an employment agreement with the new business and agreed to not compete for two years after his employment within sixty kilometres of the business. Regarding the restriction as "essential" to protect the purchase of the goodwill of the business, the court went on to rule, however, an unlimited term preventing solicitation of customers and to not engage in "similar" business as being unreasonably broad.
- *Yellowhead Petroleum Products Ltd. v. United Farmers of Alberta Co-Operative Limited:*[33] This case involved an agency agreement between two companies (as opposed to an employer/employee relationship) for the sale of fuel products. In the agreement, the plaintiff agreed to not compete within defined territories or within thirty kilometres of any point from the boundary of the territories for a period of three years

---

28   *Ibid.* at para. 34.
29   2000 CarswellOnt 851 (S.C.J.).
30   *Ibid.* at para. 6.
31   2002 BCSC 988.
32   (2003), 32 B.L.R. (3d) 306 (Ont. S.C.J.).
33   2004 ABQB 665.

after termination of the agreement. On terminating the agreement, the plaintiff sought a declaration declaring the restrictive covenant unenforceable. However, in upholding the non-competition clause, the court noted that there was no inequality of bargaining power and held the parties to their agreement:

> There is authority that requires equal contracting parties to be bound by their agreements (particularly in a case such as this where there are mutual benefits, equal bargaining strength, involvement of counsel, negotiation and re-drafting of the clause in question, express acknowledgment of reasonableness, and waiver of defenses). Accordingly, I am loathe to interfere with the bargain struck by the parties, particularly in light of [the plaintiff's] express agreement to be bound by that bargain, based on the case law and the principles surrounding restraint of trade.[34]

- *Kent Building Supplies v. Magazine du Ridge Ltée:*[35] In this case, the court upheld an agreement made by an experienced businessman when he sold his home renovation store for substantial value and had agreed to not compete for five years within 200 kilometres of Campbellton, NB:

> The facts before me would indicate that [the vendor] sold his business to Kent at a very substantial value. He was an experienced businessman and had competent independent legal advice. He knew that a part of the deal was that he would not participate in or be concerned with a business competitive with Kent. He was aware that he had agreed to avoid, either by himself or in conjunction with any other person, any act that may be detrimental to Kent's business in the Atholville area for a period of five years.
>
> There can be no doubt that the restrictive covenant set out in the non-competition agreement was enforceable as a reasonable restraint of trade.[36]

- *Anderson v. Berry-Heldt:*[37] The B.C. Court of Appeal affirmed the trial judge's decision that a one-year agreement to not compete with the travel business in the Western provinces of Canada (including Ontario) contained in a three-way shareholder's agreement was not unreasonable, especially given that the agreement was freely negotiated.

---

34 *Ibid.* at para. 81.
35 2004 NBQB 152.
36 *Ibid.* at paras. 26–27.
37 2005 BCSC 1825, aff'd 2007 BCCA 100.

Applying the factors from the foregoing cases to our client's situation would suggest that a covenant in the sale agreement by Monica Lee for her to not compete with the new business will be enforceable where she has been paid for the goodwill in the business and the time and geographic scope of any limitation on her competing with the business are reasonable to protect our client's investment.

Since, as was suggested in *Elsley*, "the test of reasonableness can be applied . . . only in the peculiar circumstances of the particular case" and "[o]ther cases may help in enunciating broad general principles but are otherwise of little assistance,"[38] the best determination of what will be reasonable in our client's situation will be what you and our client see as being necessary to protect our client's investment. There are a number of factors you should consider:

- The parties will have negotiated what will presumably be a fair value for the goodwill and will both be mutually benefitting from the transaction;
- The vendor is represented by her own counsel; and
- Given the vendor's expertise and unique teaching resources, it is reasonable for our client to want to restrict the vendor from re-deploying that expertise and those resources in a business in competition with our client.

4) Time and Geographic Restrictions

In my opinion, and based on my review of the cases, it is likely that a court would not be too concerned by a time restriction of three to five years in our client's situation. In fact, in a number of cases, a longer period of time has certainly been held to be enforceable, and if our client has any particular reason to think he will need a longer period of time, you should discuss those reasons with him and whether you should seek a longer term.

In *Connors Brothers Ltd. v. Connors*,[39] at issue was whether a covenant to not compete in the sardine business across Canada was enforceable. In ruling that the covenant was reasonable, the court suggests that where the geographic scope is reasonable, an unlimited time scope will most always be reasonable: "If the restriction as to space is considered to be reasonable it is seldom in a case where the sale of a goodwill is concerned that the restriction can be held to be unreasonable because there is no limit as to time."[40] However, the foregoing has been cited

---

38　*Elsley*, above note 13 at 923.
39　[1941] 1 D.L.R. 81 (P.C.).
40　*Ibid.* at 98.

only twice in Canadian judgments—without any particular analysis—so it may be an overstatement of the law.

As to a geographic restriction, a court would most likely hold as reasonable a restriction limiting the vendor from competing within the geographic boundaries of the seven cities in which ESL 123 currently operates. To extend the geographic restriction more broadly may require some evidence that the vendor had plans in fact to expand across the province (or to other jurisdictions).[41] When drafting the geographic scope, it is also important to accurately define the scope so that there is no ambiguity whether a particular location is included or excluded (an issue in the *Shafron* decision discussed immediately below).

5) Severance of Unreasonable Clause

One issue to consider is the risk of being greedy in seeking an overly broad time or geographic limitation in the non-competition clause. When courts determine that a particular non-competition clause is unreasonable, they are often reluctant to reduce it to terms that are reasonable since that would be re-writing the parties' contract and also creating incentives for employers to impose overly broad conditions, knowing that a court will "save the day" by reducing the conditions as needed. Indeed, this was the position taken by the Supreme Court of Canada last year in *Shafron v. KRG Insurance Brokers (Western) Inc.*:[42]

> Where the provision in question is a restrictive covenant in an employment contract, severance poses an additional concern. While the courts wish to uphold contractual rights and obligations between the parties, applying severance to an unreasonably wide restrictive covenant invites employers to draft overly broad restrictive covenants with the prospect that the courts will only sever the unreasonable parts or read down the covenant to what the courts consider reasonable.[43]

At issue in *Shafron* was a non-competition clause in an employment contract restricting an insurance broker to not compete for three years

---

41   See, for example, §475 of the Contracts title of the *Canadian Encyclopedic Digest*, which states as follows: The protected geographic area must relate to the business being sold and not to the area in which the plaintiff, subsequent to the date of the agreement, operates other businesses of which the business being sold thereafter becomes a part, because legitimate protection for potential future growth of a company may not be extended to a much greater area than that occupied at the time of sale: *McAllister v. Cardinal*, [1965] 1 O.R. 221 (H.C.J.).

42   Above note 18.

43   *Ibid.* at para. 33.

within the "Metropolitan City of Vancouver" (which is not a proper geographic description—there is no Metropolitan City of Vancouver). In ruling that the geographic scope was ambiguous, the court had to then decide whether it had power to sever the clause through "blue-pencil" severance or "notional" severance.

"Blue pencil" severance is only available where a court is able to strike out an illegal portion of the contract by drawing a line through it, leaving the portions that are not tainted by illegality, without affecting the meaning of the part remaining.[44] That was not an option in that case since simply deleting the phrase "Metropolitan City of Vancouver" would have affected the remaining part of the sentence:

> I am of the opinion that blue-pencil severance may be resorted to sparingly and only in cases where the part being removed is clearly severable, trivial and not part of the main purport of the restrictive covenant. However, the general rule must be that a restrictive covenant in an employment contract found to be ambiguous or unreasonable in its terms will be void and unenforceable.[45]

The Court also ruled that notional severance—which involves reading down an illegal provision in a contract that would be unenforceable in order to make it legal and enforceable—was also not available here because there was no "bright line" to decide what the parties intended by the phrase "Metropolitan City of Vancouver." In so doing, the court suggested that notional severance has no place in the construction of restrictive covenants in employment contracts:

> However, I am also of the view that notional severance has no place in the construction of restrictive covenants in employment contracts. In my opinion, there are at least two reasons why it would be inappropriate to extend the doctrine of notional severance to the case of restrictive covenants in employment contracts.
>
> First, there is no bright-line test for reasonableness. In the case of a contract that provides for an illegal rate of interest, for example, notional severance has been used to bring the rate down to the legal rate of 60 percent. In *Transport*, the evidence was that the parties did not intend to enter into an illegal contract, and what must be done to make the contract legal was quite clear. The Court inferred that the parties' original common intention was to charge and pay the highest legal interest rate and notional severance was applied to read down the rate to the highest legal rate.

---

44   *Ibid.* at para. 29.
45   *Ibid.* at para. 36.

In the case of an unreasonable restrictive covenant, while the parties may not have had the common intention that the covenant be unreasonable, there is no objective bright-line rule that can be applied in all cases to render the covenant reasonable. Applying notional severance in these circumstances simply amounts to the court rewriting the covenant in a manner that it subjectively considers reasonable in each individual case. Such an approach creates uncertainty as to what may be found to be reasonable in any specific case.

Second, applying the doctrine of notional severance runs into the problem identified by Lord Moulton in *Mason*. It invites the employer to impose an unreasonable restrictive covenant on the employee with the only sanction being that if the covenant is found to be unreasonable, the court will still enforce it to the extent of what might validly have been agreed to.

Not only would the use of notional severance change the terms of the covenant from the parties' initial agreement to what the court thinks they should have agreed to, it would also change the risks assumed by the parties. The restrictive covenant is sought by the employer. The obligation is on the employee. Having regard to the generally accepted imbalance of power between employers and employees, to introduce the doctrine of notional severance to read down an unreasonable restrictive covenant to what is reasonable provides no inducement to an employer to ensure the reasonableness of the covenant and inappropriately increases the risk that the employee will be forced to abide by an unreasonable covenant.[46]

There is a good argument that *Shafron* should be limited to non-competition clauses in employment contracts (and not to situations involving the sale of a business where there are not the same concerns regarding inequality of bargaining power and where there is some evidence of reasonableness, as defined by the parties). Nonetheless, there is a risk that an overly broad non-competition clause in the context of the sale of a business may be held to be unenforceable as opposed to being read down to what is reasonable.

Drafting Strategies

There are a number of possible drafting strategies you may wish to consider to help improve the enforceability of the non-compete clause. For

---

46 *Ibid.* at paras. 37–41.

example, Mark Hogan in "Drafting Non-Solicitation/Non-Competition Covenants"[47] suggests a number of tips, including:

- Put the non-compete clause in a separate agreement (but referenced in the main sale documentation) to minimize the risk of a judicial ruling of the non-compete being unenforceable affecting the validity of the main transaction.
- Have the parties expressly acknowledge in writing in the non-competition agreement that they are both represented by counsel, have carefully considered the terms of the clause, and agree that they are reasonable and mutually beneficial, and that the time and geographic restrictions on the vendor reflect the value and other consideration ascribed by both parties to the goodwill of the business.
- Have the parties agree that irreparable harm would be suffered by the purchaser if the restrictive covenant were breached and that damages would be an inadequate remedy.
- Include a standard "severability" clause in which the parties agree that if any part of the agreement is determined to be illegal or unenforceable, this does not affect the enforceability of the remaining clauses.

Other possible strategies might include the following:

- Have the parties acknowledge in a separate clause that some form of restrictive covenant is needed to protect their mutual interests, and then set out the specific time and geographic scope in the next clause. In that way, if the specific time and geographic scope were ruled to be unreasonable and hence severable, there would remain an agreement that some restriction is needed, thereby giving the court the room needed to determine what is reasonable.
- Consider having the time limitations broken down into one or more terms that are automatically renewed until their conclusion. In *Rogers Communications Inc. v. Shaw Communications Inc.*,[48] for example, the parties agreed to not compete for two consecutive periods of five years by defining the period of non-competition in these terms:

> 2(a) For a period commencing on the date hereof and ending 5 years from the date of closing, and
>
> (b) For a further period of 5 years after the end of the period referred to in paragraph 2(a).

---

47 Mark C. Hogan, "Drafting Non-Solicitation/Non-Competition Covenants" in *The Six-Minute Business Lawyer* (Toronto: Law Society of Upper Canada, 2008).

48 (2009), 63 B.L.R. (4th) 102 (Ont. S.C.J.).

Although there was no need to rule on the reasonableness of this "five and five" time restriction, the court assumed this was a deliberate technique to minimize the risk of a ten-year clause alone being struck down:

> The terms of the covenants are for five years followed by a further five years. This split into two five year periods was obviously to protect against the risk that a court might think that ten years was too long but five not.[49]

- Another technique to consider is the one used in *Burgess v. Industrial Frictions & Supply Co.*[50] In that case, the vendor sold his shares and agreed that he would not compete for five years. However, the vendor also agreed to be paid for his shares in ten annual instalments but only to the extent that he would "continuously act and conduct himself as a fiduciary" to the new business. Six years post-sale, the vendor went to work for the defendant's main competitor at which point the defendant stopped paying the annual instalment on the grounds that the vendor had breached his fiduciary duty. The majority ruling of the B.C. Court of Appeal regarded this arrangement not as a prohibition against the vendor working but as an enforceable "economic disincentive" and that if the vendor were to choose work which did not permit him to maintain his fiduciary duty to act in the best interests of Industrial, he would lose his right to payment.[51]

If interested, there is a sample non-competition agreement precedent by Jennifer Babe in *Canadian Forms and Precedents*[52] that incorporates many of the "tips" above that I will leave on your desk.

If you have any questions or concerns, please let me know.

Appendix—Resources Consulted

Books

Fridman, Gerald H.L. *The Law of Contract.* 5th ed. Toronto: Carswell, 2006.

Hall, Geoff R. *Canadian Contractual Interpretation Law.* Toronto: LexisNexis Canada, 2007.

---

49   *Ibid.* at para. 41.
50   (1987), 12 B.C.L.R. (2d) 85 (C.A.).
51   *Ibid.* at para. 29.
52   Jennifer Babe, "2F108 Non-Competition Agreement" in *Sale and Operation of a Business—Canadian Forms & Precedents*, looseleaf (Markham, ON: LexisNexis, 2007) (available on LexisNexis Quicklaw).

McCamus, John D. *The Law of Contracts.* Toronto, ON: Irwin Law, 2005.

Swan, Angela (with the assistance of Jakub Adamski). *Canadian Contract Law.* 2d ed. Toronto: Butterworths, 2009.

Trebilcock, Michael J. *The Common Law of Restraint of Trade.* Toronto: Carswell, 1986.

Waddams, Stephen M. *The Law of Contracts.* 5th ed. Aurora, ON: Canada Law Book, 2005.

Articles
Griffin, Peter H. "Non-Competition Covenants" in *The Six-Minute Business Lawyer* (Toronto: Law Society of Upper Canada, 2005).

Hassell, Jim & Rebecca Reasner. "Drafting Enforceable Non-Compete Restrictions: 'Shooting for the Moon Will Not Land You in the Stars'" (2007) 16 Can. Corp. Counsel 113.

Hogan, Mark C. "Drafting Non-Solicitation/Non-Competition Covenants" in *The Six-Minute Business Lawyer* (Toronto: Law Society of Upper Canada, 2008).

MacKillop, Malcolm J. "Enforcement of Restrictive Covenants" (2007) Spec. Lect. L.S.U.C. 297.

Nitikman, Joel. "The Nature of a Non-competition Payment" (2005) 63 Advocate (Van.) 49.

Encyclopedias
Canadian Encyclopedic Digest. 3d ed. Contracts: VII — Substantive Illegality in Contract Law 5 — Contracts in Restraint of Trade, (b) — Agreements of Employment, Sale and Partnership

Halsbury's Laws of Canada, "Contracts," paras. HCO-152

Case Law Digests
Canadian Abridgment: Commercial law: VI.4.b.iv.B.1 — Trade and commerce — Restraint of trade — Restrictive covenants — Particular situations — Sale of business — General principles (Westlaw Canada)

Canada Contracts Digest — Validity — Public Policy — Agreements in restraint of trade CTR780 (LexisNexis Quicklaw)

Canada Contracts Digest — Validity — Public Policy — Restrictive covenants CTR 785 (LexisNexis Quicklaw)

E. COMMENTS ON THE SAMPLE RESEARCH MEMO

The drafting of the memo represents the fourth and fifth stages of the FILAC legal research process discussed in Chapter 1, Section B (analysis and conclusions). What is not shown here are the detailed notes that must be taken by the researcher when reviewing the primary sources of law in Step 4 of the Legal Research Checklist.

In addition, what is not explicitly evident in the materials above is the circular or iterative nature of the legal research process. The very nature of this process reinforces the value of being as thorough as possible in following the various steps in the Legal Research Checklist since, even if you perhaps miss an obvious source in one of the steps, there is a good chance you will stumble across the reference to the source in another stage of the process.

The point here is to realize that the effective researcher will pick up on clues and references and not be shy to revisit or repeat earlier steps in the research process. At a certain point, when the same references and cases start to reappear consistently, that may be a good sign that you have come close to exhausting the research for that topic.

It is extremely useful for the research memo to contain an Appendix of resources consulted. This gives some assurance to the reader that standard materials were not overlooked and also makes it easier later for anyone needing to update the research. In addition, some law firm memos might be organized along the lines of numbered "legal issues" as opposed to using the headings in the sample research memo. Because the issues were so straightforward in this problem, it was felt to be unnecessary to use a separate, bolded heading called "Issues." In more complex problems, it can often be useful to list the issues and answer each issue individually, in order.

Here are some additional comments on the sample memo:

- Most readers want to know your conclusions right away; hence, the "Conclusions" is the first major section of the memo. This results in the "Analysis" section later in the memo being somewhat repetitive, but by this stage, the reader can quickly skim the details if she is satisfied with the information by that point.
- The summaries of cases are also somewhat repetitive but many lawyers who read memos like to get a sense of what the relevant cases are about and to get some (but not too many) quotations from actual decisions.

- You will see that I intentionally did not deal with the tax aspects of non-competition clauses (which can be complicated). I did this in part because that was not asked (and perhaps not needed).

There is no right or wrong way to organize a memo so long as the method used is logical and has some flow to it. Writing a memo can be a very organic process and the writer of the memo may very well change his organization, ideas, and even conclusions as to what the state of the law is as the memo is being drafted and revised.

Finally, equally important to what is expressed in the legal memo is what is contained in the legal research folder. Ideally, the researcher has a file containing detailed and dated notes showing what resources were consulted, what online searches were conducted (and on which databases), and what cases and legislation were consulted. Such notes, especially if the Legal Research Checklist is followed, go a long way to defeating allegations of legal research malpractice and ensuring high quality legal research results.

GLOSSARY

[Words in boldface within the definitions are defined elsewhere in the Glossary]

Abridgment: In legal literature, a summary or digest of a court case. Many publishers provide compilations of these summaries or digests organized by topic or theme. A well-known case law digest in Canada is Carswell's *Canadian Abridgment*, available in print, on CD-ROM, and on Westlaw Canada (by subscription). It has summaries of Canadian court decisions, organized by topic. LexisNexis Quicklaw has an online digest service in its Canada Digests database. See Chapter 2, Section E for more information on abridgments.

Bill: A draft piece of legislation introduced in the applicable legislature. Most often, it is the ruling party that introduces draft legislation, but members of the opposition can also introduce bills; however, opposition bills generally do not pass the requisite three readings needed to become law if they are too controversial. Bills can be public (if they are of general application) or private (if they only affect one organization or entity). A bill must pass all three readings and come into force prior to the proroguing of the legislature to become law. See also **Prorogued**.

Blog: Shorthand for "weblog," a website containing posts or entries on particular topics. Entries are usually displayed in reverse chronological order and allow comments to be added to each post. The Canadian Law Blogs List (www.lawblogs.ca) lists hundreds of Canadian law-related blogs.

Bluebook: The colloquial name of the legal **citation** guide used in the United States. Its formal name is *The Bluebook: A Uniform System of Citation* (published by the Harvard Law Review Association and revised regularly).

Boolean operators: Search commands used by Internet search engines and commercial online legal databases to allow the researcher to combine keywords. The typical Boolean operators are AND, OR, and NOT. Some search engines also allow the NEAR command (such as "wiretap NEAR unauthorized") or proximity searches, typically using the "within" command placing the words "within" so many words of each other ("wiretap /3 unauthorized"). Check the "search tips" provided with most search engines to create more precise search strategies.

Canadian Legal Information Institute (CanLII): A free online database containing legislation and case law for all Canadian jurisdictions (www.canlii.org). Similar Legal Information Institutes are available for other countries, including Australia, the United States and the United Kingdom.

Case comments: Structured "critiques" or comments on recent cases of significance. They are discussed in detail in Chapter 12, Section D.

Catchwords: Legal publishers sometimes add **headnotes** or summaries of facts and law to court cases that they publish. Above the headnote and usually after the **style of cause** (the names of the parties to the lawsuit), the publisher may add "catchwords" (often in italics) that are the keywords by which the publisher has "tagged" or identified a particular case. Browsing through the catchwords can be a quick way of getting an idea of the relevancy of the case.

C.I.F. or CIF: In legal research parlance, C.I.F. stands for "coming into force" and is used by **Queen's Printers** to indicate in a Table of Public Statutes when an amendment to the statute comes into force. Example from the *Statutes of Canada* Table of Public Statutes: CIF, 1995, c. 45 in force 01.03.96 see SI/96-23. The foregoing example tells the reader that Chapter 45 of the 1995 *Statutes of Canada* is in force on 1 March 1996, as per a government order registered as SI/96-23 (which can be found in the *Canada Gazette Part II*).

Citation, legal: Most people do not like legal citation, but it is important. It refers to the numerous technical rules for citing cases, legislation, and other law-related materials. Some of these rules can be memorized; most of them must be checked by consulting the McGill Guide, the standard legal citation guide in Canada, more formally known as the

Canadian Guide to Uniform Legal Citation. See also **Bluebook**, **McGill Guide**, and **Neutral citation**.

Competent lawyer: The Law Society of Upper Canada, in its *Rules of Professional Conduct* (discussed in Chapter 1, Section A(1)) recognize that legal research and writing are fundamental skills of a competent lawyer.

Cookies: In Internet vocabulary, cookies are strings of computer-level information communicated between your Web browser and the website you are visiting, assuming you have "enabled" your browser to accept cookies. If your Web browser is so enabled, your computer will store information in a document called "cookies.txt" about the sites you have visited. When you next visit the same sites, information from your "cookies.txt" file will be used to help identify you and your preferences to the site you are visiting. Cookies are discussed in more detail in Chapter 5, Section O.

Defendant: The person being sued by the **plaintiff** in a civil lawsuit. In the **style of cause** *Smith v. Jones*, one can assume that Jones is the defendant being sued by Smith (but this is not necessarily always the case since Smith could have originally been a defendant, and if Smith lost at trial and there was an appeal decision, the appellant in some **jurisdictions** is sometimes the first named party in the **style of cause**).

Dictionaries, legal: Provide simple definitions of law-related words, including more difficult legal or Latin phrases. They are discussed in more detail in Chapter 2, Section F(1). See also **Words and phrases**.

Ejusdem generis: Literally "of the same kind." A rule used in statutory interpretation that presumes that a general term following a list of specific terms will be limited to the more specific term — in other words, the general term will be defined to be "of the same kind" as the more specific preceding terms. See Chapter 3, Section F for an example.

Electronic footprint: Internet and Web browser technology results in data being created every time one "surfs the net." There are a variety of "electronic footprints" that one can leave when using a Web browser. Chapter 5, Section O discusses electronic footprints in more detail.

Expressio unius est exclusio alternius. Literally "to express one thing is to exclude another"; also known as the implied exclusion rule. This rule suggests that if the legislature left something out, it intended to do so since if it had wanted to include something it would have expressly set it out. See Chapter 3, Section F for an example.

Factum: A written argument or brief filed with the court that is used by a lawyer to argue a motion or case before a judge. Most **jurisdictions** have relatively strict rules regarding the contents and form of a factum. Chapter 12, Section F discusses factums in more detail.

Field or **segment**: Most online commercial legal databases organize information, whether it be a case, a **statute**, or a journal article, into fields (on LexisNexis Quicklaw, they are called segments). You may not automatically see or recognize the fields when you look at the information on the screen, but you should realize the advantage of being able to search on particular fields in order to make your search results more precise. Examples include searching for cases by a particular judge, searching for cases before or after a particular date, and searching for cases involving a particular person or company.

FILAC: The five-step approach to legal research identified by Maureen Fitzgerald (and discussed in more detail in Chapter 1, Section B). The five letters in the acronym stand for the five stages of the legal research process that researchers should address: Facts, Issues, Law, Analysis/ Application, and Conclusions.

Forms and precedents: Sample agreements and court documents produced commercially by legal publishers or privately by lawyers and law firms. Most forms and precedents use a "fill in the blank" approach, requiring users to use their own judgment in properly adapting the form or precedent to suit the particular transaction for which it is being prepared.

Gazette. An official publication of the government (provincial or federal) through which the government publishes new **regulations** and announces other official government action, including proclamation dates for new legislation.

Generalia specialibus non derogant. Literally "the general does not detract from the specific." This maxim suggests that courts prefer specific provisions over provisions of general application where the provisions are in conflict. See Chapter 3, Section F for an example.

Governor General in Council or **Lieutenant-Governor in Council**: The Queen in Canada is represented federally by the Governor General and provincially by the various Lieutenant-Governors. In legal research parlance, you will often see in **statutes** the phrase that the "Governor General in Council" or "Lieutenant-Governor in Council" be empowered to enact **regulations**. This does not mean these representatives of the Queen are themselves drafting regulations; instead the task is effectively left in the hands of Cabinet and committees of Cabinet who would carry out the regulatory-making powers and submit the necessary paperwork to the Governor General (or Lieutenant-Governor, provincially speaking) for signature.

Hansard: The official verbatim transcripts of Parliamentary debates in Canada (federal and provincial) and England. In Canada, Hansard debates are now available through the websites of the applicable government (see Table 5.10 in Chapter 5, Section H for a list of the Canadian federal and provincial government websites).

Headnote: A summary of a case provided by the publisher. A headnote typically provides a brief summary of the facts, the ruling by the court, and a summary of the reasons of the court in support of its ruling.

HeinOnline: An Internet subscription database available at www.heinonline.org that has, among other things, hundreds of full-text law journals available in PDF format, usually from the first volume of the journal. It has great historical coverage.

Invisible Web: Also known as the "deep Web." The invisible Web refers to Internet information not found by normal search engines, such as Google, and is located on a company's proprietary server instead of the free World Wide Web. There are special websites, discussed in Chapter 5, Section C, that help identify the invisible Web.

ISP (Internet Service Provider): A company that provides individuals or organizations access to the Internet through a subscription. Increasingly in Canada, ISPs offer a flat monthly rate for unlimited access (7 days a week/24 hours a day) to the Internet. ISPs are competing with each other to also provide faster Internet access through digital lines or cable modems.

Journal indexes: Used to help identify relevant journal articles. Most indexes are organized by topic or keyword, author, and title. In Canada, there are two primary journal indexes: the *Index to Canadian Legal Literature* (available in print and online) and the *Index to Canadian Legal Periodical Literature* (available in print only). Journal indexes are discussed in more detail in Chapter 2, Section B.

Judicial history: The course or path a case has taken through the court system, from a trial decision, to a court of appeal, and possibly to the Supreme Court of Canada (note that not every trial decision gets appealed). One of the reasons you "note up" a case is to ensure the case you are reading has not been reversed or varied on appeal. See also **Judicial treatment** and **Noting up**.

Judicial precedent: See *Stare decisis*.

Judicial treatment: How subsequent judges have applied, distinguished, or otherwise considered a case. Shown as "Summary of Judicial Consideration" on LexisNexis Quicklaw's Quickcite database.

Jurisdiction: At one level, jurisdiction refers to a set boundary or territory; hence, "Canada" is a jurisdiction with specific borders and defined geographic space. Jurisdiction also refers to a notion of juridical power; hence, one can speak of "federal" or "provincial" jurisdiction (based on the division of powers in the *Constitution Act, 1867*) or whether, for example, a small claims court judge has jurisdiction (i.e., legitimate power) to hear a defamation claim.

Legalese: The jargon used by some lawyers, especially in the old days (e.g., "WHEREFORE BY THESE PRESENTS . . ." at the start of an agreement). It is to be avoided.

LexisNexis Quicklaw: LexisNexis Quicklaw (www.lexisnexis.com/ca/legal/) was one of the first companies in the world to create online, searchable databases of information. Since the 1970s, Quicklaw has grown in depth and ease of use to include not only Canadian cases, legislation, journal articles, textbooks, and news, but also to include law-related material from the United States, the United Kingdom, Australia, Africa, and the Caribbean.

Library of Congress Subject Headings (LCSH) and Classification: Legal materials (typically books) need to be organized on the shelf to allow for the orderly retrieval of information. The Library of Congress in Washington, D.C. has a system for organizing material by topic that is used by major libraries throughout the world. Library of Congress Subject Headings are a controlled vocabulary used to describe the topic of a book. Thus, all books in a law library that relate to human rights law in Ontario will be assigned the subject heading "Human rights — Ontario" and searching in an online library catalogue on that specific subject heading will retrieve *all* books on that subject held by the library. Related to these subject headings are Library of Congress call numbers that are assigned to a book depending on the book's topic. The "Law of Canada" is usually assigned the starting letters "KE" followed by a number that relates to the topic (KE 850 would likely be a book on Canadian contract law). Some Canadian law libraries, however, use the "KF" letters to organize their Canadian legal materials (KF is ordinarily the "Law of America" and when Canadian law libraries use KF for Canadian materials, it is referred to as "KF Modified").

Listservs or **online discussion groups**: These groups are organized by many topics and allow one to register or subscribe using e-mail. Once one has subscribed, messages can be sent and received to all subscribers to the group. This allows for the exchange of information and ideas. Law-related listservs are discussed in more detail in Chapter 5, Section K.

McGill Guide: The colloquial name given to the *Canadian Guide to Uniform Legal Citation* (Carswell), the standard reference book in Canada to cite legal materials. The McGill Guide is discussed in detail in Chapter 1, Section D.

Netletters: Online newsletters published by Quicklaw on a variety of topics. These netletters, prepared by experts in their fields, provide regular (usually weekly) updates of all developments within a particular area of law for the preceding period.

Neutral citation: A fairly new method of citing cases by the case name, case number, and level of court. It is "neutral" citation to the extent that this basic citation would remain the same even if a commercial legal publisher later reported the same case and assigned its own publication's citation to the case. Neutral citation is discussed in more detail in Chapter 1, Section D.

Noscitur a sociis: Literally "one is known by one's associates." This maxim suggests that courts should look to the common features of words linked by "and" or "or" and limit the interpretation of those words to fit within the scope of those terms. See Chapter 3, Section F for an example.

Noting up: The process of verifying or updating your legal research. You can, and should, note up cases, legislation, and any information found in a looseleaf book where supplemental information is provided. You note up a case for two reasons: (i) to ensure it has not been reversed on appeal (you check its **judicial history**), and (ii) to see how later courts may have interpreted your case (you check its **judicial treatment**). You note up legislation to ensure that the provision you are looking at has not been amended or repealed. See also **Judicial history** and **Judicial treatment**.

Order-in-Council: An official decision or order made by Cabinet. Orders-in-Council are officially issued by the Governor General at the request of Cabinet at the Federal level.

Parallel citation: Multiple citations for the same case. In other words, important cases are often reported by more than one publisher in various case law reporters. That case will therefore have multiple citations. Each of those citations is referred to as a parallel citation since it leads you to the same case (albeit in different sources).

Plaintiff: The person who initiates a civil lawsuit by suing the **defendant**. In the **style of cause** *Smith v. Jones*, one can assume that Smith is the plaintiff being sued by Jones (but this is not necessarily always the case since Smith could have originally been a defendant, and if Smith lost at trial and there was an appeal decision, the appellant in some **jurisdictions** is sometimes the first named party in the style of cause).

Primary legal resources: Traditionally, those sources of law, such as legislation and the decisions of courts and tribunals, which have the power to directly affect people's legal rights.

Proclamation: An official announcement by the government, often through the **Governor General** or the **Lieutenant-Governor**. Some statutes will state that they come into force on proclamation. In these situations, the government will announce the proclamation date in the applicable *Gazette*.

Prorogued: When Parliament is prorogued, it means that a session has been formally ended and all Parliamentary business, including sittings of Parliament and draft **bills**, is at an end. Unless the government specifically states, prior to proroguement, that a bill will be carried over to the new session, all bills are said to "die on the Order paper" at the time Parliament is prorogued.

Queen's Printer: Traditionally a branch of government that acted as the government's official publisher and that published legislation on behalf of the government. In recent years, there has been a move by some governments to either privatize their publishing or to require their publication branches to show a profit.

Regulations: Legislation enacted by the government ordinarily only where a particular statute authorizes the government to enact such regulations. Since the **statute** usually speaks of delegating the power to enact regulations to a Minister, to Cabinet or to an appropriate statutory body, regulations are often referred to as delegated legislation. See also **Statutory instrument**.

Royal Assent: The symbolic but necessary formal approval of all federal or provincial legislation by the Queen given on her behalf by the **Governor General** (federally) or the applicable **Lieutenant-Governor** (provincially). Approval is by way of signature.

Secondary legal resources: Background material (such as textbooks, journal articles, encyclopedias, and case law digests) used to help locate **primary legal resources** (such as cases and legislation). Secondary legal resources are discussed in Chapter 2.

SOR: Stands for "Statutory Orders and Regulations" and refers to federal regulations (enacted since the most recent Consolidated version of the regulations) in the *Canada Gazette Part II*. In French, it is abbreviated DORS and stands for Décrets, ordonnances et règlements. Example: SOR/98-176 refers to the *Hazardous Products (Glazed Ceramics and Glassware) Regulations*, and it was enacted in 1998 as Regulation 176.

Standing order: The arrangement made between a legal publisher and its customer for the customer to automatically be sent the new edition or the new annual version of a publication.

Stare decisis: Literally "to stand by things decided," *stare decisis* is a rule that requires judges to follow or obey the rulings of other judges higher in the judicial hierarchy and is similar to the concept of a binding judicial precedent. When the facts in Case A are similar to Case B, the judge in Case B must follow the ruling in Case A if the judge in Case A is from a higher court in the same **jurisdiction**.

Statute: A written law debated and voted upon by elected officials. Statutes can be amended or repealed, so it is critical to ensure that one is consulting an up-to-date version of the statute. Statutes are discussed in more detail in Chapter 3.

Statutory instrument: A regulation or other order or rule created by the government (see Chapter 3, Section E for a more formal definition). In England, the term is used instead of regulation. In Canada, the term statutory instrument is broader than the term regulation. See also **Regulation** and **SOR**.

Style of cause: The names of the parties in a lawsuit. A style of cause in a civil lawsuit could be *Smith v. Jones* (meaning, most likely, that someone named Smith is suing someone named Jones). In a criminal matter, a style of cause in Canada could be *R. v. Williams*, in which the "R." stands for *Regina* (that being the symbolic name in which all prosecutions by the government against an accused are brought). (If there is a King in power, the "R." stands for *Rex*). In the foregoing example, Williams would be the accused, the person being tried by the government. The style of cause is always italicized. In online commercial databases, such as Quicklaw one can usually search for cases by the style of cause in the "case name" field.

Taxing officer: A court official (sometimes a Master, sometimes a judge, and sometimes a person specially designated as a taxing officer). This court official is given power to determine what costs, if any, a successful party is entitled to after a lawsuit has finished. Taxing officers can also settle "fees" disputes between a lawyer and her own client. In the context of legal research, there are a number of cases, discussed in Chapter 1, Section C, where the taxing officer has allowed a successful litigant to recover the costs incurred to conduct online searches on commercial online legal databases such as Quicklaw.

Time bomb: For law-related CD-ROMs, a "time bomb" is a security feature built into the software by the publisher to disable or disallow the reading of data from the CD-ROM after the expiry of the licence period for which the customer has paid for the CD-ROM.

Unreported decision: A decision of a judge that has not been published in a print case law reporter. Most decisions in Canada are in fact unreported and are only available either from the original court file, from **CanLII**, or from a commercial online legal database, such as LexisNexis Quicklaw or Westlaw Canada.

URL (Uniform Resource Locator): An URL (pronounced either "you are ell" or "earl") is a website's Web address (i.e., www.irwinlaw.com).

Words and phrases: Words and phrases dictionaries are arranged alphabetically and contain words and phrases as they have been defined or considered by the courts. Unlike law dictionaries, which usually only provide one or two definitions, words and phrases dictionaries attempt to provide multiple examples of how the words and phrases have been defined, often organized by level of court or by topic. See also **Dictionary, legal**.

TABLE OF CASES

INDEX

ABOUT THE AUTHOR

Ted Tjaden, LL.B., M.I.St., LL.M., is the National Director of Knowledge Management at McMillan LLP, a Canadian business law firm. He is called to the bar in British Columbia (1987) and Ontario (1996) and has practised law in a variety of circumstances, including as a commercial litigator, in-house counsel to Seiko Epson Corporation in Japan, and a research lawyer. In addition, his work at the University of Toronto, Faculty of Law, as a law librarian and adjunct professor, included teaching legal research at the Faculty in addition to teaching law librarianship at the Faculty of Information. He holds a Bachelor of Laws degree from Queen's University, and both a Master of Information Studies and a Master of Laws degree from the University of Toronto. His current work has is focused on the intersection of legal research, knowledge management, and technology.